# SIGNS AND WONDERS THEN AND NOW

Keith J. Hacking

# SIGNS AND WONDERS THEN AND NOW

## Miracle-working, commissioning and discipleship

APOLLOS

Apollos (an imprint of Inter-Varsity Press)
Norton Street, Nottingham NG7 3HR, England
*Email: ivp@ivpbooks.com*
*Website: www.ivpbooks.com*

*First published 2006*

**British Library Cataloguing in Publication Data**
A catalogue record for this book is available from the British Library.

UK ISBN–13: 978–1–84474–149–6
UK ISBN–10: 1–84478–149–4

Set in Monotype Garamond 11/13pt
Typeset in Great Britain by Servis Filmsetting Ltd, Manchester
Printed and bound in Great Britain by Ashford Colour Press Ltd, Gosport, Hampshire

Inter-Varsity Press publishes Christian books that are true to the Bible and that communicate the gospel, develop discipleship and strengthen the church for its mission in the world.

Inter-Varsity Press is closely linked with the Universities and Colleges Christian Fellowship, a student movement connecting Christian Unions in universities and colleges throughout Great Britain, and a member movement of the International Fellowship of Evangelical Students. Website: www.uccf.org.uk

*To Madeleine,*
*Alexandra, Josephine and Nathan*

CONTENTS

# PREFACE

Over the years I have lived in different parts of the UK and worshipped both in churches that were enthusiastically charismatic and some that were much less so. One thing they all have in common is a firm belief that the dynamic activity of God that we read about in the New Testament remains relevant for our contemporary experience in the church today. Christians do not venerate a dead guru, but follow a risen and living Lord who remains active in his church and in the lives of individual Christians, not least in his sovereign willingness to be involved in the healing of the sick.

This book is a reworking of an earlier PhD thesis submitted to the University of Durham. However, I believe the subject matter is of direct concern for Christians today, particularly in terms of the way in which our approach to the New Testament evidence influences our understanding of, and expectations for, contemporary Christian discipleship. With this in mind, it was always my hope that this project would become more widely available, and I am grateful to IVP for making this possible. Whilst I take full responsibility for the content, I would like to take this opportunity of expressing my grateful thanks to my *Doktorvater*, Professor James Dunn, who supervised the original thesis and whose astute guidance and patient, friendly encouragement spurred me on to completion during what was a very busy and difficult time. I would also like to thank the Revd Dr Dick France, the Rt. Revd Cyril Ashton and Mrs Alexandra Wilson, all of whom commented helpfully on the manuscript at various stages.

The library staff at the University of Gloucestershire together with Dr Elizabeth Magba (Tyndale House) and Mr Alan Linfield (London School of Theology) are all to be thanked for their patient and helpful forbearance, without which I could not have completed the project. I am also grateful to the Tyndale Fellowship and to the Open Theological College for help over the years in funding my research.

Almost finally, I must express my grateful thanks to my wife, Madeleine, and to our children, Alexandra, Josephine and Nathan, whose constant support and encouragement throughout have made this project possible and to whom this book is dedicated. And now, finally, thanks to my constant companion both in the study and during long reflective walks, Hector, our bulldog.

Keith J. Hacking
Easter 2006

# ABBREVIATIONS

| | |
|---|---|
| *1 En.* | *1 Enoch* |
| 11QMelch. | *Melchizedek* (Dead Sea Scrolls) |
| 1Qap Gen | *Genesis Apocryphon* (Dead Sea Scrolls) |
| 1QH | *Thanksgiving Psalms/Hymns* (Dead Sea Scrolls) |
| 1QM | *War Scroll* (Dead Sea Scrolls) |
| 1QS | *Rule of the Community* (Dead Sea Scrolls) |
| *2 Bar.* | *2 Baruch* |
| *3 Bar.* | *3 Baruch* |
| *3 En.* | *3 Enoch* |
| AB | Anchor Bible |
| *Abr.* | *On the Life of Abraham* |
| *AnBib* | *Analecta biblica* |
| *Apol.* | *Apologia* |
| *APOT* | *The Apocrypha and Pseudepigrapha of the Old Testament*, ed. R. H. Charles, 2 vols. (Oxford: Clarendon, 1913) |
| *Ass. Mos.* | *Assumption of Moses* |
| *b. Sanh.* | *Babylonian Talmud Sanhedrin* |
| *Bib* | *Biblica* |
| BibS | Biblische Studien |
| *BN* | *Biblische Notizen* |
| *BSac* | *Bibliotheca sacra* |
| *BTB* | *Biblical Theology Bulletin* |
| *CBQ* | *Catholic Biblical Quarterly* |
| CD | *Damascus Document* (Dead Sea Scrolls) |
| *Chm* | *Churchman* |
| *DPCM* | *Dictionary of Pentecostal and Charismatic Movements* |
| Ecclus. | Ecclesiasticus |
| EKKNT | Evangelisch-katholischer Kommentar zum Neuen Testament |
| ESV | English Standard Version |
| ET | English translation |
| *EvT* | *Evangelische Theologie* |

| | |
|---|---|
| *ExpTim* | *Expository Times* |
| FT | French translation |
| GNB | Good News Bible |
| GNS | Good News Studies |
| *Haer.* | *Adversus haereses* |
| *HBT* | *Horizons in Biblical Theology* |
| *HTR* | *Harvard Theological Review* |
| *Int* | *Interpretation* |
| *JBL* | *Journal of Biblical Literature* |
| *JPT* | *Journal of Pentecostal Theology* |
| JPTSup | Journal of Pentecostal Theology: Supplement Series |
| *JSNT* | *Journal for the Study of the New Testament* |
| JSNTSup | Journal for the Study of the New Testament: Supplement Series |
| *JTS* | *Journal of Theological Studies* |
| *JTSA* | *Journal of Theology for Southern Africa* |
| *Jub.* | *Jubilees* |
| *J. W.* | *Jewish War* |
| KEK | Kritisch-exegetischer Kommentar über das Neue Testament |
| LCL | Loeb Classical Library |
| *Life* | *The Life* |
| *Lig.* | *Pro Ligario* |
| LkR | Lukan redaction |
| *LS* | *Louvain Studies* |
| LXX | Septuagint version |
| Matt.R. | Matthean redaction |
| *Midr. Cant.* | *Midrash Canticles* |
| *Midr. Ps.* | *Midrash Psalms* |
| NAC | New American Commentary |
| NASB | New American Standard Bible |
| NIBCNT | New International Biblical Commentary on the New Testament |
| NICNT | New International Commentary on the New Testament |
| NIGTC | New International Greek Testament Commentary |
| NIV | New International Version |
| *NovT* | *Novum Testamentum* |
| NovTSup | Novum Testamentum Supplements |
| NRSV | New Revised Standard Version |
| NT | New Testament |
| *NTS* | *New Testament Studies* |

| | |
|---|---|
| NTTS | New Testament Tools and Studies |
| *OrSyr* | *L'orient syrien* |
| OT | Old Testament |
| PCR | Pentecostal-charismatic renewal |
| *Pelag.* | *Adversus Pelagionos* |
| Ps.-Philo | Pseudo-Philo |
| *Pss. Sol.* | *Psalms of Solomon* |
| *RTP* | *Revue de theologie et de philosophie* |
| SBLMS | Society of Biblical Literature Monograph Series |
| SBLDS | Society of Biblical Literature Dissertation Series |
| SBT | Studies in Biblical Theology |
| *ScEs* | *Science et esprit* |
| SNTSMS | Society for New Testament Studies Monograph Series |
| SP | Sacra pagina |
| *ST* | *Studia theologica* |
| SVTP | Studia in Veteris Testamenti pseudepigraphica |
| *T. Dan* | *Testament of Dan* |
| *T. Jud.* | *Testament of Judah* |
| *T. Levi* | *Testament of Levi* |
| *T. Sim.* | *Testament of Simeon* |
| *T. Zeb.* | *Testament of Zebulon* |
| *TDNT* | *Theological Dictionary of the New Testament*, ed. G. Kittel and G. Friedrich; trans. G. W. Bromiley, 10 vols. (Grand Rapids, Mich.: Eerdmans, 1964–76) |
| *Them* | *Themelios* |
| TNTC | Tyndale New Testament Commentaries |
| *TSK* | *Theologische Studien und Kritiken* |
| *TynBul* | *Tyndale Bulletin* |
| *VE* | *Vox evangelica* |
| WBC | Word Biblical Commentary |
| *ZNW* | *Zeitschrift für die neutestamentliche Wissenschaft und die Kunde der älteren Kirche* |

# 1. INTRODUCING THE ISSUES

Signs and wonders or 'doing the stuff'[1] holds an appeal for many in the church today. The quest for religious experience and the recovery of an experiential sense of the supernatural meets a need felt by many twenty-first-century Christians whose lives are besieged by contrary values associated with an all-pervading postmodern world view. John Stott has written:

> I confess to being frightened by the contemporary evangelical hunger for power, even the quest for the power of the Holy Spirit. Why do we want to receive power? Is it honestly power for witness (as in Acts 1:8), or power for holiness, or power for humble service? Or is it in reality a mask for personal ambition, a craving to boost our own ego, to minister to our self-importance, to impress, to dominate or to manipulate?[2]

These are important questions all Christians seeking to deepen their experiential relationship with God should ask themselves, but I believe the problem,

---

1. This is a popular phrase used particularly by John Wimber and colleagues to refer to a period of healing, exorcism etc. normally included during a service or conference.
2. John Stott, *Calling Christian Leaders: Biblical Models of Church, Gospel and Ministry* (Leicester: IVP, 2002), p. 41.

where it exists, arises out of more than just human weakness. In my view, it often derives from a sincere but overly simplistic understanding of the nature and authority of Scripture, where the pursuit of homogeneity at all costs is allowed to set the hermeneutical agenda. For some Christians, seeking to reproduce a New Testament world view, with its apparently uncritical acceptance of the miraculous, is one way of combating the anti-supernaturalism they see in society and within the church. Indeed, for them such miraculous activity is to be considered as normative for the contemporary church and regarded as a tangible demonstration of God's continuing activity amongst his people in much the same way, it is argued, that healings, exorcisms, signs and wonders appear within the pages of the New Testament itself.

The contemporary phenomenon of charismatic renewal has, from its inception with the Pentecostal revivals at the beginning of the twentieth century, been characterized by its claim to reproduce the earliest Christians' experience of the Holy Spirit as evidenced within the pages of the NT. The current charismatic emphasis on a theology of 'signs and wonders', associated with the so-called Third Wave[3] of contemporary Pentecostal-charismatic renewal[4] is no exception. Exponents of this theological emphasis claim to mirror in their contemporary experience, theology and praxis a biblical model or paradigm[5] based upon their understanding of the proclamation of the kingdom of God and the demonstration of its presence with signs and wonders, in the ministry of Jesus and the early church, as it is described especially in the Synoptic Gospels and Acts.

There is a sense in which the phenomenon of the Third Wave, together with its particular theological emphases, have been contextualized and absorbed into the traditions of the church.[6] This is especially true of the church in the United Kingdom, where charismatic renewal has been influential

---

3. I use the term 'Third Wave' throughout as a 'shorthand' for Christians who emphasize a theology and praxis of healings, exorcism, signs and wonders, and who represent a comparatively recent development within the contemporary Pentecostal-charismatic renewal movement.

4. Abbreviated throughout as PCR. I use this term to refer to the phenomenon of the contemporary Pentecostal-charismatic renewal that, in its broadest sense, includes Pentecostalism, neo-Pentecostalism or charismatic renewal, and the Third Wave. The overall context for the Third Wave's influence in the UK is PCR.

5. I am using the word 'paradigm' to indicate a biblical model that is used to inform contemporary faith and/or praxis.

6. I am grateful to the Rt. Revd C. G. Ashton for this insight.

in both the mainstream denominations and New Church movements. In light of this, I am not setting out simply to reiterate what others have already done with regard to the Third Wave and their theology of signs and wonders, nor am I making any particular prior judgments about the outcome.

## Scope and aims

As a *Neutestamentler* with an interest in biblical theology and a firm belief in the need for scholarship to serve the community of faith, it is my hope that the results which emerge from my examination of the NT evidence will both further our understanding of the NT texts themselves, and establish a case for a more critically sensitive approach within the church to the biblical texts and to their contemporary application to faith and praxis. In other words, my purpose is twofold: *academic*, in both an exegetical and theological sense; and *pastoral*, inasmuch as any insights gained from this study will benefit the community of faith on all sides.

I understand that, in common with other evangelical Christians, the Third Wave regard the canonical books of the NT as Scripture and, therefore, as having a particular authority within the church, not least, when it comes to informing Christian faith and praxis. Therefore, *ad hominem*, with the Third Wave, I shall also regard the NT canon as my primary source, although this will not preclude using extra-canonical sources in order to enhance our understanding of the NT texts. Whilst I am aware of the questions posed by others to this working assumption,[7] I write, nevertheless, as an evangelical addressing what is

---

7. For a variety of views held in discussing problems associated with the appropriateness of the contemporary use and application of the canon of the NT in the church today, in light of the diversity evidenced within the NT itself, as well as discussing the relationship between Scripture, canon and authority, see for example J. Barr, *Holy Scripture: Canon, Authority, Criticism* (Oxford: Clarendon, 1983); J. D. G. Dunn, 'Levels of Canonical Authority', *HBT* 4.1 (1982), pp. 13–60, and reproduced in J. D. G. Dunn, *The Living Word* (London: SCM, 1987), pp. 141–174; J. D. G. Dunn, 'Has the Canon a Continuing Function?', in idem, *Unity and Diversity in the New Testament: An Enquiry into the Character of Earliest Christianity* (London: SCM, 1977), pp. 374–388; J. Goldingay, *Models for Scripture* (Grand Rapids, Mich.: Eerdmans; Carlisle: Paternoster, 1994), pp. 77–196; *Models for Interpretation of Scripture* (Grand Rapids, Mich.: Eerdmans; Carlisle: Paternoster, 1995), pp. 87–132; R. M. Grant, 'Literary Criticism and the New Testament Canon', originally in *JSNT*

primarily an intra-evangelical issue. With this in mind, it should be noted from the outset that my purpose is also to engage with the Third Wave in such a way that I am heard by both sides – the Third Wave as well as the academy.

I have a number of reasons for wanting to engage with the Third Wave. All evangelical Christians, whether 'charismatic' or not, would claim that their theology and praxis are derived from within a biblical framework that is informed primarily by the NT and that often reflects their particular denominational or group emphasis.[8] The Third Wave's particular theological emphasis has become highly influential in PCR circles, and provides an important contemporary example of a Christian group claiming to reflect or reproduce a normative NT paradigm in their theology and praxis. As such, they clearly deserve closer attention.

Their theology of 'signs and wonders' is informed by a NT paradigm[9] that is both influential within PCR circles, as well as being potentially divisive within the wider Christian community. As such, its importance for contemporary theology and praxis in the church today approximates that of ideas about baptism in the Spirit and the manifestation of charismata that were characteristic of an earlier stage of PCR. These issues were not only controversial within the church at the time; they also attracted notable scholarly attention.[10]

---

16 (1982), pp. 24–44, and reproduced in S. E. Porter and C. A. Evans, *New Testament Interpretation and Methods* (Sheffield: Sheffield Academic Press, 1997), pp. 82–101; R. Nixon, 'The Authority of the New Testament', in I. H. Marshall (ed.), *New Testament Interpretation: Essays on Principles and Methods* (Exeter: Paternoster, 1979), pp. 334–350; C. M. Tuckett, *Reading the New Testament: Methods of Interpretation* (London: SPCK, 1987), pp. 5–20; R. W. Wall, 'Reading the New Testament in Canonical Context', in J. B. Green (ed.), *Hearing the New Testament: Strategies for Interpretation* (Grand Rapids, Mich.: Eerdmans; Carlisle: Paternoster, 1995), pp. 370–393.

8.  See for example R. T. France, 'The Church and the Kingdom of God', in D. A. Carson (ed.), *Biblical Interpretation and the Kingdom of God: Text and Context* (Exeter: Paternoster, 1984), pp. 30–44, and especially p. 42. In a similar vein, but in the context of a biblical approach to contemporary social, political and ethical concerns, see J. R. W. Stott, *Issues Facing Christians Today* (Basingstoke: Marshall, Morgan & Scott, 1984), p. 15.

9.  See chapter 2 for a discussion of the Third Wave paradigm.

10.  Here I have in mind particularly J. D. G. Dunn, *Baptism in the Holy Spirit: A Re-examination of the New Testament Teaching on the Gift of the Spirit in Relation to Pentecostalism Today* (London: SCM, 1970). This study is now something of a 'classic' and continues to provoke scholarly dialogue and discussion within PCR circles.

The way in which the Third Wave gather and use the NT evidence to inform their contemporary paradigm raises important critical, exegetical and hermeneutical issues that need to be addressed both here and, I would argue, by all Christians who believe that the NT provides normative models for the church today. It is to these hermeneutical issues relating to an appropriate methodology for interpreting and evaluating the NT evidence that we must now turn.

## Hermeneutical issues and methodology

In the 1970s James Dunn set out to engage with those involved then in PCR (as well as others) through his examination of the NT evidence for the process of Christian conversion-initiation. In so doing, he opened up a field of debate between those involved directly in PCR and the academy that continues vigorously to the present day. More importantly, Dunn pioneered dialogue at a scholarly and technical level with Pentecostals and others that has increased in both the range of subjects under discussion, and the number of scholarly contributions both from sympathetic 'outsiders' as well as from those who identify themselves as coming from within the ranks of PCR. In a sense, the purpose of this present study is to take the dialogue a stage further, by engaging in a detailed examination of the NT material offered in evidence by the Third Wave in support of their theology of 'signs and wonders'.

At an early stage in Dunn's dialogue with Pentecostalism over the issue of baptism in the Spirit and how this relates to the NT evidence for the process of Christian conversion-initiation, he raises the important methodological issue of how we are to approach the NT evidence by asking the question 'Are we to approach the NT material as systematic theologians or as biblical theologians and exegetes?'[11] Dunn answers the question by pointing out that the common error of the former is to approach the NT as an homogenous whole, selecting texts on a particular topic out of their literary context and using them to construct a theological framework or system that he deems 'extra-biblical'. For Dunn, the more appropriate approach is that taken by the latter, who treat each author and book separately with a view to identifying the particular theological emphasis and intention of the various writers before allowing a particular text to interact with others. He adds:

---

11.  Ibid., p. 39.

This means, in our case, that we cannot simply assume that the Gospels and Acts are all bare historical narratives which complement each other in a direct 1:1 ratio, nor can we assume that Luke and John have the same emphases and aims. They may, of course, but we cannot assume it without proof.[12]

Just as this methodological point was an important one to make for Dunn's study, so it is for my present study. Those with whom I shall engage also have a strong tendency to treat NT texts in a similar homogenizing fashion. It is encouraging to note that there is an increasing degree of theological expertise being brought into the various discussions between scholars associated with PCR and their partners in dialogue, and this strengthens even further the case for appropriate methodologies to be used by all sides. Indeed, there is a growing recognition that biblical scholarship, which is sympathetic to a high view of the authority of Scripture, has a crucial role to play in setting the hermeneutical agenda for evaluating biblical models that inform contemporary faith and praxis.[13]

## A new generation of PCR scholars

In retrospect, Dunn's *Baptism in the Holy Spirit* has proved to be something of a catalyst in that it has been, at least partly, responsible since the 1970s for the increasing dialogue between those associated with PCR and academic biblical scholarship. In his recent study of current trends in PCR, church historian Nigel Scotland notes that there are now a number of theological and biblical scholars who are also charismatics.[14] In an article for the *Journal for Pentecostal Theology*, Mark Stibbe traces the development of the dialogue between Pentecostal spirituality and academic theologians since the 1970s and also notes particularly the rise of a new generation of Pentecostal and

---

12. Ibid.

13. In addition to Dunn, see also, for example, M. M. B. Turner, *Power from on High: The Spirit in Israel's Restoration and Witness in Luke-Acts* (JPTSup 9; Sheffield: Sheffield Academic Press, 1996); G. H. Twelftree, *Christ Triumphant* (London: Hodder & Stoughton, 1985); and *Jesus the Miracle Worker* (Downers Grove, Ill.: IVP, 1999); R. P. Menzies, *The Development of Early Christian Pneumatology with Special Reference to Luke-Acts* (JSNTSup 54; Sheffield: JSOT, 1991).

14. N. Scotland, *Charismatics and the Next Millennium* (London: Hodder & Stoughton, 1995), p. 259.

charismatic scholars that has taken place particularly since 1983.[15] According to Stibbe, those involved in the Third Wave include more people with theological training and critical temperaments than the first two 'waves', and he concludes that the future for PCR lies in church leaders embracing a more critical emphasis in their ministries,[16] an important point with which I concur. Today, the extent of this dialogue continues to develop and it has become a fruitful area for NT research, with notable contributions from scholars such as R. Stronstad,[17] R. P. Menzies,[18] M. M. B. Turner[19] and M. W. G. Stibbe.[20]

Two further points illustrate developments taking place. Firstly, theological colleges, representing most denominations in the UK are including courses that relate to the theology and praxis of PCR, with the larger colleges offering opportunities for postgraduate work in this field.[21] Secondly, Stibbe is right to point out that the Third Wave in the United States is also producing more scholarly contributions from within its own ranks.[22] However, leading Third Wave writers from the United States have always relied to some extent on NT scholars whom they perceive to be sympathetic in some way, referring with approval especially to George Ladd, Oscar Cullmann and

---

15. M. W. G. Stibbe, 'The Theology of Renewal and the Renewal of Theology', *JPT* 3 (1993), pp. 71–90.

16. Ibid., p. 79.

17. *The Charismatic Theology of St. Luke* (Peabody, Mass.: Hendrickson, 1984).

18. *Development of Early Christian Pneumatology*.

19. *The Holy Spirit and Spiritual Gifts: Then and Now*, rev. ed. (Cumbria: Paternoster, 1996); and *Power from on High*.

20. *The Gospel of John as Literature: An Anthology of Twentieth Century Perspectives* (NTTS; Leiden: Brill, 1993).

21. Undergraduate and postgraduate courses are available at, for example, St John's College, Nottingham, Spurgeon's Baptist College, London, and the London School of Theology. It is also worth noting here that Max Turner writes in the preface to *The Holy Spirit and Spiritual Gifts*, p. xi, that the book arises out of an invitation from the Open Theological College to write a half-module for its third year BA (Hons) course in Theology.

22. Stibbe, 'Theology of Renewal', p. 79. See for example D. Williams, *Signs, Wonders and the Kingdom of God* (Ann Arbor, Mich.: Vine, 1989); J. Deere, *Surprised by the Power of the Spirit* (Eastbourne: Kingsway, 1993); C. S. Storms, 'A Third Wave View', in W. Grudem (ed.), *Are Miraculous Gifts for Today? Four Views* (Leicester: IVP, 1996), pp. 175–233.

James Dunn,[23] although the hermeneutical approach of these NT scholars is, for the most part, not reflected in contributions from Third Wave writers.[24]

Whilst applauding the positive trend within PCR to engage in dialogue with academic NT scholarship, we must also note evidence of hermeneutical ambivalence on the part of Third Wave writers that, in practice, leads to an homogenizing approach to the NT. This, I would argue, substantially weakens their case when it comes to identifying NT models to be applied to contemporary theology and praxis.

### Third Wave hermeneutical ambivalence

The first three (Synoptic) Gospels are a primary source for informing the Third Wave paradigm, their renewed interest in the Gospels being presented by the Third Wave as a corrective against what they see as evangelicalism's traditional concentration on the Pauline epistles, and the Pentecostal-charismatic concentration on the book of Acts. The primary model the Third Wave find in the Gospels is one from which they derive their theology for ministry of signs and wonders, which, they claim, is 'rooted in the ministry of Jesus as portrayed in the Gospels'.[25]

Emphasis on the Synoptic Gospels' portrayal of Jesus and his disciples opens up particular hermeneutical issues concerning the literary relationships

---

23. The two works by Dunn that are usually recommended are *Baptism in the Holy Spirit* and *Jesus and the Spirit: A Study of the Religious and Charismatic Experience of Jesus and the First Christians as Reflected in the New Testament* (London: SCM, 1975). I have also seen both books on sale in John Wimber's Anaheim Vineyard Church bookshop.

24. A recent Third Wave example that exemplifies this ambivalence is R. Nathan and K. Wilson, *Empowered Evangelicals* (Ann Arbor, Mich.: Servant, 1995), especially pp. 135–149, at the end of which G. E. Ladd's *A Theology of the New Testament* (Cambridge: Lutterworth, 1974) and Dunn's *Jesus and the Spirit* are recommended for 'further study'. Other examples may be found in G. S. Greig and K. N. Springer (eds.), *The Kingdom and the Power: Are Healing and the Spiritual Gifts Used by Jesus and the Early Church Meant for the Church Today?* (Ventura, Calif.: Regal, 1993), *passim*; Williams, *Signs, Wonders*; Deere, *Surprised by the Power of the Spirit*.

25. Nathan and Wilson, *Empowered Evangelicals*, p. 140.

that clearly exist within the Synoptic tradition and how we are to understand and interpret the evangelists in their own terms, recognizing that each evangelist handles the Jesus tradition in his own distinctive way. It is in their handling of material from the Gospels that we find the clearest evidence of the Third Wave's ambivalent attitude to more scholarly approaches to the text. On the one hand, they can affirm the need for historical-critical approaches to the text,[26] and yet their methodology has a strong tendency to treat the NT as an homogenous unit where the Gospels are used without sensitivity to the diversity of theological and Christological concerns of the individual evangelists.[27] For example, John Wimber adopts a similar homogenizing approach to the biblical material in his books and yet he can write, 'In using every critical tool at his or her disposal the evangelical's goal is to discern what Scripture meant to say to its original audience so that we can better understand what God intends to say to us today through his Word.'[28]

In light of this, it is to be regretted that actual engagement with the text evidences little use of critical tools. Indeed, the word 'critical' itself can be viewed as both negative and threatening, especially in the church, but for the academic it is a neutral word. Again, Dunn makes an important point when he writes:

> the New Testament critic must be willing to treat the New Testament texts as products of the first century, and as such be willing to analyse them in the same way as he would other historical texts. Such an examination is not antithetical or hostile to their further role as scripture.[29]

In other words, our interpretation of Scripture must rest on the assumption that each of the original authors had a specific purpose in writing in a particular way. This requires us to use the insights and methodologies of biblical scholarship in order to understand as much as we can of the author's intended meaning before we can understand what the text might mean for us today.

---

26. See for example J. Wimber, 'Introduction', in K. N. Springer (ed.), *Riding the Third Wave* (London: Marshall Pickering, 1987), p. 25.
27. See for example Williams, *Signs, Wonders, passim,* and especially pp. 105–142, where Williams sets out the NT evidence of the Third Wave paradigm for a theology of 'signs and wonders' based on the ministry of Jesus and his disciples.
28. Wimber, 'Introduction', p. 25.
29. Dunn, *Living Word,* p. 16.

## The so-called 'intentional fallacy'

I am aware of the justified criticism of the hermeneutical shift that took place in the nineteenth century away from the 'plain meaning' to the 'intended meaning' of the text, which has been identified as the 'intentional fallacy', where the intention of the author is identified as an irretrievable 'private state of mind' lying behind the text.[30]

In discussing the 'intentional fallacy', Thiselton rightly points out that in biblical studies it is both legitimate and necessary to engage in historical reconstruction, but this has nothing to do with the 'mental state' of the author or 'falling prey to the genetic fallacy', but is a 'pre-condition to the currency of the text'.[31] As Thiselton observes, 'Intention is better understood adverbially: to write in a way that is directed towards a goal.'[32] Language is intended to convey meaning and, if we are to make sense of the biblical texts, we cannot avoid the concept of meaning, nor, as Dunn rightly points out, is it necessary to dispense with the concept of authorial intention as a 'realistic goal' that we find 'entextualised'.[33]

My approach to the question of 'intentionality' on the part of the evangelists will be to understand and approach the author's 'intended meaning' only in so far as I am able to discern it through the use of critical hermeneutical tools which take as a 'given' that the authors and their readers are seeking to share meaning through the text and their shared world view. We cannot ignore the fact that when we approach the NT we face a number of immediate historical, linguistic, socio-contextual and literary-critical difficulties. These must all be faced and dealt with before we seek to apply the text to our own situation. It has also been rightly pointed out that competent scholarship must face the problem of the discontinuities between the biblical event and the present circumstances before making appeals to biblical paradigms.[34] For example, the

---

30. J. D. G. Dunn, 'What Makes a Good Exposition?', *ExpTim* 114.5 (2003), p. 151. See further A. C. Thiselton, *New Horizons in Hermeneutics* (London: HarperCollins, 1992), pp. 58–59.

31. Thiselton, *New Horizons*, pp. 558–560, and especially p. 559.

32. Ibid.

33. Dunn, 'What Makes a Good Exposition?'; and see F. Watson, *Text and Truth: Redefining Biblical Theology* (Grand Rapids, Mich.: Eerdmans, 1987), p. 118, who also makes the point that authorial intention 'is to be seen as primarily embodied in the words the author wrote'.

34. D. A. Carson, 'A Sketch of the Factors Determining Current Hermeneutical

liberation theology of G. Gutiérrez has been rightly criticized for failing to take adequate account of the discontinuities between the Exodus story in the OT and using the Exodus as a paradigm for informing revolutionary struggles against political oppressors in South America.[35] Where, then, does this leave us here in terms of an appropriate hermeneutical approach to the NT?

## Setting the hermeneutical agenda

At its most basic level, any disagreement I may have with the Third Wave is not just concerned with particular theological conclusions they derive from their reading of the NT, but with their largely uncritical and homogenizing approach to the text. Despite their tacit approval of 'sympathetic' NT scholarship, there remains an abiding methodological ambivalence on the part of Third Wave leaders and writers that eschews the use of more scholarly approaches to the NT texts, preferring to treat the NT writings as an homogenous whole from which they deduce a normative paradigm.

Against this homogenizing approach, any NT paradigm, let alone one that is absolutely central to a particular group's ethos and praxis, requires a much more careful approach to the NT evidence. Here the warning of Ernst Käsemann is apposite when he writes in the preface to his commentary on Romans, 'The impatient, who are concerned only about results or practical application, should leave their hands off exegesis. They are of no value for it, nor, when rightly done, is exegesis of any value for them.'[36]

What, then, are the barriers that prevent the Third Wave from using a more critical approach to the NT texts? I believe the answer lies in three related issues. Firstly, there is a strong tendency amongst Third Wave writers, as well as others in the church, to regard the application of critical approaches to the biblical text as being symptomatic of the historical scepticism born out of the Enlightenment, which characterized nineteenth-century liberalism, and which

---

Debate in Cross-Cultural Contexts', in D. A. Carson (ed.), *Biblical Interpretation and the Church: Text and Context* (Exeter: Paternoster, 1984), p. 26.

35. See E. A. Nunez, 'The Church in the Liberation Theology of Gustavo Gutiérrez: Description and Hermeneutical Analysis', in Carson, *Biblical Interpretation and the Church*, pp. 166–194.

36. E. Käsemann, *Commentary on Romans* (ET London: SCM, 1980), p. viii. A similar view is expressed by N. T. Wright, *The New Testament and the People of God* (London: SPCK, 1993), p. 60.

continues to influence contemporary Western rationalism.[37] Perhaps the best example of this may be found in R. Bultmann's demythologizing approach to the NT. Describing NT cosmology in terms of a three-tier universe inhabited by God, angels, Satan and demons who engage regularly in supernatural activities, both at the heavenly and earthly levels, thus ensuring that people are not master of their thoughts or actions, Bultmann concludes:

> This then is the mythical view of the world which the New Testament pre-supposes when it presents the event of redemption which is the subject of its preaching. . . . To this extent the kerygma is incredible to modern man, for he is convinced that the mythical view of the world is obsolete.[38]

With this, Bultmann sets out on his programme of demythologizing the NT in order to ensure that the saving message is not obscured by a pre-scientific world view that, he believes, the scientific mind is unable to accept.[39] Of course, the fundamental problem raised for the interpreter of the NT by this demythologizing approach is that it is difficult to know where to stop. Anything that may be regarded as supernatural or miraculous is suspect. The result of this level of scepticism is that it may not allow the interpreter of the NT to remain adequately sensitive either to historical-critical questions raised by the text, or to more recent narrative-critical ideas about assumptions being made by the implied author about his readers' prior-knowledge and their shared world view.

However, it must be pointed out here that Bultmann's historical-scepticism is no longer necessarily characteristic of contemporary NT scholarship. For example, Tom Wright is quite scathing in his criticism of earlier (and present) NT scholars who saw the Gospels as little more than founding myths baring little resemblance to what actually happened and, as such, the Gospels cannot make sense as they stand.[40] Wright suggests that such a sceptical approach to the Gospels that sees them as almost deliberately misleading smacks of G.

---

37. For Third Wave discussions, see for example Wimber, *Power Evangelism: Signs and Wonders Today* (London: Hodder & Stoughton, 1985), pp. 74–96; D. Williams, 'Exorcising the Ghost of Newton', in Springer, *Riding the Third Wave*, pp. 151–163; and especially Kraft, *Christianity with Power* (Ann Arbor, Mich.: Vine, 1989).

38. R. Bultmann, 'New Testament and Mythology', in H. W. Bartsch, *Kerygma and Myth: A Theological Debate by Rudolf Bultmann and Five Critics* (ET New York: Harper & Brothers, 1961), pp. 1–2.

39. Ibid., p. 3.

40. Wright, *New Testament and the People of God*, p. 106.

Theissen's fictional 'committee for misleading later historians'.[41] Insisting that this is not the case with the NT Gospels, Wright concludes, in a way that should encourage Third Wave exegetes to follow his excellent example and adopt a more critical approach to the evidence, that the NT evidence suggests there is a 'high probability that the earliest Palestinian Christianity continued in many important respects the sort of ministry in which Jesus himself had engaged'.[42]

Secondly, there is the Third Wave's opposition to dispensationalist cessationism[43] and what they regard as the rationalistic, anti-supernatural presuppositions that characterize its hermeneutical approach.[44] This, they argue, results in a misreading of the NT evidence that, they believe, supports a continuing expectation of the Spirit's supernatural activity in the church today. In both cases, the Third Wave reject presuppositions they consider to be 'unbiblical', and this leads us to the third of our three related issues that militate against the use of a more critical hermeneutical approach by the Third Wave – the question of 'world view'.

The Third Wave's adopted world view, which they describe in terms of a 'paradigm-shift', and its influence on their hermeneutical approach may be seen in the following:

> it is impossible to understand the Bible apart from a worldview of consistent supernaturalism. To speak of God as the Lord of nature and history and to see him on his throne executing judgement and accomplishing redemption and, at the same time, to deny the reality of his sovereign, direct intervention with signs and wonders makes the assertions about his lordship empty ('mythological'), or even worse, irrelevant.[45]

Whilst primarily seeking to guard against anti-supernaturalist presuppositions, the Third Wave's so-called 'paradigm-shift' towards an epistemological framework, which accepts uncritically a first-century world view fails to take account of the fact that a contemporary Christian world view needs necessarily

---

41. Cf. G. Theissen, *The Shadow of the Galilean: The Quest of the Historical Jesus in Narrative Form* (ET London: SCM, 1987), p. 66.

42. *New Testament and the People of God*, p. 106.

43. For discussion, see Turner, *Holy Spirit and Spiritual Gifts*, pp. 278–285. See also the classic cessationist position given in B. B. Warfield, *Counterfeit Miracles* (Edinburgh: Banner of Truth Trust, 1972).

44. See especially Deere, *Surprised by the Power of the Spirit*, pp. 45–117.

45. Williams, *Signs, Wonders*, p. 48. For a detailed discussion of 'world view' from a Third Wave perspective, see Kraft, *Christianity with Power, passim*.

to be more extensive than simply adopting a 'biblical worldview'.[46] They also fail to take account of the fact that we all bring our own 'baggage' to the text of Scripture in terms of who we are and how we have been affected by our prior experience and understanding. In other words, it is simply not possible to approach the text of the NT in isolation from one's contemporary twenty-first-century world view. At best, the Third Wave's paradigm-shift can do no more than open them up to the possibility of existential applications of the NT data to contemporary faith and praxis.

If, on the one hand, we are arguing here with Bultmann and others that pre-suppositionless exegesis is not possible, and yet on the other hand we want to remain open to understanding the NT text on its own terms, how are we to approach the hermeneutical task? Our approach can only be to take account both of the beliefs that characterized first-century Judaism, as well as the challenge to those beliefs that faced the NT writers in light of the post-Easter witness and experience of the church. We should also note here that the best approach to understanding the world view reflected in the NT is that which recognizes the socio-historical conditionedness of the texts and, in response, applies the hermeneutical tools and insights of academic NT scholarship to the task of understanding, so far as we are able, the original authors' intended meanings before seeking to construct and apply contemporary NT theologies that accurately reflect the evidence.

This is by no means the same thing as the Third Wave's attempt to adopt, uncritically, a 'biblical' world view that owes little or nothing to contemporary socio-historical, linguistic or literary-critical insights into the world of the NT writers normally associated with a more scholarly approach to the texts. Such a hermeneutical approach not only improves our pre-understanding, but is more appropriate to a view of the authoritative nature of the NT as Scripture and its continuing role of informing contemporary Christian faith and praxis.

Although Christians have, understandably, sometimes criticized the scepticism that has accompanied and governed the academy's application of historical-critical methods, it is important for us to differentiate between the methods themselves and the presuppositions that govern their application.[47]

---

46. See for example Wright, *New Testament and the People of God*, pp. 132–134, who describes a Christian world view in terms of four categories: story, answers to questions, symbols and praxis.

47. Cf. S. C. Barton, 'Historical Criticism and Social-Scientific Perspectives in New Testament Study', in J. B. Green (ed.), *Hearing the New Testament: Strategies for Interpretation* (Grand Rapids, Mich.: Eerdmans; Carlisle: Paternoster, 1995), p. 63.

In the ancient Greek world the task of the *histōr* was to act in the neutral role of an arbitrator who could look at the facts objectively.[48] It may not be possible to be entirely neutral in our approach to the text, but there is a case to be made for being open-minded in our approach to the text. Such an approach opens up the possibility of a hermeneutical dialogue with the text of the NT, allowing any questions to be asked that seem appropriate to the nature of the text, or claims to be made about the text, whilst remaining open to hearing the text speak in its own terms to us in our situation and so 'fine tune' our faith and praxis.[49]

In taking this approach to the NT evidence put forward by the Third Wave in support of their case, we bear in mind throughout two key questions: What results are yielded by the refining process involved in a more critical approach to the NT evidence and the issues raised? Does a model emerge that reflects more accurately the biblical evidence and, therefore, is more appropriate for informing contemporary theology and praxis?

But, who are the Third Wave? Where do they fit in the history and development of Pentecostal-charismatic renewal? How is the Third Wave theology of signs and wonders to relate to earlier PCR theology and practice? These are some of the questions to which we must now turn.

---

48. U. Mauser, 'Historical Criticism: Liberator or Foe of Biblical Theology?', in J. Reuman (ed.), *The Promise and Practice of Biblical Theology* (Minneapolis: Fortress, 1991), p. 102. Cf. *Iliad* 18:501, where the *histōr* is called to arbitrate between two characters who are in dispute over the 'blood price' of a man who has been killed.

49. Cf. Dunn, *Living Word*, pp. 18–19.

## 2. RIDING THE THIRD WAVE, OR JUST AZUSA STREET REVISITED?

### Enthusiastic beginnings

Christian history has, from its earliest beginnings, been punctuated by enthusiastic challenges to the religious orthodoxies of the day. Sometimes these challenges have resulted in what later generations have come to regard as 'watersheds' in the history of the church. At other times the challenge has foundered or enthusiasm has simply died out. Indeed, we may point to the characteristic enthusiasm of the post-Easter Christian communities themselves as a unifying factor to be discerned within the diversity of the writings we call the 'New Testament'. Added to this, most NT scholars would agree that earliest Christianity began as an enthusiastic Jewish sect.[1] It is certainly true that exorcisms and miraculous healings are a striking feature in the ministry of Jesus as described in all the Gospel accounts (see e.g. Matt. 4:23; Mark 1:34; Luke 4:40–41; John 4:46–54; cf. John 2:23; 20:30; Acts 2:22; 10:38). Similar phenomena occur in the ministry of the apostles, as described in Acts (cf. Acts 5:12–16; 6:8; 14:3).

In his letters Paul alludes to his own miraculous activities (Rom. 15:18–19; 2 Cor. 12:12), and discusses 'gifts of healing' with other charismata in his first

---

1. For a recent and comprehensive survey of the relationship of Christianity to Judaism, see J. D. G. Dunn, *The Partings of the Ways* (London: SCM, 1991).

letter to the church in Corinth (1 Cor. 12:9, 28). It is interesting to note here that Paul uses the plural 'gifts of healing' in relation to a single person. This probably indicates that, for Paul, each occurrence of a healing is to be regarded as an act of God effected through the healer who is gifted by the Spirit on each occasion with a healing gift, rather than healing being a gift in its own right.[2] Elsewhere in the NT, church leaders are clearly expected to exercise a healing ministry of prayer and anointing with oil (Jas 5:16; cf. Mark 6:13).

## Challenges to orthodoxy

Immediately following the apostolic era, there was a growing tendency towards 'catholicity' within the church – the beginnings of which are evidenced within the NT itself – which came to regard outbreaks of enthusiasm, such as second-century Montanism,[3] as a challenge to ideas of authority that are an integral feature of any move towards catholicity.[4] In the West, following the sixteenth-century Reformation, a frequent consequence of enthusiasm has been schism, resulting in an increasing multiplicity of denominations within Protestantism. Notable examples in this country are the Quakers in the seventeenth century, led by George Fox (1624–91), and in the eighteenth century the Methodists, led by John Wesley (1703–91).

An important feature of post-apostolic Christian enthusiasm has been its appeal to a first-century ideal that, it is claimed, is evidenced by the NT and is, therefore, somehow normative for later situations. Examples of this appeal to a NT ideal may be seen in the insistence on believers' baptism by the

---

2. See further G. D. Fee, *God's Empowering Presence: The Holy Spirit in the Letters of Paul* (Peabody, Mass.: Hendrickson, 1994), p. 169; J. D. G. Dunn, *Jesus and the Spirit: A Study of the Religious and Charismatic Experience of Jesus and the First Christians as Reflected in the New Testament* (London: SCM, 1975), p. 211; G. H. Twelftree, 'Healing, Illness', in G. F. Hawthorne, R. P. Martin and D. G. Reid (eds.), *Dictionary of Paul and his Letters* (Leicester: IVP, 1993), p. 380.

3. See further D. E. Aune, *Prophecy in Early Christianity and the Ancient Mediterranean World* (Grand Rapids, Mich.: Eerdmans, 1983), pp. 313–316; D. F. Wright, 'Why Were the Montanists Condemned?', *Them* 2.1 (1976), pp. 15–22.

4. For a discussion of developing catholicity within the NT, see the seminal essay by Ernst Käsemann, 'Paulus und der Frühkatholizismus', *ZTK* 60 (1963), pp. 75–89; ET 'Paul and Early Catholicism', in idem, *New Testament Questions of Today* (London: SCM, 1969), pp. 236–251.

Anabaptists, and the form of ecclesiastical polity that characterizes Presbyterianism.[5] Occasionally, a group's particular appeal to the NT is reflected in the name of the resultant movement. Such is the case with the Pentecostal movement that began with the Azusa Street revivals in Los Angeles, California, in 1906.

Church historian Nigel Scotland traces the development of early Pentecostalism from the influence of the Welsh revival of 1904, associated with Evan Roberts, upon an American Baptist minister, Joseph Smale. When Smale returned to Los Angeles, he in turn influenced a black preacher, William Seymour, who, from 1906, began to hold services in an abandoned warehouse in Azusa Street, Los Angeles. These resulted in reports of powerful spiritual experiences by members of the congregation, including glossolalia (speaking in tongues).[6] In September 1907 a Norwegian Methodist, T. B. Barratt, who had himself been affected by the Azusa Street meetings, was invited to hold a series of meetings in All Saints Parish Church, Sunderland, after which Pentecostal groups began to meet all over the UK.[7] As the name suggests, the particular emphasis of Pentecostalism is its appeal to the events of the day of Pentecost (Acts 2:1ff.) as being a normative paradigm for Christian experience today. The features they have traditionally emphasized are Spirit-baptism, as a

-------

5. The *Oxford Dictionary of the Christian Church* notes that during the sixteenth and seventeenth centuries, the proponents of this form of ecclesiastical polity regarded it as 'a re-discovery of the apostolic model found in the NT, and many of them held it to be the only permissible form of government and thus permanently binding upon the Church' (F. L. Cross and E. A. Livingstone, 'Presbyterianism', *The Oxford Dictionary of the Christian Church* [Oxford: Oxford University Press, 1974], p. 1118).

6. N. Scotland, *Charismatics and the Next Millennium: Do they Have a Future?* (London: Hodder & Stoughton, 1995), p. 5.

7. For a survey of the development of Pentecostalism in the UK leading to charismatic renewal in the 1960s and the influence of the Third Wave from the 1980s, see Scotland, *Charismatics and the Next Millennium*. For details of Pentecostal churches, see for example Cross and Livingstone, *Oxford Dictionary of the Christian Church*, p. 1062. See also W. J. Hollenweger, *The Pentecostals*, 3rd ed. (ET Peabody, Mass.: Hendrickson, 1988); R. Massey, *Another Springtime: The Life of Donald Gee, Pentecostal Pioneer* (Guildford: Highland, 1992), pp. 14–22; C. M. Robeck, Jr., 'Pentecostal Origins from a Global Perspective', in H. D. Hunter and P. Hocken (eds.), *All Together in One Place: Theological Papers from the Brighton Conference on World Evangelization* (Sheffield: Sheffield Academic Press, 1993), pp. 166–180.

second experience subsequent to conversion, glossolalia as initial evidence for Spirit-baptism, a general restoration of NT charismata (1 Cor. 12:8–11, 28; Rom. 12:6–8; Eph. 4:11–12) and, in particular, divine healing.

Healing ministries have been a significant, if somewhat controversial, aspect of Pentecostalism, usually centred on particular individuals thought to posses a special gift of healing, with some (such as William Branham, Aimee Semple McPherson, Kathryn Kuhlman and Oral Roberts) even becoming household names in North America.[8] The most significant point about Pentecostalism here is its responsibility for, and influence upon, the phenomenon of twentieth-century PCR.[9]

## The charismatic movement

According to Scotland,[10] the link between Pentecostalism and the charismatic movement came through the ecumenical efforts of Pentecostal spokesman David du Plessis (1905–87), who attended the Second Assembly of the World Council of Churches held in Evanston, Illinois, in 1954.[11] From the 1960s and throughout the 1970s the emerging charismatic movement, with its emphasis on 'baptism in the Spirit' and the practice of spiritual gifts as normative for the contemporary church, began to have a spectacular influence on just about every major branch of the church throughout the world, both Protestant and

---

8. For a fuller account, see P. G. Chappell, 'Healing Movements', in S. M. Burgess and G. M. McGee (eds.), *Dictionary of Pentecostal and Charismatic Movements* (Grand Rapids, Mich.: Zondervan, 1988), pp. 353–374 (abbreviated hereafter as *DPCM*).

9. Articles covering the history and development of PCR can be found in *DPCM*. See also Massey, *Another Springtime*; E. D. O'Conner, *The Pentecostal Movement in the Catholic Church* (Notre Dame, Ind.: Ave Maria Press, 1971); P. Hocken, *Streams of Renewal: The Origins and Development of the Charismatic Movement in Great Britain* (Exeter: Paternoster, 1986); Scotland, *Charismatics and the Next Millennium*.

10. Nigel Scotland has written what is probably the most up-to-date account of developments within PCR since the 1970s.

11. For a short biography of this significant Pentecostal leader, see R. P. Spittler, 'Du Plessis, David Johannes', *DPCM*, pp. 250–254. Fuller treatments can be found in D. J. du Plessis, *The Spirit Bade Me Go* (Oakland: published by the author, 1963); and M. Robinson, 'To the Ends of the Earth: The Pilgrimage of an Ecumenical Pentecostal, David J. du Plessis 1905–1987' (unpublished PhD thesis, University of Birmingham, 1987).

Catholic. This development within PCR later came to be designated by commentators as the 'second wave' of the Holy Spirit.[12] In addition to its influence within the historic denominations, PCR was largely responsible for the emergence of the so-called 'house church' movement, which has attracted very large numbers to its ranks with its emphasis on a restorationist theology that seeks to restore to the contemporary church a NT pattern for ministry and structure, including the practice of spiritual gifts.[13]

## Enter the Third Wave

In the 1980s PCR began to feel the impact of what has been called the 'Third Wave' of the Holy Spirit.[14] In the United States the most significant Christian group to be influenced by the Third Wave were conservative evangelicals who formerly held to a dispensationalist/cessationist theology that denies the contemporary validity of the charismata, exorcisms and miraculous healings, associated with Pentecostalism and the later charismatic movement. Initially, under the influence of John Wimber and other members of the faculty of the School of World Mission at Fuller Theological Seminary in the United States, attitudes to the place of charismata and signs and wonders[15] in contemporary mission changed through those who were influenced by Wimber's teaching and writing, who sometimes describe themselves as 'empowered evangelicals' as a way of separating themselves from earlier 'waves' of PCR.[16] A course, conducted at Fuller by Wimber and featuring practical demonstrations of 'signs and wonders' in the classroom, not surprisingly, became a cause célèbre. Not all members of the faculties at Fuller were in agreement with the emerging

---

12. Scotland, *Charismatics and the Next Millennium*, pp. 6–10.

13. Ibid., p. 11.

14. According to John Wimber, 'Introduction', in K. N. Springer (ed.), *Riding the Third Wave* (Basingstoke: Marshall Pickering, 1987), pp. 30–31, the phrase was coined by C. P. Wagner, Professor of Missions at Fuller Theological Seminary, California, and long-time associate of John Wimber and other American leaders of the Third Wave. Wagner identifies Pentecostalism and the charismatic movement as waves one and two respectively.

15. Normally used by the Third Wave as a 'catch all' for healings, exorcisms and miracles associated with Jesus and his followers.

16. Cf. R. Nathan and K. Wilson, *Empowered Evangelicals* (Ann Arbor, Mich.: Vine, 1995).

Third Wave teaching, and this led to public disagreements between faculty members, resulting in the eventual withdrawal of the MC105 course 'The Miraculous and Church Growth', taught largely by Wimber, despite its attracting record numbers of students.[17]

In the United Kingdom, where the charismatic movement has continued to develop, the Third Wave has had an enormous influence upon this development across the denominations, as well as in the house-church movement. It is worth noting here that estimated numbers of Christians involved in PCR run into the millions worldwide, with an estimated number of over eight million involved in the Third Wave in Europe alone.[18] The huge numbers of Christians being influenced by the Third Wave and their theology of signs and wonders make this renewal movement of great significance in any study of contemporary Christianity. Little wonder it has attracted considerable attention from a variety of commentators,[19] although none of these has engaged in the detailed exegetical analysis of the relevant NT material I propose here.

Under the influence of John Wimber and others associated with the Vineyard Christian Fellowship churches, signs and wonders, exorcisms and miraculous healings have played a central role in the theology and praxis of those associated with the Third Wave. Wimber's influence has been well

---

17. For details of the internal discussions between Fuller staff that led to the withdrawal of Wimber's course, see L. B. Smedes, *Ministry and the Miraculous: A Case Study at Fuller Theological Seminary* (Pasadena, Calif.: Fuller Theological Seminary, 1987).

18. See further D. B. Barrett, 'Global Statistics', in *DPCM*, pp. 810–830; and C. P. Wagner, 'Church Growth', in *DPCM*, pp. 180–195. For an earlier indication of the influence of Pentecostalism, especially in the Third World, see W. J. Hollenweger, *The Pentecostals*.

19. See for example J. R. Coggins and P. G. Hiebert, *Wonders and the Word: An Examination of Issues Raised by John Wimber and the Vineyard Movement* (Winnipeg: Kindred, 1989); N. Geisler, *Signs and Wonders* (Wheaton, Ill.: Tyndale House, 1988); J. Gunstone, *Signs and Wonders: The Wimber Phenomenon* (London: Daybreak, 1989); D. Lewis, *Healing: Fiction, Fantasy or Fact?* (London: Hodder & Stoughton, 1989); N. Scotland, *Charismatics and the Next Millennium*; T. Smail, A. Walker and N. Wright, *Charismatic Renewal: The Search for a Theology* (London: SPCK, 1993); C. P. Wagner (ed.), *Signs and Wonders Today* (Altamonte Springs, Fla.: Creation House, 1987); E. E. Wright, *Strange Fire: Assessing the Vineyard Movement and the Toronto Blessing* (Darlington: Evangelical, 1996).

documented both in his own writings and by others,[20] and from the early 1980s Wimber's ministry had a tremendous impact on Christians associated with PCR in the United Kingdom. During conferences and in his writings Wimber presented a contemporary model for a theology and praxis of signs and wonders, based upon a paradigm derived from his understanding of the NT evidence for the ministry of Jesus and his disciples, which insists that this should be considered normative for all Christians, rather than being restricted to a few 'gifted' individuals.

## The Great Commission and healing

In an earlier generation A. J. Gordon, who was a leading apologist for divine healing in the United States and who was also associated with the Keswick Movement in the United Kingdom,[21] argued in a book that became popular on both sides of the Atlantic[22] that Jesus' ministry was twofold: healing the sick, and forgiving sinners. From here, Gordon argued on the basis of Psalm 103:3 and Matthew 8:17 that physical healing was to be understood as being provided for in the atonement and that an ongoing healing ministry within the church was integral to the so-called Great Commission, based particularly on Mark 16:18.[23] Clearly, considerable hermeneutical issues are raised here about the way in which Scripture may be used legitimately to inform contemporary praxis, but the important point to note is that Gordon attempts to set out a biblical model for the ongoing healing ministry of the church that he grounds

---

20. See for example biographical notes in J. Wimber, *Power Evangelism: Signs and Wonders Today* (London: Hodder & Stoughton, 1985), *passim*; and *Power Healing* (London: Hodder & Stoughton, 1986), *passim*; together with biographical notes *passim* in the works cited above, n. 9, and especially Gunstone, *Signs and Wonders*, pp. 1–20.

21. The Keswick Movement was born out of an annual convention that began meeting in Keswick, Cumbria, in 1875 for Bible study and addresses and that sought to promote 'practical holiness'. The movement continues to the present day and attracts a worldwide following. See further D. D. Bundy, 'Keswick Higher Life Movement', in *DPCM*, pp. 518–519, and bibliography.

22. A. J. Gordon, *The Ministry of Healing* (1882), cited by Chappell, 'Healing Movements', p. 362.

23. The longer ending of Mark's Gospel is often referred to in this context and usually considered to be authoritative by Third Wave writers. For a detailed discussion, see chapter 11.

in the Great Commission – an important point of contact that becomes central to later Third Wave thinking.

Pentecostalism, followed by the later charismatic renewal, also viewed its theology of healing and associated phenomena as being based upon the commissioning of the apostles both during Jesus' earthly ministry (Matt. 10:1–17; Mark 6:7–12; Luke 9:1–6) and post Easter (Matt. 28:16–20; Mark 16:14–18; Luke 24:44–49). R. F. Martin, a Catholic NT scholar and theologian associated with the charismatic movement, concludes in his article 'The Gift of Healing', 'It is obvious then that healing and deliverance from demonic power are integral parts of evangelization.'[24] However, in charismatic renewal this particular NT model did not really hold centre stage as the primary informant for their theology and praxis of healing, particularly at the local level, until the advent of Wimber. Earlier charismatic teaching focused more on the Pauline idea of individuals receiving various gifts in order to play their part in the life of their Christian community, with the Acts narrative being used, somewhat uncritically, to re-enforce their understanding of a contemporary Spirit-filled charismatic community. We should also note that the idea of spiritual warfare and exorcism has never been very far from the PCR agenda![25] Nevertheless, until comparatively recently, the theological focus within charismatic circles in the UK has been on the role of the Spirit in Christian conversion-initiation, together with an emphasis on the practice of charismata during worship services, and with special attention being given to gifts of utterance such as tongues, interpretation of tongues and prophecy.

## Conclusions

The NT evidence for the role of the Spirit in Christian conversion-initiation continues to be debated, as does the NT evidence for and against a dispensationalist doctrine of cessationism, which has characterized non-charismatic evangelical critiques of PCR theology and praxis.[26] However, under the

---

24. *DPCM*, p. 353.

25. See M. Harper, *Spiritual Warfare* (London: Hodder & Stoughton, 1970); and cf. the collection of articles on demon possession and exorcism in *Chm* 94.3 (1980).

26. For examples of the ongoing debate, see in addition to Dunn, *Baptism in the Holy Spirit*, recent further discussion in J. D. G. Dunn, 'Baptism in the Spirit: A Response to Pentecostal Scholarship on Luke-Acts', *JPT* 3 (1993), pp. 3–27, with responses in R. P. Menzies, 'Luke and the Spirit: Reply to James Dunn', *JPT* 4 (1994), pp. 115–138,

considerable influence of the Third Wave, there has been a resurgence of interest in the contemporary practice of healing and exorcism informed by the Third Wave's development of earlier Pentecostal ideas, which argued that in the Great Commission, and elsewhere in the NT, such a ministry was normative for the church both during and following the apostolic era.

Whilst clearly owing much to aspects of Pentecostal theology, the Third Wave has sought to avoid earlier theological conflicts associated with Pentecostalism's two-stage theology of conversion-initiation and the importance placed upon speaking in tongues.[27] Unlike earlier Pentecostalism, they have become more open to theological dialogue and have become conscious of the need to be more discerning in their presentation of theological emphases, making use of biblical scholars from within their own ranks. In other words, it would be unfair to the Third Wave to regard them as simply 'Azusa Street revisited'. The Third Wave have provided the vanguard for more recent developments and theological emphases in PCR, especially in the United Kingdom, where their influence has been across the denominations and so, in light of their contribution to the development of PCR, it is fair to describe them more positively as 'riding the third wave'.[28]

But what are the particular theological emphases associated with the Third Wave? What contribution does their 'kingdom theology' make to the way in which the ministry of Jesus and his disciples is understood to inform their paradigm for contemporary ministry?

---

and J. B. Shelton, 'A Reply to James D. G. Dunn's Baptism in the Spirit: A Response to Pentecostal Scholarship on Luke-Acts', *JPT* 4 (1994), pp. 139–143. See also R. P. Menzies, *The Development of Early Christian Pneumatology with Special Reference to Luke-Acts* (JSNTSup 54; Sheffield: JSOT, 1991); M. M. B. Turner, *Power from on High: The Spirit in Israel's Restoration and Witness in Luke-Acts* (JPTSup 9; Sheffield: Sheffield Academic Press, 1996); *The Holy Spirit and Spiritual Gifts: Then and Now* (Carlisle: Paternoster, 1996); J. Ruthven, *On the Cessation of the Charismata: The Protestant Polemic on Postbiblical Miracles* (JPTSup 3; Sheffield: Sheffield Academic Press, 1993); W. Grudem (ed.), *Are Miraculous Gifts for Today? Four Views* (Leicester: IVP, 1996).

27. See J. Wimber, *The Dynamics of Spiritual Growth* (London: Hodder & Stoughton, 1990), pp. 129–163.

28. For common use of this expression, see Springer, *Riding the Third Wave*.

## 3. KINGDOM THEOLOGY AND THE THIRD WAVE

There has never really been a satisfactory theology of power to show us where God's power fits into the Church's role in history. Kingdom theology provides a vehicle for such an understanding.

– J. White

So writes John White, a prominent Third Wave writer and conference speaker, in the foreword to former New Testament Professor Don Williams's book *Signs, Wonders, and the Kingdom of God*.[1] In New Testament scholarship today, all are agreed that the central feature of the message of Jesus of Nazareth was his proclamation of the kingly rule of God (see e.g. Mark 1:15; Matt. 4:17; Luke 4:43; Matt. 5:3//Luke 6:20; Matt. 10:7//Luke 10:9).[2] The centrality of

---

1. J. White, in D. Williams, *Signs, Wonders, and the Kingdom of God* (Ann Arbor, Mich.: Vine, 1989), p. ix. Don Williams is now the pastor of a church in San Diego, California, but was formerly Professor of New Testament at Fuller Theological Seminary, Pasadena, California.

2. Most recently noted by J. D. G. Dunn in *The Partings of the Ways* (London: SCM, 1991), p. 164. I do not propose here to give an historical survey of research into the meaning of 'kingdom of God' in the Gospels. This task has been more than adequately carried out by others in the past. See for example B. Chilton (ed.), *The*

this fact for the theology of contemporary Pentecostal-charismatic renewal is affirmed by Peter Kuzmic, writing on 'kingdom of God' in the *Dictionary of Pentecostal and Charismatic Movements* as follows: 'The biblical motif of the kingdom of God provides the essential theological framework for understanding the contemporary Pentecostal-charismatic phenomenon.'[3]

For the Third Wave in particular, their understanding of the kingdom of God in the NT provides the theological undergirding for their contemporary application of NT models taken from the ministry of Jesus and the early church. Their understanding of the kingdom of God in the teaching of Jesus and its implications for contemporary ministry is summarized in what follows. But what is 'kingdom theology'? How is kingdom theology understood and articulated by those associated with the Third Wave? What are the implications, with particular reference to the use of NT paradigms, of their understanding of kingdom theology for contemporary Third Wave belief and praxis?

## Power and presence

The Third Wave's understanding of the kingdom of God is developed particularly from the perspective of G. E. Ladd: the kingdom of God should be understood as the 'kingly rule of God' and is both present and future.[4] In other words, it is the kingdom power and presence of God and is to be understood as God's dynamic kingly rule in the hearts and lives of his people.[5] Through Jesus, the rule of God is being established in the hearts of those who respond

---

*Kingdom of God in the Teaching of Jesus* (London: SPCK, 1984); G. Lundström, *The Kingdom of God in the Teaching of Jesus: A History of Interpretation from the Last Decades of the Nineteenth Century to the Present Day* (ET Edinburgh: Oliver & Boyd, 1963); N. Perrin, *The Kingdom of God in the Teaching of Jesus* (London: SPCK, 1963); G. R. Beasley-Murray, *Jesus and the Kingdom of God* (Grand Rapids, Mich.: Eerdmans; Exeter: Paternoster, 1986).

3. P. Kuzmic, 'Kingdom of God', *DPCM*, p. 526.

4. G. E. Ladd, *A Theology of the New Testament* (Cambridge: Lutterworth, 1974); *The Presence of the Future: The Eschatology of Biblical Realism* (London: SPCK, 1974).

5. J. Wimber, 'Power Evangelism: Definitions', in C. P. Wagner and F. D. Pennoyer (eds.), *Wrestling with Dark Angels* (Eastbourne: Monarch, 1990), p. 25. Cf. G. Cray, 'A Theology of the Kingdom', *Transformation* 5.4 (1988), p. 25; B. Chilton, *Jesus and the Ethics of the Kingdom* (London: SPCK, 1987), p. 48.

appropriately to the message of the in-breaking kingdom. Having said this, the Third Wave emphasis on the contemporary manifestation of signs and wonders means that they also understand that the presence of the rule of God is visibly revealed in healings and exorcisms.[6]

## Present and future

According to Williams, in heralding the kingdom of God (Mark 1:15), we are to understand that Jesus proclaimed a kingdom that is both future and present.[7] In the NT accounts we find that the time of eschatological fulfilment has dawned (Matt. 8:11) with the return of the prophetic Spirit. This is evidenced in Luke's Gospel in the prophetic activity of Zechariah (Luke 1:67–79), Simeon (Luke 2:25–35), Anna (Luke 2:36–38), John the Baptist (Luke 1:15) and supremely in Jesus himself (Luke 4:18–21). Williams argues that Jesus believed in the re-establishment of God's rightful rule, firstly over Israel and then over the Gentile nations,[8] and that his mission was the inauguration of that rule. While God's direct rule was present and manifest in Jesus (Matt. 12:27–28//Luke 11:19–20), there will also be a future fulfilment when Satan, sin and death are completely destroyed.[9]

Today there is nothing controversial in this understanding of the kingdom of God in the Gospels. All are agreed that within the NT we have an eschatological tension between the 'now' and the 'not yet'. The Third Wave understanding of this eschatological tension is clearly articulated by Williams, who writes that a correct understanding of this eschatological tension explains

> both our sense of triumph in Christ and the continuing spiritual warfare which we fight on many fronts. It explains the reality that we have died with Christ and, at the same time, that the flesh still wars against the spirit. It explains why people are dramatically healed today by the power of God and also continue to get sick and die.[10]

---

6. G. S. Greig, 'The Purpose of Signs and Wonders in the New Testament', in G. S. Greig and K. N. Springer (eds.), *The Kingdom and the Power: Are Healing and the Spiritual Gifts Used by Jesus and the Early Church Meant for the Church Today?* (Ventura, Calif.: Regal, 1993), p. 157.

7. Williams, *Signs, Wonders*, p. 10.

8. The question arises whether this issue is really so clear in the Synoptic Gospels.

9. Williams, *Signs, Wonders*, p. 107.

10. Ibid., p. 108.

## Realized eschatology

According to the Third Wave, 'kingdom theology' teaches that until the final consummation of the kingdom of God, Christians experience the eschatological tension found in the NT because they must live under two kingdoms – the kingdom of God and the kingdom of Satan. Many of those associated with the Third Wave quote with approval Oscar Cullmann's argument that, in the coming of Christ, the division of time between the 'now' and the 'not yet' occurs. Cullmann writes:

> The decisive battle in a war may already have occurred in a relatively early stage of the war, and yet the war still continues . . . But the war must still be carried on for an undefined time, until 'Victory Day' . . . that event on the cross, together with the resurrection which followed was the already concluded decisive battle.[11]

Again, many would find little to argue with here in the Third Wave's theological presentation of NT eschatology. However, there remains a degree of tension between the Third Wave's theological presentation and its practical application. Practically speaking, the Third Wave emphasis tends to be almost wholly concentrated on the present reign of God, which is to be understood 'spatially' in that the kingdom of God is within reach, and our broken humanity is being restored to God's original order.[12]

In the final analysis, we may have to say that the Third Wave's theology of the kingdom is faulty due to their (over)emphasis on the presence of the kingdom, but that this is due more to 'effect' (in terms of their experience of signs and wonders etc.) rather than its being the 'cause'. Nevertheless, the question arises as to how far there is a tendency towards a pragmatic dualism in the Third Wave position that appears to be inherent in their theology of spiritual warfare and that, in turn, fails to reflect properly the eschatological tension found in the NT. This concentration on the present aspect of the

---

11. O. Cullmann, *Christ and Time* (ET London: SCM, 1951), p. 84. For Third Wave references, see for example C. Kraft, *Christianity with Power* (Ann Arbor, Mich.: Vine, 1989), p. 177; Williams, *Signs, Wonders*, pp. 107–108; J. White, *When the Spirit Comes with Power: Signs and Wonders among God's People* (London: Hodder & Stoughton, 1988), p. 36; Wimber, *Power Evangelism*, p. 23; and J. Wimber, *Kingdom Come: Understanding what the Bible Says about the Reign of God* (London: Hodder & Stoughton, 1989), pp. 19–20.

12. Williams, *Signs, Wonders*, p. 111.

kingdom of God, particularly by John Wimber, has attracted criticism. For example, D. L. Smith writes:

> Wimber's doctrine of the kingdom is either defective or somewhat premature in its expectations . . . He anticipates that all believers should be mediating sensational 'power' gifts which will throw Satan on his back to the canvas and will destroy the works of evil.[13]

It is at this point that problems, so far as Third Wave kingdom theology is concerned, arise out of their (over)emphasis on the present aspect of the kingdom of God. In practice, the Third Wave appear to be so taken up with the idea of living now in the 'presence of the future',[14] that they tend to project on to the biblical evidence, which informs their faith and praxis, understandings that serve their kingdom theology rather than allowing the biblical evidence to speak for itself in its own terms and, where appropriate, to (re)shape their theology.

The most serious argument against the Third Wave's theology of signs and wonders is not simply one that denies contemporary demonstrations of the miraculous per se – such arguments are dismissed by the Third Wave as theologically liberal and rationalistic and, therefore, a sign of unbelief. It is, rather, the argument by some fellow evangelicals who claim that biblical miracles are not recorded to provide a contemporary paradigm for ministry, but are there to authenticate God's revelation. Therefore, they are to be found in the Bible 'clustered' around significant redemptive events such as the Exodus and the ministry of Jesus.[15] This primary argument that signs and wonders are given to authenticate revelation, is levelled especially against the Third Wave idea of the contemporary manifestation of signs and wonders accompanying the proclamation of the Christian gospel.

Against this view, the Third Wave argue first that the coming of the kingdom involves a clash between the kingdom of God and the kingdom of

---

13. D. L. Smith, 'Third Wave Theology: The Vineyard Movement', in idem, *A Handbook of Contemporary Theology* (Wheaton, Ill.: Victor, 1992), p. 236.

14. Cf. Ladd, *Presence of the Future*.

15. See for example D. A. Carson, 'The Purpose of Signs and Wonders in the New Testament', in M. Scott-Horton (ed.), *Power Religion: The Selling out of the Evangelical Church?* (Chicago: Moody, 1992), pp. 89–118; L. B. Smedes, *Ministry and the Miraculous: A Case Study at Fuller Theological Seminary* (Pasadena, Calif.: Fuller Theological Seminary, 1987).

Satan, and the reality of this clash is demonstrated in displays of signs and wonders. Second, in the NT, signs and wonders frequently attest the identity and authority of Jesus and his disciples. Their purpose is to establish ministry and, more controversially, not just the ministry of Jesus and the early church. So far as the key elements in the ministry of Jesus that serve as a contemporary paradigm for ministry are concerned, it could be argued against the Third Wave that in Jesus' ministry the forgiveness of sins plays a more central role than casting out demons and healing the sick. In defence of the Third Wave position, Williams makes the point that in the Gospel summaries of Jesus' ministry (Matt. 4:23; Luke 4:18–21), 'forgiveness' is never included,[16] and to place forgiveness at the forefront of Jesus' works is to make a theological judgment rather than an historical observation.[17] But, how far is this really the case? Evidence for the place of forgiveness of sins in Jesus' ministry amounts to more than explicit incidents where sins are forgiven,[18] and this bears out the need for a more detailed examination of the NT evidence used by the Third Wave in support of their case for signs and wonders being normative for the contemporary church.

## A paradigm for contemporary ministry

In terms of the contemporary application of their theology of signs and wonders, the Third Wave believe that Christians are inheritors of the ministry of Jesus and that this is clearly reflected in the experience and praxis of the early church. Christians are to continue, in each generation, to proclaim and demonstrate the presence of the kingly rule of God. The historical and theological arguments mounted by the Third Wave are based on three factors. Firstly, the relationship described in the Gospels between Jesus and his disciples. Secondly, Jesus' restoration of charismatic leadership and his giving to those whom he calls the task of being his representatives. Thirdly, the idea of the disciples being sent out in mission during Jesus' lifetime and their subsequent 'commissioning' by the risen Christ with its mandate to continue the ministry of the earthly Jesus in proclaiming and demonstrating, with signs and wonders, the kingdom of God.

---

16. Williams appears to ignore here Mark 1:14–15!

17. Williams, *Signs, Wonders*, p. 111.

18. See for example J. Jeremias, *New Testament Theology Volume One: The Proclamation of Jesus* (ET London: SCM, 1971), pp. 113–114.

According to the Third Wave, there is a twofold pattern to be discerned in the way Jesus delivered his message of the kingdom of God. Jesus not only proclaimed the arrival of the kingdom of God; he also demonstrated its presence through healings, exorcisms and various other 'power encounters'. In other words, the kingdom of God is seen as both a 'message' and a 'ministry', a point, Wimber argues, the institutional church has often failed to grasp (Matt. 4:23–25; 9:35).[19] According to Wimber, in the proclamation and demonstration of the kingdom of God by Jesus, we have the 'decisive turning point of all history'.[20] Just as in the Gospels, where we read that the supernatural is to be expected as part of the presence of the kingdom of God,[21] for the Third Wave, when the finger/Spirit of God touches you, the kingdom of God is manifestly present.[22]

From here, it is asserted that this twofold pattern identified in the ministry of Jesus provides a paradigm for contemporary ministry in that the church, as inheritors of the ministry of Jesus, should also proclaim the present reality of the kingly rule of God and demonstrate this reality through signs and wonders. It is the life and experience of Jesus, as we have it described in the Gospels, that provided the principal paradigm for his disciples and for the early church, and now provides the principal paradigm for Christians today. Confirmation for the contemporary validity of the paradigm is sought particularly in the experience of the disciples of Jesus being sent out in mission by him in both the pre and post-Easter situations. The followers of Jesus have been commissioned by him to be inheritors of his ministry, both then and now.

That Christians are commissioned to continue this ministry, using Jesus as

---

19. Wimber, 'Power Evangelism', pp. 24–25. Also, J. Wimber, *The Kingdom of God* (Cassette Series; Vineyard Ministries International, 1985), cassette 1, side 1.

20. Ibid.

21. Williams, *Signs, Wonders*, p. 108. Once again, this raises hermeneutical issues for our handling of the NT texts and the question of the need to be sensitive theologically to differences that exist between pre- and post-Easter situations. This sensitivity appears often to be lacking, especially in the handling of the biblical material and also in the subsequent identification of biblical paradigms and the resulting theology of ministry. In the NT, the pivotal point of history occurs with the death and resurrection of Jesus and it is from a post-resurrection perspective that the NT documents have been written. Once again, I would argue that only a critical handling of the text will allow for the necessary sensitivity required to do justice to the intended meaning of the authors.

22. Wimber, *Kingdom of God*, cassette 1, side 1.

the primary paradigm for ministry, can be seen in the model of discipleship used by Jesus; the commissioning and sending out of the disciples and the Seventy (Luke 10:1–16; Matt. 9:37–38; 10:7–16); and especially in the Great Commission by the risen Jesus to go out into the world and make disciples and so on (Matt. 28:18–20; cf. Mark 16:9–20).[23] For the Third Wave, 'commissioning' contains within it the idea of a linear development from the historical Jesus to the Twelve (Matt. 10:6),[24] to the wider circle of disciples (Luke 10:1–16) to the apostles/disciples who received the post-resurrection commissioning on behalf of the church (Matt. 28:18–20).[25] In addition to explicit commissionings, implicit within the NT presentation of discipleship is the idea of following, emulating and representing the teacher/sender.[26] It is pointed out that in the ancient world the word 'apostle' carries with it the idea of being commissioned to be the legal and authoritative representative of another, and that this accords with the rabbinic idea that 'the one sent by a man is as the man himself'.[27] In calling the Twelve, unlike the rabbis, who wait for disciples to ask to join them,[28] Jesus takes the initiative and calls individuals to follow him.[29] Williams points out that in calling his disciples/apostles, 'Jesus restores charismatic leadership to Israel in order to carry out both his message and his ministry.'[30]

Furthermore, the proclamation and demonstration of the kingdom of God

---

23. Considerable weight is placed on the longer ending to Mark's Gospel, despite the weight of manuscript evidence testifying to the lateness of Mark 16:9–20. This issue is discussed in detail in chapter 11.

24. K. L. Sarles, 'An Appraisal of the Signs and Wonders Movement', *BSac* (January–March 1988), pp. 57–58, argues that the commission in Matt. 10:6 specifically restricted the activity of the Twelve to Israel. Therefore, it is inappropriate to find a wider contemporary application here – a point we will need to return to in a more detailed treatment of the NT 'commissionings'.

25. One is almost tempted to see this as a Third Wave alternative to apostolic succession!

26. John Wimber also views the NT concept of discipleship as critical for understanding the Great Commission (Matt. 28:18–20). See Wimber, 'Power Evangelism', pp. 25 and 29–30.

27. Williams, *Signs, Wonders*, p. 124. Cf. K. H. Rengstorf, ἀποστέλλω, ἀπόστολος, *TDNT* 1, p. 415.

28. E. Schweizer, *Jesus* (ET London: SCM, 1971), p. 40.

29. Williams, *Signs, Wonders*.

30. Ibid., p. 125. Cf. M. Hengel, *The Charismatic Leader and His Followers* (ET Edinburgh: T. & T. Clark, 1981), p. 88.

was not just restricted to the Twelve, as is evidenced by Jesus' sending out the Seventy (Luke 10:1ff.). Jesus' subsequent ecstatic vision of the fall of Satan (Luke 10:17–20) serves to emphasize his intention of commissioning a wider following. Here Williams concludes 'from these passages that Jesus' kingdom ministry, his word and his work, is first exhibited by him and then reproduced in his followers'.[31]

This intention by Jesus is further evidenced in the Great Commission (Matt. 28:18–20) where, Williams argues, the whole thrust in the idea of making disciples is again for Jesus to 'reproduce' himself and his kingdom ministry in his followers.[32] To facilitate this process, the exalted Lord continues to 'gift' his church with 'charismatic leaders'[33] (cf. Eph. 4:7–12; Acts 6:5, 8; 8:6–8; 13:8–12). In other words, for the Third Wave, there is no dispensational restriction to the 'Apostolic Age': charismatic leaders who are raised up by the Spirit are to continue to reproduce themselves in their disciples, which means that the ministry of proclaiming and demonstrating the kingdom of God will continue to be an ongoing process until the end of the age.[34]

## Kingdom and kerygma

Throughout this discussion of the Third Wave's kingdom theology, a vitally important point, by which much of Third Wave kingdom theology could stand or fall, has emerged. As we have seen, the Third Wave has identified the proclamation and demonstration of the kingdom of God as a continuing and prominent theme for the post-Easter community. This being the case, it is argued, then by extension (and commission) we have a paradigm for the contemporary message of the church. Central to that message today should be the message proclaimed by Jesus (the kingly rule of God) and that proclamation should be accompanied, as with Jesus, by signs and wonders. The Third Wave position can be summarized as follows:

---

31. Williams, *Signs, Wonders*, pp. 125–126. Interestingly, O. Cullmann, *Christ and Time* (ET London: SCM, 1951), p. 71, sees an eschatological emphasis here on the anticipation of the final end-time victory over Satan rather than an example of discipleship. He argues that Luke 10:17–20 indicates that already in his lifetime Jesus sees Satan's downfall, although the final victory over Satan is still in the future.

32. Williams, *Signs, Wonders*, p. 129.

33. Ibid.

34. Ibid., p. 131.

Not only was the kingdom a prominent theme before the resurrection, but ample evidence exists in Scripture that it was a very important theme thereafter. In Acts 1:3 we read that during the 40 days between the time Jesus was raised from the dead and His ascension, He spoke to His disciples about 'the kingdom of God'. When Philip evangelised Samaria, he 'preached the good news about the kingdom of God' (Acts 8:12). In Rome, Paul 'spoke boldly, arguing and pleading about the Lord Jesus Christ quite openly and unhindered' (Acts 28:31). Paul, Peter, James and the author of Hebrews all mention the kingdom in their epistles.[35]

In other words, just as the kingdom of God was central to the kerygma of Jesus, according to the Third Wave the NT evidence clearly suggests that it should also continue to be central to the kerygma of the church.[36] But is this really the case? Does the weight of NT evidence support such a direct correlation between the ministry of Jesus and the early church? Alternatively, is the Third Wave position undermined because it virtually ignores the radical change in perception that was occasioned by the resurrection? The scholarly consensus detects a vital change between the content of the kerygma of Jesus and the kerygma of the post-Easter communities. This change is summarized succinctly by James Dunn, who writes:

> Jesus proclaimed the kingdom, the first Christians proclaimed Jesus; Jesus called for repentance and faith with respect to the kingdom, the first Christians called for faith in Jesus; Jesus held out the offer of God's forgiveness and acceptance, the first Christians held out a similar offer but as mediated through Jesus. Quite clearly, Jesus stands at the centre of the post-Easter kerygma in a manner which is not really paralleled in Jesus' own kerygma.[37]

If, on the one hand, there are substantial differences between the kerygma of Jesus and the post-Easter kerygma, and yet, on the other hand, there is a unity between the historical Jesus and the kerygmatic Christ,[38] what are the

35.  J. Wimber, 'Theological Foundation: The Kingdom of God', in idem, *Signs, Wonders and Church Growth* (Vineyard Teaching Manual; Placenta, Calif.: Vineyard Ministries International, 1984), Part 1, Section 2, pp. 7–8.

36.  This appears to be the general perspective shared by others associated with the Pentecostal-charismatic renewal. See for example Kuzmic, 'Kingdom of God', p. 526.

37.  J. D. G. Dunn, *Unity and Diversity in the New Testament: An Enquiry into the Character of Earliest Christianity* (London: SCM, 1977), p. 31.

38.  Ibid., p. 228.

implications for Third Wave kingdom theology? Here we should also note particularly how surprising is Paul's treatment of the kingdom, and, if the Third Wave are correct, what are we to make of John's silence?[39]

## Conclusions

I have set out in broad terms the Third Wave's understanding of the kingdom of God; how they see it relating to the miraculous in the ministry of Jesus and the early church, as well as how they believe it provides a paradigm for the ministry of Christians today with an emphasis on the contemporary manifestation of signs and wonders. We have noted a number of specific NT issues arising out of the Third Wave's kingdom theology that need to be followed up in more detail. These include, for example, the relationship in the ministry of Jesus between the authority to forgive sins and the miraculous; the purpose of signs and wonders; the evangelists' presentation(s) of the disciples and discipleship, and the consequent understanding we are to derive for the nature and purpose of discipleship today; the contemporary relevance of the commissioning of the disciples and their being empowered by the Spirit. These issues in turn, raise questions about the uniqueness of Jesus and continuity/discontinuity between the experience of Jesus as he is presented in the Synoptic Gospels and that of the post-Easter church as Luke presents it in Acts – issues I will address in the following chapters, beginning with Matthew's Gospel and the Great Commission.

---

39. Dunn, *The Theology of Paul the Apostle* (Edinburgh: T. & T. Clark, 1998), pp. 190–191, draws attention to the relative paucity of references to the kingdom of God by Paul (14 times) when compared to Jesus in the Synoptics (around 105 times). He points out that for Paul, Jesus' emphasis on the kingdom of God has given way to an emphasis on righteousness (Paul 57 times; Jesus in the Synoptics 7 times) and the Spirit (Paul 110-plus times; Jesus in the Synoptics 13 times). Nevertheless, he asserts, Paul's references to the kingdom of God are in line with Jesus' teaching. Paul clearly acknowledges the presence of the kingdom (e.g. Rom. 14:7), although the majority of Paul's references are to the future eschatological rule of God.

# PART ONE

# THE GREAT COMMISSION ACCORDING TO MATTHEW: A CONTEMPORARY PARADIGM FOR SIGNS AND WONDERS?

## Introducing the issues

Absolutely central to the Third Wave's paradigm for contemporary Christian discipleship is their particular understanding of Matthew's Great Commission. Is it really the case, as the Third Wave argue, that whilst authority to heal is not mentioned specifically in the Great Commission according to Matthew (28:16–20), it may be implicitly assumed on the grounds that this authority had already been granted to Jesus' disciples when he sent them out in mission (Matt. 10:1, 5–10; cf. Mark 6:7–13; Luke 9:1–6; Luke 10:1–20) – an understanding of the Great Commission, that has proved contentious.[1]

Key questions for us to consider here include the following. How far does

---

1. See for example the critique of the Third Wave position set out in L. B. Smedes (ed.), *Ministry and the Miraculous: A Case Study at Fuller Theological Seminary* (Pasadena, Calif.: Fuller Theological Seminary, 1987), which, unfortunately, also takes an homogenizing approach to the biblical evidence. For a Third Wave response, see D. Williams, 'Following Christ's Example: A Biblical View of Discipleship', in G. S. Greig and K. N. Springer (eds.), *The Kingdom and the Power* (Ventura, Calif.: Regal, 1993), pp. 175–196; and in the same volume, see appendix 3: 'Matthew 28:18–20 – The Great Commission and Jesus' Commands to Preach and Heal', pp. 399–403.

Matthew intend his portrayal of the disciples to be paradigmatic for the church? What are the characteristics of Christian discipleship that emerge from Matthew's Gospel? What evidence is there that Matthew implies for his readers a place for signs and wonders and the miraculous in the post-Easter mission of the church? Does Matthew intend the Great Commission to be understood by his first readers to include authority to heal, as the Third Wave claim?

## Key Matthean themes

As we read through Matthew's Gospel, it is difficult to ignore its overall shape, where we have five major sections reminiscent of the Pentateuch. Furthermore, emphasis on the place of the law can be seen in the way Matthew presents Jesus as a new Moses figure (cf. Deut. 18:15–18).[2] Throughout his Gospel, the First Evangelist constantly reminds his readers that events concerning Jesus, or words and actions by Jesus, fulfil Old Testament prophecy (see 1:22; 2:15, 17, 23; 8:17; 12:17; 13:25; 21:4; 26:54, 56; 27:9). We are told that all the law is binding (5:17–19), and hypocrisy is constantly attacked (cf. 6:2, 15–16; 7:5; 15:7; 16:3; 22:18; 23:13–14; 24:51). When we ask why this is so, we must answer, because the seal of authority has been set upon these things by Jesus (7:29). With this thought in mind, as the Matthean Jesus climbs a mountain to deliver his discourse on the law (Matt. 5:1; cf. Luke 6:17), it is not difficult for readers of the First Gospel to see the Sermon on the Mount in the context of the giving of the law on Mount Sinai, particularly in the series of antitheses that begin with an authoritative 'You heard that it was said to those of ancient times . . . but I tell you' by Jesus (5:21–48; my trans.).

At the end of the sermon the crowds are 'amazed at his teaching' because he is said to teach as one who has authority (*exousia*), unlike their teachers of the law (7:29). In Matthew's narrative this comment concerning Jesus' authority is followed immediately by two healing stories that immediately demonstrate Jesus' authority in action.[3] The first, the cleansing of the leper, which

---

2. Cf. G. Bornkamm, 'End Expectation and Church in Matthew', in G. Bornkamm, G. Barth and H. J. Held, *Tradition and Interpretation in Matthew* (ET London: SCM, 1963), p. 35.

3. If chapters 5–7 may be regarded as an anthology of the Messiah's *exousia* expressed in word, then chapters 8–9 may be regarded as being largely a parallel anthology of the Messiah's *exousia* expressed in action. I am grateful to the Revd Dr R. T. France for this insight.

Matthew found in Mark (Matt. 8:1–4//Mark 1:40–45), shows Jesus aligning himself with Torah (Matt. 8:4; cf. Lev. 14:1ff.). The second, the healing of the centurion's servant, which the evangelist found in Q (Matt. 8:5–13//Luke 7:1–9), pointedly discusses the question of 'authority' in order to stress the legitimacy of the authority of Jesus, which is recognized even by a Gentile. In summary, Matthew presents Jesus' authority in terms of both word and miraculous activity.

All this, in turn, suggests that Matthew is not only (re)telling the Jesus tradition, but intends his Gospel to be used as a reference point by his church for what it means to be a follower of Jesus, and how they should apply Jesus' teaching to their own situation. Matthew clearly has a high regard for the law, as taught by Jesus (cf. Matt. 5:17–19), and he is keen to point out the way in which law-keeping relates to 'righteousness' (*dikaiosynē*)[4] for Jesus' followers (Matt. 5:20). Matthew's extensive use of the verb 'to do' (*poiein*) indicates that, for the First Evangelist, law-keeping is an active process where only those who do the will of the Father will be called great / enter the kingdom of heaven (5:19; 7:21; 19:16–17; 25:40, 45). Those who fail to keep the law are accused in Matthew's Gospel of being *anomia*, 'lawless' (7:23; 13:41; 23:28). This term of condemnation occurs only in Matthew and is clearly his own formulation.[5] These, and other issues relevant to our investigation arising out of the complexity of Matthew's Gospel, will be discussed further as we proceed.

---

4. *Dikaiosynē* occurs seven times in Matthew (3:15; 5:6, 10, 20; 6:1, 33; 21:32) against once in Luke (Luke 1:75) and twice in John (John 16:8, 10).

5. J. D. G. Dunn, *Unity and Diversity in the New Testament: An Enquiry into the Character of Earliest Christianity* (London: SCM, 1977), p. 247. For a comparison with Luke's Hellenizing 'workers of righteousness' (Matt. 7:22–23//Luke 13:25–27), see R. H. Gundry, *Matthew: A Commentary on His Literary and Theological Art* (Grand Rapids, Mich.: Eerdmans, 1982), pp. 132–133.

## 4. MATTHEW, JESUS AND DISCIPLESHIP

In the Great Commission (Matt. 28:19), Jesus tells the eleven disciples to go and make disciples, and this imperative raises the question 'How, according to Matthew, are we to understand the role of the disciples and the nature of discipleship?' Is Matthew interested in the disciples only in so far as they accompanied Jesus during his earthly ministry? Alternatively, does Matthew use the disciples to provide a paradigm for his church and, by extension, the church to the 'end of the age' (Matt. 28:20), for what it means to be a disciple of Jesus?

In redaction-critical studies of Matthew's Gospel that examine Matthew's understanding and presentation of the ministry of Jesus and his disciples, two opposing views have emerged. The first is described as 'historicizing' and regards Jesus and the disciples as confined to a holy, unrepeatable past. The second argues for 'transparency', where the disciples act as role models for Matthew's church.

### Historicizing

In his essay 'The Concept of History in Matthew', Georg Strecker, who is the chief proponent of the historicizing approach, aimed to present a redaction-critical study of Matthew's concept of history as it relates to his presentation of the Jesus tradition.[1] According to Strecker, Matthew's understanding of history was governed by his second-generation perspective,[2] and that his presentation of the Jesus tradition was aimed at serving the needs of his community as it faced the theological situation brought about by the delay of the parousia.[3]

Strecker writes, 'The first inference from our recognition of the theological-historical background of the Synoptic redactions is that there was a "*historicizing*" of the traditional material by the redactor Matthew.'[4]

What exactly is meant by 'historicizing'? For Strecker, historicizing means that Matthew deliberately set out to give the appearance of history to the Jesus tradition by using both chronology and geography to provide an historical context in which to locate the tradition.[5] For example, Strecker interprets Matthew's use of the formula 'from then' (*apo tote*) as being one that the evangelist deliberately inserts to act as a chronological 'sign post' (Matt. 4:17; 16:21; 26:16). He also points to Matthew's identification of Mark's reference to Capernaum (Mark 2:1) as Jesus' 'own town' (Matt. 4:13; cf. 9:1), where the First Evangelist also identifies the house in which Jesus heals the paralytic (Mark 2:1–12 pars.). Strecker concludes that 'originally topological ideas have become geographically limited'.[6]

He also argues that Matthew uses OT quotations to indicate that the 'promises of God have found fulfilment in the life of Jesus'.[7] From here, Strecker suggests that the quotations are linked to temporal and geographical statements that mark different stages in Jesus' life, together with biographical details (e.g. performance of miracles or entry into Jerusalem). He explains, 'This means that Matthew uses formula-quotations to interpret the history of Jesus as unique event, temporally and geographically distant from his own situation.'[8]

Strecker notes that Matthew is the only Evangelist to restrict the mission of the disciples to Israel, although Matthew himself is clearly aware of the universal mission of the church (Matt. 28:18–20). He argues that this can be

---

1. First published as 'Das Geschichtsverständnis des Matthäus', *EvT 26* (1966), pp. 57–74; ET republished as 'The Concept of History in Matthew', in G. Stanton (ed.), *The Interpretation of Matthew* (London: SPCK, 1983), pp. 67–84.

2. Matthew is probably writing during the 80s AD.

3. Strecker, 'Concept of History', pp. 69–70.

4. Ibid., p. 70.

5. Ibid.

6. Ibid., pp. 71–72.

7. Ibid., p. 72.

8. Ibid.

explained only in terms of Matthew deliberately reflecting the historical situation in the lifetime of Jesus and the disciples. Strecker concludes that Matthew understood history in terms of three periods or epochs (the time of preparation, the time of Jesus, and the time of the church),[9] and that both Jesus and the disciples belong to 'a unique, unrepeatable, holy, and ideal epoch in the course of history'.[10] Indeed, the disciples are very much a part of the 'uniqueness' of this central epoch, and Strecker is keen to argue that this is particularly emphasized by Matthew when he restricts the term 'disciple' (*mathētēs*) to the Twelve, although, as France points out, this is not always the case (cf. 8:19, 21; 10:42).[11] Also, as I will discuss further below, Matthew's use of the verb *mathēteuō* is used to describe the continuing mission of the church.[12]

If we accept Strecker's view, then the unique time-conditionedness of the activity of Jesus and (especially) the disciples suggests that the miracle-working activities associated in this Gospel with the disciples and their being commissioned to take part in Jesus' mission to the 'lost sheep of the house of Israel' could not have been intended by Matthew to be paradigmatic for his church and its mission to all nations (Matt. 28:19). How, then, did Matthew intend the tradition to remain relevant for his church and their own socio-historical context?

According to Strecker, Matthew has subjected the tradition to a process of 'ethicization', by which he means that for Matthew, Jesus' mission is characterized primarily by his proclamation of an ethical demand that signifies the presence of the eschatological reign of God. This proclamation has been shaped redactionally by Matthew to meet the institutionalizing demands of his community, and continues during the period of the church. It provides the

---

9. An understanding of history attributed to Luke some years earlier by H. Conzelmann, *Die Mitte der Zeit* (Tübingen: Mohr, 1953); ET *The Theology of St. Luke* (London: SCM, 1960).

10. Strecker, 'Concept of History', p. 73.

11. G. Strecker, *Der Weg der Gerechtigkeit: Untersuchung zur Theologie des Matthäus*, 3rd ed. (Göttingen: Vandenhoeck & Ruprecht, 1971), pp. 191–193. Strecker, 'Concept of History', p. 73; R. T. France, *Matthew: Evangelist and Teacher* (Exeter: Paternoster, 1989), p. 261.

12. France, *Matthew: Evangelist and Teacher*, pp. 261ff., who argues contra Strecker that *mathētēs* as used by Matthew is 'a term which is appropriate to all who follow Jesus, past, present and future'. This verb occurs elsewhere in the NT in Acts 14:21 but is used only as an imperative here by Matthew.

continuity between the past time of Jesus and the present time of the church, until the 'end of the age' (Matt. 28:20).[13] Examples of this can be seen in Matthew's insertion of the clause 'except on the ground of unchastity' in Jesus' teaching on divorce (Matt. 5:32; 19:9; cf. Mark 10:11–12) and a reversal by Matthew of the prohibition by Jesus on oath-taking (Matt. 5:33–37; cf. 23:16–22).[14]

On this reading, the paradigm Matthew intends for the church, as it relates to the manifestation of the presence of the kingdom of God, is to be found in the continuing ethical proclamation of the church. Strecker's understanding of Matthew as 'historicizing' his tradition, with Jesus and the disciples as belonging to a holy and unrepeatable past, leaves little or no room for a Third Wave paradigm that sees the church's continuing proclamation of the kingdom of God being accompanied by signs and wonders.

## Transparency

The alternative view to Strecker's *historicizing* is to understand Matthew's literary intentions in terms of *transparency*. This applies particularly to the way in which Matthew presents the disciples as primary vehicles for transparency.[15] It is the experience of the disciples that provides a paradigm for Matthew's church. Schuyler Brown describes transparency in the following way:

> Since the term 'disciple' is not restricted to a follower of the earthly Jesus but applies to any Christian, the Matthean identification between 'the Twelve' and 'the disciples' makes the 'twelve disciples' into a transparency for the members of Matthew's own community. . . . Everything addressed to the twelve disciples is intended for all Jesus' future disciples.[16]

---

13. Strecker, 'Concept of History', p. 79.
14. It should be noted here that there is no universal agreement on the interpretation of Matt. 5:33–37 adopted here by Strecker. For alternative views, see R. H. Gundry, *Matthew: A Commentary on His Literary and Theological Art* (Grand Rapids, Mich.: Eerdmans, 1982), pp. 91–93; and D. A. Hagner, *Matthew 1–13* (WBC 33A; Dallas, Tex.: Word, 1993), pp. 126–129.
15. See especially U. Luz, 'The Disciples in the Gospel according to Matthew', in Stanton, *Interpretation of Matthew*, pp. 99–105.
16. S. Brown, 'The Mission to Israel in Matthew's Central Section (Matt. 9.35–11.1)', *ZNW* 69 (1977), pp. 74–75.

It is argued that transparency can be detected in Matthew's Gospel in the way in which the story of Jesus' conflict with Israel is mirrored in the experience of Matthew's own community (cf. Matt. 5:11–12; 10:23; 23:23), particularly as relationships between church and synagogue became increasingly strained.[17] It is argued that the disciples are imitators of Jesus and, at the same time, are paradigmatic for Matthew's community, thus allowing Matthew's readers to be contemporary with Jesus and the twelve disciples.[18] The church's experience, particularly as described in the mission discourse (Matt. 10:1–42), is to reflect that of Jesus in terms of homelessness, poverty (10:9–10) and, above all, their destiny as they take up the cross (cf. Matt. 10:17–18, 23, 38–39; cf. John 9:22, 34, 35).[19]

Transparency is further evidenced in Matthew's retelling of the miracle stories, which are intended by the Evangelist to be 'transparent for the present'.[20] According to Luz, Matthew's community did witness and experience miracles themselves. However, the way in which Matthew primarily intends the miracle stories to be transparent is in a 'spiritualized' way. For example, 'blindness' refers not only to physical blindness but also to the way in which Matthew's community is led from blindness to knowledge by Jesus. This, in turn, sets Jesus and the disciples apart from the Pharisees who are themselves 'blind guides' (15:14; 23:16–26).[21] Similarly, in Matthew, the healing of the lame man (9:2–8) becomes directly transparent in terms of the community's own experience of the forgiveness of sins.[22]

---

17. U. Luz, *The Theology of the Gospel of Matthew* (ET Cambridge: Cambridge University Press, 1995), pp. 64–66. For a detailed discussion of the emergence of Christianity from Judaism, see J. D. G. Dunn, *The Partings of the Ways* (London: SCM, 1991).

18. Luz, *Theology of the Gospel of Matthew*, p. 92.

19. Ibid., pp. 77ff. For a discussion of the way in which Matthew links discipleship to following Jesus and taking up one's cross, see France, *Matthew: Evangelist and Teacher*, pp. 262–264. See also J. D. Kingsbury, 'The Verb *akolouthein* ("to follow") as an Index of Matthew's View of his Community', *JBL* 97 (1978), pp. 56–73; M. Hengel, *The Charismatic Leader and His Followers* (ET Edinburgh: T. & T. Clark, 1981), *passim*.

20. Luz, *Theology of the Gospel of Matthew*, p. 66. For a detailed example, see especially G. Bornkamm, 'The Stilling of the Storm in Matthew', in G. Bornkamm, G. Barth and H. J. Held, *Tradition and Interpretation in Matthew* (ET London: SCM, 1963), pp. 52–57.

21. Luz, *Theology of the Gospel of Matthew*, pp. 68–69. Luz points out that in Jewish tradition 'blindness' can refer to spiritual blindness (p. 68). For the recurrence of Jesus' healing of blind persons in Matthew's Gospel, see 9:27–31; 12:22–24; 20:29–34; 21:14.

22. Ibid.

Nevertheless, Luz argues, Matthew does not remove the miracles from the corporeal altogether. Indeed, it is lack of the ability to perform miracles that Luz identifies as being the reason for their 'little faith' (Matt. 16:8; 17:14–20). For Luz, transparency in Matthew's retelling of the miracle stories becomes what we might describe as a merging of two horizons – the corporeal and the spiritual – as can be seen from the following:

> That Jesus first healed Israel's sick and cast out its demons is significant to Matthew not only because it thereby demonstrates that Israel truly experienced all that the Messiah is capable of accomplishing. No, the real importance lay elsewhere. For the miracles embodied a true core of the mission of Jesus and his [Matthew's] community: 'salvation' – healing – takes place, if not exclusively, then at least initially in the realm of the corporeal. . . . The experience undergone by Matthew and his community, initiated by Jesus' miracles, were signs that the Lord really is with his community 'always to the end of time'.[23]

If, then, we are to understand discipleship in the First Gospel as being 'transparent' in the sense that Matthew regards the church as somehow 'embodied' in the disciples,[24] what are the key features that provide the essence of Matthew's intended paradigm for discipleship? Are disciples meant to be imitators of Jesus in terms of proclaiming and demonstrating, with acts of power, the kingdom of God, as the Third Wave argue? Alternatively, does Matthew present us with a more complex paradigm?

## The essence of discipleship according to Matthew

Matthew portrays Jesus as a Mosaic prophet who fulfils the law (5:17–18), interprets the law according to the 'Golden Rule' (7:12), demands action as well as words (5:20), and whose authority to teach is ratified by his charismatic activity (cf. 11:4–5). Throughout his Gospel Matthew makes the point that discipleship is related to the teaching of Jesus.[25] Indeed, discipleship is, by definition, about learning (13:52; 27:57; 28:19); disciples are to hear and understand Jesus' words (13:13–25, 51–53) and obey them (21:5, 28–32; 28:20).[26]

---

23. Ibid., p. 70.

24. G. Barth, 'Matthew's Understanding of the Law', in Bornkam, Barth and Held, *Tradition and Interpretation*, p. 100 n. 2.

25. Luz, 'Disciples in the Gospel According to Matthew', p. 105.

Matthew's presentation of discipleship is also firmly linked to the idea of 'righteousness' (*dikaiosynē*) resulting from doing the will of God, which amounts to keeping the law (rightly interpreted by Jesus), and this is crucial for our understanding of the complexity of the Matthean paradigm of discipleship.

The noun *dikaiosynē* occurs redactionally seven times in Matthew's Gospel: the reason given for Jesus' baptism by John is 'to fulfil all righteousness' ( Matt. 3:15); the Matthean beatitudes are described as being for 'those who hunger and thirst for righteousness' (Matt. 5:6; cf. Luke 6:21); blessings come to those who are persecuted for 'righteousness' sake' (Matt. 5:10; cf. Luke 6:22); Jesus' followers are not to practise their acts of piety (*dikaiosynē*) for public approval (Matt. 6:1); the disciples are to seek God's kingdom first and 'his righteousness' (Matt. 6:33; cf. Luke 12:31); and finally, in Matthew 21:32, where Jesus, who has publicly endorsed the teaching of John the Baptist (Matt. 21:32), now describes that teaching as 'the way of righteousness' (Matt. 3:2; cf. 4:17 and 21:32).[27] Those who fail to display a righteousness that exceeds that of the scribes and Pharisees will not enter the kingdom of heaven (Matt. 5:20).

Throughout the Gospel, Jesus continually instructs the disciples whose ability to understand goes hand in hand with 'little faith' and doubt (e.g. 5:1; 13:10; 15:12–20; 16:5–12; 17:10–13, 19–20; 28:17). Matthew's stress on the understanding of the disciples does not serve to idealize the disciples, but rather to accentuate the teaching of Jesus.[28] Indeed, Matthew's portrayal of the disciples is thoroughly realistic, rather than idealistic,[29] and in this they serve as an appropriate model for a church where some act righteously and others do not (Matt. 13:24–30). Importantly, for Matthew, Jesus' authority to interpret the demands of the law is passed on to the disciples/community (16:19; 18:18), although there is clearly a tension in the way Matthew presents the disciples as inheritors of Jesus' authority (*exousia*) and, at the same time, as those of little

---

26. Gundry, *Matthew*, p. 7. For a detailed examination of the idea of 'understanding' as it relates to the disciples in Matthew's Gospel, see Barth, 'Matthew's Understanding of the Law', in Bornkamm, Barth and Held, *Tradition and Interpretation*, pp. 105–125.

27. For discussion of the idea of *dikaiosynē* in Matthew's Gospel, see for example Strecker, *Weg der Gerechtigkeit*, pp. 149–158, 179–181; 'Concept of History', pp. 74–77; B. Przybylski, *Righteousness in Matthew and in his World of Thought* (SNTSMS 41; Cambridge: Cambridge University Press, 1980), pp. 13–76.

28. M. J. Wilkins, *The Concept of Disciple in Matthew's Gospel: As Reflected in the Use of the Term Μαθητής* (NovTSup 59; Leiden: Brill, 1988), p. 165.

29. Cf. Ibid., p. 169.

faith (Matt. 10:1; 28:18–20; cf. 6:30; 8:26; 14:31; 16:8). Nevertheless, for Matthew it is, as Bornkamm asserts, 'in following Jesus that the perfection demanded by the law is fulfilled'.[30]

According to Matthew, the righteousness demanded of those who follow Jesus is to exceed that of the Pharisees and scribes (Matt. 5:20) as a result of obedience to all the law (Matt. 5:17–19; cf. Ps. 119:141–144). Whilst he acknowledges that the scribes and Pharisees 'sit in Moses' seat' (Matt. 23:2), the disciples are not to be hypocrites like them, displaying their righteousness before men (23:2). By all means tithe mint and dill (v. 23a), but Jesus' disciples are to make sure they do not neglect the basic covenant concepts of justice, mercy and faithfulness (v. 23b). The way to righteousness for the followers of Jesus is to manifest inwardly the qualities inherent in the law, whilst outwardly meeting all its demands (v. 23c). In Matthew 19:28, Matthew inserts a Q saying (cf. Luke 22:30b) which emphasizes that discipleship is not only linked to fulfilling the law here and now, but is also linked to a promise that will be realized eschatologically. Leaving all to follow Jesus will bring its rewards, but discipleship is also concerned with cross-bearing and suffering. The disciples are to follow their Lord, who, in his passion, has set them the example par excellence of the righteous person being made to suffer (Matt. 27:20; 5:11–12; cf. Wisdom 1–5) and who, as the Risen One, is himself the final proof that God will vindicate and reward righteousness.

### Beware of self-deception (Matt. 7:21–23)

At the end of the Sermon on the Mount, the 'Golden Rule' (Matt. 7:12) summarizes how the law is to be fulfilled by the followers of Jesus.[31] From here, Matthew presents us with four 'vignettes' that demonstrate clearly how to differentiate between true and false disciples.[32] Set against the context of final

---

30. G. Bornkamm, 'Christology and Law', in Bornkamm, Barth and Held, *Tradition and Interpretation*, p. 29.

31. E. Schweizer, *The Good News According to Matthew* (ET London: SPCK, 1976), p. 176.

32. France, *Matthew: Evangelist and Teacher*, p. 276. For arguments that support the structural unity of Matt. 7:15–20 and 21–23, see W. D. Davies and D. C. Allison Jr., *A Critical and Exegetical Commentary on The Gospel According to Saint Matthew*. Vol. 1: *Introduction and Commentary on Matthew I–VII* (Edinburgh: T. & T. Clark, 1988), pp. 693–694, 701–703.

judgment, they conclude with a dire warning to those who regard charismatic activity as a defining mark of Christian discipleship rather than obeying the commands of Jesus (7:21–23; cf. 13:36–43; 25:31–46). The warnings are introduced in 7:13–14 with a saying about entering by the 'narrow gate' (cf. 5:20). In 7:15–20, Jesus uses the two metaphors of wolves in sheep's clothing and trees that fail to bear good fruit, in order to illustrate the true nature of the false prophets.[33] It is clear that a thematic relationship exists between the false prophets of 7:15, who present themselves as members of the Christian community but whose true identities are revealed by their actions (7:16–20), and the charismatics envisaged in 7:21–23.[34] According to Schweizer, the false prophets referred to in 7:15 and 24:12, and whom Matthew presents as Christians who may or may not be members of his own community, are those who have turned away from the law as rightly interpreted by Jesus.[35] They have the appearance of being like other members of Matthew's community but are deceivers (7:15; cf. 7:21). In Matthew's portrayal of a mixed community where the 'righteous' and the 'lawless' coexist together (13:24–30; 47–50), doing the will of the Father opens the way through the narrow gate (7:13–14), and it is only at the Last Judgment that the true nature of the false prophets will be revealed.[36]

Crucially for our understanding of Matthew's portrayal of Christian discipleship the object of the warning in 7:21–23 is the charismatic life of Matthew's community. Matthew is not opposed to charismatic activity as such, as the references to prophets in Matthew 5:12, 10:41 and 23:3 makes clear.[37] Nevertheless, all who claim to be disciples of Jesus, whether charismatics or not, are equally bound by the injunction to obey all that Jesus has commanded (28:20a). Discipleship for Matthew is characterized by the 'Golden Rule' (Matt. 7:12) rather than by charismatic activity. In 7:21–23 the Matthean Jesus makes his meaning indisputably clear. The address 'Lord, Lord' in 7:21 appears in Matthew's Gospel only on the lips of those who are either followers of Jesus or sincerely seeking his help. In contrast, during the betrayal scene in 26:25, 49, Judas calls Jesus 'Rabbi' – a form of address reserved by Matthew

---

33. R. A. Guelich, *The Sermon on the Mount: A Foundation for Understanding* (Waco, Tex.: Word, 1982), p. 393.

34. Ibid.

35. E. Schweizer, 'Matthew's Church', in Stanton, *Interpretation of Matthew*, p. 138.

36. E. Schweizer, 'Observance of the Law and Charismatic Activity in Matthew', *NTS* 16 (1969–70), p. 225.

37. Schweizer, *Good News According to Matthew*, p. 179.

for outsiders.[38] Furthermore, in 23:34 Matthew makes it clear that Jesus will send prophets, wise men and teachers who are part of the Christian community and, as Guelich concludes, the use of 'Lord' here implies that the false prophets were accepted as part of the Christian community.[39]

In Matthew 7:22a the phrase 'in those days' clearly alludes to the Last Judgment and sets the scene for 7:22b–23,[40] where the invocation of Jesus' name serves to guarantee the presence of the risen Jesus (cf. 28:20b; 18:20) and should be understood here as 'in your power'.[41] Mention of the 'many' provides confirmation of the relationship between the false prophets of 7:15 and those 'many false prophets' encountered here in 7:22.[42] Guelich comments that the invocation of Jesus' name in the course of their charismatic ministry is also reminiscent of the earlier charge that the false prophets are like wolves in sheep's clothing (7:15). This leads to their acceptance within the community, but not ultimately by the Matthean Jesus (7:23),[43] for whom charismatic deeds are not 'definitive pointers' to authentic faith/discipleship.[44] Rather, judgment is pronounced against them on the grounds that they are workers of 'lawless-

---

38. R. T. France, *The Gospel According to Matthew: An Introduction and Commentary* (Leicester: IVP; Grand Rapids, Mich.: Eerdmans, 1985), p. 148; A. J. Saldarini, *Matthew's Christian-Jewish Community* (Chicago: University of Chicago Press, 1994), p. 187. Guelich, *Sermon on the Mount*, pp. 398–399, also draws attention to examples of Matthew changing the form of address used by outsiders, notably Matt. 8:25//Mark 4:38 and Matt. 17:15//Mark 9:17. U. Luz, *Matthew 1–7: A Commentary* (ET Edinburgh: T. & T. Clark, 1989), p. 444, comments that the double use of *kyrie* (lord) in the context of eschatological judgment is 'especially expressive and imploring'.

39. Guelich, *Sermon on the Mount*, p. 399.

40. Gundry, *Matthew*, p. 131; Hagner, *Matthew 1–13*, p. 187; cf. G. Delling, ἡμέρα, *TDNT* 2, pp. 943–953. Hagner makes the point that the future tense 'will enter into the kingdom of heaven' points to the 'last judgement' (p. 186).

41. O. Michel, "The Conclusion of Matthew's Gospel: A Contribution to the History of the Easter Message', in Stanton, *Interpretation of Matthew*, p. 41 n. 9; Barth, 'Matthew's Understanding of the Law', p. 162; and cf. H. Bietenhard, ὄνομα, in *TDNT* 5, pp. 276–277. For a discussion of the use of Jesus' 'name' in Acts, see Part Three.

42. Guelich, *Sermon on the Mount*, p. 400, suggests that there may also be an allusion here to the many false prophets mentioned in Matt. 24:11.

43. Guelich, *Sermon on the Mount*, p. 400.

44. Davies and Allison, *Matthew I–VII*, p. 714.

ness' (*anomia*). Whilst Matthew's use of *anomia* in 7:23c (cf. Luke 13:27: *adikia*, unrighteousness) emphasizes the link with Psalm 6:8, *anomia* is a word favoured by Matthew and, in the Synoptic tradition, peculiar to his Gospel where it has particularly negative connotations (cf. Matt. 13:41; 23:28; 24:12). For Matthew *anomia* is a most serious charge that can be brought against those claiming to be followers of Jesus, and is the very antithesis of all that characterizes true discipleship.

To summarize, those who are condemned by Jesus in 7:21–23 claim to be his followers but they prize the working of miracles and exorcisms over and above what is required by Jesus of those who would follow him. They refuse to take the narrow gate of true discipleship and the hard road that leads to life (7:13–14). Their ultimate fate, already described in the colourful language of the 'road that leads to destruction' (7:13) and the tree that fails to bear good fruit being 'cut down and thrown into the fire' (7:19), is spelled out in the starkest way in 7:23 where their eschatological fate translates into final denial and banishment rather than acknowledgment by Jesus in the heavenly assize (7:22, 23; cf. 10:2).

## Conclusions

In our examination of Jesus and discipleship according to Matthew, we looked at two approaches to understanding how Matthew intends his readers to understand the way in which he presents Jesus and the disciples. We saw that the historicizing approach consigned Jesus and the disciples to a holy, unrepeatable past and that this left little room for the Third Wave paradigm that views the experience of Jesus and the disciples acting as a continuing model for the church. A more fruitful approach, that of transparency, regards Matthew as removing the gulf between the disciples before and after the resurrection so that all concerning the nature of discipleship that is addressed to the disciples of Jesus during his earthly ministry is also addressed to Matthew's church, who are thus able, as a community, to identify with the disciples and embody their experience.

Given Matthew's intended transparency, does this mean that all that is addressed to the disciples by Jesus during his earthly ministry is also addressed to Matthew's church and, by extension, to the church today? If this is the case, then any attempt at contemporary application must take account of the fact that the paradigm for discipleship Matthew presents here is a sophisticated one, where the essence of being a disciple of Jesus is to be understood in terms of learning, understanding and obeying the words of Jesus. Importantly for the Third Wave, we have seen that Matthew portrays Jesus as a Mosaic prophet who rightly interprets the law, and whose authority to teach is ratified by his charismatic activity. In describing the miracles of the earthly Jesus we have seen that Matthew has a tendency to spiritualize them, presenting them in terms of 'salvation', and that the Matthean Jesus is highly critical of charismatic activity not rooted in obedience to his teaching (Matt. 7:21–23).

## 5. MATTHEW'S READERS AND THE GREAT COMMISSION

### Introduction

The foundational commissioning text for the Third Wave's theology of signs and wonders is the Great Commission, which concludes Matthew's Gospel (Matt. 28:16–20). It is the Third Wave's understanding of the content and function of these verses that provides them with a filter through which they understand and interpret other commissionings in the Synoptic Gospels and Acts.[1] Our focus in this chapter will be on Matthew 28:16–20 and the questions these verses raise for the contemporary exegete. How do these concluding verses relate to the First Gospel as a whole?

In his preface to the commands that follow, the risen Jesus makes the extraordinary claim that 'all authority in heaven and on earth has been given to me'

---

1. See for example G. S. Greig and K. N. Springer, 'Appendix 3: Matthew 28:18–20 – The Great Commission and Jesus' Commands to Preach and Heal', in idem (eds.), *The Kingdom and the Power: Are Healing and the Spiritual Gifts Used by Jesus and the Early Church Meant for the Church Today?* (Ventura, Calif.: Regal, 1993), pp. 399–403; J. Wimber, *Power Evangelism: Signs and Wonders Today* (London: Hodder & Stoughton, 1985), p. 42; K. Blue, *Authority to Heal* (Downers Grove, Ill.: IVP, 1987), pp. 158–159.

(Matt. 28:18a). This raises the question 'How does Matthew understand the way in which the authority (*exousia*) of Jesus relates to the disciples and their commission?' The core command of the risen Jesus to his disciples in the Great Commission is that they should go themselves and 'make disciples'. What can we learn about Matthew's understanding of Christian discipleship from his portrayal of the earthly Jesus and his disciples that helps us to understand what is meant here? Is Matthew's portrayal of Jesus and his disciples intended to be paradigmatic and provide a model for later Christian generations, and, if so, how? How does the command to make disciples relate not just to Christian initiation/ baptism, but also to teaching them to obey all that Jesus commanded?

It is striking that in Jesus' words of commission there is no specific mention of signs and wonders, and we must ask what exactly is the remit of the authority (*exousia*) passed on to the disciples by Jesus? How would the Great Commission have been understood by those for whom Matthew is writing? Is there any evidence that Matthew implies a place for signs and wonders and the miraculous in the post-Easter mission of the church? With all these questions in mind, we must begin by asking how Matthew's readers would have understood Matthew 28:16–20 and its background.

## The importance of *Gattung*

The most common attempt to uncover the 'theological heart' of Matthew's intended meaning in Matthew 28:16–20 has been to determine the *Gattung* (German for 'literary genre') that lies behind the pericope.[2] A clear indication of the complexity of the issues raised can be seen from the way in which the contemporary scholarly debate about the question of *Gattung* has developed. Importantly for us here, this complexity serves as a cautionary tale against taking an homogenous approach to biblical texts in order to inform contemporary paradigms for theology and praxis.

---

2. Cf. T. L. Donaldson, *Jesus on the Mountain* (JSNTSup 8; JSOT, 1985), p. 175. For a full and stimulating discussion of the importance of identifying *Gattung* in NT studies, see J. L. Bailey, 'Genre Analysis', in J. B. Green (ed.), *Hearing the New Testament: Strategies for Interpretation* (Grand Rapids, Mich.: Eerdmans; Carlisle: Paternoster, 1995), pp. 197–221. Earlier examples of *Gattung* analysis include H. Gunkel and J. Begrich, *Einleitung in die Psalmen*, 2 vols. (Göttingen: Vandenhoeck & Ruprecht, 1928–33); M. Dibelius, *From Tradition to Gospel*, 2nd ed. (ET London: Clarke, 1971); R. Bultmann, *History of the Synoptic Tradition* (ET New York: Harper & Row, 1976).

It has long been recognized by NT specialists that in Matthew's Great Commission we are not simply confronted with straightforward history or reportage. The presence of both language and style pointing to Matthean redaction indicates that the First Evangelist has carefully crafted the conclusion to his Gospel and this, in turn, raises crucial questions as to how Matthew's conclusion relates to the rest of his Gospel. Bailey defines *Gattung* as being

> the conventional and repeatable patterns of oral and written speech, which facilitate interaction among people in specific social situations. Decisive to this basic definition are three aspects: patternedness, social setting, and rhetorical impact.[3]

According to Bailey, *Gattungen* are used to convey the experiences and insights of a previous generation to the next generation. Bailey cites the example of Jesus' use of the picture of God's vineyard (Mark 12:1–12), which he suggests would have evoked the 'love song' genre found in Isaiah 5:1–7.[4] In other words, implicit within the choice of *Gattung* are interpretative clues to the author's intended meaning. In seeking to understand both the meaning of Matthew 28:16–20 as well as its relationship to the rest of Matthew's narrative, the contemporary exegete must bear in mind that Matthew is writing in what is now an alien culture, using interpretative clues that, for the modern reader, can seem obscure.

## Quest for the *Gattung* of Matthew 28:16–20

Even a brief overview of the scholarly quest to identify the literary family (*Gattung*) to which Matthew 28:16–20 belongs reveals a rich variety of proposals, none of which has proved to be conclusive. During the earlier part of the twentieth century, biblical scholarship, with its primary interest in form criticism, regarded Matthew 28:16–20 as a typical example of a 'cult legend' reflecting first-century Hellenistic Christian instructions concerning baptism that also presupposes a universal mission about which earliest Palestinian Christianity knew nothing.[5] This treatment of the pericope must be judged

---

3. Bailey, 'Genre Analysis', p. 200.

4. Ibid., p. 202.

5. M. Dibelius, *Die Formsgeschichte des Evangeliums*, 4th ed. (Tübingen: Mohr, 1961), pp. 282–285; R. Bultmann, *History of the Synoptic Tradition* (ET Oxford: Blackwell, 1963), pp. 286–289.

inadequate because it fails to take account of the individual elements contained within the pericope. Nor does it take adequate account of the literary form of the whole of Matthew 28:16–20.[6]

Still concentrating on verses 18–20, Strecker[7] maintains that Matthew 28:18–20 contains a mix of traditional and redactional elements and identifies the following elements as being already present in Matthew's tradition: reference to the authority (*exousia*) of the risen Christ (v. 18b); the command to baptize (v. 19b); the promise of Jesus' abiding presence with his disciples (v. 20b).[8] According to Strecker, the baptismal command, with its triadic formula, was not composed by Matthew but provides the clue to the *Sitz im Leben* for the pre-Matthean material; namely, the liturgical life of Matthew's church.[9] Apart from his failure to engage with verses 16–17, a major criticism of this proposal is that it is unlikely that in the pre-Matthean tradition identified by Strecker the sayings of the risen Jesus declaring universal authority (v. 18b) and the promise of his abiding presence (v. 20b) were present only to provide authority for the community's baptismal practice.[10]

An alternative approach to locating the *Gattung* of Matthew 28:18–20 in the liturgical life of Matthew's church is the suggestion, made by Otto Michel[11] and developed further by Joachim Jeremias,[12] that these verses should be understood in terms of enthronement and as a reshaping of Daniel 7:14 (LXX). According to Michel, Matthew 28:18–20 reflects the liturgical pattern of an early Christian enthronement hymn, similar in form to the Christological hymn in Philippians 2:5–11, and based upon the enthronement of kings in the ancient Near East.[13] Jeremias turns to texts describing ancient Egyptian coro-

6. Many earlier commentators fail to take adequate account of the contextual setting provided by vv. 16–17.
7. G. Strecker, *Der Weg der Gerechtigkeit: Untersuchung zur Theologie des Matthäus* (Göttingen: Vanenhoeck & Ruprecht, 1962).
8. Ibid., p. 210.
9. Ibid., p. 209.
10. So B. J. Hubbard, 'The Matthean Redaction of a Primitive Apostolic Commissioning' (PhD thesis, University of Iowa, 1973), p. 7.
11. O. Michel, 'The Conclusion of Matthew's Gospel: A Contribution to the History of the Easter Message', in G. N. Stanton (ed.), *The Interpretation of Matthew* (London: SPCK/Fortress, 1983), pp. 30–41; ET from the original German article 'Der Abschluss der Matthäusevangeliums', *EvT* 10 (1950–1), pp. 16–26.
12. J. Jeremias, *Jesus' Promise to the Nations* (ET London: SCM, 1967).
13. Michel, 'Conclusion of Matthew's Gospel', p. 36.

nation rituals in an attempt to develop Michel's thesis for an enthronement background providing the underlying literary form for Matthew 28:18–20, but presents no convincing evidence in confirmation of his case.[14]

Whilst few would now deny that Daniel 7:14 (LXX) probably lies somewhere in the background of Matthew 28:16–20, precisely to what extent continues to be debated.[15] The evidence is insufficient for regarding the Great Commission as an enthronement hymn along the lines of Philippians 2:5–11 with its primarily Christological emphasis. The emphasis in Matthew 28:16–20 is Christological, to be sure, but it is a Christology that serves primarily as an authoritative context for the building of the church through universal mission. Whereas enthronement is all about the bestowal of power, Matthew's Christological starting point in verse 18 is that Jesus already possesses 'all authority in heaven and on earth', and central to these verses is the idea of Jesus' commissioning of others rather than the enthronement/exaltation of Jesus himself.

Ferdinand Hahn[16] also considers exaltation to be the dominant theme of Matthew 28:18–20, but acknowledges the fact that the *exousia* saying in verse 18b assumes that enthronement has already been accomplished.[17] For Hahn, it is Psalm 109 (LXX), rather than Daniel 7:14, that provides the primary OT background for Matthew 28:18–20. He argues that this messianic psalm was particularly influential on Hellenistic-Jewish Christianity's ideas about the lordship of Christ (cf. Phil. 2:9–11; Rev. 14:6–7). Hahn also suggests that Matthew has substituted the disciples' post-Easter mission to the Gentiles, linked to Jesus' teaching about observing the law, for the traditional OT theme of the 'subjugation of the nations'.[18]

The weakness in Hahn's case is that he stresses, incorrectly, Matthew's intention to link the lordship of Christ, expressed in the *exousia* saying, and the promise of Christ's abiding presence with the disciples. Rather, the link

---

14. Jeremias, *Jesus' Promise to the Nations*, pp. 38–39.

15. A most thorough and recent examination of the Danielic background to Matt. 28:16–20 is by J. Schaberg, *The Father, The Son and The Holy Spirit: The Triadic Phrase in Matthew 28.19b* (SBLDS 61; Chico, Calif.: Scholars Press, 1982), who concludes (pp. 335–336) that the triadic phrase in Matt. 28:19b is a traditional midrash that has developed from the triad found in Daniel 7 (Ancient of Days, one like a son of man, and angels.)

16. F. Hahn, *Mission in the New Testament* (ET SBT 47; London: SCM, 1965).

17. Ibid., p. 66.

18. Ibid., pp. 65–66.

for Matthew is with missionary activity, with the Greek word translated 'therefore' in verse 19a providing the syntactical link with what follows in verses 19b–20. Also, Hahn's case that Psalm 109 (LXX), rather than Daniel 7:14 (LXX), is the primary OT text influencing Matthew is again weakened to a considerable extent by the fact that his argument depends on the incorrect assumption that Matthew stresses the idea of enthronement rather than a (post-enthronement) commission by the risen Christ for the church to engage in a universal mission.

At this point, the scholarly discussion takes more serious account of verses 16–17 and moves away from ideas of an enthronement *Gattung* for Matthew's Great Commission. C. H. Dodd,[19] identifies Matthew 28:16–20 as a 'concise' type of resurrection narrative[20] characteristic of oral folk-traditions, where an often-repeated story is refined down to its essentials.[21] According to Dodd, verse 18b begins with a Christologizing of the fact of Jesus' resurrection by alluding to enthronement language found in Daniel 7:14, thus establishing Jesus' resurrection as the basis for his possession of universal *exousia*. Dodd also notes that in Matthew 28:20 the resurrection narrative has been used to introduce a form of church order comparable with Matthew 18:15–20.[22]

Dodd is the first to draw attention to the element of 'doubt' and this is an important insight that has led some scholars to conclude that in the mention of doubt in Matthew 28:17 we have 'a genuine historical echo'.[23] However, Dodd places the elements of fear/doubt together under a single form-critical classification, and this is highly questionable. Here, and elsewhere in the appearance tradition, these two elements occur separately and serve different

---

19. C. H. Dodd, 'The Appearances of the Risen Christ: An Essay in Form Criticism of the Gospels', in idem, *More New Testament Studies* (Manchester: Manchester University Press, 1968), pp. 102–133. This essay was first published in 1957 as one of a series of essays in memory of R. H. Lightfoot and this earlier date is important for our sensitive understanding of the positive contribution (and limitations) of Dodd's contribution to the debate at this point.

20. Ibid., p. 102.

21. Ibid., p. 103.

22. Ibid., p. 106.

23. J. D. G. Dunn, *Jesus and the Spirit: A Study of the Religious and Charismatic Experience of Jesus and the First Christians as Reflected in the New Testament* (London: SCM, 1975), p. 124. For a list of scholars who favour this position and those against, see p. 392 n. 124.

literary purposes. The element of doubt, unlike the element of fear, requires more than just verbal reassurance.[24] In terms of tradition-history, 'doubt' may well have belonged to the earliest stratum of the tradition, but form-critically it serves to inform the reader that the risen Jesus appeared in a form that was qualitatively different from that of an angel or spirit/ghost.[25]

The fear/alarm theme is common to supernatural appearance stories in the NT featuring angels as well as Christophanies.[26] In each case the fear theme is presented as an appropriate reaction by human beings to a supernatural appearance and is often, but not always,[27] accompanied by a word of reassurance. In other words, form-critically in the Gospels the fear theme serves a different purpose to the doubt theme, although both feature in the appearance tradition.

A further important development in the form-critical debate about the *Gattung* of Matthew 28:16–20 is to be found in the more recent work of scholars who have sought parallels in OT commissioning stories. Parallels identified by W. Trilling,[28] occur in Deuteronomy,[29] whilst for B. J. Malina,[30] the OT model is to be found in the decree of Cyrus (2 Chron. 36:23),[31] which

---

24. For example, the words of commission following Matt. 28:17 in Matt. 28:18; the proof from Scripture during the walk to Emmaus, followed by the disciples' recognition of the risen one in the breaking of the bread (Luke 24:13–35; John 21:12–13); the invitation to touch the risen Jesus (Luke 24:36–40; John 20:19–20, 24–28), followed by his eating with the disciples – a sure proof that the heavenly person before them was not an angel (cf. Tobit 12:15–19). See further the discussion in Part Three below.

25. Hubbard, 'Matthean Redaction', p. 62, identifies the fear theme as a reaction to the presence of God or his angel in eight of the OT commissionings he examines, but in no case is there a conflation of fear/doubt (cf. Gen. 17:3; 28:16–17; Exod. 3:3, 6; Num. 22:31; 1 Kgs 19:13; Isa. 6:5; Ezek. 1:28).

26. Here I am using Christophany in a general sense to include all appearances of the risen Christ.

27. See for example Matt. 28:4.

28. W. Trilling, *Das Wahre Israel – Studien zur Theologie des Matthäusevangeliums*, 3rd ed. (Munich: Kösel, 1964).

29. For example, the revelatory word of Deut. 5:6 followed by commandments that are to be obeyed; the promise to Joshua of God's presence (Deut. 31:5–8, 23).

30. B. J. Malina, 'The Literary Structure and Form of Matt. XXVIII.16–20', *NTS* 17 (1970), 87–103.

31. Ibid., pp. 91–92.

marks the end of the Masoretic text of the Hebrew scriptures. This is some-what surprising, since, as K. Stendahl has shown, Matthew's church almost certainly used the LXX, which, unlike the MT, ends with Malachi.[32] More importantly, J. P. Meier has pointed out that an examination of the texts in question reveal a considerable number of dissimilarities as well as the similar-ities identified by Malina,[33] which prompts Meier to conclude that 'Cyrus is not the answer'.[34]

The quest for OT parallels reaches its zenith with the comprehensive con-tribution of B. J. Hubbard, who argues more broadly that the structure of the closing verses of Matthew's Gospel conform to a 'Hebrew Bible commission-ing *Gattung*', basing his case on the evidence of twenty-seven OT commission-ings involving patriarchs and prophets. Problems arise when he attempts to apply his OT commissioning *Gattung* to Matthew 28:16–20, which contains only five out of the seven elements Hubbard identifies. Although the OT pas-sages examined by Hubbard do contain elements of commissioning, there seems no reason to designate them specifically as commissioning stories rather than, say, angelophanies or theophanies.[35] For example, J. E. Alsup, in an equally detailed analysis of all of the appearance stories,[36] relates Matthew 28:16–20 to anthropomorphic theophanies found in the OT and intertesta-

---

32. See K. Stendahl, *The School of St. Matthew and its Use of the Old Testament*, 2nd ed. (Philadelphia: Fortress, 1968), who concludes, 'The dominant use of the LXX, however, shows the authority of the LXX as the accepted edition of the O.T. in everyday church life' (p. 205). More recently, this widely held view based on Stendahl's careful analysis of the use of the OT in Matthew's Gospel has been criticized by G. N. Stanton, 'Matthew's Use of the Old Testament', in *A Gospel For a New People: Studies in Matthew* (Edinburgh: T. & T. Clark, 1992), pp. 346–363, and especially pp. 353–363. Stanton, who concentrates on redactional passages in Matthew's Gospel – an approach developed since Stendahl's study – argues that the results of his analysis of Matthew's redaction of OT quotations in Mark and Q suggest that it is no longer certain that the LXX was 'Matthew's Bible' (Stanton, 'Matthew's Use of the Old Testament', p. 355).

33. For details, see J. P. Meier, 'Two Disputed Questions in Matt. 28:16–20', *JBL* 96.3 (1977), p. 419. See also, Hubbard, *Matthean Redaction*, p. 22.

34. Meier, 'Two Disputed Questions', p. 419.

35. Cf. H. K. McArthur, 'Review of B. J. Hubbard, "The Matthean Redaction of a Primitive Apostolic Commissioning"', *CBQ* 38 (1976), pp. 107–108.

36. J. E. Alsup, *The Post-Resurrection Appearance Stories of the Gospel Tradition* (Calwer Theologische Monographien 5; Stuttgart: Calwer; London: SPCK, 1975).

mental literature and designates it a 'Group Appearance Gattung'.[37] In other words, it could just as easily be argued that Matthew drew on the post-Easter appearance story tradition that already contained a form of commissioning by the risen Jesus, redacting it in the direction of an OT commissioning.[38]

## Conclusions

Arising out of our study of the debate about *Gattung*, we can make some important initial conclusions about Matthew 28:16–20. We can say that Matthew is basing the concluding verses to his Gospel on traditional material that linked accounts of appearances of the risen Jesus with the idea of commissioning the (eleven) disciples. Form-critically, this pericope echoes (but no more) other commissionings found in the OT as well as the idea of enthronement and receipt of universal authority found in Daniel 7. Traditionally, in accounts of resurrection appearances, there was a strong element of doubt and recognition present, as well as an element of fear normally associated in the Bible with the manifestation of heavenly personages.

At the end of the day the evidence for a particular literary form providing an exact model for Matthew 28:16–20 is not conclusive and proposals as to *Gattung* can only provide a speculative starting point for our understanding of Matthew's purpose. More importantly, Meier is surely right when he points out that there is a tendency when applying *Gattungen* to Matthew 28:16–20 to ignore the post-resurrectional nature of the epiphany and not to allow this to enter into the choice of *Gattung*.[39] It is for this reason more than any other that we must conclude with Meier that the reason why no single *Gattung* proposed so far adequately fits Matthew 28:16–20 is that the pericope is primarily *sui generis*. Whilst Matthew is undoubtedly dependent upon traditional material

---

37. Ibid., pp. 211ff., and see especially the 'Text Synopsis' attached to the back of the book. Noted also by McArthur, 'Review of B. J. Hubbard', p. 108.

38. So Meier, 'Two Disputed Questions', p. 423. Alsup, *Post-Resurrection Appearance Stories*, p. 212, notes that where the element of commissioning occurs, 'the words of the resurrected One are cast entirely in the style, vocabulary and theological intention of the three evangelists [Matthew, Luke and John] in question'. Indeed, Hubbard himself argues convincingly for the existence of just such a primitive apostolic commissioning, which Matthew has redacted in line with the OT commissioning tradition ('Matthean Redaction', pp. 98–133).

39. Meier, 'Two Disputed Questions', p. 423.

arising out of accounts of appearances of the risen Jesus to his followers, in
its present form Matthew 28:16–20 is largely the product of Matthean redaction.[40]

The concluding verses in 28:16–20 form the climax to Matthew's Gospel
and bring together key Matthean themes, such as mission/universalism, discipleship and Christology, which feature throughout the Gospel.[41] Given the
largely redactional nature of the pericope, the lack of consensus as to *Gattung*
and its *sui generis* nature, we are forced back to an examination of the words of
commission themselves, together with other material within the wider context
of Matthew's Gospel, and it is to this examination that we must now turn.

According to Matthew, Jesus' authority to interpret the demands of the law
is passed on to his disciples (16:19; 18:18), although we saw that here there is
a tension in the way Matthew presents the disciples as at the same time inheritors of Jesus' *exousia* and those of little faith. How does Matthew envisage the
way in which Jesus' delegated authority works? Are we to understand that, like
Jesus, the disciples, as inheritors of Jesus' *exousia*, are also to expect that their
authority to interpret the law is to be ratified by charismatic activity? In order
to answer these questions we will look at two 'case studies' from Matthew's
Gospel where we have important examples of delegated authority: the sending
out of the Twelve on mission to Israel (Matt. 10:1ff.), and the giving of the
keys of the kingdom to Peter (Matt. 16:18–20).

---

40. Ibid., p. 424.
41. See especially D. R. Bauer, *The Structure of Matthew's Gospel* (Sheffield: Almond, 1989),
    pp. 109–128.

# 6. THE DISCIPLES' MISSION TO ISRAEL

## Introduction

In the first of our two case studies, the commissioning and sending of the twelve disciples out in mission to Israel (Matt. 10:1, 5–15), the first important point to note is that Matthew is the only Synoptic Evangelist to insist on the disciples' mission being limited to Israel (cf. Matt. 15:24). How, if at all, does the restriction in Matthew 10:5–6 to go only to the 'lost sheep of the house of Israel' help us to understand the extent of the authority delegated to the disciples in the Great Commission? In light of this restriction, are there also indications in the mission discourse which suggest that Matthew intends the discourse to be transparent for his church? How does the authority/*exousia* granted by Jesus to the disciples as he commissions them to go only to Israel compare to that given to the eleven disciples by the exalted Lord in the Great Commission (Matt. 28:16–20)? Is the continuation of *exousia* to heal and exorcise (and even raise the dead!)[1] clearly implied in the Great Commission? Alternatively, does the evidence here favour opponents of the Third Wave for whom the granting of *exousia* to

---

1. J. Wimber, *Power Evangelism*, 2nd ed. (London: Hodder & Stoughton, 1992), pp. 182–185.

the disciples by Jesus is regarded as being strictly limited to an 'unrepeatable holy past'?


## Commissioning the disciples

Half a century ago, T. W. Manson wrote that 'The mission of the disciples is one of the best-attested facts in the life of Jesus.'[2] There are four accounts in the Synoptic Gospels of Jesus sending his followers out in mission, all of which F. Hahn has shown to derive from just two sources (Mark 6:7–12 and Luke 10, derived from Q).[3] Matthew's account conflates material concerning the mission of the Twelve found in both the Markan and Q traditions. According to James Dunn, Matthew retains here the limited view of a mission to Israel only envisaged by the pre-Easter Jesus.[4] Similarly, Graham Twelftree detects an original pre-Easter *Sitz im Leben* for Jesus' sending of his followers out on mission and that, originally, preaching the kingdom would have included exorcism for Jesus and his disciples.[5] Although our concern here is with Matthew's account of the mission, it is helpful to note here elements that were already present in the tradition Matthew has used.

We noted earlier that Matthew's Gospel is structured around five major discourses, the second of these being located in the 'central section' of his Gospel (9:35 – 11:1),[6] where the mission to Israel plays a pivotal role in Matthew's narrative. Choosing twelve disciples clearly has an eschatological significance for Israel and her traditional twelve tribes (cf. Matt. 19:29//Luke 22:29–30),[7] and

---

2. T. W. Manson, *The Sayings of Jesus* (London: SCM, 1957), p. 73. See more recently G. H. Twelftree, *Jesus the Exorcist: A Contribution to the Study of the Historical Jesus* (Peabody, Mass.: Hendrickson, 1993), pp. 122–127.

3. F. Hahn, *Mission in the New Testament* (ET SBT 47; London: SCM, 1965), pp. 41–46. See also J. Jeremias, *New Testament Theology Volume One: The Proclamation of Jesus* (ET London: SCM, 1971), p. 231.

4. J. D. G. Dunn, *Unity and Diversity in the New Testament: An Enquiry into the Character of Earliest Christianity* (London: SCM, 1977), p. 250.

5. Twelftree, *Jesus the Exorcist*, p. 125.

6. Identified by S. Brown, 'The Mission to Israel in Matthew's Central Section (Matt. 9.35–11.1)', *ZNW* 69 (1977), pp. 73–90.

7. Matthew editorially identifies Mark's 'the Twelve' with the disciples, so they become 'the twelve disciples'. See M. J. Wilkins, *The Concept of Disciple in Matthew's Gospel: As Reflected in the Use of the Term* Μαθητής (NovTSup 59; Leiden: Brill,

they now participate in the distinct eschatological mission of Jesus to the 'lost sheep of the house of Israel' (Matt. 10:5; cf. 15:24).[8]

In Jesus' commissioning of the disciples to go out on mission to Israel we find that they are to reflect Jesus' own ministry of announcing the dawn of God's rule and, in their charismatic activity, to reflect the miracles of Jesus that have been described in the preceding chapters (8–9) even to the point of raising the dead (Matt. 10:8).[9] Whilst the delegation by Jesus to the disciples of his *exousia* results in quite spectacular charismatic power, it is crucial to note that at this stage in Matthew's story, 'teaching', which will be an explicit feature of the post-Easter commission, remains the preserve of the earthly Jesus. The disciples are to continue to develop their understanding under Jesus' tutelage and be 'discipled' by him in preparation for the commission they will receive from the risen Lord and the authority they are then to exercise in his abiding presence (Matt. 28:18–20; 16:16–20; 18:18–20).

Are there any indications in the mission discourse which suggest that Matthew intends the discourse to be transparent for his church? At first glance it appears that the *exousia* granted to the disciples to perform miracles as they go out on mission to Israel is limited to the mission of the disciples during the lifetime of Jesus. However, as we read the mission discourse we find that Matthew includes material clearly intended for the ongoing missionary situation facing his community in the post-Easter situation, where the disciples of Jesus share both his mission and his suffering (cf. Matt. 10:16ff.). In doing this, Matthew clearly intends to provide a model for mission for his church rather than just a narrative account of what happened on this particular occasion, as in Mark 6:12–13.[10] This also explains the fact that, unlike Mark 6:7–30 and Luke 10:1–20 where the disciples are described specifically as being sent out on mission by Jesus, in Matthew's account, following a long discourse on mission, the narrative then makes it clear that it is Jesus himself who then sets out to teach and preach the good news (Matt. 11:1).[11]

---

1988), p. 133. See also Jeremias, *New Testament Theology*, p. 234. See also J. Jeremias, *Jesus' Promise to the Nations* (ET London: SCM, 1967), p. 21.

8. Cf. B. F. Meyer, *The Aims of Jesus* (London: SCM, 1979), p. 157.

9. Cf. Matthew's 'has just died' (Matt. 9:18) with Mark's 'is at the point of death' (Mark 5:23).

10. Cf. U. Luz, 'The Disciples in the Gospel According to Matthew', in G. Stanton (ed.), *The Interpretation of Matthew* (London: SPCK/Fortress, 1983), p. 108.

11. U. Luz, *The Theology of the Gospel of Matthew* (ET Cambridge: Cambridge University Press, 1995), p. 76.

A further clue indicating that the mission discourse is intended by Matthew to be transparent for his own situation can be seen in the ban on taking payment (Matt. 10:8b), a point reflected elsewhere in the life of the early church and in rabbinic Judaism where the prohibition refers to teaching Torah.[12] The connection in rabbinic Judaism between payment and teaching the law may also reflect the contemporary interests of Matthew and his church, particularly when, as we shall see, the delegated authority to teach is reserved for the post-Easter situation.

Further indications of transparency can be seen in verses 9–10, where the ban on provisions is updated by Matthew to meet the needs of an ongoing situation where itinerant missionaries have a right to expect hospitality and nourishment (10:10b).[13] In 10:17–25 the missionaries are warned that persecution will accompany their witness to the Gentiles (cf. 10:5–6); warnings are given about division of families (= Mark 13:12), which is indicative of the apocalyptic woes to be expected at the end of the age (2 Esdras 5.9; 6.24; 13.31; *Jub.* 23.19; *2 Bar.* 70.3; *1 En.* 56.7; 99.5; 100.1).[14] Both in their charismatic activity and in their suffering, followers of Jesus identify with their Lord (10:25b; 10:38) and their suffering is emphasized in the anachronistic imagery of cross-bearing (cf. 16:24), which is a further indication that Matthew intends his mission discourse for disciples of his own day.[15]

---

12. 2 Cor. 11:7; cf. 1 Cor. 9:3–18; Didache 11–12; *Abot* 1.13; 4.7. See also the later ethical rabbinic tractate *Derek Eretz Zuta* 4.2, where we read, 'Teach the Law gratis, and take no fee for it: for the words of the Law no fee must be taken, seeing that God gave the Law gratis. He who takes a fee for the Law destroys the world' (ET in C. G. Montefiore and H. Loewe [eds.], *A Rabbinic Anthology* [New York: Schocken, 1974], p. 128).

13. The reference to 'food' is Matt.R. Cf. Mark's ban on taking bread (Mark 6:8) followed by Luke (Luke 9:3).

14. L. Sabourin, 'Traits apocalyptiques dans L'Évangile de Matthieu', in *ScEs* 3.3 (1981), p. 362, who comments, 'Le conflit social figure souvent dans les représentations apocalyptiques des tribulations de la fin des temps.'

15. D. A. Hagner, *Matthew 1–13* (WBC 33A; Dallas, Tex.: Word, 1993), p. 292; R. H. Gundry, *Matthew: A Commentary on His Literary and Theological Art* (Grand Rapids, Mich.: Eerdmans, 1982), p. 200. M. Davies, *Matthew* (Sheffield: JSOT, 1993), p. 85, points out that the cross does not otherwise come into view in Matthew's Gospel until 16:21. J. C. Anderson, *Matthew's Narrative Web: Over, and Over, and Over Again* (Sheffield: JSOT, 1994), p. 158, views Matt. 10:38 as a 'clear anticipation' addressed to the disciples alone and 'integrated into the plot'. Whatever the case, as Hagner,

We have seen that there are clear indications that the disciples' ministry is to parallel closely that of Jesus, and this identification of the disciples with the ministry of Jesus extends transparently to the experience of Matthew's own community as it engages in mission. But what about the all-important question of Matthew's understanding of authority/*exousia*? Is there anything in Matthew's use of *exousia* to indicate that he intends his readers to understand his meaning and application of *exousia* differently in the pre- and post-Easter situations? Are the Third Wave correct in their assumption that the emphasis remains the same in both commissionings? Is there any evidence to support the claim that Matthew intends the Great Commission to be understood by his readers to include authority/*exousia* to heal?

## Matthew's use of *exousia*

In ordinary Greek usage *exousia* can mean simply the ability to perform an action without hindrance. The *exousia*/authority of Jesus during his earthly ministry comes from God, denoting his divinely given authority to act and is of the same essence as that shared by the apostles.[16] Occurring nine times in Matthew's Gospel, *exousia* is used to describe both the limited authority of the earthly Jesus and the unlimited authority of the exalted Lord (7:29; 9:6; 21:23ff.; 28:18). The first occurrence of *exousia* in the First Gospel is in 7:28–29. Matthew uses this saying from Mark 1:22 as an authoritative finale to the Sermon on the Mount and where Jesus' authoritative teaching 'astounds' the crowds.[17] In his omission of Mark 1:23 Matthew clearly intends his reference to the *exousia* of Jesus to be linked to his teaching alone.[18]

As the narrative progresses, we find that Matthew's succinct telling of the story of the healing of the centurion's servant (Matt. 8:5–13; cf. Luke 7:1–10) serves primarily to remind his readers that Jesus, like the centurion, is a man under authority (Matt. 8:9). This is followed in Matthew 9:2–8, where Jesus

---

*Matthew 1–13*, p. 293, points out, it is clearly a call to 'radical obedience that entails self-denial'.

16. For a full discussion of *exousia* in Greek, Jewish (LXX) and NT usage, see W. Foerster, ἐξουσία, *TDNT* 2, pp. 562–574.

17. The Greek verb *ekplēssō* occurs four times in Matthew's Gospel (7:28; 13:54; 19:25; 22:33), where in each case the astonishment is in reaction to Jesus' teaching.

18. Cf. with Mark's rather different context where Jesus' *exousia* to teach is closely linked with and demonstrated by his *exousia* over unclean spirits.

heals a paralytic, and again the healing is used as a context for a further amplification of Matthew's presentation of the *exousia* of Jesus. In this healing story Matthew shifts the focus from the healing itself to the even more extraordinary fact that Jesus has *exousia* to forgive sins, something to be borne in mind when making judgments about how Matthew intends his readers to understand the scope of the mandate to the Eleven, standing behind their commission at the conclusion of Matthew's Gospel.

In Matthew 10:1 Jesus delegates his *exousia* to the Twelve before commissioning them for mission to the 'lost sheep of the house of Israel'. The focus of the delegated authority here is very clearly on healing and exorcism and is linked in verses 5–6 with proclaiming the nearness of the kingdom of heaven. Mark uses *exousia* only as 'authority over unclean spirits' (Mark 6:7) or, in the context of sending out the Twelve, 'authority to drive out demons' (Mark 3:15), whereas Matthew deliberately widens the scope of the *exousia* given here to the disciples by adding to Mark's 'unclean spirits' the 'formulaic' phrase 'to cure every disease and every sickness'.[19]

This expansion reflects an earlier description of the ministry of Jesus (Matt. 9:35; cf. Luke 9:1) and serves to emphasize the fact that, for Matthew, the disciples are in solidarity with Jesus in their sharing of his *exousia* and mission, as well as in the accusations made in reference to the source of their *exousia* (Matt. 10:24–25). Later, when the question about Jesus' authority is raised by his opponents (Matt. 21:23ff.; cf. Mark 11:27–33 par.), Matthew places the focus on Jesus' teaching (v. 23; cf. Luke 20:1). However, by retaining Mark's reference to 'these things' Matthew clearly expects his readers to take account of the events of the preceding day: the triumphal entry into Jerusalem, the clearing of the temple and the healing of blind and lame persons who, by virtue of their deformity, would have been excluded from full participation in the worship of the temple (Matt. 21:1–16, and especially v. 14).

It could be argued, against the Third Wave, that in the restriction in the mission charge to go only to the 'lost sheep of the house of Israel' we should understand the disciples' mission and delegated authority to heal and exorcize as temporary, belonging strictly to the past and not intended by Matthew to be applicable to his church. For example, Hagner grants that the commands would have been understood literally in Jesus' day, but asserts (without evidence!) that the commands to heal and exorcize would have been taken in a 'spiritual sense' in Matthew's day, being understood as what happens to individuals when they receive and accept the good news of the kingdom. He

---

19. So Hagner, *Matthew 1–13*, p. 265.

concludes, 'The Commission in its literal terms applied fully only to the apostolic age.'[20]

## Then and now?

The evidence at this point is rather mixed. On the one hand, it seems very likely that Matthew's restriction to go only to the 'lost sheep of the house of Israel' was already present in his source material, and yet throughout the mission discourse there are clear indications that Matthew is addressing his own community who now take a more universalistic view of mission (Matt. 28:19a). This suggests that Matthew is widening the scope of Jesus' mission discourse so that it applies to his readers, and that Matthew does not intend to restrict the idea of delegated *exousia* to an unrepeatable past event in the lives of Jesus and the disciples.

On the other hand, Matthew often presents Jesus' miracles as fulfilment of OT prophecy (e.g. Matt. 8:17; 11:5–6; 12:18–21) and so, Christologically, thoroughly bound up with the mission of the earthly Jesus. Also, in his use of the title 'son of David' in connection with the miracle stories (9:27; 12:23; 15:22; 20:30–31) Matthew shows that the miracles are a demonstration of Jesus' messiahship. Therefore, they are to be interpreted primarily as part of the fulfilment of Jesus' specific mission to Israel. This would explain why, in Matthew's account of the Twelve being commissioned by Jesus, the disciples do not actually go out on mission, much less describe their experience of healings and exorcisms (cf. Mark 6:15; Luke 9:6; 10:17). It is also worth noting that later in Matthew's narrative when some of the disciples do attempt to engage independently in healing an epileptic boy, they fail miserably (17:14–20)! Nevertheless, the fact remains that Matthew 10:24–25 identifies the charismatic activity of the disciples with that of Jesus, and the mission discourse itself provides a 'transparent window' for viewing the church's post-Easter mission to the Gentiles.[21]

In Matthew 28:18–20 the emphasis is very much on the universal mission

---

20. Ibid., pp. 271–272. See also for example L. B. Smedes, *Ministry and the Miraculous: A Case Study at Fuller Theological Seminary* (Pasadena, Calif.: Fuller Theological Seminary, 1987), pp. 29–30; P. May, 'Focussing on the Eternal', in J. Goldingay (ed.), *Signs, Wonders and Healing* (Leicester: IVP, 1989), pp. 39–40; J. Goldingay, 'Analysing the Issues', in *Signs, Wonders and Healing*, pp. 179–180.

21. See D. R. Catchpole, *The Quest for Q* (Edinburgh: T. & T. Clark, 1993), p. 166.

of the church to make disciples (Matt. 28:19a), initiate them into the community (Matt. 28:19b), and here, significantly, for the first time the disciples are given what has previously been reserved for Jesus alone; that is, authority to teach all that Jesus has commanded (Matt. 28:20a). Given what appears to be a clear and intended emphasis on delegated authority to teach in the Great Commission, together with the lack of any specific mention of signs and wonders, the question remains: are there any indicators that Matthew intends his readers to understand the *exousia* to heal and exorcize as being in any way implied by the Great Commission, given its antecedents in the Gospel as a whole?

We have seen that Matthew clearly emphasizes Jesus' teaching ministry throughout his Gospel, especially as it relates to law-keeping and the superior righteousness that comes from obeying Jesus' ethical demands. We have also seen how Matthew is not content only to emphasize healing and exorcism in relation to the *exousia* of Jesus. When he is not focusing his readers' attention on Jesus' authority to teach, Matthew's portrayal of the *exousia* of Jesus includes the authority to forgive sins. It is here that we find a further indication that the authority delegated to the followers of Jesus is understood by Matthew to include activities beyond just those described specifically in the words of the Great Commission. Is there specific evidence that Matthew considered the forgiveness of sins to be part of his community's ongoing activity, thus reflecting both the ministry of the earthly Jesus and an acknowledgment of the continuing presence of the exalted Lord?

## The theme of forgiveness

In chapter 1 we saw that opponents of the Third Wave argue that the Third Wave's case is weakened by their not taking account of the authority of Jesus to forgive sins. In defence of the Third Wave position, Williams rather weakly points out that forgiveness is not included in the summaries we have of Jesus' ministry in the Gospels.[22] Evidence for the place of the forgiveness of sins in the ministry of Jesus amounts to more than explicit incidents where sins are forgiven.[23] Whilst Matthew omits Mark's reference to 'forgiveness of sins' in his description of the preaching of John the Baptist (Matt. 3:2; cf. Mark 1:4),

---

22. D. Williams, *The God who Reigns* (Basingstoke: Marshall Pickering, 1989), p. 126; *Signs, Wonders, and the Kingdom of God* (Ann Arbor, Mich.: Vine, 1989), p. 111.

23. See further for example Jeremias, *New Testament Theology*, pp. 113–114.

the First Evangelist ensures that it is transparently present in the ministry of Jesus (e.g. 6:12–15; 9:2–6; 18:23–35; 26:28).

Most importantly, forgiveness is explicitly taught to the disciples, who, as we have seen, are presented by Matthew as a learning community who transparently embody the church.[24] Matthew's redaction of the words of institution at the Last Supper – where he adds to Mark's 'This is my blood of the covenant, which is poured out for many' (Mark 14:24) the words 'for the forgiveness of sins' (Matt. 26:28b) – appears to be a clear indication that, linked with Matthew 18:18, Matthew's church practised the forgiveness of sins within a community context, and this was (at least) one of the ways in which they experienced (and expressed?) the presence of the exalted Jesus (Matt. 18:20; 28:20). In Matthew 18:18 the authority to forgive sins is widened to the community, where it is linked to the authority to 'bind and loose' given earlier to Peter (16:19).

But how would Matthew and his readers have understood this idea of 'binding and loosing'? Is it simply a matter of authority to forgive sins, or is there more to be understood by this enigmatic phrase? To answer these questions, we must now turn to our second case study in Matthew 16:13–20 and ask, 'What further clues does this offer for our understanding of the way in which Matthew conceives the extent to which the authority delegated by Jesus is operative in his church?'

---

24. G. Barth, 'Matthew's Understanding of the Law', in G. Bornkamm, G. Barth and H. J. Held (eds.), *Tradition and Interpretation in Matthew* (ET London: SCM, 1963), p. 100 n. 2.

# 7. PETER AND THE KEYS OF THE KINGDOM OF HEAVEN (MATT. 16:18–20)

## Introduction

It is clear on any reading of Matthew's Gospel that Peter plays a central role, acting as both a typical disciple as well as spokesman for the group.[1] There are three particular Petrine cameos (Matt. 14:28–31; 16:16b–19; 17:24–27) that serve to promote Peter as a central character within the First Gospel. Here we will concentrate on Peter's role in Matthew 16:18–20 in order to answer a number of questions. For example, what are the most likely ways Matthew intends his readers to understand the nature of the delegated authority to 'bind and loose'? What light does this pericope shed on our understanding of how Matthew views the extent and scope of the delegated *exousia*/authority to be exercised by his community? Can we find any evidence to support the Third

---

1. See Matt. 14:28–31; 15:15; 17:24–27; 18:21–22. See further for example R. H. Gundry, *Matthew: A Commentary on His Literary and Theological Art* (Grand Rapids, Mich.: Eerdmans, 1982), p. 9; U. Luz, 'Das Primatwort Matthäus 16.17–19 aus Wirkungsgeschichtlicher Sicht', *NTS* 37 (1991), pp. 422 and 427; *The Theology of the Gospel of Matthew* (ET Cambridge: Cambridge University Press, 1995), p. 94; M. J. Wilkins, *The Concept of Disciple in Matthew's Gospel: As Reflected in the Use of the Term* Μαθητής (NovTSup 59; Leiden: Brill, 1988), pp. 143–144.

Wave's contention that the authority delegated to the church in the Great Commission might have been understood by Matthew to include authority over the demonic?

Of the three Synoptic Evangelists, Matthew's account of Peter's confession at Caesarea Philippi is the only one to contain a reference to the 'keys of the kingdom of heaven' (Matt. 16:13–20//Mark 8:27–30//Luke 9:18–21). Matthew's expansion of his Markan source is considerable throughout this pericope. Following Peter's declaration that Jesus is the Christ, 'the son of the living God' (v. 16b), the First Evangelist continues with his special material that refers in verse 19a to the 'keys of the kingdom of heaven' (Matt. 16:17–19). In Matthew 16:19b, 19c, repeated in Matthew 18:18, we have a parallelism that suggests a Semitic style which could have originated with Jesus himself.[2] Peter frequently acts as spokesman for the disciples/community (Matt. 15:15; 17:24–27; 18:21–22; cf. 14:28–31),[3] and in verse 19a, Jesus' promise to Peter of the keys of the kingdom of heaven is clearly linked to the authority to 'bind and loose'. The representative nature of Peter's role is further evidenced when the authority to bind and loose is extended in 18:18 to Matthew's church. To what does this authority relate within the context of Matthew's Gospel? Does it include authority to make definitive teaching pronouncements and to forgive sins, as we saw was the case with Matthew's understanding of Jesus authority? If so, can we also assume that the authority delegated to the disciples/church will also be validated through miraculous activity? Is there any evidence

---

2.  R. E. Brown, K. P. Donfried and J. Reumann (eds.), *Peter in the New Testament* (London: Chapman, 1974), p. 96. Also, J. Jeremias, *New Testament Theology Volume One: The Proclamation of Jesus* (ET London: SCM, 1971), pp. 20–35, who notes the strongly Semitic character and poetic rhythm when the logion is translated back into Aramaic. O. Cullmann, *Peter: Disciple, Apostle, Martyr* (ET London, SCM, 1953), p. 176, does not rule out the possibility of the logion having originated with the historical Jesus. See further B. F. Meyer, *The Aims of Jesus* (London: SCM, 1979), pp. 185 ff.; M. Wilcox, 'Peter and the Rock: A Fresh Look at Matthew xvi.17–19', *NTS* 22 (1975–6), pp. 73–78; B. P. Robinson, 'Peter and his Successors: Tradition and Redaction in Matthew 16.17–19', *JSNT* 21 (1984), pp. 85–104; C. Rowland, *Christian Origins: An Account of the Setting and Character of the Most Important Messianic Sect of Judaism* (London: SPCK, 1985), p. 153; J. Marcus, 'The Gates of Hades and the Keys of the Kingdom (Matt. 16.18–19)', *CBQ* 50 (1988), pp. 443–455.

3.  Cf. T. L. Donaldson, 'Guiding Readers – Making Disciples: Discipleship in Matthew's Narrative Strategy', in R. N. Longenecker (ed.), *Patterns of Discipleship in the New Testament* (Grand Rapids, Mich.: Eerdmans, 1996), p. 32.

connected with the idea of 'binding and loosing' to suggest that healings and/or exorcisms might be envisaged?

## Isaiah 22:22

It is commonly maintained by commentators that in verse 19a the keys of the kingdom of heaven should be viewed as being synonymous with the 'key of David' referred to in Isaiah 22:22,[4] and that Matthew 23:13[5] confirms this interpretation.[6] In Matthew 23:13 the Evangelist does use the verb 'to shut/lock', indicating dependence upon the key imagery that occurs both in Isaiah 22:22 and Matthew 16:19a. It is argued that this link is strengthened further by the connected idea of 'binding and loosing' (Matt. 16:19b, 19c; cf. Isaiah 22:22) and the statement made by Jesus in Matthew 23:13 that teachers of the Law 'lock people out of the kingdom of heaven'. However, this interpretation ignores the important Christological imagery of Jesus as the holder of the keys of heaven (Matt. 16:19a), which suggests a further development of the Isaiah 22:22 tradition based upon ideas current in Jewish angelogical traditions that Matthew used here to heighten both the Christological and ecclesiological import of this pronouncement by Jesus. It should also be noted that the phrase 'the keys of the kingdom' does not occur in Matthew 23:13, a fact that serves to weaken the argument that Matthew 23:13 confirms that Matthew 16:19a refers to the 'key of David' found in Isaiah 22:22. Some exploration of this further development is clearly called for here so that we can assess its effect on our understanding of the nature and scope of the *exousia* implicit in the granting of the keys to Peter with their associated authority to 'bind and loose' (Matt. 16:19b, 19c; 18:18).

It appears that in the granting of the keys to Peter we have a foreshadowing of the Great Commission, with Matthew giving his readers a glimpse of the exalted Jesus in his role as heavenly key-bearer, to whom all authority in heaven and on earth has been given (cf. 28:18). Here Jesus passes the keys to the kingdom of heaven on to Peter as representative of the disciples and forebear of Matthew's own community. If this is the case, then the associated

---

4. A reference to the authority as royal steward to be conferred upon Eliakim, the son of Hilkiah, who replaced Shebna during the reign of King Hezekiah.

5. Cf. Luke 11:52 and the reference to the 'key of knowledge'.

6. See for example E. Schweizer, *The Good News According to Matthew* (ET London: SPCK, 1976), p. 343.

sharing in the *exousia* to 'bind and loose' may be regarded as particularly indicative of their experiencing the abiding presence of the exalted Jesus in the community (cf. Matt. 28:20).

## The influence of Jewish sources

In Matthew 16:19 the phrase 'the keys of the kingdom' is inextricably linked with the idea of exercising delegated authority, and in this there is indeed a parallel with Isaiah 22:22. However, in Isaiah 22:22 the authority is passed on only at the earthly level and is concerned with purely mundane affairs. In contrast, for Matthew the authority is of heavenly origin, is concerned (at least) with the law and community discipline, and contains an explicit heavenly–earthly correspondence. These important developments suggest strongly that the key imagery Matthew uses in 16:19a is best understood as being more dependent upon contemporary Jewish ideas associated with angelic key-holders, and especially the archangel Michael.[7] This being the case, we have here what appears to be a substitution of Jesus in place of Michael, which makes the important Christological point that the earthly Jesus is also God's heavenly plenipotentiary,[8] thus replacing the archangel Michael in his traditional role as God's chief agent with special responsibility for Israel, the people of God (cf. Matt. 10:23; 15:24; 19:28).[9] Of course, this substitution does not mean that for Matthew and his community the risen Jesus was an exalted angel. Rather, this is an example of an early Christian community using traditions and imagery from Jewish angelology to help them come to terms theologically with the exalted Christ.[10]

---

7. For recent treatments of the relevance of Jewish angelology for the origins of Christology, see especially J. D. G. Dunn, *Christology in the Making: A New Testament Enquiry into the Origins of the Doctrine of the Incarnation* (London: SCM, 1980), pp. 149–159; C. Rowland, *The Open Heaven: A Study of Apocalyptic in Judaism and Early Christianity* (London: SPCK, 1982), pp. 94–113. See also, L. W. Hurtado, *One God, One Lord: Early Christian Devotion and Ancient Jewish Monotheism* (London: SCM, 1988), pp. 71–90.

8. This substitution also serves to underline the risen Jesus' claim in Matt. 28:18 that 'all authority in heaven and on earth has been given to me'.

9. Note also how in Matt. 27:42 Matthew's removing Mark's 'Christ' (cf. Mark 15:32//Luke 23:35) from the words spoken by those mocking Jesus on the cross serves to emphasize more starkly for his readers Jesus' association with Israel.

10. Cf. Hurtado, *One God, One Lord*, p. 74.

Further evidence of Matthew's tendency to adapt Jewish traditions by sub-stituting the name of Jesus in order to make a Christological point can be seen in Matthew 18:20. Here the Christological substitution appears to be based on a rabbinic tradition found in *Abot* 3.3, which reads, 'R. Hanina b. Teradion said: If two sit together, and words of Torah are between them, the *Shechinah* rests between them . . .'[11]

In Matthew's adaptation, it is the *name* of Jesus,[12] as the one who now fulfils and rightly interprets Torah that replaces the (pre-Jesus) Halachic interpret-ations of Torah, and the (risen) presence[13] of Jesus substitutes for the *shekinah* presence of God. It is also possible that further evidence of Matthew's being influenced here by contemporary Jewish sources may be seen in *Berakot* 6a, where we have a similar saying that reads, 'Where three sit and judge, the *Shekinah* is in their midst' (cf. Matt. 18:28).[14] This rabbinic aphorism also pro-vides contextual light on Matthew 18:19, where the Matthean context pro-vided in verse 18 is also about the reassurance of God's presence during the exercising of communal governance.

Elsewhere in the NT we find that it is the exalted Christ who is the keeper of the keys (Rev. 3:7), although here at least, there appears to be a direct depen-dence upon Isaiah 22:22. In both instances (Rev. 3:7 and Isa. 22:22) 'key' is sin-gular, whereas in Matthew 16:19a we have the plural. The use of the plural here is possibly an indication of a closer dependence by Matthew upon traditions found in *3 Baruch* featuring the archangel Michael, rather than a direct depen-dence upon Isaiah 22:22. It is worth exploring more carefully how the key-imagery found in the apocalypse of *3 Baruch* might shed light on our understanding of Matthew 16:19.

Texts of *3 Baruch*, in which the prophet Jeremiah's scribe, Baruch, weeps over the destruction of the temple and city of Jerusalem, have been found in both Greek and Slavonic, with the Slavonic text being a translation from a now lost original Greek text.[15] As to date and provenance, the weight of scholarly opinion favours a Jewish provenance with evidence for Christian interpolation

11. C. G. Montefiore and H. Loewe (eds.), *A Rabbinic Anthology* (New York: Schocken, 1974), p. 23.

12. Cf. Schweizer, *Good News According to Matthew*, pp. 374–375.

13. Or (Holy) Spirit.

14. Schweizer, *Good News According to Matthew*, pp. 374–375.

15. H. E. Gaylord (trans.), '3 [Greek Apocalypse of] Baruch', in J. H. Charlesworth (ed.), *The Old Testament Pseudepigrapha*. Vol. 1: *Apocalyptic Literature and Testaments* (London: Darton Longman & Todd, 1983), p. 653.

at various points in the text,[16] and with Syria being the most recently suggested place of origin.[17] The date for *3 Baruch* is thought to be somewhere between the late first and early second century AD,[18] which may indicate that the traditions preserved here were current from at least the beginning of the first century AD, and possibly earlier.

The central angelic figure in this apocalypse is Michael, who is described as commander-in-chief of the angelic host and who, in Jewish tradition, is firmly associated with Israel, where he replaces YHWH as the guardian of Israel and advocate of the Jews (Dan. 10:13; 12:1; cf. Sirach 17.17). Michael leads Israel against her enemies (*Ass. Mos.* 10.2); he descends to earth in order to accept human prayers (*3 Bar.* 11.4); presents the merits of the righteous to God (*3 Bar.* 14.2), and in this he has close affinities with Raphael in the much earlier book of Tobit (Tobit 12.12–15). Importantly here, according to *3 Baruch* 11.2, Michael acts as the keeper of the keys of the gates to the kingdom of heaven. He also functions as priest in the heavenly temple.[19] According to the apocalypse, Baruch and his angelic guide arrive at the gate of the fifth heaven, which is closed. Baruch asks the angel if they might enter, but the angel responds in *3 Baruch* 11.2, 'We are unable to enter until Michael the holder of the keys of the kingdom of heaven comes.'[20]

Jeremias has argued that *3 Baruch* 11.2 is the result of a Christian interpolation on the grounds that the phrase 'the kingdom of heaven' is not found elsewhere in the literature.[21] Whilst there is evidence for Christian interpolation throughout this apocalypse, I would argue that the non-Christian nature of *3 Baruch* 11.2 may be deduced from the following:

1  According to Matthew 16:19a it is Jesus who is keeper of the keys of the kingdom of heaven and, as such, is in a position to hand them on to Peter, who will act as Jesus' plenipotentiary at the earthly level; whereas

---

16. For detailed arguments, see ibid. See also L. Sabourin, 'Traits apocalyptiques dans L'Évangile de Matthieu', in *ScEs* 33.3 (1981), p. 363.

17. Ibid. and note.

18. G. W. E. Nickelsburg, *Jewish Literature between the Bible and the Mishnah: A Historical and Literary Introduction* (London: SCM, 1981), p. 303.

19. Cf. Hebrews 7:15 ff.

20. My translation from the Greek.

21. J. Jeremias, κλείς, *TDNT* 3, p. 749. For arguments against the view that 'kingdom of heaven' is a Christian interpolation, see *APOT* 2, p. 539, and note.

in *3 Baruch* 11.2 it is Michael rather than Jesus who is the keeper of the heavenly keys.[22]

2  Given the probable dating and provenance of *3 Baruch* (late first to early second century AD), it is quite likely that Christian interpolators would be aware of Matthew's portrayal of Jesus as keeper of the heavenly keys and would hardly miss the opportunity to replace Michael with Jesus at this point.

In *3 Baruch* 11.12 Michael receives men's prayers in the fifth heaven (Paradise)[23] from lesser angels.[24] Michael, as keeper of the heavenly keys, has direct access to God in a similar way to that ascribed to Raphael in Tobit 12.15 and, significantly, Jesus in the Q tradition (Matt. 10:32–33//Luke 12:8–9).[25] There are, however, important differences between the pseudepigraphical literature and Matthew's Gospel. In the pseudepigraphical literature the keys remain in the possession of the heavenly personage, whereas in Matthew 16:19a the keys of heaven are passed from a heavenly personage (Jesus, in the light of the coming post-Easter situation, cf. 28:18) to an earthly steward (Peter, as representative of the earthly *ekklēsia*). The authority to bind and loose is then placed in juxtaposition to possession of the heavenly keys (v. 19b, 19c).

Similar ideas are in the rabbinic literature. In 1 Kings 17:1 Elijah prophesies a drought that will end only as a result of his prayer (1 Kgs 18:42–45). The Babylonian Talmud (*b. Sanh.* 113a) attributes this to Elijah having been given the heavenly 'key of rain' by God, so that he has the ability to unlock what is already present in that heavenly repository. Here we have not only the use of heavenly-key imagery, but also what may be described as a heavenly–earthly correspondence connected to the idea of 'binding and loosing'.

To summarize, the complexity of ideas associated with Michael as the bearer of the heavenly keys appears to have influenced Matthew in a number of ways that help us to understand the nature and scope of the delegated authority

---

22.  Cf. Rev. 3:7.

23.  Cf. Luke 23:43.

24.  *APOT* 1, pp. 788–789. In *T. Levi* 2.7 – 3.8 the fifth heaven is also the place to which lesser angels carry the prayers of men to the angels of the presence, of whom Michael is one.

25.  Reference to angels is not present in Matt. 10:32–33 (cf. Luke 12:8–9), but see Matt. 18:10, where angelic representatives of members of the *ekklēsia* have direct access to God.

entrusted to Matthew's church. We have seen that in Matthew 16:19a the phrase 'the keys of the kingdom' was probably not directly dependent on Isaiah 22:22, but reflects a development of ideas found in contemporary Jewish sources. Here the heavenly keys are associated with the archangel Michael who is God's chief agent with particular responsibility for Israel / the people of God, and where the authority represented by the keys has a heavenly origin.

In presenting Jesus as the keeper of the keys, Matthew evokes for his readers familiar imagery associated with the archangel Michael. In this way, prior to the resurrection appearances at the end of the Gospel, Matthew foreshadows the heavenly–earthly authority to be claimed by the risen Jesus in the final commissioning scene (28:18) and which underwrites the instructions given in the Great Commission. The ideas represented here by Matthew in terms of key-imagery associated with binding and loosing are clearly important for our understanding of the nature and scope of the delegated authority envisaged by Matthew as being entrusted by the risen Jesus to the evangelist's community and, transparently, to later Christian generations.

Given the close association suggested here between the keys to the kingdom of heaven, symbolizing authority to bind and loose, and Matthew's Great Commission, what support, if any, do our findings offer for the Third Wave in their contention that the Great Commission includes authority to heal? And how, exactly, are we to understand the nature and scope of the delegated authority to bind and loose? With these questions in mind, let us now turn to Matthew 16:19b, 19c.

## Binding and loosing (Matt. 16:19b, 19c)

Commentators are divided as to how the idea of 'binding and loosing' should be understood. J. Marcus argues that clues to understanding what Matthew means here are to be found in the directional flow of the saying together with the future perfect tense Matthew uses here.[26] In Matthew 16:17 it is the Father in heaven who revealed Jesus' true identity to Peter at the earthly level, added to which the literal meaning of verse 19b, 19c also indicates a heaven–earth directional flow. We read, 'whatever you [singular] bind on earth will have been bound in heaven, and whatever you loose on the earth will have been loosed in heaven'.[27]

---

26. Marcus, 'Gates of Hades', pp. 443–455.
27. My trans.

Marcus argues that if the use of the future perfect tense (lit. 'shall be having been bound' and 'shall be having been loosed') is taken seriously, then it points to a directional flow where events in heaven precede events on earth.[28] C. F. D. Moule prefers what he considers to be the more natural reading, 'shall have been bound' on the grounds that the NT does not always follow classical Greek usage in such cases where periphrastic future perfects are better understood as being equivalent to simple futures.[29] Against Moule, Marcus sees no grammatical reason to assume that Matthew deviates here from classical Greek and points out that the significance of the perfect tense is that it usually indicates 'a past action with a present result'.[30] According to Marcus, in Matthew's Gospel futures are not just intentional (I will . . .) but refer to 'an apocalyptic change that will alter the entire cosmos, including the law'.[31]

Such an 'apocalyptic change' would be very much in line with an understanding of the symbolism of the heavenly keys, where the earthly *ekklēsia*, represented here by Peter,[32] has access to a true understanding of Torah that has been eschatologically redefined by Jesus as the new Moses and who now, as the Risen One, is the holder of all authority (Matt. 28:18). As with rabbinic tradition, where 'binding and loosing' refers to Halachic decisions about what is and what is not permitted by Torah, so here in Matthew, 'binding and loosing' also refers to authority to interpret the law. By handing the heavenly keys to Peter, the Matthean Jesus delegates authority to open the heavenly realm and gain insight into the true (eschatological) meaning of Torah and so ensure that the righteousness of the earthly *ekklēsia* continues to exceed that of the scribes and Pharisees, until the Son of Man returns (16:13b).

The authority to teach, reserved for the earthly Jesus prior to the resurrection, is conferred on the disciples by the risen Jesus in the final commission (Matt. 28:20a). Along with the universal missionary outlook, this is a striking reversal of the pre-Easter situation. In light of the Great Commission,

---

28. Marcus, 'Gates of Hades', p. 448.

29. C. F. D. Moule, *An Idiom Book of New Testament Greek*, 2nd ed (Cambridge: Cambridge University Press, 1959), p. 18. Moule cites as examples Matt. 16:19; Luke 12:52; Heb. 2:13.

30. Marcus, 'Gates of Hades', p. 448.

31. Ibid., p. 453.

32. G. Bornkamm, 'The Authority to "Bind and Loose" in the Church'; ET in G. Stanton (ed.), *The Interpretation of Matthew* (London: SPCK, 1983), pp. 93–95, makes the point that here Peter's role is that of teacher and guarantor through whom Matthew's community knows itself to be founded on the teaching of Jesus.

Matthew's understanding of the authority to 'bind and loose' clearly extends beyond mere *halakah*. The (transparent) command to the Eleven to teach members of the community to observe all that Jesus commanded (28:19) must now be understood to include, for Matthew, the authoritative interpretation of the law, the exercising of community discipline (18:15–20) and forgiveness of sins (18:21–22; cf. 26:28).

The Third Wave argue that Jesus' instruction in the Great Commission to teach disciples to obey all that Jesus commanded includes authority to heal and exorcize.[33] It would be easy to dismiss their claim here on the grounds that it is based on a highly dubious hermeneutical approach to the NT evidence, and that the words of the Great Commission do not explicitly refer to healing/ exorcism. It is true to say that as it stands, based on their homogenizing approach to the evidence, the Third Wave's argument is not convincingly supported by the evidence to which they appeal. However, we have already seen that, in light of our understanding of the delegated authority to 'bind and loose', Jesus' command to teach Christians to obey all that he commanded is clearly intended by Matthew to be applied more widely than just to provide an imprimatur for a Christian *halakah*. And so, finally, here we will ask if we can find any evidence that might incidentally support the Third Wave's assertion about the Great Commission and healing/exorcism.

Interestingly, we do have a further reference to 'binding and loosing' that is broadly contemporary with Matthew's Gospel, which is found in the Qumran literature (CD 13.10). Here the reference to binding and loosing occurs in connection with freedom from demonic oppression, and this may also be reflected in Matthew's idea of the community's sharing in the authority of the exalted Jesus. If this is the case, then it broadens still further the scope of Matthew's understanding of the authority delegated to the disciples/church so that it also includes authority to heal and cast out demons.

From here it would be fair to say that the authority to heal and cast out demons cannot be dismissed from Matthew's understanding of the remit and scope of authority delegated by the risen Jesus. Indeed, it may even be assumed to be implicit in the delegated *exousia* underpinning Matthew's Great Commission,

---

33. See for example G. S. Greig and K. N. Springer, 'Appendix 3: Matthew 28:18–20 – The Great Commission and Jesus' Commands to Preach and Heal', in idem (eds.), *The Kingdom and the Power: Are Healing and the Spiritual Gifts Used by Jesus and the Early Church Meant for the Church Today?* (Ventura, Calif.: Regal, 1993), p. 401; and J. Wimber, *Power Evangelism: Signs and Wonders Today* (London: Hodder & Stoughton, 1985), pp. 42–43.

and to which the abiding presence of the exalted Jesus acts as guarantor of the legitimacy of the community's authority to act (28:20b; cf. 18:20). Whilst this suggestion is attractive and lends considerable weight to the Third Wave's case, based on the evidence available it remains no more than a possibility.

## Conclusions

We have seen that in Matthew 16:19 there appears to be a conflation of ideas that may have influenced Matthew and which suggest that the First Evangelist had in mind a broad scope for the remit of his community's *exousia* to 'bind and loose'. Whilst for Matthew the primary emphasis in the Great Commission is to make disciples and teach them to obey all that Jesus commanded, it is quite plausible that Matthew's first readers would have understood the church's *exousia* to 'bind and loose' also to include authority to forgive sins and quite possibly authority to heal/exorcize.

On this last point, however, the Matthean Jesus warns of the most dreadful consequences for those whose claim to be disciples relies on their use of Jesus' name, and the authority it invokes, to engage in spectacular charismatic activity (Matt. 7:21–23). In light of Matthew's intentional transparency, this remains as much a warning for Christians today as it did in the first century for Matthew and his community.

## 8. CONCLUSIONS TO PART ONE

Our brief overview of the scholarly attempts to identify the *Gattung* of Matthew 28:16–20 led us to conclude that Matthew's Great Commission should be regarded as *sui generis* and, therefore, to be understood uniquely with reference to the rest of Matthew's Gospel. The source material used by Matthew for his Great Commission already contained a conflation of appearance traditions linked to the idea of the commissioning of the Eleven for a mission by the risen Jesus. As it stands, Matthew 28:16–20 reflects Matthew's later perception of the missionary task facing his church. In terms of its literary function, Matthew's Great Commission serves as a climax to the Gospel and, as such, brings together key Matthaean themes present throughout his Gospel.

In view of Jesus' command to 'make disciples', which lies at the heart of the Great Commission, we set out to discover what Matthew is saying to the church about the essence of Christian discipleship. We saw that the historicizing approach to Matthew's Gospel, which consigns Jesus and the disciples to a holy, unrepeatable past, leaves little room for the Third Wave paradigm, which regards the experience of Jesus and the disciples as a continuing model for the contemporary church. A more widely accepted, and fruitful, approach is that of 'transparency', which considers all that is addressed to the disciples by Jesus during his earthly ministry as being also addressed to Matthew's community, who are thus able to identify with the disciples and embody their experience.

With this in mind, we saw that Matthew presents us with a sophisticated paradigm for discipleship, where the essence of being a disciple of Jesus is to be understood primarily in terms of learning, understanding and obeying the words of Jesus. Matthew portrays Jesus as a Mosaic prophet who rightly interprets the law, and whose authority to teach and to forgive sins is validated by his charismatic activity. However, in presenting the miracles of the earthly Jesus, we saw that Matthew's tendency is both to spiritualize them (by presenting them in terms of 'salvation') and to cast them in terms of the fulfilment of OT prophecy, which suggests that there is a sense in which the First Evangelist wants to locate Jesus' miracle-working in the historic past. Nevertheless, it is clear that, for Matthew, Jesus' authority to interpret the demands of the law is passed on to his disciples (16:19; 18:18), although there is a tension in the way Matthew presents the disciples as being at the same time inheritors of Jesus' *exousia* as well as those of little faith.

In our examination of the mission of the Twelve (Matt. 10:5–6) we saw that the effect of choosing twelve disciples and authorizing them to go only to the 'lost sheep of the house of Israel' was to show that they shared in the eschatological mission of the earthly Jesus. Given the universal outlook of Matthew 28:19, in the restriction to go only to Israel, it could be argued that Matthew's intention here is to place this incident firmly in an unrepeatable past. However, we saw that in Matthew's account he is not concerned to record that the disciples actually go out on mission, much less describe their success in healings and exorcisms (cf. Mark 6:13; Luke 9:6; 10:17). In the First Gospel at least, the mission of the Twelve is to be regarded as being transparent in that it acts as a vehicle through which Matthew widens Jesus' missionary discourse to include material that takes account of the universal outlook reflected in 28:19. This is clearly intended for the ongoing missionary situation facing his community, where they continue to share not only in Jesus' mission, but also in his suffering (cf. 10:16ff.). And here there is clearly a lesson for the church today.

According to Matthew, authority to teach, which lies at the heart of the Great Commission, was the sole preserve of Jesus until the post-Easter commissioning of the Eleven (28:18). However, we have seen that Matthew had in mind a wider scope for his community's *exousia* to 'bind and loose' than just community discipline and authority to teach. It was also understood by Matthew as authority to forgive sins, which is reflected in the uniquely Matthean Jesus' words at the Last Supper (Matt. 26:28; cf. Mark 14:24; Luke 22:20; 1 Cor. 11:25). Importantly for the Third Wave, there is evidence to suggest that Matthew's community may have also regarded the *exousia* delegated to them to bind and loose as also including authority over the demonic. In this connection, an important qualification is to be seen in the dire warning given by the Matthean Jesus against charismatic activity that is not rooted in obedience to his teaching (Matt. 7:21–23). In view of what we have seen of Matthew's intentional transparency, this remains as much a warning for Christians today who regard signs and wonders as normative as it did in the first century for Matthew and his community.

And so, what sort of a model for Christian discipleship does Matthew provide for the church in the twenty-first century? How does it differ from the model proposed by the Third Wave? We have in Matthew's Gospel evidence that can be understood as supporting the Third Wave paradigm with regard to the Great Commission and authority to heal/exorcize. However, this is evidence that is not presented by the Third Wave, nor is it readily accessible to their homogenous hermeneutical approach to the text. In seeking a paradigm from Matthew's Gospel for contemporary Christian discipleship we have found that the great weight of evidence goes a considerable way beyond the narrow confines of just proclaiming and demonstrating, with acts of power, the nearness of God's heavenly rule. Discipleship for Matthew is a much richer concept than this. Yes, it involves sharing in the *exousia* of the exalted Jesus, making disciples and teaching all that Jesus commanded, but at its heart it also involves living lives that demonstrate the superior righteousness appropriate to followers of Jesus who claim their part in the eschatological people of God. Matthew's paradigm for discipleship also makes room for the expectation of suffering and persecution (Matt. 10:16–32), the forgiveness of sins (6:12, 14; 18:21–22; 26:27–28) as well as exercising authority, as a community, in temporal and spiritual matters.

Healings and exorcisms continue to have a part to play in the community's experience of the outworking of the delegated *exousia* entrusted to all disciples, but they must by no means be the predominant characteristic of those who follow Jesus. Indeed, Matthew clearly subordinates healings and exorcisms to doing God's will, even when they are performed in Jesus' name (Matt. 7:21–23). If our reading of the link between the risen Jesus' promise of his abiding presence (Matt. 28:20b) and his authoritative presence in connection with binding and loosing (Matt. 18:20) is correct, then the contemporary model for healings/exorcisms suggested here is one where the invocation of Jesus' name is practised in a (formal?) setting (Matt. 18:15–20), where the success or otherwise of the claim to authority for healing/exorcism is transparently open to ratification by the church acting in light of their belief in the abiding presence of the risen Jesus/Holy Spirit. Clearly, for Matthew, this could never be at the expense of subordinating what truly characterizes Christian discipleship to simply 'doing the stuff'!

# PART TWO

# COMMISSIONING AND DISCIPLESHIP
## ACCORDING TO MARK

## Introducing the issues

In his discussion of appropriate methods for interpreting Mark's Gospel Christopher Marshall points out that, in light of the widespread scholarly acceptance of Markan priority within the Synoptic tradition, an increasing number of scholars have come to accept the need to move away from a polarization of methods employed in the study of Mark.[1] The need now is to adopt an eclectic approach that is more appropriate to the 'methodological pluralism' required by the text.[2] In contrast to form criticism, with its understanding of Mark as the product of Mark's 'community', redaction criticism understands the present form of the Gospels as the work of a single author. However, the limitations of redaction criticism for the interpretation of Mark have been ably demonstrated by Clifton Black in his examination of redaction-critical studies of the role of the disciples in Mark, and it must now be recognized that the application of *Redaktionsgeschichte* alone to the Second Gospel is far from a precise science.[3]

---

1. E.g. form criticism, redaction criticism etc.
2. C. D. Marshall, *Faith as a Theme in Mark's Narrative* (SNTSMS 64; Cambridge: Cambridge University Press, 1989), p. 8.
3. C. C. Black, *The Disciples According to Mark: Markan Redaction in Current Debate*

Black demonstrates the point by focusing on the work of three representative scholars, each holding different theological presuppositions: conservative,[4] median[5] and liberal.[6] Building on the seminal work of Willi Marxsen,[7] they each arrive at rather different conclusions about the role of the disciples in Mark. The reason for this, Black insists, is due to inconsistencies in their application of redaction-critical criteria resulting in differing conclusions about what they judge to derive from Mark's tradition and what may be assigned to Markan redaction. Given the limitations of redaction-criticism, it is now recognized that the interpreter of Mark must take account of the Gospel narrative as a whole drawing on insights from secular literary criticism in order to take better account of Mark's theological and literary integrity.[8] As we saw with respect to Matthew 28:16–20, methods best suited to the interpretation of a literary text depend very much on the question of genre. Marshall writes:

> While there is much disagreement over the precise literary genre that best accommodates Mark's gospel, or whether it is in fact *sui generis*, all would agree that

----

(JSNTSup 27; Sheffield: JSOT, 1989), pp. 17–38 and 60. For a useful article that discusses and contextualizes Markan *Redaktionsgeschichte* within the history of Synoptic studies, see C. C. Black, 'The Quest of Mark the Redactor: Why Has it Been Pursued, and what Has it Taught us?', *JSNT* 33 (1988), pp. 19–39. Here Black raises the important question (which he pursues in considerable detail in his *Disciples According to Mark*) of the value of this approach in light of Markan priority. Arising out of his discussion of the pros and cons, Marshall gives the reader a profile of the redaction-critical method, placing it in its scholarly *Sitz im Leben*. He concludes that although redaction criticism sought to cast light on the Evangelists' historical and social settings, and those of the communities for which they were writing, the point of entry lay with identifying the redactor's theology and from here his intended meaning.

4. R. P. Meye, *Jesus and the Twelve: Discipleship and Revelation in Mark's Gospel* (Grand Rapids, Mich.: Eerdmans, 1968). See further Black, *Disciples*, pp. 65–97.

5. E. Best, *Following Jesus: Discipleship in the Gospel of Mark* (JSNTSup 4; Sheffield: JSOT, 1981). See further Black, *Disciples*, pp. 99–125.

6. T. J. Weedon, *Mark – Tradition in Conflict* (Philadelphia: Fortress, 1971). See further Black, *Disciples*, pp. 128–157.

7. W. Marxsen, *Mark the Evangelist: Studies on the Redaction History of the Gospel* (ET Nashville, Tenn.: Abingdon, 1969).

8. Marshall, *Faith as a Theme*, p. 14.

the fundamental category to which it belongs is that of narrative. By narrative we mean a story or an account of events and participants who move through time and space, a recital with a beginning, middle and end. The most fruitful literary approach to Mark, then, is one which takes seriously the narrative or story mode he uses to communicate his message, an approach which may be called *narrative criticism*.[9]

## Mark as narrative

With respect to (implied) authorial intent,[10] narrative criticism assumes that Mark tells a coherent story which involves the skilful use of his tradition about Jesus and the disciples in order to create a narrative which previously did not exist.[11] Mark's redaction of traditional material, together with the assumed coherence and integrity of his Gospel narrative, indicates a unity of story that may be entered into and experienced by the reader.[12] The key question for us here is, what does Mark intend to say to his first readers about Jesus and the disciples in order to inform their (and our) understanding of what it means to be a follower of Jesus?

Reading through his Gospel, it is clear that Mark portrays the disciples in both a favourable and unfavourable light. The disciples are called by Jesus to be 'fishers of men', they remain with Jesus until his arrest and are privy to Jesus' teaching about discipleship, yet they constantly show their lack of understanding. In narrative-critical terms, the reader is clearly meant to identify with the disciples who act as a foil for Jesus' teaching, affording him the

---

9. Ibid., p. 15. Cf. D. Rhoads and D. Michie, *Mark as Story: An Introduction to the Narrative of a Gospel* (Philadelphia: Fortress, 1982), p. 3.

10. According to A. Stock, *Call to Discipleship: A Literary Study of Mark's Gospel* (GNS 1; Delaware: Glazier; Dublin: Veritas, 1982), p. 206, the implied author of Mark is a Christian who, in narrating the public life of Jesus, 'shapes his narrative to be of maximum benefit to his Christian readers'.

11. Cf. Marshall, *Faith as a Theme*, pp. 16–20.

12. R. C. Tannehill, 'The Disciples in Mark: The Function of Narrative Role', in W. Telford (ed.), *The Interpretation of Mark* (Philadelphia: Fortress; London: SPCK, 1985), p. 141, goes further when he writes, 'The decision of the author to write a Gospel, including the story of the first disciples, rests on the assumption that there are essential similarities between the situation of these disciples and the situation of the early Church, so that, in telling a story about the past, the author can also speak to his present.'

opportunity to correct their demonstrably wrong notions about true disciple-ship.[13] According to Augustine Stock, several perspectives borrowed from secular literary studies are helpful in reading Mark as a unified narrative, an important concept, which is particularly relevant here, being that of 'commis-sion'. Stock explains, 'A commission is accepted by a narrative character and this results in a unified narrative sequence as the narrator tells us how the char-acter fulfils that commission or fails to fulfil it.'[14]

This insight can be applied to Mark where Jesus receives his commission from God as Son of Man/Messiah/Son of God, and the disciples receive their commission to discipleship from Jesus. Stock explains that it is common for an implied author to 'instil' or 're-enforce' values that are important for him in the narrative, and a recognition of these values gives the clue to the author's purpose in writing. Importantly, he notes that a tension is set up in the narra-tive whenever a character acts in a way which is contrary to those values.[15]

In Mark's Gospel, we find that Jesus corrects his followers' wrong notions of discipleship, and Mark's readers are clearly intended to evaluate the disci-ples' behaviour in light of the words and actions of Jesus. Stock points out that an *internal* tension is set up in the narrative between Jesus and the disciples whenever the disciples fall short of Jesus' standard. Here the implied reader is invited by the text to give a negative judgment against the disciples, and this in turn contributes to the *external* tension set up between the author's values and those of the implied reader.[16]

In terms of the overall structure, Mark's Gospel can be divided into Mark 1:14 – 8:26 and Mark 8:27 – 16:8, with the Christological turning point in the story being Peter's recognition and confession of Jesus' messiahship at Caesarea Philippi (Mark 8:27–30). However, the turning point for Mark's teaching about discipleship comes at 8:31–33, where, in the face of Jesus' teaching that the Son of Man must suffer and Peter's objection to this, Jesus' rebuke in verse 33b is particularly significant. From this point in the Gospel, the key to a right understanding of discipleship is clearly for the reader to view the disciples from Jesus' own self-sacrificing, heavenly perspective rather than a power-seeking, earthly perspective. Mark's explicit teaching about disciple-ship is linked to three passion predictions (Mark 8:31–33; 9:30–32; 10:32–34). From here the disciples are presented in a largely negative light and their ideas

---

13. Cf. Rhoads and Michie, *Mark as Story*, pp. 122–123.

14. Stock, *Call to Discipleship*, p. 154.

15. Ibid., pp. 154–155.

16. Ibid., p. 155.

about discipleship are radically turned around by Jesus. Unlike the Third Wave paradigm with its primary focus for contemporary discipleship centred on being commissioned and empowered to perform exorcisms and healings, Mark's teaching on discipleship is concerned more with what we might call today the 'spirituality' of Christian discipleship.

With all the above in mind, our examination of Mark's view of commissioning and discipleship will concentrate on the call of disciples and their being sent out on mission; Mark's central section (8:27 – 10:45); the endings of Mark's Gospel and what they add to (or detract from) Mark's model for authentic Christian discipleship. The key question we need to ask is what paradigm for discipleship does Mark present for his readers, and how does this compare with the Third Wave paradigm, particularly as it is informed by their appeal to evidence in Mark's Gospel?

## 9. JESUS CALLS AND COMMISSIONS HIS DISCIPLES

### Called by Jesus for mission

The idea of being called by Jesus is foundational for the paradigm of disciple-ship that Mark unfolds throughout his Gospel. We may assume that Mark is writing for readers who are already followers of Jesus and who can identify particularly with Jesus' disciples as they read the Gospel. The paradigm Mark presents to his readers is concerned with the consequences of discipleship and how that shapes and affects the lives of those individuals who aspire to being true followers of Jesus.[1] The primary informant for this paradigm is Jesus himself, who, in his obedience and loyalty to God's call as well as in his teaching of the disciples, acts as the basis for the pattern of discipleship presented here by Mark.[2]

---

1. Cf. J. R. Donahue, *The Theology and Setting of Discipleship in the Gospel of Mark* (1983 Pere Marquette Theology Lecture; Milwaukee: Marquette University Press, 1983), p. 14.
2. P. L. Danove, *The End of Mark's Story: A Methodological Study* (Leiden: Brill, 1993), p. 213, recognizes the important connection between Christology and discipleship in Mark, where 'a proper understanding of discipleship requires a proper understanding of Jesus, the Christ, the Son of Man who must suffer, be rejected,

At the beginning of Mark's Gospel, following the arrest of John the Baptist, we have a summary statement describing Jesus' activity and message (Mark 1:14–15). Marshall argues for the paradigmatic significance of this summary statement, which provides a pattern for others in the story to emulate.[3] This is demonstrated by Mark in the way in which the role of the disciples is presented as an extension of Jesus' role unfolding from their call to follow Jesus (1:16–20; 2:14); their being commissioned to share Jesus' ministry (cf. 1:14–15); their preaching the same message as Jesus and casting out demons (6:12; 3:14; cf. 1:39).[4] Robert Meye notes how in 1:17, 3:13–19 and 6:7–13, 30 Mark develops the link between Jesus and his disciples.[5] Similarly, in his study of discipleship in Mark, Donahue also concentrates here when he examines the three narratives of the call and commissioning of the disciples. He makes the point that, despite the negative portrayal of the disciples, especially later in the Gospel, Jesus nevertheless calls, commissions and grants them the same authority (*exousia*) as himself in order to empower them to go out as his agents sharing in his mission.[6]

The fundamental nature of discipleship can be detected in the pattern of

---

be put to death, and rise on the third day'. In a similar vein, R. C. Tannehill, 'The Disciples in Mark: The Function of Narrative Role', in W. Telford (ed.), *The Interpretation of Mark* (Philadelphia: Fortress; London: SPCK, 1985), p. 143, writes, 'In important ways Jesus represents the positive alternative to the failure of the disciples. He not only calls the disciples to save their lives by losing them and to be servants, but he follows this way himself.'

3. C. D. Marshall, *Faith as a Theme in Mark's Narrative* (SNTSMS 64; Cambridge: Cambridge University Press, 1989), p. 39.

4. Ibid., p. 40.

5. See his discussion in R. P. Meye, *Jesus and the Twelve: Discipleship and Revelation in Mark's Gospel* (Grand Rapids, Mich.: Eerdmans, 1968), pp. 106–110. Danove, *End of Mark's Story*, notes the generation of a model of discipleship developed by Mark as follows: 1:16–20; 3:13–19; 6:6b–32; 8:27–30; 8:34 – 9:1; 9:35–41; 10:42–45; 13:5–37.

6. Donahue, *Theology and Setting*, p. 12. L. W. Hurtado, 'Following Jesus in the Gospel of Mark – and Beyond', in R. N. Longenecker (ed.), *Patterns of Discipleship in the New Testament* (Grand Rapids, Mich.: Eerdmans, 1996), p. 18, has noted that this sharing with Jesus by the disciples is underlined philologically throughout the Gospel by Mark's use of plural verbs. See also C. H. Turner, 'Marcan Usage: Notes, Critical and Exegetical, on the Second Gospel', *JTS* 26 (1925), pp. 225–231.

the call itself, which always comes at the initiative of Jesus, who demands total allegiance.[7] In Mark's narrative this makes the final desertion of Jesus by the disciples all the more shocking for the reader in that it is not only an abandonment of his person, but of all that is implicit in their divine call to share with him in the eschatological family of God. However, the shocking nature of the reality of their desertion has already been softened somewhat by Mark with Jesus' prediction in 14:27 followed by the promise of restoration in 14:28. According to Marshall, Jesus' calling of his disciples is analogous to YHWH's calling of the prophets in the OT and, as such, displays for Mark's readers Jesus' unique messianic authority.[8] Jesus' interpretation of the demands of God with respect to family ties, property and response to the call to discipleship is made exclusively in the light of the imminent coming of the kingdom of God. The position has been summarized succinctly by Rudolf Bultmann, who writes, 'Now is the last hour; now it can be only: either – or. Now the question is whether a man really desires God and His reign or the world and its goods; and the decision must be drastically made.'[9]

The outstanding OT example is of Elisha's being called to follow Elijah (1 Kgs 19:19–21), where the prophet Elijah finds Elisha working on the family farm, ploughing with a team of oxen (1 Kgs 19:19a). Elijah asserts his claim over his prospective disciple by symbolically casting his mantle upon Elisha (1 Kgs 19:19b). Before going with Elijah, Elisha requests permission to say goodbye to his family, and his request is granted. Before leaving home, Elisha distributes his belongings amongst his people (1 Kgs 19:21). In comparing this OT account with the call of the disciples we find that, like Elijah, Jesus also takes the initiative in calling his disciples (Mark 1:17; 2:14), but whereas Elisha takes time to settle family matters, there is no time permitted for those whom Jesus calls to be his disciples (Mark 1:19b).[10]

---

7. J. D. Kingsbury, *Conflict in Mark: Jesus, Authorities, Disciples* (Minneapolis: Fortress, 1989), pp. 89–90.

8. Marshall, *Faith as a Theme*, p. 137. See further Hengel, *The Charismatic Leader and His Followers* (ET Edinburgh: T. & T. Clark, 1981), pp. 67–71.

9. R. Bultmann, *Theology of the New Testament*, vol. 1 (ET London: SCM, 1952), p. 9.

10. In the Q tradition this is presented even more strongly when Jesus refuses permission to attend even to the most pressing family matters (Matt. 8:21–22//Luke 9:59–60). For a detailed discussion of this pericope, see Hengel, *Charismatic Leader*, pp. 3–15.

Amongst the rabbinic schools like those of Hillel and Shammai it was the pupil who first approached his teacher. The prospective rabbinic disciple was not committed in any permanent way to the rabbi of his choice, and a degree of movement from rabbi to rabbi was common. Here Jesus differs radically from our OT example, and, as K. H. Rengstorf has pointed out, it is a fundamental mark of the disciple in the Jesus tradition that the initial call should come from Jesus himself.[11] Also, with Jesus there is a permanence in the relationship, which follows naturally from the total commitment Jesus demands of his disciples. Furthermore, in the case of a pupil who belongs to one of the rabbinic schools, the honour that attaches itself to such a pupil is shared by his family.[12] Not so in the Gospel tradition, where family ties are not just relegated to a subordinate position in the face of a call by Jesus – they are completely overridden. Martin Hengel suggests that the best parallels to Jesus and his disciples are to be found in the charismatic-prophetic-eschatological contexts.[13] Gerd Theissen goes further and suggests that not only was Jesus a 'charismatic wanderer' but that the role of charismatic wanderer was prominent in the early years of the post-Easter communities.[14]

Discipleship for Mark has mission as its purpose. This can be seen both in the early missionary activity of Jesus and that of the disciples (Mark 1:14), and then envisaged in the post-Easter situation (cf. Mark 13:10; 14:9).[15] We see this particularly in the appointing of the Twelve (Mark 3:13–19) and their being sent out in mission by Jesus (6:6b–13). Following the call of Jesus' first disciples, Mark establishes the authority of Jesus' teaching both in the presence of the disciples and before the synagogue congregation in Capernaeum with his description of Jesus exorcizing the man with the unclean spirit (Mark 1:23–27). It has been noted how Mark's positioning of

---

11. K. H. Rengstorf, ἀποστέλλω, ἀπόστολος, *TDNT* 1, p. 444.

12. Ibid.

13. Hengel, *Charismatic Leader*, p. 67, and see further pp. 16–37, 71–72. Also see *Didache* 9.

14. G. Theissen, *The Sociology of Early Palestinian Christianity* (ET Philadelphia: Fortress, 1978), p. 190. Geza Vermes, *Jesus the Jew: A Historian's Reading of the Gospels* (London: SCM, 1983), pp. 69–80, also views Jesus as a charismatic healer in the same vein as Honi the Circle Drawer (BC) and especially the Galilean Hanina ben Dosa (AD), who was known as a miracle-worker and teacher of wisdom who paid little regard for legal regulations.

15. Cf. Kingsbury, *Conflict in Mark*, p. 91.

this pericope at the beginning of Jesus' ministry indicates both its paradigmatic and programmatic nature.[16] During the course of the exorcism, Mark establishes again Jesus' messianic identity when he is recognized by the unclean spirit (Mark 1:24; cf. 1:1, 11). Following the healing, Mark concludes by describing how those who witness the exorcism are 'all amazed' (v. 27a), not just by the exorcism itself but by its function as authoritative validation of Jesus' teaching.[17] When the disciples are sent out to proclaim Jesus' message to Israel, they too will receive similar validation of their message (cf. Mark 6:7, 12–13).

## The role of the Twelve in Mark

The role of the Twelve in Mark has been seen as something of a problem in that Mark uses two principal terms for those who follow Jesus: 'the Twelve' (15 times) and 'disciples' (46 times).[18] In terms of establishing a NT pattern from the commissioning of the Twelve, we should note the important link between call and commission.[19] In the appointing of the Twelve, Mark's use of the verb 'to send' (*apostellein*) probably reflects OT usage, were the Hebrew verb *šālaḥ* is translated *apostellein* in the LXX.[20] Hengel suggests that in the fusion between the Jesus tradition and community formulations as they appear in the Gospel tradition of the sending out of the Twelve, there is evidence of a 'conscious awareness' at this point of the continuity between Jesus' activity and that of the later activities of the community.[21] Mark's presentation of the Twelve points towards a communal aspect to discipleship. This communal aspect may be understood variously in terms of the Twelve representing the

---

16. Cf. G. H. Twelftree, *Jesus the Exorcist: A Contribution to the Study of the Historical Jesus* (Peabody, Mass.: Hendrickson, 1993), p. 57.

17. That the conclusion to this pericope (Mark 1:27b–28) is Mark's is suggested by the typically Markan vocabulary and grammar, although the description of the crowd's amazement may have been a stereotype conclusion to a miracle story that Mark found in his tradition. Cf. Twelftree, *Jesus the Exorcist*, p. 59.

18. Donahue, *Theology and Setting*, p. 5.

19. Noted by E. Best, *Following Jesus: Discipleship in the Gospel of Mark* (JSNTSup 4; Sheffield: JSOT, 1981), p. 181, and a point to which we will return in our examination of Luke-Acts in Part Three.

20. Noted by Hengel, *Charismatic Leader*, p. 83.

21. Ibid.

twelve tribes of Israel as the eschatological people of God, or that the Twelve originate in the post-Easter situation as witnesses to the resurrection and thus represent for Mark the 'nucleus of a new community'.[22]

The situation is complicated further by the fact that Mark portrays the Twelve as having both a positive and negative role. The Twelve are accorded special status by the Markan Jesus, and they also appear to serve as representatives of Jesus' wider circle of followers – which also extends to Mark's readers. According to Hurtado, the failures of the Twelve are also representative of the failures of the larger group of Jesus' followers, and so, he concludes:

> Thus no distinction between the Twelve and the larger circle of disciples as to blameworthiness need be postulated in Mark, and no attempt need be made to play off the Twelve against another group of disciples that might represent alternative factions of early Christians.[23]

In assessing the role of the Twelve, are we to assume that they were considered leaders of the community, and, if so, how are we to understand the way in which their leadership functions for Mark? In two passages (Mark 3:13–19 and 6:7–13) it is clear that the Twelve are depicted as 'missionary leaders', whereas elsewhere in the Gospel they are simply representative disciples and bearers of Jesus' teaching (6:34; 13:3ff., 13, and cf. 31).[24]

---

22. Donahue, *Theology and Setting*, p. 7.

23. Hurtado, 'Following Jesus', p. 17. A minority of scholars, most notably T. J. Weedon, insist that Mark was written for a polemical purpose that involved discrediting the Twelve, who represented a false understanding of Jesus as a 'divine man' whose miracle-working powers are the key to understanding the nature of his messiahship. Mark saw this view as heretical and set out to discredit the Twelve, who, according to this view, are the founding figures of the *theios anēr* Christology to which Mark is opposed. See further T. J. Weedon, *Mark – Tradition in Conflict* (Philadelphia: Fortress, 1971). For a discussion of Mark's presentation of the disciples as 'fallible' and Jesus' correctives being strengthened by the behaviour of minor characters in the narrative, see E. S. Malbon, 'Fallible Followers: Women and Men in the Gospel of Mark', *Semeia* 28 (1983), pp. 29–48.

24. E. Best, *Mark: The Gospel as Story* (Edinburgh: T. & T. Clark, 1983), p. 49.

## Commissioning and sending out the Twelve

Implicit within the NT idea of being sent is that those being sent are not just given a specific task, but act as legally empowered to exercise the authority of the sender. At this point in Mark's narrative the apostles are commissioned by Jesus and designated 'apostles' (3:14–15) to share in his own ministry to proclaim the kingdom of God and to have authority to heal and exorcize.[25] As we will see, later in his narrative Mark ensures that his readers are made aware that such charismatic activity is not what is particularly characteristic of his model of discipleship. Even here Mark foreshadows what is to come later when he introduces a negative note with his description of Judas as Jesus' betrayer (Mark 3:19).

At this point in Mark's narrative, the reader is already aware that Jesus' own authority has been amply demonstrated in both his teaching and exorcisms (Mark 1:21–32; 2:1–12; 3:1–12). Now, having given the apostles authority – Jesus' own authority to cast out demons – the validity and source of that authority is immediately called into question not only by the religious authorities from Jerusalem, but even by Jesus' own family (3:21–22).[26] Mark's introduction to the Beelzebub controversy is quite shocking for the reader. Jesus returns home only to be thought mad by his family, who then seek to restrain him (3:21; cf. John 10:19–21). Against those who accused him of being in league with Satan,[27] Mark's purpose here is clearly to emphasize that the source of Jesus' authority over demons is a heavenly one and is firmly connected with his proclamation of the kingdom of God (v. 29). The community of disciples have become Jesus' (eschatological) family (3:31–35; 10:28–30), pointing beyond itself in Mark's narrative to the (Markan) post-Easter community.

The purpose in commissioning the Twelve[28] is set out by Mark (3:14–15) as

---

25. Cf. D. R. A. Hare, *Mark* (Louisville, Ky.: Westminster John Knox, 1996), p. 48.

26. We should note that although the phrase used here to translate 'family' can also mean 'adherents', most commentators understand this as a reference by Mark to Jesus' own family. See for example C. S. Mann, *Mark* (AB 27; New York: Doubleday, 1986), p. 252.

27. Here it may be that we have evidence of a lingering accusation against Jesus and the source of his charismatic powers. Cf. ibid.

28. Here I am concerned with the role of the Twelve as it relates to Mark's model of discipleship rather than their eschatological role as it relates to the restoration/

follows: to be with him (3:14b); to be sent out to proclaim the message (3:14c); and to have authority to cast out demons (3:15). For Mark, the Twelve are both disciples and apostles, intimates of Jesus and members of his wider (eschatological) family. As disciples, they are naturally described as being with Jesus in order to learn from him before being sent out as his representatives in mission.[29] In verse 14c the Twelve are sent out to proclaim what was presumably the same message that Jesus proclaimed, of the imminent kingdom of God, and to have authority over demons. Mark makes it clear that the Twelve also share in the authority that lies behind Jesus' own mission. Their mission is an extension of Jesus' own ministry (cf. 6:1 with 1:14–15; 6:30 with 1:21–22 and 6:6; 6:13 with 1:34; 3:10 and 6:13 with 1:34, 39).[30] The only parallel lacking at this point between the Twelve and Jesus is in the use of oil to anoint the sick, and this probably reflects later practice in the post-Easter community (cf. Jas 5:14). In other words, Mark makes it clear that the ones being sent out in mission truly represent the sender (Jesus), and this, in turn, provides a sense of continuity between Jesus' activities and those of the community, particularly with reference to people sent in mission.[31]

## The mission of the Twelve

In Mark 6:7 Jesus commissions the Twelve and delegates to them a share in his own kingdom *exousia*. Unlike Matthew's Great Commission, Mark does not explicitly extend this to the post-Easter situation,[32] although in 14:9 Jesus does

---

renewal of Israel. For a discussion of the issues raised, see for example E. P. Sanders, *Jesus and Judaism* (London: SCM, 1985), especially pp. 95–116; and, more recently, N. T. Wright, *Jesus and the Victory of God* (London: SPCK, 1996), p. 300, who notes, 'The very existence of the twelve speaks, of course, of the reconstitution of Israel; Israel had not had twelve visible tribes since the Assyrian invasion in 724 BC, and for Jesus to give twelve followers a place of prominence, let alone to make comments about them sitting on thrones judging the twelve tribes, indicates pretty clearly that he was thinking in terms of the eschatological restoration of Israel.'

29. Cf. C. E. B. Cranfield, *The Gospel According to St. Mark* (Cambridge: Cambridge University Press, 1959), p. 128.

30. Noted by Kingsbury, *Conflict in Mark*, p. 95.

31. Cf. Hengel, *Charismatic Leader*, p. 83.

32. See my discussion of the endings to Mark's Gospel below.

refer to the universal mission of the church and the gospel being 'proclaimed in the whole world'. Jesus' authoritative summoning of the Twelve is reflective of his earlier calling of the disciples and reflects Mark's depiction of his (in Hengel's terms) charismatic authority. More importantly, it also serves to emphasize for Mark's readers the idea that being summoned and sent out in mission by Jesus is paradigmatically associated with Jesus' own authority to preach and cast out demons, and that the missionary task has a special role in the community over and above the more general call to discipleship. If this, in fact, is the case, then we should not underplay the need to test this notion of individuals being summoned to mission by Jesus when we attempt to apply NT paradigms for discipleship in the church today, especially where there is an expectation that an individual's call may be charismatically validated by 'signs and wonders'.

The sending out of the missionaries in pairs reflects post-Easter missionary activity and serves to bear out the paradigmatic nature of this tradition for later missionary activity in the church (cf. 1 Cor. 9:5–6; Acts 8:14; 13:1–2; 15:22, 39–40).[33] It is also reflective of Jewish ideas about the need for more than one witness in order for testimony to be valid (cf. Deut. 17:6; 19:15).[34] The idea that Mark is setting out here a paradigm not so much for discipleship but for the missionary activity of the church is borne out further by the fact that the instructions that follow the commissioning of the Twelve (vv. 8–11) make sense in terms of itinerant missionary work only, where the very pragmatic emphasis appears to be on rules governing the practice of hospitality rather than on casting out demons (cf. *Didache* 9).[35] However, at the end of the mission charge we do have a summary of the disciples' activity in verses 12–13 which informs the reader that the Twelve preached a message of repentance and that the success of their mission was indicated by the many exorcisms and healings they performed.

The evidence from Mark's Gospel examined so far indicates that exorcisms performed by the Twelve belong firmly within the context of the latters' mission. If, as the Third Wave argue, power to perform exorcisms is ongoing and integral to Mark's paradigm for discipleship per se, why do the disciples who have just been described as extremely successful missionary-exorcists

33. So Donahue, *Theology of Discipleship*, pp. 18–19.

34. See for example Cranfield, *St. Mark*, p. 198; V. Taylor, *The Gospel According to Mark*, 2nd ed. (London: Macmillan, 1966), p. 303; and Mann, *Mark*, p. 292.

35. In M. Staniforth, '*Didache*', in idem (ed.), *Early Christian Writings: The Apostolic Fathers* (Harmondsworth: Penguin, 1968).

have difficulty when they attempt, independently, a single exorcism later in Mark's narrative?[36]


## Conclusions

What have we learnt so far about Mark's paradigm for discipleship from our examination of the call and mission of the Twelve? Our major finding has been that Mark intended the mission of the Twelve to be a model not for discipleship per se, but for the sending out of missionaries by his own community. That Mark has his own community in mind is indicated further in 6:13, which is the only reference in the Gospels to anointing the sick with oil. It is also interesting to note that Mark associates the practice of anointing the sick with oil with the Twelve, who, for his readers, may be viewed as the embryonic leaders of the post-Easter community (cf. Jas 5:14). When the Twelve report back to Jesus in 6:30, Mark describes the successful missionaries as 'apostles', and this title is used here by Mark not to describe a church office but very much in the context of mission.[37]

In what we have seen so far, 'signs and wonders' are envisaged by Mark as being primarily given to authenticate the mission of the church and its message rather than being an integral, everyday part of his paradigm for discipleship. From a Markan perspective, it is crucial that this is borne in mind by any who would seek validation here for a contemporary theology that argues for a normative link between signs and wonders and Christian discipleship. It should also be noted that the essential details of Mark's paradigm for discipleship rather than centring on call and commission come later in his central section 8:27 – 10:45. This being the case, then the evidence so far calls into serious question the Third Wave paradigm, at least from a Markan standpoint.

In demonstrating that the disciples are chosen by Jesus and are sent out in mission as his empowered representatives, Mark has set the stage for his central section. In contrast to the more spectacular activities of healing and exorcism that marked the successful mission of the Twelve, Mark now sets out clearly what he considers to be the more important aspects of his paradigm for discipleship, in stark contrast to the negative example of the Twelve. Indeed, the very success of the mission of the Twelve and their participation in the

---

36. The question of what Mark may be saying to his readers in 9:14–29 will be examined in chapter 9.

37. Best, *Following Jesus*, p. 193.

missionary deeds / *exousia* of Jesus serves to make the Twelve's subsequent lack of understanding and hardness of heart all the more ironic (Mark 6:52; 7:18; 8:14–21; 9:17–18), and is indicative of the point Mark emphasizes consistently throughout the rest of his Gospel; namely, that success in proclaiming the kingdom of God with acts of power does not necessarily lead to a proper understanding and practical outworking of authentic Christian discipleship.

## 10. MARK'S CENTRAL SECTION AND TEACHING ON DISCIPLESHIP

The majority of scholars recognize that the critical way in which Mark presents the disciples, and especially the Twelve, is not meant just to attack them but serves as a device that enables Mark to present his understanding of the true nature of Christian discipleship as articulated and modelled by Jesus. According to Best, in using the disciples' mistakes as a device to allow Jesus to issue corrective teaching, Mark is following a literary precedent already well established by stories of philosophers in the ancient world who also teach through their followers' failure to understand. In the second half of the Gospel, Mark portrays the disciples in an increasingly negative light, ending finally in Jesus' betrayal by one of the Twelve and his being abandoned by the rest.

Prior to 8:27 Mark has depicted the disciples as engaging in the same activities as Jesus; namely, preaching (3:15; 6:12), teaching (6:30), healing (6:13) and exorcism (3:15; 6:7).[1] After their previous success as missionaries (cf. 6:13), why did Mark present the disciples in such a negative light, particularly in his central section? What does this say to Christians today about Mark's presentation of the disciples as a post-Easter paradigm for the church? Donahue argues that the key to understanding the disciples in Mark is found in the

---

1. J. D. Kingsbury, *The Christology of Mark's Gospel* (Philadelphia: Fortress, 1983), p. 93.

dynamic tension that exists between the text and the reader.[2] Here, in narrative terms, we have the clue to the reason for Mark's negative treatment of the disciples in his central section, where Jesus' correctives on the true nature of discipleship overrule the misunderstandings of the disciples. These correctives are aimed not just at the disciples themselves but at Mark's own community and, by extension, serve to inform the contemporary church's understanding of what it means to be a true follower of Jesus.

## Teaching on authentic discipleship

The central section of Mark, which extends from 8:27 to 10:45,[3] depicts Jesus journeying to Jerusalem (cf. 8:27; 9:33; 10:17, 32, 52) and provides the setting for a right understanding of Jesus' forthcoming passion.[4] In exercising control over the ordering of his material, Mark is able to shape the gospel story in ways that give positional emphasis to subjects especially important to him. This applies particularly to the teaching on discipleship, which is grouped around three passion predictions made by Jesus, which are crucial for what Mark wants to say to his community.[5]

The journey towards Jerusalem can be divided into three stages, each marked by a passion prediction with the repeated pattern of Jesus predicting his forthcoming death and resurrection, and the disciples failing to accept any notion of suffering on the part of Jesus or to understand his subsequent corrective teaching on discipleship. This, in turn, is particularly significant for Mark's readers, for if Jesus is required to suffer in furtherance of the kingdom of God, then suffering will also be required of his followers (8:31; 9:31; 10:33). As Hurtado notes succinctly:

---

2. In J. R. Donahue, *The Theology and Setting of Discipleship in the Gospel of Mark* (1983 Pere Marquette Theology Lecture; Milwaukee: Marquette University Press, 1983), p. 29.

3. See R. T. France, *Divine Government: God's Kingship in the Gospel of Mark* (London: SPCK, 1990), p. 49.

4. Ibid.

5. Mark 8:31–33 with 8:34–38; 9:31–32 with 9:33–37; 10:35–40 with 10:41–45. See E. Best, *Mark: The Gospel as Story* (Edinburgh: T. & T. Clark, 1983), p. 54; also R. C. Tannehill, 'The Disciples in Mark: The Function of Narrative Role', in W. Telford (ed.), *The Interpretation of Mark* (Philadelphia: Fortress; London: SPCK, 1985), p. 148.

Just as Mark emphasises that a proper understanding of Jesus requires doing justice to his crucifixion as the culminating revelation of his mission and significance, so Mark insists that discipleship must be conformed to the pattern of Jesus' own ministry of obedience and sacrifice.[6]

Throughout the narrative, we encounter the theme of following Jesus 'on the way', and Mark underlines the importance of this central section for his readers' understanding of the true nature of discipleship at key points.[7] An overall narrative framework is provided by two healings of blind persons whose eyes are opened by Jesus (8:22–26; 10:46–52), with the second of these healings ending with Bartimaeus setting an example by following Jesus 'on the way' (10:52).[8] During the dramatic transfiguration scene, the heavenly voice orders those accompanying Jesus to 'listen to him'.[9]

Although the teaching on discipleship and suffering is aimed at the disciples, in 8:34 Jesus calls the crowd and addresses them along with the disciples, indicating that, for Mark, Jesus' subsequent foundational teaching for a right understanding of discipleship is to have a more universal application.[10] Boring suggests that the crowd represents the church,[11] whereas Gundry argues that

----

6.  L. W. Hurtado, 'The Gospel of Mark', in S. M. Burgess and G. B. McGee (eds.), *Dictionary of Pentecostal and Charismatic Movements* (Grand Rapids, Mich.: Zondervan, 1988), p. 578.

7.  E. Best, *Disciples and Discipleship: Studies in the Gospel According to Mark* (Edinburgh: T. & T. Clark, 1986), p. 6. R. T. France, *The Gospel of Mark: A Commentary on the Greek Text* (NIGTC; Grand Rapids, Mich.: Eerdmans, 2002), p. 339, points to the recurrent use of 'on the way' and related language in 8:27; 9:33–34; 10:17, 32, 52.

8.  C. D. Marshall, *Faith as a Theme in Mark's Narrative* (SNTSMS 64; Cambridge: Cambridge University Press, 1989), p. 123. A. Stock, *Call to Discipleship: A Literary Study of Mark's Gospel* (GNS 1; Delaware: Glazier; Dublin: Veritas, 1982), p. 148, makes the point that here the restoration of sight by Jesus should be understood in terms of 'salvation'.

9.  Tannehill, 'Disciples in Mark', p. 149.

10. C. A. Evans, *Mark 8:27–16:20* (WBC 34B; Nashville, Tenn.: Nelson, 2001), p. 25. France, *Gospel of Mark*, p. 339, draws attention to Mark 4:10, where Jesus also addresses the wider circle of those who are with him when making an important revelation, on this occasion about the nature of parables.

11. M. E. Boring, *Sayings of the Risen Jesus: Christian Prophecy in the Synoptic Tradition* (SNTSMS 46; Cambridge: Cambridge University Press, 1982), p. 200.

Mark intends the crowd to represent non-Christians who are 'summoned to Christian discipleship'.[12] More cautiously, Schweizer suggests that the inclusion of the crowd indicates that the teaching is conditional upon 'everyone' who would follow Jesus.[13]

In the three passion announcements (8:31; 9:31; 10:33–34) Jesus' teaching points firmly to his own forthcoming suffering and sacrificial service, thus providing the model upon which Jesus' followers must be prepared to base their discipleship (especially 8:34–35; 10:45).[14] Whilst the three passion predictions with their appended teaching on discipleship vary in detail, each emphasizes that for the Markan Jesus authentic discipleship cannot be understood apart from his passion and the fact that suffering is God's way for them.

Following Peter's messianic confession at Caesarea Philippi (8:27–30; 31–33; 34–35), Jesus makes the first passion prediction, where he tells of his forthcoming suffering, crucifixion and resurrection (8:31), and which is completely misunderstood by Peter, despite his recent insight into Jesus' messianic status (8:29b). Jesus' strong rebuke of Peter in 8:33 opens the way in the narrative for the first major section of teaching on discipleship (8:34–35). The key to understanding the different perspectives being presented here by Mark can be seen in the final phrase of Jesus' rebuke to Peter at Caesarea Philippi, when he gives the following reason for the sharpness of the rebuke: 'For you are setting your mind not on divine things but on human things' (Mark 8:33b). It is through these conflicting heavenly–earthly perspectives that the reader is to understand and identify with Jesus' correctives on the true nature of discipleship.

## Suffering and self-denial

In Mark 8:34 we have the first of the three pericopes where Mark emphasizes the idea that following Jesus is inextricably tied to suffering and self-denial, and characterized by cross-bearing and losing one's life in order to gain it (Mark

---

12. R. H. Gundry, *Mark: A Commentary on His Apology for the Cross* (Grand Rapids, Mich.: Eerdmans, 1993), p. 452. For a similar view, see H. Anderson, *The Gospel of Mark* (London: Oliphants, 1976), p. 217.

13. E. Schweizer, *The Good News According to Mark* (ET London: SPCK, 1971), p. 175.

14. Tannehill, 'The Disciples in Mark', p. 148; Best, *Disciples and Discipleship*, p. 6; France, *Gospel of Mark*, p. 339.

8:34b).[15] For the disciples this is a far cry from the triumphal proclamation and exorcisms Mark describes in 6:13. The open-ended warning in 8:38 suggests that Mark is widening the scope to more than just the disciples or the crowd Jesus addresses in the narrative, to include the readers of his Gospel.[16] Stock suggests that Mark has deliberately delayed teaching about discipleship linked to suffering until this point so that, in addition to the teaching itself linked with the three passion predictions, Jesus may be seen to be tangibly pointing the way as he himself journeys towards Jerusalem.[17]

Jesus' teaching 'on the way' about self-denial and taking up one's cross clarifies how his death and resurrection are to be understood (8:31),[18] and the application of this understanding is fundamental to Mark's view of discipleship.[19] According to Cranfield, Mark's use of the aorist imperative of the verb 'to deny' in 8:34b indicates that a once-and-for-all decision to sever the former relationship with self-interest is being required here by Jesus.[20] The finality of the abandonment is then graphically illustrated in the invitation to take up one's cross (8:34b),[21] and here France is correct to insist that we should not attempt to 'domesticate' the saying.[22] In other words, Mark makes it abun-

---

15. Best, *Mark*, p. 28.

16. Hurtado, 'Following Jesus', p. 11.

17. Stock, *Call to Discipleship*, pp. 140–141, 146.

18. Schweizer, *The Good News According to Matthew* (ET London: SPCK, 1976), p. 175; Evans, *Mark 8:27–16:20*, p. 24.

19. France, *Gospel of Mark*, p. 339, draws attention to *opistō mou* (after me) used alongside *akolouthein* (to follow) in 8:34 and elsewhere by Mark (1:18; 2:14), and comments that here we have a 'basic condition' of discipleship. For a detailed discussion, see E. Best, *Following Jesus: Discipleship in the Gospel of Mark* (JSNTSup 4; Sheffield: JSOT, 1981), pp. 33–34 and 36–39.

20. C. E. B. Cranfield, *The Gospel According to St. Mark* (Cambridge: Cambridge University Press, 1959), pp. 281–282. Cf. France, *Gospel of Mark*, p. 340.

21. Best, *Mark*, p. 87. Cf. Gundry, *Mark*, p. 452, who argues that the placement of this saying between the first passion prediction and the transfiguration is so that Mark's audience would not be scandalized by the cross.

22. France, *Gospel of Mark*, p. 340; and see Best, *Following Jesus*, pp. 38–39, for different views on the meaning here. For a discussion of the figurative use of the idea of cross-bearing, see J. Schneider, σταυρός, *TDNT* 7, pp. 577–579. For a detailed study of crucifixion in the Roman world, see M. Hengel, *Crucifixion in the Ancient World and the Folly of the Message of the Cross* (ET republished in *The Cross of the Son of God*; London: SCM, 1986), especially pp. 114–155.

dantly clear to his readers that authentic discipleship inevitably and inexorably involves denial of self and taking up one's cross (8:34–35).[23] In verses 35–36 we have a 'reversal of values', where the result, paradoxically, is that the self-abandonment demanded of those who would follow Jesus results in their finding (eternal) life.[24]

## A reversal of earthly values

Following on from Peter's messianic confession at Caesarea Philippi, the reader is confronted with an even more powerful revelation of Jesus' true identity, in the transfiguration (Mark 9:2–8). After this there can be little doubt as to who Jesus really is, for he has already been identified for the reader's benefit in 1:1 as 'Son of God' and again at his baptism as 'my son, the beloved' (1:11), words which are repeated here by the heavenly voice adding, significantly for Mark's readers, 'listen to him', indicating that from this point in the narrative Mark's readers (as they identify with the disciples) are to pay special attention to the words of Jesus. After the transfiguration scene (9:2–8), where Moses and Elijah appear together with Jesus (9:4–5), we have a discussion of the eschatological significance of the appearance of Elijah (9:9–13) that links to the discussion of Jesus' forthcoming passion (9:9, 12b).

In 9:14–29 there is an extended narrative describing the disciples' failure to exorcise a boy with a spirit,[25] followed by the second passion prediction in verses 30–32, which is followed by further teaching about discipleship. Here Jesus again takes the initiative[26] by asking the disciples what they have been discussing amongst themselves, but they refuse to answer (9:33–34). For Mark's readers, the disciples' attitude is still far from reproducing the humility previously demanded by Jesus of his followers in 8:34–35. Their reluctance to answer appears to reflect the fear they felt in the face of Jesus' second passion prediction (9:32). There is also a hint that the disciples are undergoing a dawning realization that Jesus' demand for authentic discipleship necessitates a reversal of the earthly values to which they are still clinging – a conflict that continues to speak to the human condition.

---

23. Cf. H. C. Waetjen, *A Reordering of Power: A Socio-Political Reading of Mark's Gospel* (Minneapolis: Fortress, 1989), p. 146.

24. Schweizer, *Good News According to Mark*, p. 177.

25. Discussed further below.

26. Cf. Mark 8:1, 27, where Jesus also takes the initiative.

Jesus, who (presumably) discerns that the disciples have been discussing amongst themselves the issue of status calls the Twelve[27] and teaches them further about the contrary values of the kingdom.[28] In 9:35b Jesus responds to the issue of status in a direct and unequivocal way, where earthly values are again turned upside down. The contrast is between first and last, and the contrast is emphasized further with the words 'last of all' and 'servant of all'. If 'first' and 'last/servant' are to be associated with rank and influence in society,[29] then the contrast with 'servant' as a person without any rank, particularly when taken with the descriptive 'of all' is stark indeed.

It is this very question of pre-eminence within the community of Jesus' followers that is now dealt with explicitly by Mark in 10:32ff. Mark has already made it clear that seeking pre-eminence and rank at the earthly level is not to be considered a characteristic of the authentic discipleship that seeks its model in the example of Jesus, and this can be seen most explicitly in the third passion prediction (10:32–34) and the teaching on discipleship that follows (10:35–41, 42–45).

### Slavery as the price of pre-eminence

Attached to Jesus' final passion prediction is the story of the request for preferred status from James and John (10:35–45), which reflects the concerns raised previously in Mark 9:33.[30] In light of the disciples' continued failure to grasp what Jesus is talking about when he refers to his forthcoming passion,[31]

---

27. In contrast to the disciples and crowd addressed in 8:34ff.
28. See also for example Mark 4:1; Luke 4:20; 5:3; Matt. 5:1; 12:41, 43; cf. 23:2. For the association of sitting and teaching, see discussions in, for example, Gundry, *Mark*, pp. 190–191, 508, 517; Hagner, *Mark 8:27–16:20*, p. 61; V. Taylor, *The Gospel According to Mark*, 2nd ed. (London: Macmillan, 1966), p. 404.
29. So Hagner, *Mark 8:27–16:20*, p. 61, who suggests that 'first' here should be understood in terms of rulers, aristocrats, chief priests.
30. Cf. Matt. 20:20, where it is the mother of James and John who approaches Jesus with the request. According to Taylor, *Gospel According to Mark*, p. 440, the phrase *en tē doxē sou* (in your glory) refers to the parousia (see also C. S. Mann, *Mark* [AB 27; New York: Doubleday, 1986], p. 412). Cranfield, *St. Mark*, p. 337, cautions that *en tē doxē sou* is to be distinguished from the kingdom of God, commenting that at this point the disciples are 'apparently thinking of the Messiah's rule' (cf. Acts 1:6).
31. This despite 8:31; 9:12, 31; 10:33–34; cf. especially 9:32.

or to understand his teaching on the nature of true discipleship, the reference here to the parousia seems odd. The important point here is that the brothers' request for pre-eminence in the coming messianic kingdom clearly reflects their own expectation of the messianic 'glory' that is to come, rather than the messianic suffering just described for the third time by Jesus (10:32–33). The presumption of the sons of Zebedee angers the other disciples (10:41) and this provides Jesus with a further opportunity to address the question of authentic discipleship, anchoring his teaching firmly in the model he himself provides (10:45).

Jesus' teaching in 10:42–44 is most explicit. Appealing to Jewish antipathy towards Gentiles, Jesus points out that the disciples' lust for status and pre-eminence is more characteristic of the pretentious behaviour associated with Gentile views of leadership and the behaviour of their 'great men'. For Mark's readers, this also recalls the disciples' earlier discussion amongst themselves in 9:33–34. The model for Jesus' disciples to follow is not that commonly found amongst the rulers of the Gentiles, which would be very evident to Mark's community as they moved out in mission, establishing Christian communities amongst Gentiles.[32] Initially, Jesus' contrast is between greatness and taking on the role of a servant (10:43). In 10:43 the phrase 'to become great' has replaced the 'first' of 9:35 but the contrast remains rooted in the alternative characteristic of service (10:43), which is then further amplified by Jesus in 10:44. In 10:44 Jesus' words recall his use of the phrase 'of all' in 9:35 but now draw an even more shocking contrast in that for those who seek a pre-eminent position within the community of Jesus' followers, the role of 'servant' must be downgraded further to that of 'slave of all' (10:44), a person without any claim to rights over even his or her own life.[33]

Finally, the 'ransom' saying in 10:45 brings the characteristics of humble service outlined in verses 42–44 into relationship with the example of Jesus himself, thus providing a fitting conclusion to this long section that began in 8:27 and which teaches the alternative values and attitudes that are to characterize

---

32. Gundry, *Mark*, p. 479, is correct to note how the 'great ones' in 10:42 reflects the discussion about greatness reported in 9:34 and looks forward to 10:43. See also W. H. Kelber, *The Kingdom in Mark: A New Place and A New Time* (Philadelphia: Fortress, 1974), pp. 45–66, who argues that in Mark's Gospel the Gentile mission is anticipated through Jesus' activity in Gentile territory.

33. Cf. Best, *Following Jesus*, p. 126, and Gundry, *Mark*, p. 581, who notes the contrast between the personal character of service associated with 'servant' and the obligatory character of service associated with 'slave'.

authentic Christian discipleship. Whilst Jesus acts as the exemplar of true discipleship par excellence for Mark, there is an important distinction made here, which would not be lost on Mark's readers – that only Jesus is called upon to give his life as 'a ransom for many' (10:45b).[34] Indeed, the culmination of Jesus' mission is to give his life for others.[35] As Gundry succinctly comments:

> Thus the Marcan apologetics of miraculous ability, of didactic authority, and of predictive power metamorphose into an apologetic of beneficial service. The Cross will not bring shame to its victim but salvation to his followers.[36]

To summarize, the disciples who have shared in Jesus' ministry must now abandon their earthly values and adopt the heavenly values, characterized by suffering and self-denial, that Jesus advocates for all who would follow him. And yet, despite Jesus' teaching on what is required for authentic discipleship, in 14:32ff., at the crucial point of Jesus' need for their support, his closest disciples fall asleep whilst he agonizes in the garden, and matters worsen when one of the Twelve betrays him and the rest desert him. In light of this complete failure on the part of the disciples, is there more we can learn from Mark about, on the one hand, sharing in Jesus' *exousia* to heal/exorcize, and, on the other hand, reflecting Mark's paradigm for authentic Christian discipleship?

## Exorcism in context

Returning to Mark chapter 9, of particular interest here due to both their subject matter and positioning by Mark, are two important pericopes that follow Jesus' first and second passion predictions (Mark 9:14–29 and 9:38–41). Both pericopes involve Jesus' disciples and are concerned with exorcism, and both pericopes serve to counterbalance the exorcistic successes described in 6:13.

As if to emphasize further the relative unimportance of 'signs and wonders' for true discipleship, in the first incident as Jesus and his companions descend the mountain of transfiguration, they are confronted with the failure of the

---

34. Best, *Following Jesus*, p. 127. Mann, *Mark*, p. 410, understands this as 'ransom for the community', thus reflecting Isa. 53:10–12 LXX.

35. P. J. Achtemeier, *Mark* (Proclamation Commentaries; Philadelphia: Fortress, 1975), p. 98.

36. Gundry, *Mark*, p. 581.

remaining disciples to cast out a dumb spirit from a boy. Mark has already fore-shadowed earlier the failure of the disciples to cast out the dumb spirit in the face of unbelief (9:19) with his description of Jesus' experience in Nazareth (6:5–6). The disciples' failure to cast out the spirit from the boy appears in stark contrast to the success they enjoyed when they were sent out in mission by Jesus.[37] Is Mark intending here to say something of conclusive importance about the relationship between discipleship and signs and wonders? In our dis-cussion of the commissioning and sending out of the disciples in mission (Mark 3:13–15; 6:6–13), we saw that Mark describes the Twelve as 'apostles' commissioned and sent out by Jesus to preach the message of the kingdom and whose success in doing so is summarized with the words 'They cast out many demons' (Mark 6:13a). This makes their inability to perform a single exorcism independently here all the more interesting in terms of Mark's model of discipleship. What light do these two passages (Mark 9:14–29; 38–41) shed on the Third Wave argument that power to perform exorcisms is integral to the paradigm for discipleship modelled by Jesus and the first disciples? Is Mark using these two incidents to ensure that such spectacular 'power encounters' may on occasion have their place in the church's ministry (e.g. exercised in the context of mission) but are not of first importance in terms of his paradigm for true discipleship?

## The boy with the spirit (Mark 9:14–29)

The pericope begins with Jesus, Peter, James and John returning from the mountain of transfiguration and rejoining the other nine disciples. On seeing Jesus, the crowd are described as being awestruck. It has been suggested that the reason for this was because Mark was seeking to link Jesus' transfiguration with the OT tradition of Moses' face glowing after he returned from receiv-ing the law on Mount Sinai (Exod. 32 – 33).[38] It is argued that the use of the word 'amazed' (v. 15) to describe the crowd's reaction on seeing Jesus' approach may be accounted for by the whiteness of Jesus' garments and so provide the reader with an allusion to the Moses tradition. To posit such a link

---

37. So, ibid., p. 487. Also, D. E. Nineham, *Saint Mark* (Pelican Gospel Commentaries; Harmondsworth: Penguin, 1963), p. 245. Best, *Following Jesus*, p. 69, thinks that Mark is drawing attention to the disciples' failure in order to pick up from 3:15 and 6:7 and to say more about how exorcisms are to be performed.

38. Best, *Following Jesus*, p. 68.

seems to me both speculative and unnecessary, as Mark's narrative has clearly moved on to another subject – that of further instruction of the disciples.[39] Indeed, it seems more likely here that the crowd's astonishment is due more to Jesus' unexpected, opportune arrival on the scene.[40]

When Jesus arrives, the nine are surrounded by a large crowd and are arguing with some scribes. Although Jesus asks what the argument is about, the substance of the argument is never described. Instead, the story is redirected by the father's interjection when he explains that he had brought his son to Jesus in order that the dumb spirit possessing the boy might be exorcized. In the absence of Jesus himself, the father's request to the disciples seems perfectly reasonable. The disciples would be regarded as Jesus' representatives and the expectation would be that they were possessors of Jesus' power to exorcize and heal (cf. Mark 6:13).[41] Jesus' charge of faithlessness in verse 19 is addressed to all present and, as I indicated earlier, we have here a similar situation of unbelief to the one Jesus faced in Nazareth (cf. Mark 6:3). Jesus' response on that occasion was to move on because time was short (Mark 6:6), whereas here the instruction to pray probably reflects the post-Easter situation facing Mark's own community.[42]

The demon's powerful grip on the boy is described graphically in the story and this emphasizes for the reader Mark's main point that all things are possible for faith.[43] Faith is the necessary characteristic for those about to be healed, and faith expressed in prayer is a necessary characteristic of Jesus' fol-

---

39. So ibid., p. 68.

40. So, Cranfield, *St. Mark*, p. 300.

41. Noted by W. L. Lane, *The Gospel of Mark* (NICNT; Grand Rapids, Mich.: Eerdmans, 1974), p. 332.

42. Cranfield, *St. Mark*, p. 301, thinks that the charge is directed primarily at the disciples, whose lack of faith had been highlighted by their failure. Alternatively, it could be argued that Mark's redactional activity at 9:14 and 28–29, which focuses the reader's attention on the disciples, may also indicate that originally the accusation of faithlessness now directed at the disciples/crowd was originally directed at the father, who was seeking healing for his son (cf. Mark 2:5 and 5:36 for friends of the sick persons, and 5:34 and 10:52 for the sick persons themselves). So G. H. Twelftree, *Jesus the Exorcist: A Contribution to the Study of the Historical Jesus* (Peabody, Mass.: Hendrickson, 1993), p. 94.

43. A theme that Mark is to develop further (Mark 11:20–25). For a discussion of 'faith' in Mark, see M. A. Beavis, 'Mark's Teaching on Faith', *BTB* 16 (1986), pp. 139–142.

lowers. This is especially so when they are engaged in the difficult ministry of exorcism.[44] In verse 23 the faith under discussion is 'faith that prays',[45] and Mark makes it clear for his readers that discipleship, healing and exorcism in the post-Easter situation is to find its power base in prayer.

To summarize, any share in Jesus' *exousia* that is enjoyed by his disciples / the church is not theirs to control as they will, but only becomes available to them from God through prayer.[46] For Mark it is fair to say that so far as Jesus is concerned, signs and wonders are firmly linked to Christology (Jesus' identity as Messiah / Son of God), whereas for Jesus' disciples signs and wonders are primarily functional and, as we saw in 6:13, their successful outworking is normally linked to mission.

From here we may conclude that the thrust of this pericope, within the overall context of Mark's teaching on discipleship, shows that the earlier spectacular successes on the part of the disciples sent out by Jesus in mission should not be regarded by Mark's readers as the everyday norm for the church. Whilst signs and wonders have their place in the church's mission, such power encounters are of relatively little importance when compared to the essentials that characterize true discipleship. That this is the case is further evidenced, not only by the clear correctives to false ideas about discipleship in Mark's central section, but also by the incident involving the strange exorcist (9:38–41).

## Another exorcist (Mark 9:38–41)

It is difficult to see why this incident has been placed here by Mark, interrupting as it does the flow of Jesus' discourse on becoming like a child (9:35–37ff.).[47]

---

44. Best, *Following Jesus*, p. 69, concludes here that 'the father's faith in v. 25 is linked so lightly to the need for the healing of his child that its understanding as "saving faith" stands out'.

45. Lane, *Gospel of Mark*, p. 335; and see discussion in Beavis, 'Mark's Teaching on Faith', pp. 139–141.

46. Cf. Mann, *Mark*, p. 371; and Schweizer, *Good News According to Mark*, p. 189. Nineham's suggestion (*Saint Mark*, p. 245) that the conclusion to the story reflects the early church's difficulty with some exorcisms and this being attributed to 'spiritual deficiencies' on the part of the exorcists seems less likely to me.

47. For a full discussion of the original *Sitz im Leben* for this pericope, see Gundry, *Mark*, pp. 519–524.

However, the climax in verse 41 indicates that the pericope is concerned with right attitudes towards Jesus,[48] which links with the same theme expressed in verse 37 and the clear allusion there to disciples as missionaries representing Jesus as he, in turn, represents God.

In this pericope Mark concludes his teaching on exorcism as it relates to discipleship, and in so doing may be reflecting a contemporary problem for his church.[49] It has been argued that Mark is primarily drawing attention to the disciples' exclusive understanding of Jesus' mission in that they saw themselves as a narrow, authorized circle of Jesus' followers who were (alone) commissioned to confront Satan.[50] However, this seems unlikely in light of Mark's concentration in his central section on the meaning of true discipleship, which is clearly intended for his wider readership. What then is Mark saying here about the relationship between discipleship and the working of miracles?

John's complaint is significant here,[51] for it does draw the reader's attention back to the fact that only the Twelve had been commissioned by Jesus to cast out demons in his name. This explains, in turn, why John and his fellow-

---

48. Mann, *Mark*, p. 377.

49. In Acts 19:13ff. it is evident that the early church was concerned with incidents of non-Christians using the name of Jesus to heal and perform exorcisms (cf. Acts 8:18ff.); see further discussion in chapter 5 below. Cranfield, *St. Mark*, p. 309, rejects the view that this pericope is a product of the early church on the grounds that such a tolerant attitude as that displayed by Jesus was unlikely in the early church and that the association with John suggests a traditional origin. Both he and Taylor, *Gospel According to Mark*, pp. 407, find no reason to suppose that Jesus' name was not also used by others during his lifetime.

50. Lane, *Gospel of Mark*, p. 343.

51. This is the one occasion in Mark where John plays a special role on his own, which for Schweizer, *Good News According to Mark*, p. 194, indicates a strong link with the dominical tradition. In a recent study of the 'anatomy of envy' as it occurs in Mark's Gospel, which uses insights from cultural anthropology and the evidence of ancient sources, Hagedorn and Neyrey suggest that John's motivation here is envy of a rival and that in forbidding the other exorcist to use Jesus' name the disciples were showing loyalty to their patron. By refusing to react, Jesus models an alternative approach to the quest for honour that characterizes the value-system of their culture, where Jesus' disciples simply do not participate in honour-seeking. See further A. C. Hagedorn and J. H. Neyrey, "'It Was out of Envy That they Handed Jesus over" (Mark 15.10): The Anatomy of Envy and the Gospel of Mark', *JSNT* 69 (1998), pp. 15–56, and especially p. 48.

disciples had tried unsuccessfully to stop the exorcist.[52] As Lane notes, the irony here is that the disciples had so recently proved incapable themselves of casting out the dumb spirit from the boy.[53] It is true that in verse 39 Jesus' rebuke is in response to the disciples' intolerance, because, as Jesus himself points out, the use of his name by the exorcist indicates a lack of hostility towards Jesus and the miracles he performed.[54] The exorcist clearly does not belong to Jesus' circle of followers or for that matter to Mark's community. Nevertheless, his use of the name of Jesus indicates that he is by no means anti-Christian.

Mark's point appears to be that exorcism in Jesus' name need not necessarily involve (true) discipleship[55] and, as such, should be regarded by his readers as being of relatively minor importance in terms of what characterizes true discipleship.[56] Nevertheless, a right attitude towards Jesus and those who follow him (v. 41) is important, as has already been pointed out in verse 37. What remains of minor importance is the ability to perform exorcisms in the name of Jesus that have little, if anything, to do either with being a true disciple of Jesus or even being commissioned by him for mission. Rather, Mark is keen to convey to his readers that the right attitudes taught by Jesus are what characterize true discipleship and so provide a paradigmatic legacy for the church of his day for what it means to be a follower of Jesus.


## Conclusions

A Markan paradigm for contemporary discipleship that also seeks to understand the role of signs and wonders in relation to mission must begin with a fundamental question for Mark and his original readers: 'What does it mean to follow Jesus?'

So far as providing evidence for a contemporary theology of signs and wonders is concerned, we have seen how the earlier spectacular success of the

---

52. Note *eidomen* (we saw) and *ekōluomen* (we were preventing him) in v. 38, and see further, Marshall, *Faith as a Theme*, pp. 157–158.

53. Lane, *Gospel of Mark*, p. 343.

54. Cranfield, *St. Mark*, p. 310, who also points to a similar sentiment expressed by Caesar in Cicero, *Lig.* 11, and suggests that Jesus' response in v. 40 may reflect a contemporary popular saying.

55. This certainly appears to be the case with Matthew (cf. Matt. 7:21).

56. Cf. M. D. Hooker, *Mark The Message of Mark* (London: Epworth, 1983), p. 229.

disciples when they are commissioned and sent out in mission by Jesus is not to be regarded by Mark's readers as the everyday norm for the church. Any share in Jesus' *exousia* that is enjoyed by his disciples – together with the post-Easter church both then and now – is not theirs to control as they will, but becomes available to them from God through prayer only. For Mark, it is fair to say that so far as Jesus is concerned, signs and wonders are firmly linked to Christology (Jesus' identity as Messiah / Son of God), whereas for Jesus' disciples signs and wonders are primarily functional and their successful outworking is normally linked to mission. In other words, signs and wonders have their place in the church's mission but, compared to the essentials that characterize true discipleship, such power encounters are of relatively little importance.

In Mark's central section we have seen that the evangelist's critical presentation of the disciples serves as a device to enable Mark to present his understanding of the true nature of Christian discipleship as articulated and modelled by Jesus. Jesus' correctives on the true nature of discipleship overrule the disciples' misunderstandings and are aimed not just at the disciples themselves, but at Mark's own community and, by extension, serve to inform the contemporary church's understanding of what it means to be a true follower of Jesus. Christian discipleship, according to Mark, requires utter commitment, a servant spirit, willingness to suffer and a focus not on religious orthodoxy[57] but on doing the will of God – all characteristics modelled by Jesus himself and emphasized as part of the 'messianic corrective' that may be understood as the primary goal for Mark's narrative of 'the good news of Jesus Christ, the Son of God' (Mark 1:1).

---

57. In Mark's Gospel represented by the religious orthodoxy of the Pharisees.

## 11. THE ORIGINAL ENDING TO MARK'S GOSPEL?

Against the idea that the original ending of Mark's Gospel is now lost or that the so-called longer ending (Mark 16:9–20) was penned by the Second Evangelist, the vast majority of NT scholars have come to believe that Mark intended to end his Gospel at 16:8. Even so, the longer ending attached to Mark's Gospel is one of the most frequently cited references to Mark by the Third Wave in support of their contemporary theology of signs and wonders being integral to Christian discipleship and normative for today. Here, it is argued, we have a further confirmation of the Great Commission in Matthew 28:16–20.

### The longer ending to Mark's Gospel (Mark 16:9–20)

Although opinions as to the authenticity of these verses vary amongst Third Wave writers they are, nevertheless, often considered authoritative in terms of providing evidence that (at least) reflects the experience of the early church and, it is argued, give further confirmation of Jesus' mandate to his disciples to exercise a ministry of signs and wonders that continues to apply to the contemporary church. For example, K. Bottomly, who holds a postgraduate degree in theology from Princeton, cites Mark 16:17–20 as evidence that Jesus commissioned all his disciples to 'do power ministry'.[1] More specifically, John

Wimber understands the post-Easter commission in Mark 16:14–20 as being entirely consistent with the disciples' 'training', adding, 'I find it remarkable that many Western Christians are surprised by the emphasis on signs and wonders in this commissioning.'[2]

To be fair, Wimber acknowledges that some have challenged the authenticity of Mark 16:9–20, but he, nevertheless, continues, 'This raises a question: Why was such a text added – if it were, as the evidence suggests (but does *not* confirm) – in the second century? . . . why did Irenaeus cite Mark 16:9? And why did Justin refer to Mark 16:20 as authoritative?'[3]

For Wimber, the inclusion of these verses in many manuscripts is best explained in terms of their reflecting the actual ongoing experience of the early church, which is also the position adopted by another Third Wave writer, Sam Storms.[4] For Jack Deere, Mark 16:20 provides evidence from the experience of the early church that the purpose of miracles is to authenticate the 'message about Jesus'.[5] Whilst conceding that the majority of NT scholars do not consider the longer ending to be an original part of Mark's Gospel, which he believes to be now lost, he nevertheless can write, 'At the very least . . . these verses reflect what the early church thought about the purpose of miracles, even if these verses are not considered part of the original Scriptures.'[6]

Similarly, Greig points out that

> The wide dissemination of the long ending, seen in the manuscript evidence, suggests that the Early Church readily agreed that Jesus' commission to the disciples did include the expectation that supernatural signs would accompany the preaching of the gospel.[7]

---

1. K. Bottomly, 'Coming out of the Hangar: Confessions of an Evangelical Deist', in G. S. Greig and K. N. Springer (eds.), *The Kingdom and the Power* (Ventura, Calif.: Regal, 1993), p. 273.

2. Wimber, 'Power Evangelism: Definitions', in C. P. Wagner and F. D. Pennoyer (eds.), *Wrestling with Dark Angels* (Eastbourne: Monarch, 1990), p. 27.

3. Ibid.

4. Ibid. and cf. C. S. Storms, 'A Third Wave View', in W. Grudem (ed.), *Are Miraculous Gifts for Today? Four Views* (Leicester: IVP, 1996), p. 214.

5. J. Deere, *Surprised by the Power of the Spirit* (Eastbourne: Kingsway, 1993), p. 103.

6. Ibid., p. 277.

7. G. S. Greig, and K. N. Springer (eds.), *The Kingdom and the Power: Are Healing and the Spiritual Gifts Used by Jesus and the Early Church Meant for the Church Today?* (Ventura,

More cautiously, Wagner and Pennoyer, whilst conceding that the longer ending to Mark's Gospel dates from the first half of the second century AD and is, therefore, a later addition to the Gospel, maintain that these verses reflect 'an early post-biblical understanding of Jesus' post-resurrection commission to His disciples and to all "those who believe" (Mark 16:17), which, as the manuscript evidence suggests, was widely accepted in the Early Church'.[8]

Here it seems to me that the 'wide acceptance' was of Mark 16:9–20 as an integral part of Mark's Gospel by Christians who assumed that these verses formed the legitimate ending to their copy of this Gospel. Whilst the earliest manuscripts support the conclusion of Mark at 16:8[9] many early manuscripts do contain Mark 16:9–20. For example, Tatian's *Diatessaron* (c. AD 140) knew this ending and Irenaeus (died AD 202) accepted verses 9–20 as part of Mark's Gospel.[10] Lane argues that the form, language and style of these verses militate against Markan authorship[11] and, text-critically, the majority of scholars would argue that Mark 16:9–20 can be shown to be secondary. However, evidence of early patristic witness to the longer ending clearly indicates that these verses were attached to the end of Mark's Gospel at the latest by the beginning of the second century.

It has been suggested that these verses may have been used independently for some time as a catechetical summary before being attached to Mark's Gospel.[12]

---

Calif.: Regal, 1993), p. 167 n. 25. Greig makes special mention of the gift of tongues with reference to Mark 16:17 but makes no mention of 16:18a!

8. Greig and Springer, 'Appendix 3: Matthew 28:18–20 – The Great Commission and Jesus' Commands to Preach and Heal', in idem, *Kingdom and the Power*, p. 401.

9. The two earliest parchment codices are Vaticanus (B) and Sinaiticus (Aleph). See also miniscules 304 and 2386. Noted for example in W. L. Lane, *The Gospel of Mark* (NICNT; Grand Rapids, Mich.: Eerdmans, 1974), p. 601; and H. Anderson, *The Gospel of Mark* (London: Oliphants, 1976), p. 358.

10. *Haer.* 3.10.6.

11. A, C, D, K, L, W, X, D, Q, P, y, f, 28, 33, 274, 565, 700, 892, 1009, latt, sy, c, p, h, pal, coppt. Omitted by Aleph, B, k, sys and by some arm., eth. and geo mss. For further discussion of the manuscript evidence, see for example Lane, *Mark*, p. 604; and C. E. B. Cranfield, *The Gospel According to St. Mark* (Cambridge: Cambridge University Press, 1959), p. 471. A particularly comprehensive survey is to be found in W. R. Farmer, *The Last Twelve Verses of Mark* (SNTSMS 25; Cambridge: Cambridge University Press, 1974), pp. 3–75.

12. Cranfield, *St. Mark*, p. 472. See also E. Schweizer, *The Good News According to Mark* (ET London: SPCK, 1971), p. 374. Anderson, *Gospel of Mark*, considers them to have been an independent appearance story originally, which was later attached to

Others suggest that because verses 16–20 are largely composed of fragments found in the other Gospels and Acts, they are to be understood as a carefully constructed 'rounding off' of the Gospel.[13] Against this idea of rounding off Mark's Gospel, Morna Hooker points out that, although verses 9–20 are clearly an attempt to 'complete' the Gospel, these final verses do not, in fact, deal with the questions posed by Mark 16:1–8 in terms of the women's silence and Jesus' promise to meet with the Eleven in Galilee (cf. Matt. 28:16–17).[14] Finally, an examination of the vocabulary of Mark 16:9–20 proves somewhat inconclusive. Whilst these verses include some sixteen words not used previously by Mark,[15] according to W. R. Farmer, verses 9, 11, 13, 15, and particularly verse 20, do use vocabulary found elsewhere in Mark.[16]

In addition to the evidence against the authenticity of verses 9–20, the problem has been compounded further by the rather surprising ending of Mark's Gospel at verse 8, which commentators have often refused to accept as the original ending intended by Mark. What, then, are we to make of Mark 16:9–20? How, if at all, is the longer ending related to the rest of Mark's Gospel? Do these verses provide any legitimate evidence for the Third Wave paradigm for contemporary discipleship, more importantly here from a Markan standpoint?

## The appearance to Mary Magdalene (Mark 16:9–11)

The writer of these verses almost certainly knew Luke's Gospel and was

---

Mark's Gospel in order to bring it into line with the other Gospels. See also C. L. Blomberg, *Jesus and the Gospels* (Leicester: Apollos, 1997), p. 75.

13. See for example B. van Iersel, *Reading Mark* (ET Edinburgh: T. & T. Clark, 1989), p. 216.

14. M. D. Hooker, *The Gospel According to Saint Mark* (London: A. & C. Black; Peabody, Mass: Hendrickson, 1991), p. 389.

15. These include 'to go on one's way' (16:10, 12, 15); 'mourning' (16:10); 'to be seen' (16:11, 14); 'to view attentively' (16:11, 16); 'another' (16:12); 'form' (16:12); 'but later' (16:14); 'eleven' (16:14); 'will accompany' (16:17); 'to pick up' (16:18); 'deadly (poison)' (16:18); 'to injure/hurt' (16:18); 'to be taken up' (16:19); 'work with/together' (16:20); 'confirm' (16:20); 'accompanying' (16:20). See P. L. Danove, *The End of Mark's Story: A Methodological Study* (Leiden: Brill, 1993), pp. 122–124.

16. Farmer, *Last Twelve Verses of Mark*, p. 103. For a comparative analysis between Mark 1:1 – 16:8 and 16:9–20, see pp. 83–103.

possibly familiar with John's Gospel.[17] The appearance to Mary Magdalene clearly begins *de novo*. The lack of homogenous relationship to the rest of Mark's Gospel can be seen from the fact that these verses take no account of Mary's earlier appearance at 16:1. Instead, she is introduced here as if for the first time,[18] as the one from whom Jesus had cast out seven demons. This echoes Luke 8:2 and is entirely superfluous, for Mark himself clearly did not need to include such an explanatory note about Mary (cf. Mark 15:40, 47; 16:1).[19] The statement in verse 11 about the disciples' disbelief at hearing female testimony to the resurrection is also reminiscent of Luke 24:11, where the women's story is dismissed as an 'idle tale' and may also reflect the more general theme of disbelief found in Matthew 28:17 and John 20:25.

All the indications are that verses 9–11 were not written by the author of Mark and thus have no direct bearing on Mark's view of discipleship. What we may have here is a first indication that the writer of these verses was concerned about growing unbelief in the Easter story either in his own community or more generally in the church of his day (16:11). As we shall see, this appears to be borne out further in verses 14ff.

## The appearance to the two travellers (Mark 16:12–13)

In verse 12 the Greek verb 'to appear'[20] is not the same as that normally used in

---

17. V. Taylor, *The Gospel According to Mark*, 2nd ed. (London: Macmillan, 1966), p. 610. In addition to the echo of Luke 8:2, Schweizer, *Good News According to Mark*, p. 375, suggests that these verses may be dependent on John 20:11–18. Cf. also Cranfield, *St. Mark*, p. 472. D. E. Nineham, *Saint Mark* (Pelican Gospel Commentaries; Harmondsworth: Penguin, 1963), p. 451, grants that this may be possible but contends that it cannot be shown that the author of the long ending of Mark was familiar with John's Gospel.

18. The clumsiness of the connection with vv. 1–8 is noted by most commentators. See for example Cranfield, *St. Mark*, p. 472.

19. Cf. Matt. 4:18, where Matthew adds an explanatory note about Simon, 'the one called Peter' – here a first indication of the special representative role Peter is to play in Matthew's Gospel. For Schweizer, *Good News According to Mark*, p. 375, this is a clear indication that this was not written by Mark, who may not have been familiar with the story of Mary's exorcism by Jesus. Also 'cast out/from' is not found elsewhere in the NT. Noted by Taylor, *Gospel According to Mark*, p. 611.

20. Lit. 'he was manifested'.

the primitive kerygmatic formulae of 1 Corinthians 15:3–5, 6–8[21] although, interestingly, it does occur twice in John 21:1 and 14, which is also probably a later addition to the original conclusion to the Fourth Gospel, which appears to end quite naturally at John 20:31. Taylor notes that the phrase 'And after these things' at the beginning of verse 12 occurs frequently in John, but is not used by Mark.[22] The narrative at this point clearly echoes Luke 24:13–35 and the journey to Emmaus, although neither the vocabulary nor style of verses 12–13 is Markan.[23]

Of rather more interest is the phrase 'in another form'. According to Taylor, this suggests that Jesus appears here in a different form from that in which he appeared to Mary in verse 9.[24] Schweizer maintains that this phrase is intended to differentiate between the earthly Jesus and the appearance of the risen Jesus here to Mary Magdalene.[25] More plausibly, Cranfield argues that the description of the risen Jesus during the walk as being 'in another form' probably reflects Luke 24:16, understood in terms of the subjective experience of those to whom Jesus appeared, rather than that Jesus literally took on a different form.[26]

In verse 13 we again have a stress on the motif of disbelief, which was clearly important for the author of the longer ending.[27] So far as the theme of discipleship is concerned, we learn very little except that we have yet a further indication of the writer's concern with unbelief (16:13).


### The commissioning of the Eleven (Mark 16:14–18)

In verse 14 the writer stresses for the third time the unbelief of the disciples,

---

21. For example, 1 Cor. 15:5; lit. 'he was seen by Cephas'.
22. Taylor, *Gospel According to Mark*, p. 611.
23. Cf. for example Taylor, *Gospel According to Mark*, p. 611; and Schweizer, *Good News According to Mark*, p. 375.
24. Taylor, *Gospel According to Mark*, p. 611.
25. Schweizer, *Good News According to Mark*, p. 375.
26. Cranfield, *St. Mark*, p. 472. See also Nineham, *Saint Mark*, p. 451. It should be noted that Luke appears to be conscious of the need to make it clear that the risen Jesus was both recognizable apart from subjective experience, and was neither a ghost (24:37–43) nor an angel (Acts 12:15). John also makes the same point with the risen Jesus, although on this occasion Jesus is not described as eating the fish (cf. John 21:1–14). For evidence of heavenly beings appearing in an unrecognizable form but only pretending to eat, see Tobit 12.11–19.
27. See below on v. 14 for further comment on this issue.

to the point where the same risen Jesus who is about to commission them upbraids them for their unbelief. Schweizer suggests that their unbelief and hardness of heart reflects Mark's theme of blindness of the disciples.[28] In light of what we have seen so far, however, it seems more likely that it reflects Luke 24:38 and serves as a further rebuke aimed at lack of Easter belief. This point is strengthened when we consider that Mark 16:14 is the only occurrence in the appearance tradition where Jesus upbraids the disciples for their failure to believe those to whom he has already appeared.[29] Once again the evidence points to an emerging theme within these verses of the lack of belief in the early apostolic witness in the writer's own church or the wider Christian community, and that the writer felt it necessary to provide a longer (polemical) ending to Mark's Gospel in defence of the apostolic witness.[30] If this is the case, then we have an important clue to the way in which the writer intends his readers to understand his addition to the ending of Mark's Gospel.

---

28. Schweizer, *Good News According to Mark*, p. 375.

29. Anderson, *Gospel of Mark*, p. 359; and, more strongly, Nineham, *Saint Mark*, p. 451. Taylor, *Gospel According to Mark*, pp. 611–612, notes that 'unbelief' (*apistia*) is a word Mark himself uses in the context of hostility towards Jesus (cf. Mark 6:6; 9:24), and comments further, 'So strong a rebuke can be understood only by the supreme importance attached to the Resurrection by the writer, who has in mind the conditions of his own day.'

30. J. Jeremias, 'The Freer Logion', in E. Hennecke, *New Testament Apocrypha*, vol. 1 (ET London: SCM, 1963), pp. 188–189, and see notes 1–9 for possible NT echoes noted by Jeremias. This logion appears in the Gospel MS W (from Egypt, fourth or fifth century) and is quoted by Jerome, *Pelag.* 2.15 and is reflective of a number of other NT passages noted by J. Jeremias, who provides a translation of this saying in 'Freer Logion', p. 189, as follows.

   [*Mark 16:14*: 'Afterward he appeared to the eleven as they reclined at table and reproached them for their unbelief and hardness of heart, for they had not believed those who had seen him after he rose] And they excused themselves with the word, "This aeon (age) of lawlessness and unbelief is under Satan, who through the unclean spirits does not allow the true power of God to be comprehended. Therefore," they said to Christ "reveal your righteousness now." And Christ replied to them, "The measure of the years of Satan's power is filled up. But other fearful things draw near, also (for those) for whom I, because they have sinned, was delivered to death, that they might turn back to the truth and sin no more in order to inherit the spiritual and imperishable glory of righteousness (preserved) in heaven."'

   The passage then continues with v. 15, 'Now go into all the world . . .'

At this point after verse 14, Codex W includes the so-called 'Freer Logion', but this is a later interpolation into the longer ending, although it has been suggested that these verses may have been used independently for some time as a catechetical summary before being attached to Mark's Gospel. Interestingly, the interpolator's purpose appears to be to provide an explanation for the 'unbelief' that features so prominently in Mark 16:9–14. Note also here how the later copyist responsible for the 'Freer Logion' shows respect for the disciples by defending them, something that is often lacking in the earlier Gospel tradition.[31]

Following his rebuke, the risen Jesus commissions the disciples to go into all the world, thus reflecting the universalism already latent in Mark 13:10 and 14:9 as well as that found explicitly elsewhere in the NT church (Matt. 28:19–20; cf. Rom. 1:8; Col. 1:23).[32] In Mark 16:15 the appropriate response to believing the good news is baptism (16:15; cf. Matt. 28:19; Acts 2:38)[33] and at this point the writer delivers his *coup de grâce* against Easter scepticism; namely, that those who believe will be saved but those who do not believe will face eschatological condemnation.

From here in verses 17–18, and most importantly for the Third Wave, we find a list of 'signs' that will accompany those who believe.[34] Taylor's suggestion that the idea of signs 'accompanying/following' is Johannine (cf. John 14:12) is not convincing. In John 14:12 the writer refers to 'works' (*erga*) rather than 'signs' (*sēmeia*). Also, in Mark's Gospel the idea that signs are a legitimate validation of Jesus' ministry/message is treated in a wholly negative fashion (Mark 8:11, 12; 13:22). In the case of Mark 13:4 the sign given is not a miraculous healing or exorcism of the type described in Mark 16:16–20 but a very negative prophetic utterance by Jesus.

---

31. Cranfield, *St. Mark*, p. 472. See also Schweizer, *Good News According to Mark*, p. 374. Anderson, *Gospel of Mark*, considers them to have been an independent appearance story originally that was later attached to Mark's Gospel in order to bring it into line with the other Gospels. See also Blomberg, *Jesus and the Gospels* (Leicester: Apollos, 1997), p. 75.

32. Anderson, *Gospel of Mark*, p. 360, notes rightly that here the universalism found in Matthew's commission gives way to a narrower and exclusivist formula.

33. Hooker, *Gospel According to Saint Mark*, p. 390.

34. Taylor, *Gospel According to Mark*, p. 612. Anderson, *Gospel of Mark*, p. 360, suggests that the promise of charismatic gifts to those who believe suggests that the writer belonged to a church that considered such practices to be 'ongoing marks of authentic Christian faith'.

In 16:17a the promised accompanying signs are explained in detail. Exorcisms and healing have already been attributed in Mark's narrative to Jesus' disciples (Mark 3:15; 6:13) and others (cf. Mark 9:38–41). Mark also mentions the use of oil by Jesus' disciples, reflecting the practice of the early church, but this is lacking here (Mark 6:13; Jas 5:14–15). In 16:17b glossolalia is mentioned but is not found elsewhere in the Gospel tradition, although it is described elsewhere in the NT as part of the experience of the early church (see e.g. Acts 2:3–4; 10:46; 19:6; 1 Cor. 12:28).

In 16:17c, 17d handling snakes probably reflects Acts 28:3–4 (cf. Luke 10:19 and possibly Isa. 11:8), but drinking poison with impunity is not mentioned elsewhere in the NT.[35] At this point we have clearly moved away considerably from what we have identified in Mark's narrative as his intended paradigm for discipleship, towards the very model of discipleship that Mark condemns! Morna Hooker summarizes the position succinctly when she writes:

> The emphasis now is on the mighty works for their own sake, as demonstrations of the power of Christ's name – the Lord ... confirming their message through the signs that accompanied them (v. 20) – rather than as an integral part of the gospel. Like Jesus, the disciples are to cast out demons and heal the sick; but, unlike him, they are to speak in tongues and be preserved from physical danger.[36]

## The ascension and the heavenly court (Mark 16:19–20)

Again the vocabulary and ideas are post-Markan. The name 'the Lord Jesus' is not used elsewhere in the Gospels, although it is used frequently in Acts and (less frequently) by Paul who prefers the fuller designation 'the Lord Jesus

---

35. Taylor, *Gospel According to Mark*, p. 613, mentions several post-NT references to characters drinking poison without harm. Some extreme contemporary Christian sects (e.g. snake handlers in southern Appalachia) handle deadly snakes in their religious gatherings. H. D. Hunter, 'Serpent Handling', in S. M. Burgess and G. B. McGee (eds.), *Dictionary of Pentecostal and Charismatic Movements* (Grand Rapids, Mich.: Zondervan, 1988), p. 777, writes, 'The principle [*sic*] text is Mark 16:18, and none of those people know [*sic*], or would believe, that this is not part of the original text of the Gospel of Mark.' This practice, together with drinking poison, is conveniently forgotten by the Third Wave when referring to the longer ending of Mark in support of contemporary paradigms for discipleship!

36. M. Hooker, *Gospel According to Saint Mark*, p. 390.

Christ'.[37] Jesus' ascension recalls similar scenes in Luke and Acts (Luke 24:51; Acts 1:9–10), and mention of Jesus at the right hand of God recalls Stephen's vision during his martyrdom (Acts 7:56).[38] Linked to Jesus' ascension in verse 19 is a heavenly court scene where Jesus is described as sitting down at the right hand of God (cf. Ps. 110:1), which is common elsewhere in the NT (see e.g. Acts 7:55–56; Rom. 8:34; Eph. 1:20; Col. 3:1; Heb. 1:3; 8:1; 10:12; 12:12; 1 Pet. 3:22; Rev. 3:21).

The longer ending closes with a summary that depicts the ascended Jesus continuing to help his disciples from his heavenly throne as they go out in mission, which may be derived from Matthew 28:20b (as well as the work of the Spirit described in Acts), although Matthew has previously made it clear how this works in relation to Christ's teaching and the community's missionary activity.[39] The final part of verse 20 is of particular interest here because it suggests that 'while the Lord worked with them and confirmed the message by the signs that accompanied it' is firmly linked to the missionary activity of the Eleven and it is their going out in mission that forms the final conclusion for the writer of the longer ending.[40]

### Conclusions to discussion of Mark 16:9–20

Whilst many early manuscripts do contain Mark 16:9–20, the earliest manuscripts support the conclusion of Mark's Gospel at Mark 16:8. During our examination of the longer ending to Mark's Gospel we have seen indications that the writer was concerned about growing unbelief in the Easter story either in his own church or more generally in the wider church. This may have been his reason for adding his longer ending to Mark's Gospel, which does reflect (probably unintentionally) aspects of Mark's association of missionary activity with healings and exorcisms.

---

37. For example, 1 Cor. 1:3 etc.
38. The difference being that in Mark 16:19 Jesus sits at the right hand of God, indicating his earthly mission is accomplished, whereas in Acts 7:56 Jesus stands at the right hand of God to receive his first martyr. The suggestion by Schweizer, *Good News According to Mark*, p. 378, that v. 19 also echoes OT language associated with the heavenly ascension of Elijah (1 Kgs 2:11) seems less likely, as the ascension of Elijah is depicted in particularly graphic language that is totally absent here.
39. See my previous chapter for a discussion of this point.
40. Cf. Schweizer, *Good News According to Mark*, p. 378.

However, the writer of the longer ending goes much further than Mark in his graphic description of signs and wonders. At best these verses summarize material already present elsewhere in the NT and need to be understood apart from the rest of Mark's Gospel. In other words, Mark 16:9–20 was not penned by the author of Mark's Gospel, does not reflect Mark's teaching on discipleship and simply will not bear the weight placed upon it by Third Wave commentators. Rather, Mark's contribution to our contemporary understanding of Christian discipleship reminds us that there are other, more profound, aspects to the example Jesus articulates and models for those who would follow him.

If we must rule Mark 16:9–20 out of court so far as a Markan paradigm for commission and discipleship is concerned, how then are we to understand the abrupt ending to Mark's Gospel at 16:8? How does it relate to Mark's Gospel as a whole, and particularly to his teaching on discipleship?

### The original ending to Mark's Gospel (Mark 16:1–8)

There is no escaping the enigmatic and puzzling nature of Mark 16:8. Even so, the vast majority of NT scholars now believe that Mark intended to end his Gospel at this point and this consensus is now reflected in the majority of modern English translations of the NT where it is pointed out that verses 9–20 are not original to Mark.[41] Former arguments that the original ending to Mark's Gospel is now lost, or that the so-called longer ending (Mark 16:9–20) was penned by the Second Evangelist have been discounted, as has the argument that it was not possible to end a book, or even a paragraph with the word 'for'.[42] Evidence that this is, in fact, a legitimate way for Mark's Gospel to end has been produced by R. H. Lightfoot[43] and more recently Paul Danove,[44] Thomas Boomershine[45] and Nicholas Denyer.[46]

---

41. Some notable examples include the NIV, NASB, GNB, NRSV and ESV.
42. See, Hooker, *Gospel According to Saint Mark*, p. 391. The Greek reads literally 'they were afraid for'.
43. R. H. Lightfoot, *The Gospel Message of Mark* (Oxford: Clarendon, 1950), pp. 80–97.
44. Danove, *End of Mark's Story*.
45. T. J. Boomershine and G. L. Bartholemew, 'The Narrative Technique of Mark 16.8', *JBL* 100.2 (1981), pp. 213–223. In a subsequent article, Boomershine ['Mark 16:8 and the Apostolic Commission', *JBL* 100.2 (1981), pp. 197–211] sets out to show that 16:8 gives a coherent ending to Mark in light of the preceding narrative,

A further argument against Mark having ended his Gospel at 16:8 is that the ending appears to demand a resurrection appearance (cf. 16:7), but, argues Hooker, Mark's readers clearly knew the final outcome (their community being founded on resurrection faith) and so it is quite feasible that Mark deliberately intended to involve his readers and their knowledge of the outcome as he ended his Gospel.[47] On a slightly different tack, David Catchpole argues that the ending at 16:8b is wholly in line with an established tradition that belongs to the structure of epiphany (the appearance of a heavenly being).[48] Alternatively, Burdon bases his argument in favour of the ending at 16:8 on the fact that chapters 13 and 16 already make it clear in their different ways that the disciples of Jesus now live in the time of the 'absent Christ' and are to engage in their mission whilst awaiting the parousia.[49]

In seeking a purpose for the ending of Mark's Gospel N. Q. Hamilton, who regards Mark's Christology from a Hellenistic, 'god-man' (*theios anēr*) view-point, argues that the empty tomb narrative was a deliberate creation by Mark who was seeking to satisfy Graeco-Roman expectations that would have been aroused by his Son of God Christology, where his empty tomb would suggest a removal, indicative of the expected fate of a hero, rather than a resurrec-tion.[50] A similar view was put forward by E. Bickermann who argued that Mark's empty tomb should be understood in terms of a 'translation' that would not require a resurrection appearance.[51] Against this sceptical view-point, Bolt argues that Mark 16:1–8 does not fit the pattern of empty tomb translation stories in either the Hellenistic traditions or intertestamental liter-ature. Rather Mark's story clearly points to Jesus' resurrection on the grounds that Mark goes to great pains to ensure that his readers understand that Jesus

---

providing a 'climactic reversal' of the messianic secrecy motif in Mark, and is in line with the endings of the other Gospels in that Mark too ends with an apostolic commissioning to 'proclaim the gospel'.

46. N. Denyer, 'Mark 16:8 and Plato, *Protagoras* 328D', in *TynBul* 57.1 (2006), pp. 149–150.

47. Hooker, *Gospel According to Saint Mark*, p. 392.

48. D. R. Catchpole, 'The Fearful Silence of the Women at the Tomb: A Study in Markan Theology', *JTSA* 18 (1977), p. 9.

49. C. Burdon, '"Such a Fast God" – True and False Disciples in Mark's Gospel', *Theology* 7.34 (1987), pp. 89–97.

50. N. Q. Hamilton, 'Resurrection Tradition and the Composition of Mark', *JBL* 84 (1965), p. 418.

51. E. Bickermann, 'Das leere Grab', *ZNW* 23 (1924), pp. 218–291; see especially pp. 286ff.

had joined the ranks of the dead (15:42–47) rather than avoiding death by translation or apotheosis.[52]

Importantly, from a narrative point of view, Mark's readers have already been forewarned of the possibility of a resurrection appearance to the disciples in Galilee (14:28).[53] With this in mind, the need for continued vigilance has been stressed in Gethsemane (14:32–42). The promise of 14:28 is now repeated in 16:7, where the context of the former saying (14:27) about scattering of shepherdless sheep would be dramatically recalled by Mark's readers. In 16:8 Boomershine identifies three emotional responses of the women (fear, astonishment and trembling), which, he concludes, are positive. Whereas the flight of the women and their failure to obey the angel's command to report back to the disciples are negative,[54] Mark's readers would condemn the women's action whilst having sympathy for their fear in the face of an angelic appearance. In other words, any negative reader response to the women intended by Mark is to the women's response rather than to the women themselves, and any interpretation of the end of Mark's Gospel must take account of this.[55]

According to Marxsen, the primary motif at the end of Mark's Gospel is the tension between speech and silence, which he links with the messianic secrecy theme in Mark.[56] Marxsen argues that the proclamation of Jesus' resurrection by the angel (16:6–7) is a reversal of the secrecy theme in view of the delay of the parousia.[57] Building on Marxsen's proposal of a tension between proclamation and silence, Reginald Fuller discusses the three types of conclusion normally associated with the abrupt ending of Mark at 16:8: accidental premature conclusion due, for example, to the death of the author; the mutilation hypothesis, where an original ending beyond 16:8 and in fulfilment of 16:7 was removed/lost before it reached either Matthew or Luke; the deliberate conclusion hypothesis, where Mark intended to end his

---

52. P. G. Bolt, 'Mark 16:1–8: The Empty Tomb of a Hero?', *TynBul* 47.1 (1996), p. 37.

53. E. Best, *Mark: The Gospel as Story* (Edinburgh: T. & T. Clark, 1983), p. 55, notes interestingly here how the idea of Jesus going ahead of the disciples links back to 10:32.

54. See the negative use of 'everyone left' in Mark 14:50–52 to describe the desertion of the disciples and the flight of the naked young man.

55. Boomershine, 'Mark 16:8 and the Apostolic Commission', pp. 200–205.

56. Marxsen, *Mark the Evangelist: Studies on the Redaction History of the Gospel* (ET Nashville, Tenn.: Abingdon, 1969), pp. 111–116.

57. Ibid., p. 113.

Gospel at 16:8.[58] Fuller settles for the latter, maintaining that Mark 9:9 had already pointed forward to the resurrection as the *'terminus ad quem* for the preservation of the messianic secret'.[59] Based on conjecture that Mark did not have available to him a resurrection tradition on which to draw, Fuller argues that Mark was, therefore, unable to narrate such a tradition.[60] This, in my view, seems highly unlikely in light of, for example, 1 Corinthians 15:5ff. Nevertheless, Fuller concludes that in light of 9:9 (cf. 9:31 and 10:33–34), 16:7 simply points forward to appearances to the disciples and Peter as the basis for the inauguration of the church's mission.

Both Marxsen and Fuller are primarily dependent on a redaction-critical analysis of Mark 16:7 for their conclusions. Using the same redaction-critical approach, David Catchpole arrives at a very different, and much more plausible, conclusion. He points out that in Mark 14:27 Jesus predicts that all the disciples will become deserters, and this is exactly what happens in 14:50.[61] In 16:7 we have the promise of reversal and restoration for all the disciples, including Peter. Catchpole argues that it is precisely the reversed situation from 14:50 that 16:7 is intended by Mark to confirm, making the point that 'the perspective which shows in 16:7 sees contact with Jesus as cancelling the failures of the past and opening up a new and hopeful era'.[62]

Catchpole argues further that the probable background to 16:7–8 envisaged by Mark involves stories of heavenly beings 'on the move' and offers examples from the OT, Apocrypha and NT,[63] concluding that Mark 16:7–8 is simply another example.[64] In light of this understanding of Mark 16:7, Catchpole argues that Mark would never have envisaged that the message did not reach the disciples. The fear motif attributed to the women in 16:7 clearly indicates a 'heavenly manifestation' and suggests that Mark 16:8b can be interpreted in the light of 'established tradition', which, in turn, suggests that the reaction of the women in 16:8 (fear and silence) is appropriate both to the angelic appearance (16:5) and the message they receive (cf. 16:8a).[65] From here Catchpole

---

58. See further R. H. Fuller, *The Formation of the Resurrection Narratives*, 2nd ed (London: SPCK, 1980), pp. 24–25.

59. Ibid., p. 67.

60. Ibid.

61. Catchpole, 'Fearful Silence', p. 4.

62. Ibid.

63. Gen. 16:1–2, 4–14; 18:1–16a; 19:1–23; Tobit 5.4ff.; Mark 6:45–52; Luke 24:13–35.

64. Catchpole, 'Fearful Silence', p. 5.

65. Ibid., p. 9.

concludes that the expectation to be taken from the messenger's words in 16:6b ('he has been raised') is that Mark's readers are to expect a further epiphany when the risen Jesus restores Peter and the other disciples and recommissions them (cf. 16:7).[66]

As we saw earlier, Clifton-Black has warned against overdependence upon the results of a redaction-critical approach to Mark's Gospel. Based on the hypothesis that Mark intended his work to be read aloud, Boomershine[67] argues that the narrative structure of the ending (16:1–8) is built on Mark's passion narrative and the earlier passion/resurrection predictions, and concludes:

> Mark's final comment ['for they were afraid'], the shortest and most enigmatic of his concluding comments, provokes his listeners to reflect on the future response of Jesus' followers, including themselves, to the commission to proclaim the gospel.[68]

This analysis by Boomershine is too conjectural in my view. The most commendable aspect is the attempt to link the ending at 16:8 with a generally known apostolic commission stated in more explicit terms in the other Gospels, which was clearly known earlier to Paul (1 Cor. 15:3–7). That Mark was aware of the Gentile mission seems clear from indications of a post-Easter proclamation of the gospel that appear in his narrative (cf. 8:35; 10:28–31; 13:5–23; 14:9). What is not clear is that Mark was aware of a similar commissioning of the Eleven along the lines of Matthew 28:16–20.

And so, we are left with a positive proclamation of the resurrection to the women (16:6), followed by an angelic commission to the women, indicating reinstatement of the disciples and Peter, together with a repeat in 16:7 of the promise made by Jesus in 14:28 that after the resurrection he would meet the disciples in Galilee. The fear and silence of the women in 16:8 provides a climactic conclusion to the proclamation of Jesus' resurrection and emphasizes its epiphanic nature.

## Conclusions

The evidence throughout Mark's Gospel clearly suggests that the evangelist has presented his readers with a portrait of the disciples as progressively

---

66. Ibid., pp. 9–10.

67. Boomershine, 'Mark 16:8 and the Apostolic Commission', pp. 208–209.

68. Ibid., p. 210.

uncomprehending and self-seeking, who finally betray, desert and deny Jesus. The disciples' failure is immediately overridden by the heavenly figure's message in 16:7, where the women are told to go and tell Peter and the other disciples that Jesus is risen and will meet them in Galilee. Nevertheless, the narrative ends in 16:8 not with the delivery of the angel's message by the women but enigmatically with their silence. With consummate artistry Mark leaves his readers with a promise of reinstatement in light of the resurrection (16:7) and the possibility (already foretold in 13:10) that the disciples will be commissioned once again to engage in the mission of Jesus – it only remains for Mark's readers to fill in the gaps for themselves from what they already knew to be the case.

# 12. CONCLUSIONS TO PART TWO

In Part Two we have seen that Mark's Gospel portrays the disciples in both a favourable and an unfavourable light. With respect to (implied) authorial intent, we saw that narrative criticism assumes that Mark tells a coherent story that involves the skilful use of his tradition about Jesus and the disciples in order to create a narrative that previously did not exist. In narrative-critical terms, the reader is clearly meant to identify with the disciples, who act as a foil for Jesus' teaching and afford him the opportunity to correct their demonstrably wrong notions about true discipleship.

Unlike the Third Wave paradigm, Mark's teaching on discipleship concentrates on more than just calling, commissioning and empowering of the disciples to perform healings and exorcisms. In Mark's Gospel the commissioning and charismatic empowering of the Twelve is not aimed at Christians per se, but is intended by Mark to apply to Christians engaged in mission. Here the emphasis is not so much on signs and wonders, but more on Jesus' instructions about how his representatives are to conduct themselves (Mark 6:8–11). In other words, for Mark, signs and wonders are to be regarded as being given primarily to authenticate the (pioneering?) evangelistic mission of the church and its gospel message rather than being an integral, everyday part of his paradigm for discipleship. That the earlier missionary success of the disciples in healing and exorcism is not to be regarded as normative by Mark's readers is underlined when, acting independently, they fail to heal the boy with an evil spirit (Mark 9:14–29). Any share in Jesus' *exousia* that is enjoyed by his disciples/the church is not theirs to control as they will, but becomes available to them from God through prayer only. Signs and wonders have their place in the church's mission, but, compared to the essentials that characterize true discipleship, such power encounters are of relatively little importance. That this is the case is further evidenced by the incident that follows, involving the strange exorcist (9:38–41).

In the central section of Mark's Gospel the Evangelist's critical presentation of the disciples serves as a device to enable him to present his understanding of authentic Christian discipleship as articulated and modelled by Jesus. Jesus' correctives on the true nature of discipleship overrule the disciples' misunderstandings and are aimed not just at the disciples themselves, but at Mark's own community – and, by extension, serve to inform the church today about what it means to be a true follower of Jesus. In essence, Christian discipleship, according to Mark, requires utter commitment, a servant spirit, willingness to suffer and a focus not on a pietistic religious orthodoxy, but on doing the will of God. These are all characteristics modelled in the Gospel by Jesus himself and emphasized as part of the 'messianic corrective', which may be understood as the primary goal for Mark's narrative of 'the good news of Jesus Christ, the Son of God' (Mark 1:1).

Having concluded that Mark 16:9–20 is not original to Mark, and therefore cannot bear the weight placed upon it by the Third Wave, we turned to what most scholars consider to be the original ending to Mark's Gospel. Here we found that Mark leaves us with a positive proclamation of the resurrection to the women (16:6), followed by an angelic commission to the women indicating reinstatement of the disciples and Peter together with a repeat, in 16:7, of Jesus' promise in 14:28 that after the resurrection he would meet the disciples in Galilee. The fear and silence of the women in 16:8 is intended by Mark to provide a dramatic climactic conclusion to the proclamation of Jesus' resurrection, and emphasizes its epiphanic nature.

In terms of contemporary application from a Markan perspective, the emphasis is clearly on what characterizes authentic Christian discipleship. Mark's paradigm for discipleship is derived from the example of Jesus himself and the correctives we find in Mark's often-negative portrayal of the disciples. For Mark, Christian discipleship is not particularly characterized by spectacular charismatic activity, although he does hint at a more formalized healing ministry involving church leaders anointing the sick with oil (Mark 6:13; cf. Jas 5:14). In the end, the model for discipleship that Mark's readers are left with – then and now – is one where, despite weakness, misunderstanding and failure, the disciples are called again by the risen Jesus to continue to follow him on the way. This is a model of discipleship that would have brought comfort to Mark's community, and resonates easily with contemporary Christian experience.

PART THREE

# SIGNS AND WONDERS, COMMISSIONING AND DISCIPLESHIP ACCORDING TO LUKE-ACTS

## Introducing the issues

Empowerment to perform signs and wonders is very definitely subsumed, so far as Matthew and Mark are concerned, under the primary Christological focus for the church's proclamation that Christ is risen and the implications this has for both the message and the nature of Christian discipleship. It is in the light of this core Christological focus for the church's mission that a fore-taste of God's resurrection power becomes manifest in healings, exorcisms and other signs and wonders that may, from time to time, accompany the out-working of the Great Commission. Can the same be said for Luke?

Of the three Synoptic Evangelists Luke is unique in providing us with a second volume in addition to his Gospel in which he narrates the early experi-ence and missionary progression of the post-Easter church, beginning in Jerusalem and ending with Paul's arrival in Rome. There is a substantial amount of material in Luke-Acts that is relevant to our investigation, and we will begin by looking at Luke's presentation of discipleship and commissioning in his Gospel, concentrating on the period of the earthly ministry of Jesus. From here we will move on to the post-Easter period, examining the post-Easter commissioning of the disciples by the risen Jesus in Luke's Gospel and in Acts. Finally, we will consider Luke's understanding of the role of signs and wonders and their relationship to discipleship in the early church as he presents it in Acts.

Turning to Luke's Gospel, we find that Third Wave commentators rely heavily on the commissioning and sending out of the Seventy(-Two) disciples for support of their paradigm for contemporary discipleship. This incident, which occurs only in Luke (Luke 10:1–20), and, when taken together with the mission of the Twelve (Luke 9:1–6, 10a), is considered pivotal by Third Wave commentators for confirmation of their argument that Jesus intended his ministry of proclaiming the kingdom of God and demonstrating its manifest power with signs and wonders to be 'inherited' not just by the Twelve, but potentially by all Christians. This, they argue, is evidenced further by the subsequent activities of Christians described in the book of Acts. Referring particularly to the two missions described by Luke in relation to the contemporary practice of signs and wonders, Charles Kraft of Fuller Theological Seminary writes, 'Practice confirms belief. Jesus taught his disciples first through example. . . . Then he sent them out to practise it for themselves (Luke 9:1–6; 10:1–12).'[1]

Opinions differ occasionally within the Third Wave as to the way in which this NT evidence should be understood and applied today. For example, in discussing the mission of the Seventy(-Two), Jack Deere acknowledges that this may have been a temporary mission with a temporary empowering. Nevertheless, he still goes on to argue that Luke's inclusion of the mission of the Seventy(-Two) militates against the notion that Jesus intended the power to heal and exorcize to be restricted just to the apostles. Less cautiously, Kirk Bottomly argues that Jesus sent out the Twelve and Seventy(-Two) 'to preach the kingdom of God and heal the sick and to demonstrate the power of God to reclaim His kingdom'.[2] In other words, the primary purpose of the missions of the Twelve and the Seventy(-Two) was to demonstrate God's miraculous power. But is this really Luke's intention here?

In his rejection of dispensationalist arguments for the cessation of signs and wonders at the end of the 'apostolic age' (whenever that was!), Don Williams also relies heavily on Luke 9:1ff.//Matthew 10:1ff., followed by Luke 10:1ff. as NT evidence against any understanding that restricts the performance of signs and wonders to the Twelve. Williams, who regards the sending out the Seventy(-Two) as being of special importance for the Third Wave's case, rejects the notion that the two missions might have been limited in terms

1. C. H. Kraft, *Christianity with Power* (Ann Arbor, Mich.: Vine, 1989), p. 87.

2. K. Bottomly, 'Coming out of the Hangar: Confessions of an Evangelical Deist', in G. S. Greig and K. N. Springer (eds.), *The Kingdom and the Power* (Ventura, Calif.: Regal, 1993), p. 265.

of their objectives[3] and argues on the basis of Luke 10:1ff. that Jesus' intention was to share his ministry more widely than just with the Twelve.[4] Based on the evidence of Luke 10:16 he concludes that Jesus also intends his disciples to become 'extensions of himself'.[5] Ignoring the obvious Christological difficulties this raises, Williams quotes, with approval, NT scholar Joachim Jeremias in further support of his case when he writes, 'Authority over the spirits recurs constantly in the mission sayings and is virtually a characteristic of them.'[6] Williams concludes that Jesus deliberately set out to reproduce his 'kingdom ministry' in his disciples, and after Pentecost, throughout the church.[7]

However, Jeremias makes a further important point that Williams chooses to ignore. According to Jeremias, Luke 19:19–20 and parallels belong to early pre-Easter tradition, and differ markedly from the (post-Easter) mission charge to the early Christian missionaries in that their message is characterized by its Christological content.[8] In other words, Williams ignores the theological significance of the pre- and post-Easter situations that is a 'given' for the authors of the NT, and is particularly insensitive to Luke's programme of unveiling epochs of salvation-history as a key to understanding the Evangelist's narrative progression as it unfolds in his two-volume work.

Traditionally, for Pentecostal and charismatic Christians, Luke-Acts has been a primary source for what may be considered normative for contemporary understandings of the role and activity of the Spirit in the life of the church today. Third Wave commentators have also placed much weight on selected material in Luke-Acts, but, as we shall see, Luke also has his own view of miracles and their place in the life of the church. With this in mind, we shall begin our study of Luke by asking, 'What does it mean for Luke to be a follower of Jesus?'

---

3. Ignoring here the fact that in Matthew's Gospel Jesus specifically limits the missionary activities of the Twelve to the 'lost sheep of Israel' (Matt. 10:5).

4. D. Williams, *Signs, Wonders, and the Kingdom of God* (Ann Arbor, Mich.: Vine, 1989), pp. 125–127.

5. Williams, *Signs, Wonders*, p. 129.

6. J. Jeremias, *New Testament Theology Volume One: The Proclamation of Jesus* (ET London: SCM, 1971), p. 95.

7. D. Williams, 'Following Christ's Example: A Biblical View of Discipleship', in G. S. Greig and K. N. Springer (eds.), *The Kingdom and the Power* (Ventura, Calif.: Regal, 1993), p. 183.

8. Jeremias, *New Testament Theology*, p. 95.

## 13. OVERVIEW OF DISCIPLESHIP IN LUKE

What are Luke's chief concerns in his presentation of the disciples and discipleship? Does the evangelist offer clues about these concerns through his handling of his source material? Can particular paradigmatic themes, which relate to Luke's view of discipleship, be detected?

### Luke's use of his sources

According to Fitzmyer, Luke's shift in salvation-historical perspective, from the earlier expectation that the eschaton was imminent to the longer-term present,[1] enabled the evangelist to present his own view of discipleship as a model to be followed by his readers as they came to terms with the delay in the parousia and the need to continue to function in the world as followers of the Way.[2] It is clear that Luke's redactional activity demonstrates a pragmatic approach to discipleship that is geared to following Jesus in the longer term. Two examples of this tendency in Luke's handling of Q can be seen in his

---

1. Already evidenced in Paul's earlier correspondence (see 1 Thess. 4:13ff.).
2. J. A. Fitzmyer, *The Gospel According to Luke (I–IX)* (AB 28; New York: Doubleday, 1981), p. 235.

presentation of the Beatitudes (Luke 6:20b–26//Matt. 5:3–12), and in his expansion of the sayings concerning the conditions for following Jesus (Luke 9:57–62//Matt. 8:18–22).

Matthew's Sermon on the Mount contains nine 'blessings' that spiritualize the qualities required of Jesus' followers. In contrast, Luke's Sermon on the Plain has only four 'blessings' plus four 'woes', all of which provide a much starker presentation of the mundane conditions facing disciples on a day-to-day basis. For Matthew, the qualities that attract God's blessing are being 'poor in spirit', and 'hungering and thirsting after righteousness' (Matt. 5:3, 6), whereas Luke is clearly much more concerned with conditions likely to face disciples in his own generation, such as poverty and hunger (Luke 6:20–21). Both evangelists are conscious of the likelihood that disciples will be persecuted (Luke 6:22–23//Matt. 5:11–12), but again Luke is more explicit about the form persecution is likely to take in terms of exclusion, and followers of Jesus being considered evil.[3]

A second example from Q sets out the conditions required of those who would follow Jesus (Luke 9:59–62//Matt. 8:21–22). Luke's version is expanded so that the person who requests permission to go and bury his father (Luke 9:59//Matt. 8:21) is not only told to leave the dead to 'bury their own dead', which is probably best understood as reflecting an earlier sense of immediacy present in Q, but is also told by the Lukan Jesus to go and 'proclaim the kingdom', which, for Luke, is very much an ongoing missionary task for disciples of Jesus (cf. Acts 8:12; 19:8; 20:25; 28:23, 31). Similarly, in Luke 14:26 those who would follow Jesus are told that their attitude to family ties, in contrast to their commitment to following Jesus, must be one of hatred. Marshall maintains the view that the use of the verb 'to hate' (*miseō*) should be understood in terms of 'loving less' rather than hatred.[4] However, Nolland, who accepts that the language is typical of Semitic hyperbole (e.g. Prov. 13:24; cf. Gen. 29:30–33), insists that the language of hate used in Luke 14:26 is intended to be understood 'with all seriousness' (cf. Ps. 139:21–22; 1QS 1.10; 9.21).[5]

---

3. I. H. Marshall, *The Gospel of Luke: A Commentary on the Greek Text* (Exeter: Paternoster, 1978), p. 252, suggests that Luke is referring here to social ostracism (cf. 1QS 5.18) rather than the practice of exclusion from the synagogue (cf. John 9:22), which was instituted c. AD 85.

4. Marshall, *Gospel of Luke*, p. 592.

5. J. Nolland, *Luke 9:21–18:34* (WBC 35B; Dallas: Word, 1993), p. 762. J. Denney, 'The Word "Hate" in Luke xiv.26', *Exp. Tim* 21 (1909–10), p. 41, draws attention to similar ideas contained in a war song of Tyrtaeus (v. Bergk, *Poetae Lyrici Graeci*,

However, from the context of cross-bearing (14:27) and counting the cost prior to making the radical commitment demanded by Jesus (14:28–33), it is clear that Luke intends his readers to understand the thrust of Jesus' words in the sense of 'renunciation' as a prerequisite for discipleship.[6]

Perhaps the most significant example of the way in which Luke's redaction of his sources sharpens his presentation of discipleship is his addition to Mark 8:34 of 'daily' (9:23). For Mark, the attitude of the disciple is to be one of initial self-renunciation, exemplified in the metaphorical image of condemned persons taking up their cross.[7] However, for Luke, discipleship is understood as being lived out in the context of an ongoing situation. For this reason, it is little wonder that for Luke, disciples of Jesus must first count the cost of completing their course (cf. 14:28). The demand by the Lukan Jesus for his disciples to 'carry their own cross' (my trans.) (14:27) is a commitment to self-denial that he has already made clear must be renewed on a daily basis (9:23).

## Jesus and his followers

It is clear from reading both Luke and Acts that the Third Evangelist has a particular view of discipleship that, through his narrative, he presents to his readers in terms of ideal qualities to be attained by those who are disciples of Jesus of Nazareth. In the Gospel, Luke uses Jesus as the pre-eminent exemplar. As Talbert notes, Jesus is the supreme paradigm for Luke as both the originator and example of a way of life that disciples must emulate.[8] In Acts we see further examples of ideal discipleship presented by Luke primarily through the apostles and other leading characters, all of whom may fairly be described as Luke's 'heroes of the Spirit'.[9]

Luke is the only evangelist who clearly depicts Jesus having crowds of followers, both men and women, all of whom Luke regards as disciples (6:17;

---

ii.P.15), which compares a man's life in battle with 'his enemy' for the honour of Sparta and 'the black doom of death as dear as the beams of the sun'.

6. Cf. O. Michel, μισέω, *TDNT* 4, pp. 690–691; and Marshall, *Gospel of Luke*.

7. Cf. Marshall, *Gospel of Luke*, p. 374.

8. C. H. Talbert, 'Discipleship in Luke-Acts', in F. F. Segovia (ed.), *Discipleship in the New Testament* (Philadelphia: Fortress, 1985), p. 74.

9. We will follow up the implications of this for Luke's understanding of the purpose of signs and wonders and their relationship to discipleship in Acts in later chapters.

10:1; 19:37).[10] In 6:17 Luke mentions a 'great crowd' of disciples who are part of a greater multitude of the people, and in 19:37 Luke tells us that Jesus is greeted by a 'multitude' of disciples. Like his fellow Synoptic Evangelists, Luke concentrates on the Twelve, but he also indicates his widening of the circle of disciples who gather around Jesus by mentioning a number of women who are followers of Jesus, some of whom he names (Luke 8:1–3; 24:10).[11] Importantly, Mary Magdalene and the other women are portrayed by Luke as exhibiting loyalty to Jesus as an ideal quality of discipleship.[12]

According to Luke, when the Twelve are chosen, they are named 'apostles' from the outset by Jesus. Private instruction given to the disciples by Jesus, which is characteristic of Mark, is played down by Luke, who creates scenes where instruction given by Jesus to his disciples takes place in the presence of larger groups such as the crowd (12:1; 20:45) or a larger group of Jesus' disciples (e.g. Luke 6:17, 20).[13] This may well reflect Luke's ecclesiology, where leaders operate within the wider community and are recognized for special tasks by that community (e.g. Acts 1:15ff.; 6:2ff.; 13:1ff.). Freyne perhaps overstates the case when he maintains that the instruction about disciples striving to be like their teacher given in Luke 6:40 is aimed specifically at the Twelve as 'leaders', for there is no evidence to suggest that the explicit context to disciples in general given in 6:1 and 17 has changed. It is true that, following a night of prayer (6:12), Jesus chooses the Twelve from amongst his wider circle of disciples, but immediately following this, Luke explicitly sets the Sermon on the Plain before 'a great crowd of his disciples and a great multitude of people from all Judea, Jerusalem, and the coast of Tyre and Sidon' (6:17).

Beginning in the Gospel with the ministry of John the Baptist in 3:1–6, Luke points embryonically towards two key themes that are central to his presentation of discipleship in the Gospel and Acts: proclamation of the message of God, and the universality of the gospel.[14] Jesus sends out his newly

---

10. Noted also by S. Freyne, *The Twelve: Disciples and Apostles* (London: Sheed & Ward, 1968), p. 208.

11. B. Witherington III, 'On the Road with Mary Magdalene, Joanna, Susanna, and Other Disciples – Luke 8.1–3', *ZNW* 70 (1979), p. 247, makes the point that for Luke, women are also called to be disciples and witnesses. However, Luke clearly has some residual difficulty with the idea of women as witnesses (cf. Luke 24:10–11)!

12. Ibid., p. 244.

13. Freyne, *The Twelve*, p. 209.

14. R. N. Longenecker, 'Taking up the Cross Daily: Discipleship in Luke-Acts', in idem

appointed and empowered apostles to proclaim the kingdom of God (Luke 9:1–2), and in Luke's Gospel alone this missionary activity extends to a larger group chosen from those who follow the Lukan Jesus. Here Jesus appoints Seventy(-Two) of his disciples to act as emissaries, sharing in his mission of healing, exorcism and proclamation of the kingdom of God, as he makes his way towards Jerusalem (10:1). This exemplifies further the requirement upon disciples to preach the kingdom of God with a universal perspective that is central to Luke's story of the expansion of the church in Acts.

## The journey theme

As Sweetland has observed, it is a characteristic of Luke's understanding of discipleship that it involves a journey – from Galilee to Jerusalem (Luke's Gospel) and from Jerusalem to 'the ends of the earth' (Acts 1:7).[15] In Luke's Gospel the disciples follow Jesus along the road from Galilee to Jerusalem. Fitzmyer notes how Lukan redaction indicates that this is also paradigmatic, in a figurative way, for his readers. He writes, 'for Luke Christian discipleship is portrayed not only as the acceptance of a master's teaching, but as the identification of oneself with the master's way of life and destiny in an intimate, personal following of him'.[16]

The idea of following Jesus is presented by Luke as both a model (the Gospel) and a metaphor (Acts), where Jesus' disciples are described as followers of the Way (Acts 9:2; 19:9, 23; 22:4, 14, 22; cf. 18:25–26). According to Fitzmyer, Luke uses akolouthein (to follow) as a generic term for people who physically follow Jesus (e.g. Luke 7:9; 9:11; 18:43; 22:10, 39, 54; 23:27; Acts 12:8, 9; 13:43; 21:36), as a metaphor for discipleship (Acts 9:23, 49, 57, 59, 61; 18:22, 28), and in a corporate sense in Acts where the primitive Christian community are designated followers of 'the way'.[17] The link between following Jesus and being a witness is brought out particularly in Acts when Judas' place is taken by Matthias, whose primary qualification is that he is a witness to both the earthly ministry and resurrection of Jesus (Acts 1:22). This idea of bearing

---

(ed.), *Patterns of Discipleship in the New Testament* (Grand Rapids: Eerdmans, 1996), pp. 57–58.

15. D. M. Sweetland, 'Following Jesus: Discipleship in Luke-Acts', in E. Richard (ed.), *New Views on Luke-Acts* (Collegeville, Minn.: Liturgical, 1990), p. 109.

16. Fitzmyer, *Luke (I–IX)*, p. 241.

17. Ibid., p. 242.

witness is an important aspect of discipleship for Luke. It is emphasized at the end of the Gospel (Luke 24:48) and is then carried forward as a central theme in Acts (1:8; cf. 2:32; 3:15; 5:32; 10:39–41; 13:31).[18]

## Material possessions

An emphasis in Luke's Gospel that reflects God's Old Testament bias towards the poor is brought out in a number of ways. Beginning with Jesus' 'Nazareth manifesto' (Luke 4:18–19), it also manifests itself in parables about the rich and poor (e.g. 12:13–21; 14:15–24; 16:19–31) as well as in other material (e.g. 1:52–53; 6:20–21, 24–25; 14:12–14; 18:18–25). It has been argued that the communal aspect of discipleship which manifests itself explicitly in Acts is foreshadowed in the Gospel at 8:1–3 and is further implied in the two missions (9:1–6; 10:1–24).[19] Jesus' disciples are those who have left everything for the sake of the Gospel (18:28), and, when the early post-Easter community is formed in Jerusalem, they share their material possessions (Acts 4:44–45; cf. 5:1–11) and explicitly meet the needs of the poor (Acts 6:1).[20] Elsewhere in his Gospel Luke makes it clear that Jesus' disciples are to help others (10:25–37), be persistent in prayer (11:5–13; 18:1–8), have a right attitude to possessions and true riches (12:13–34; 16:19–31), have a proper attitude to serving God (19:11–27) and reflect in their attitude to others God's love for the lost (15:8–10, 11–32).[21]

The above brief sketch of Luke's understanding of the qualities required in followers of Jesus, provides us with a Lukan context for a more detailed examination of issues raised by the Third Wave's use of Luke-Acts in support of their paradigm for contemporary discipleship and theology of signs and wonders.

---

18. Ibid., p. 243.
19. Talbert, 'Discipleship in Luke-Acts', p. 72.
20. For a detailed discussion of Luke's attitude to material possessions, see for example M. Hengel, *Property and Riches in the Early Church: Aspects of a Social History of Early Christianity* (ET London: SCM, 1974); L. T. Johnson, *The Literary Function of Possessions in Luke-Acts* (Missoula: Scholars Press, 1977); P. F. Esler, *Community and Gospel in Luke-Acts: The Social and Political Motivations of Lucan Theology* (Cambridge: Cambridge University Press, 1987).
21. Longenecker, 'Taking up the Cross Daily', p. 67.

## 14. THE COMMISSIONING OF JESUS

### The baptism – a paradigm?

In examining Luke's presentation of the baptism/commissioning of Jesus, my purpose here is twofold. Firstly, to provide an important Lukan context for the sending out of the Twelve and the Seventy(-Two) in mission. Secondly, to ask, in what ways, if at all, can we say that Luke's portrayal of the baptism of Jesus is intended to be paradigmatic for the church?

Luke has made a number of redactional changes to his Markan source, but few of them contribute significantly to an understanding of Luke's presentation of the baptism of Jesus as being intentionally paradigmatic for informing subsequent generations of Christian praxis. Luke arranges his narrative so that the reader is told of the imprisonment of John the Baptist before he relates the story of Jesus' baptism and pneumatic anointing. Hans Conzelmann made much of this feature, claiming that it should be understood in terms of Luke's understanding of salvation-history, where John the Baptist and Jesus belong to two separate epochs.[1] More recently, Conzelmann's tightly

---

1. Conzelmann understands Luke's salvation-historical scheme in terms of three distinct epochs: the period of Israel, the period of Jesus, the period of the church. H. Conzelmann, *The Theology of St. Luke* (ET London: SCM, 1960), *passim*.

drawn three-epoch *heilsgeschichtliche* hypothesis has been criticized at several points.[2] In any case Luke shows a distinct tendency elsewhere to neatly round off his narrative concerning the activities surrounding one major character before moving on to another (e.g. Luke 1:80; 3:19–20; 24:50–53; Acts 1:9; 12:17). Nevertheless, Conzelmann's basic three-epoch scheme with the middle period covering Jesus and his earthly ministry to Israel is a helpful aid to understanding Luke's redactional interests here.[3]

Luke begins by placing Jesus' baptism in the context of his being identified with others associated with the Baptist's repentance movement, and explicitly shows Jesus (following the example of other baptismal candidates?) praying after his baptism.[4] Luke tells us that Jesus' baptism took place 'when all the people were baptized' (Luke 3:21). Eduard Schweizer suggests that Luke's intention here is to show that the word which comes to Jesus declaring him to be 'Son of God' occurs in the presence of 'all the people'.[5] However, this assertion is not altogether supported by the evidence. Luke's contextual reference to 'all the people' is better understood in terms of Jesus' identifying himself, and his mission, with the people of Israel/God.[6] Schweizer's suggestion about the significance of the heavenly voice is again not entirely supported by Luke's narrative, which suggests rather that the events following Jesus' baptism (the descent of the Spirit and the heavenly commissioning) occurred in the context of a subjective vision following prayer (cf. Luke 10:18; Acts 10:9ff.). Therefore, it appears here that Luke is emphasizing Jesus' strong identification and solidarity with the people of Israel/God within the overall context of his being commissioned by God.[7]

This understanding is strengthened further when viewed as part of the

---

2. See for example I. H. Marshall, *Luke: Historian and Theologian* (Exeter: Paternoster, 1970). For a critique of Conzelmann with reference to John the Baptist and the three epochs, see S. G. Wilson, *The Gentiles and the Gentile Mission in Luke-Acts* (Cambridge: Cambridge University Press, 1973), pp. 60–67.

3. Viewed less rigidly than Conzelmann's Satan-free period (Luke 4:14 – 22:3).

4. Cf. *T. Levi* 4.2. Luke's presentation of prayer and discipleship is discussed further in chapter 13.

5. E. Schweizer, *The Good News According to Luke* (ET London: SPCK, 1984), p. 79.

6. Apart from two occasions (Acts 15:14 and 18:10) where the context makes it clear that Gentiles are being included in the people of God, Luke always uses the singular *laos* to refer to Jews only. See Wilson, *Gentile Mission*, p. 35.

7. Cf. R. L. Brawley, *Luke-Acts and the Jews* (SBLMS; Atlanta, Ga.: Scholars Press, 1987), p. 23.

wider narrative, where Jesus returns to Nazareth in the power of the Spirit and identifies himself with Isaiah's prophecy, thus setting the agenda for his earthly ministry (Luke 4:18–19; cf. Isa. 61:1–2a). The context provided here for the Nazareth pericope clearly focuses on the key Lukan theme of the power of the Spirit, and Luke introduces Jesus' public ministry by presenting him as a spirit-empowered teacher/healer whose mission is to proclaim YHWH's Jubilee. Twelftree notes that an important clue to Luke's understanding of Jesus' ministry is to be found in the close connection Luke makes between Jesus' ministry of teaching and healing and his being anointed with the Spirit.[8] It is, therefore, all the more shocking for Luke's readers when, after initial approval (Luke 4:22), Jesus' countrymen become so outraged by his assertions that they seek to kill him (4:29–30).

The underlying narrative purpose appears to be that Luke wants to establish his motif of the rejection of Jesus from the outset. If this is the case, then it clearly mitigates against a paradigmatic understanding of Luke's portrayal of Jesus' baptism and pneumatic anointing. Rather, they should be understood as being, for Luke, a unique event in salvation-history. In other words, from the outset Luke has established for his readers the uniqueness of the earthly ministry of Jesus within salvation-history. This in turn cautions against any cavalier tendency to treat the words and actions of the Lukan Jesus as normative for today. That is not to say that Luke does not provide clear models for Christian discipleship in his presentation of Jesus and those with whom Jesus interacts. It is simply that any claim for a Lukan paradigm that may be considered normative for today must be measured against the 'given' of the unique place the earthly Jesus and the apostles hold for Luke in salvation-history.

## The importance of prayer

Luke's explicit mention of Jesus praying following his baptism may possibly reflect later Christian baptismal practice, but more likely is placed there by the Evangelist for the following reasons:

1 To emphasize the importance of prayer for Luke (Luke 3:21; 5:16; 6:12; 9:18, 28–29; 11:1; 22:41; 23:46; Acts 1:24; 6:6; 8:15; 9:11; 9:40; 10:9; 11:5; 12:12; 13:3; 16:25; 20:36; 21:5; 22:17; 28:8).

---

8. G. H. Twelftree, *Jesus the Miracle Worker* (Downers Grove, Ill.: IVP, 1999), p. 146.

2  To establish the link between prayer and heavenly visions (Luke 1:10ff.; 9:28–36; 22:39–46; Acts 1:14; 2:1ff.; 10:9ff.).

3  To show that prayer is the precursor for receiving or being empowered by the Spirit (Luke 11:13; Acts 1:14; 2:1–4; 2:21, 39; 4:23–31; 8:15–17; 22:16).

Immediately following the baptism of Jesus, the descent of the Spirit is described, followed by the verbal commissioning. The eschatological significance of these events is considerably heightened by Matthew when he replaces Mark's graphic description of the heavens being 'torn apart' (Mark 1:10) with the stylized apocalyptic introduction 'and behold, the heaven was opened' (my trans.) (Matt. 3:16//Luke 3:21).[9] Luke's use of the verb, *anoigō* (to open) indicates that he is also aware of the apocalyptic significance of the event from his likely knowledge of LXX parallels,[10] although, being more concerned here with the descent of the Spirit, he does not expand this in quite the same vivid way as the First Evangelist.

Luke's more objective description of the descent of the (Holy) Spirit and God's voice is to emphasize for his readers the reality of the experience.[11] In verse 22, as heaven opens, the Holy Spirit 'descends in bodily form as a dove' (my trans.). Again, this is different from Mark's absolute 'the Spirit', although we might expect Luke to use 'Holy Spirit', which occurs twelve times in his Gospel and forty-one times in Acts.[12] However, there is nothing here to

---

9.  Matthew uses the more usual plural form 'and behold, the heavens were opened' (see e.g. Ezekiel 1:1 LXX; *T. Levi* 18:6–7; *T. Judah* 24:2), whereas Luke uses the singular 'the heaven' (Luke 3:21).

10. In discussing the eschatological role of the Spirit, J. D. G. Dunn, 'Baptism in the Spirit: A Response to Pentecostal Scholarship on Luke-Acts', *JPT* 3 (1993), p. 21, makes the important point, also relevant here, that whilst Luke was very familiar with the LXX, it is doubtful that he had detailed knowledge of either Jewish apocalyptic writings, Qumran literature or rabbinic tradition, as these do not appear to inform his theological background to the same extent as the LXX does.

11. Schweizer, *Good News According to Luke*, p. 78. J. Nolland, *Luke 1–9:20* (WBC 35A; Dallas: Word, 1989), p. 161. This appears to be a Lukan tendency. See for example Luke's description of the risen Jesus' appearance to the apostles (Luke 24:36–51, and especially vv. 39–43) and Peter's escape from prison (Acts 12:6–17, and especially vv. 7 and 9).

12. Cf. Mark four times, Matthew five times, John three times. Of the twelve occurrences in Luke, all except for four occurrences – Luke 3:16 (= Mark

suggest that Luke is presenting a paradigm for the experience of receiving the Spirit.[13] Luke's emphasis is rather on Jesus being anointed with the Spirit in fulfilment of Isaiah 61:1 (cf. Luke 4:18).

So far I have suggested that any paradigmatic intentions by Luke appear to stress the centrality of prayer as the natural precursor to important events. As such, the significance of Jesus' prayer here should be taken in context with other similar examples of prayer that occur in Luke and Acts. In Luke's use of the term 'Holy Spirit' there is a parallel with the post-Easter experience of Jesus' followers, but not a direct paradigm. In the case of Jesus' pneumatic anointing, there is a unique fulfilment of OT prophecy that at best foreshadows, but is not necessarily paradigmatic for, the expectation[14] and experience of the post-Easter community (Acts 2:4 and *passim*). That this is the case seems to be confirmed further by Luke's description of the Holy Spirit descending 'in bodily form'.

There has been much speculation about the intended meaning of the dove-imagery found in all four Gospel accounts (Matt. 3:16; Mark 1:10; Luke 3:22; John 1:32), but there is no consensus.[15] Whatever the original meaning of this imagery, Luke's use of graphic language may be understood as foreshadowing his equally graphic wind and fire imagery at Pentecost (Acts 2:2–3).[16] In other words, we may say no more than what happened to the disciples at Pentecost was foreshadowed or 'patterned after Jesus' experience at Jordan'.[17]

As a further counterbalance against the danger of overshadowing the uniqueness of Jesus' baptism and reception of the Spirit in order to force Luke's paradigmatic intentions, it is worth looking briefly at two suggestions

---

1:8//Matt. 3:11), Luke 11:13 (= Q; cf. Matt. 7:11), Luke 12:10 (= Mark 3:29//Matt. 12:32) and Luke 12:12 (= Mark 13:11) – are unique to Luke.

13. So Nolland, *Luke 1–9:20*, p. 161.

14. Acts 1:5. Cf. Matt. 28:19; John 20:22.

15. For a summary of the many suggestions, see Marshall, *Luke*, pp. 153–154; and for a much fuller treatment, see Keck, 'The Spirit and the Dove', *NTS* 17 (1970–1), pp. 41–67.

16. Schweizer, *Good News According to Luke*, p. 78, suggests that the more graphic and corporeal descent of the Spirit in bodily form as described by Luke is typical of Luke's 'special language of the Spirit' (Acts 2:4; 4:31; 10:44–46; cf. 8:17–19).

17. B. Aker, 'New Directions in Lukan Theology: Reflections of Luke 3:21–22 and Some Implications', in P. E. Elbert (ed.), *Faces of Renewal* (Peabody, Mass: Hendrickson, 1988), p. 123.

(out of many) that have been made concerning the underlying meaning behind Luke's use of dove-imagery and that serve to highlight the uniqueness of the event for Luke. The first regards the dove as a symbol for Israel.[18] Given the likely dominical origin[19] of the tradition, an original Semitic background seems almost certain.[20] In Jewish tradition the dove was a symbol for Israel[21] and it has been suggested that Mark (Mark 1:10), invoking the servant imagery of Isaiah 41:2, intended his readers to understand that with the reception of the Spirit, Jesus became the representative of Israel,[22] which fits

---

18. Marshall is too dismissive of Luke's possible use of dove-imagery being aimed by Luke at the Graeco-Roman world, on the grounds that the imagery should be understood in terms of a Semitic background. Although an original Semitic background seems likely, Marshall is even more dismissive of the view that the dove is a symbol for Israel (Marshall, *Luke*, p. 153).

19. As a visionary experience of Jesus (cf. Luke 10:18). So for example J. D. G. Dunn, *Jesus and the Spirit: A Study of the Religious and Charismatic Experience of Jesus and the First Christians as Reflected in the New Testament* (London: SCM, 1975), p. 65.

20. Against L. Morris, *The Gospel According to Luke* (Leicester: IVP, 1974), p. 99, who allows that in rabbinic sources the dove was a symbol for Israel but who, nevertheless, insists here that the dove-imagery must be taken as a piece of early Christian symbolism rather than something taken over from Jewish or Hellenistic sources. It must be noted here that Morris offers no arguments to substantiate his claim.

21. H. L. von Strack and P. Billerbeck, *Kommentar zum Neuen Testament aus Talmud und Midrasch*, vols. 1–7 (Munich: Beck, 1922–61), vol. 1, pp. 123–125. Cf. Hos. 11:11; Pss. 68:13; 74:19. *Midr. Cant.*; 1:15 (93b); 2:14 (10a). Commenting on the phrase 'As the wings of a dove covered with silver', the writer of *Midr. Ps.* 68:13 asks, 'Why is *Israel* compared to a dove?' C. G. Montefiore and H. Loewe (eds.), *A Rabbinic Anthology* (New York: Schocken, 1974), p. 261; italics mine. In Ps.-Philo we find in retelling the OT story of the ninth judge of Israel, Jephthah (Judg. 11:1–12), Ps.-Philo 39:5 reads, 'And the people said to him [Jephthah], "Let the dove to which Israel has been compared teach you . . ."' Ps.-Philo is possibly to be dated as early as 135 BC, although most probably during the first century AD. See further D. J. Harrington, 'Pseudo-Philo', in J. H. Charlesworth (ed.), *The Old Testament Pseudepigrapha* (London: Darton Longman & Todd, 1985), vol. 2, p. 299.

22. So J. D. G. Dunn, *Baptism in the Holy Spirit: A Re-examination of the New Testament Teaching on the Gift of the Spirit in Relation to Pentecostalism Today* (London: SCM, 1970), p. 30.

well with Mark's idea of Jesus as the suffering servant (cf. Mark 10:45//Matt. 20:28). However, this does not guarantee that Luke understood the dove-imagery found in his Markan source in the same way, although it would also fit well with Luke's efforts to restrict the ministry of Jesus to Israel (cf. Luke 7:1–10//Matt. 8:5–13). It is also tempting to think that Luke could be drawing particular attention to the descent of the Spirit in dovelike bodily form as a symbol of Israel to underline the fact that Jesus' (unique) mission was to Israel.

The second suggestion looks at the impact of dove symbolism in the Graeco-Roman world. According to C. H. Talbert, Luke's description of the descent of the Spirit upon Jesus 'in bodily form like a dove' would evoke for his Graeco-Roman readers the Roman use of the flight of birds to discern the omens – good or bad.[23] 'For the Holy Spirit to come to Jesus in the form of a dove would say to Mediterranean hearers that Jesus was beloved of God.'[24]

This is certainly in line with the heavenly affirmation that, following the descent of the Spirit, Jesus is 'the beloved' and again serves to emphasize the uniqueness of the occasion. At the same time a parallel is drawn with the graphic imagery describing the descent of the Spirit at the time of Pentecost (Acts 2:2–3), which now speaks of eschatological judgment (cf. Luke 3:16//Matt. 3:11).

### Conclusions

We set out to answer the question 'In what way, if at all, can Luke's description of Jesus' baptism be considered as paradigmatic for the church?' The evidence suggests that Jesus' commissioning for ministry at Jordan was portrayed by Luke as an experience unique to Jesus and, consequently, a unique event in salvation-history. Also for Luke, Jesus' pneumatic anointing marks him out as the representative man in terms of his receiving the Spirit.[25] Whilst Jesus' pneumatic anointing foreshadows, to a certain extent, the experience of his adherents at Pentecost, Luke's description of Jesus' baptism is not intended by him to provide a paradigm that should be considered normative for the

---

23. C. H. Talbert, *Reading Luke: A Literary and Theological Commentary on the Third Gospel* (New York: Crossroad, 1984), p. 40.

24. Ibid.

25. Cf. Dunn, *Baptism in the Holy Spirit*, p. 41.

church. Rather, it has the effect of establishing, from the beginning of Jesus' ministry, the unique place held by the earthly Jesus in the salvation-historical scheme that overarches Luke's two-volume work, and already allotted to Jesus by Luke in the birth narrative when he tells us that Jesus was conceived by the Spirit (1:39).

# 15. LUKE AND THE TWELVE (LUKE 6:12–16)

## Jesus – a man under authority

Luke's rendering of the call of the first disciples appears in Mark and Matthew in a different form (Luke 5:1–11; cf. Mark 1:16–20//Matt. 4:18–22). Evans maintains that the whole section (Luke 5:1 – 6:11) is of 'fundamental importance' for our understanding of Luke's treatment of discipleship in Luke-Acts.[1] Perhaps most significantly, from Luke 5:1 onwards we read of occasions when Jesus begins to share his ministry of preaching, healing and exorcism with chosen disciples (Luke 9:1–6, 10; 10:1–20) and these occasions foreshadow for Luke's readers the way in which Jesus' ministry will eventually extend beyond Israel to the whole world through the agency of the apostles and other chosen men of the Spirit.

Luke has delayed the calling of the Twelve until 5:1ff. in order to establish for his readers the beginning of (and *raison d'être* for) Jesus' ministry (4:14–44).

---

1. C. F. Evans, *Saint Luke* (London: SCM, 1990), p. 287, who notes particularly the principal role of Peter and his companions in both the Gospel and the life of the early church (Luke 8:51; 9:28, 54; Acts 3:1; 4:13; 8:14ff.; 12:2), and especially Peter as the leader of the apostolic band and missionary to the Gentiles (Luke 9:2; 22:31; Acts 2:14–37; 5:29; 10–11; 15:14).

Jesus directs the fishing activity of the putative disciples with its miraculous results and thus demonstrates the 'power' (*dynamis*) at work in him, and which Luke's readers already know is effective in exorcisms and healings.[2] Luke has highlighted this feature of Jesus' ministry for his readers from 4:14, when Jesus, filled with the power of the Spirit, returns from the wilderness to Galilee and begins to gain a reputation as a teacher and healer (4:15, 23). Following his rejection in Nazareth, Jesus returns to Capernaum, where he continues to teach and perform exorcisms (4:31ff.).

In concluding the story of the healing of the man with an unclean spirit, Luke uses the questions raised by the crowd about the nature of Jesus' authority to perform exorcisms as a rhetorical device for his readers (4:36). For Luke, it is important to establish that Jesus is a man under authority and this is made clear throughout his Gospel (e.g. Luke 4:32, 36; 5:24; 7:7b–8), with the nature of this authority being debated more fully in Luke 11:14–23 (cf. 20:1–8). Just as Jesus is presented by Luke as a man under authority, so too are those whom Jesus commissions to share in his authority (cf. 9:1; 10:1, 19; 24:49). In other words, the idea of being 'under authority' is the key to understanding the way in which Jesus' disciples share his ministry in Luke's Gospel, including their being empowered to perform signs and wonders.

### Called to be fishers of men

Luke first introduces his readers to Simon Peter when Jesus visits Simon's house and heals his mother-in-law (4:38–39). By reordering his text in this way,[3] Luke gives the impression that Simon was already known to Jesus. Leaney's suggestion that Simon was already a disciple has the effect of rendering Luke's deliberate reordering of his source material somewhat redundant and must, therefore, be rejected.[4] Following the healing of Peter's mother-in-law, Luke tells us that Jesus heals many, and his true identity as Messiah and Son of God is acknowledged by the demons he has cast out (cf. Mark 1:32–33). Thus it is only after Jesus' reputation as a teacher, healer and

---

2. Cf. L. T. Johnson, *The Gospel of Luke* (SP 3; Collegeville, Minn.: Liturgical, 1991), p. 89.

3. Mark waits until Jesus has called his first disciples – Simon, Andrew, James and John – before relating the healing of Simon's mother-in-law (Mark 1:16–20, 29–30).

4. A. R. C. Leaney, *The Gospel According to St. Luke* (London: A. & C. Black, 1958), p. 124.

exorcist has been firmly established by Luke that his narrative turns to the call of the first disciples.

Importantly, Luke adds to his Markan source for the story of the call of Peter (Mark 1:16–20) the element of a 'divine call'. This element of divine call we saw was present in the commissioning of Jesus and is characteristic of Lukan commissionings here and in Acts.[5] In order to heighten the dramatic effect, Luke adds to his setting for the call of Jesus' first disciples the story of the miraculous catch of fish, which is also found in a different form in the 'appendix' to John's Gospel (21:1–8), where it introduces an extended resurrection appearance.[6] In using the miracle story as his context, Luke associates this important call to discipleship with a revelation to Peter of the divine authority of the one who is calling him and his companions to follow him (5:1–11 and especially v. 8). In a similar way later in Acts, Paul's call to discipleship is also accompanied by a heavenly revelation that guarantees the authoritative nature of Paul's vocation. Confronted with their respective revelations of Jesus' heavenly authority, both Peter and Paul fall to the ground.[7]

Luke concludes both his call narrative here, and the call of Levi in 5:27–31, by referring to themes he considers important. In 5:9 the amazement of the onlookers is indicative of Jesus' divine authority; the reference in 5:10 to 'catching people' foreshadows the missionary activity that is integral to the ministry of Jesus in the Gospel and that of his followers in Acts; the immediacy of the response of Peter and his companions in leaving everything and following Jesus together with Levi's response to Jesus' call to repentance illustrate what is, for Luke, the appropriate response to Jesus' call to follow him (cf. 14:33; 18:28).[8] By the time we reach Luke 6:12, Jesus has an expanded band of followers from whom he is able to choose the Twelve.

Although Luke has introduced Jesus' ministry in terms of teaching, healing and exorcism, like the other Synoptic Evangelists Luke also makes it clear throughout his Gospel and Acts that discipleship amounts to much more than proclaiming the kingdom and performing signs and wonders. In presenting

---

5. Discussed further in chapter 5.

6. Cf. John 20:31, which appears to indicate the original ending of the Fourth Gospel. For a detailed discussion of Luke's calling of the disciples within the context of the miraculous catch of fish, see J. Delorme, 'Luc v.1–2: analyse structurale et histoire de la rédaction', *NTS* 18 (1971–2), pp. 331–350.

7. Noted by Evans, *Saint Luke*, p. 28, who points out that similar language is used in Luke 5:8 and in Acts 9:4.

8. In contrast to the rich ruler portrayed later in 18:18–25 and cf. vv. 28–30.

Jesus to his readers as a model or paradigm for discipleship, Luke clearly shows Jesus to be a teacher concerned with the personal qualities of those who would follow him. In so doing, Luke deliberately uses the wider context in which he sets the call of the first disciples to emphasize prayer as an important characteristic of discipleship. Jesus is presented by Luke as a man of prayer, and here he serves as a paradigm for his followers.

## Prayer and discipleship

In Luke's Gospel the word 'prayer' and the verb 'to pray' occur forty-seven times, whereas they occur only seventeen times in Matthew and twelve times in Mark.[9] In addition to occasions where material on prayer occurs elsewhere in Luke's sources, there are also a significant number of occasions that occur only in Luke, when Jesus is found at prayer (Luke 3:21; 5:12–16; 6:12–16; 9:18–22, 28–29; 22:32; 23:34; cf. 11:5–8; 18:1–8; 9–14). Luke's didactic theme of prayer continues to be exemplified in the life of the early church (e.g. Acts 1:12–14, 24–25; 2:42, 46–47; 4:23–31; 6:2–4, 6; 7:59–60; 8:14–17, 22; 9:11, 13–14, 17, 40; 10:19; 12:5, 12; 13:1–3, 48; 14:23; cf. 16:13–16; 20:36; 21:5; 22:17–18; 24:11; 28:8). Lane notes a number of occurrences of thematic parallels between the prayers of Jesus in Luke's Gospel and the prayers of the early church in Acts.[10]

The importance of prayer for Luke can be seen from the beginning of Jesus' ministry, where it is only Luke who portrays Jesus praying at his baptism (3:21). From here, Luke 'punctuates' Jesus' ministry with the same motif at other key points throughout his Gospel (e.g. 5:16; 6:12; 9:18, 28–29; 11:1; 22:42, 44–45; 23:46).[11] Following the call of the first disciples and the healing of the leper (5:12–14), Luke inserts another summary of Jesus' activity with an inter-

---

9.  T. J. Lane, *Luke and the Gentile Mission: Gospel Anticipates Acts* (European University Studies 571; Frankfurt am Main: Lang, Europäischer Verlag der Wissenschaften, 1996), p. 66.

10.  Lane, *Luke and the Gentile Mission*, p. 67. Examples include prayer and reception of the Spirit (Luke 3:21–22; Acts 1:12–14; 2:1–4; 4:31; 8:15) and prayer before making a decision (Luke 6:12–13/Acts 1:15–26; 6:1–6). Also, Jesus' words of resignation to the will of God (Luke 22:42) are echoed by Paul's companions in Acts 21:14, and Jesus' words at the point of death (23:46) are echoed by Stephen, the first Christian martyr.

11.  Johnson, *Gospel of Luke*, p. 69.

esting biographical reference to Jesus' habit of withdrawing to quiet places to pray (5:16). In doing this, Luke clearly uses Jesus as an example to inform Christian discipleship. Prior to Jesus' selecting the Twelve from his wider circle of followers, Luke tells us that Jesus spends the night in prayer (6:12).[12] It has been suggested that in setting the scene in the mountains, Luke is alerting his readers to the importance of what is about to take place. According to Green, Luke's topographical setting suggests that he is reflecting the practice found in the OT where mountains are often the location for theophanies and divine revelation.[13] In contrast, Evans suggests that the location is to be understood theologically rather than topographically, the reference being to a new Sinai.[14] Alternatively, it may be that the mountains here are simply a descriptive representation of the 'deserted places' referred to in Luke's previous intriguing comment in 5:16. Whatever the case may be, there can be no other conclusion than that Luke's emphasis on prayer in the ministry of Jesus is clearly intended to have a didactic purpose for his readers.

Green suggests that for Luke, the night of prayer, which precedes the appointment of the Twelve, provides a model for the idea of the divine will being discerned through prayer.[15] This model is further demonstrated in Acts, for example, when the Seven are appointed in order to enable the Twelve to devote themselves 'to prayer and to serving the word' (Acts 6:4), and when Paul and Barnabas are commissioned as missionaries by the church in Antioch (13:3).[16]

Finally, Jesus tells a parable that occurs only in Luke, making the point that persistence in prayer is necessary in order to effect a change in the circumstances (Luke 18:1–8). Elsewhere in the Gospel, Jesus makes similar points about the need for persistence in prayer (11:5–8, 9–13). Persistence in prayer is then demonstrated in Acts when we are told that, following the death of James, and Peter's subsequent imprisonment, the church gather together and

---

12. This all-night prayer vigil is indicated by Luke's use of *dianyktereuōn* (lit. 'he was spending the whole night'), which occurs only here in the NT (cf. Job 2:9c LXX), noted by D. L. Bock, *Luke 1:1–9:50* (Grand Rapids, Mich.: Baker, 1994), p. 540.

13. J. B. Green, *The Gospel of Luke* (Grand Rapids, Mich.: Eerdmans, 1997), p. 258.

14. Evans, *Saint Luke*, p. 319.

15. Green, *Gospel of Luke*, p. 258. For Luke's view of the need for persistence in prayer, see especially Luke 18:1–8 (cf. 22:46).

16. For a detailed analysis of prayer in Luke-Acts, see A. A. Trites, 'The Prayer Motif in Luke-Acts', in C. H. Talbert (ed.), *Perspectives on Luke-Acts* (Edinburgh: T. & T. Clark, 1978), pp. 168–185.

offer earnest prayer to God on Peter's behalf (Acts 12:5). They continue in prayer, not knowing of Peter's escape until he arrives at the home of John Mark where they are gathered, and even then can hardly believe that their prayers have been answered (Acts 12:15).

For our purpose here, the overriding point is not so much that prayer occurs frequently in Luke-Acts, or that it is an important Lukan theme (although both are true); its importance lies in the fact that by persistently focusing on prayer in his Gospel and Acts, Luke shows it to be an important characteristic of discipleship, and this alone alerts us to the fact that Luke has more to say about discipleship than just signs, wonders and power encounters.

## The Twelve as apostles

So far, I have argued that in his presentation of the calling of the Twelve Luke makes significant editorial changes to his source material, all of which throw light on his presentation of Christian discipleship. Unlike Mark and Matthew, and in addition to his redactional reference to Jesus praying, Luke makes it clear that the Twelve have been chosen from amongst a larger group of Jesus' followers (6:13, 17). Luke also makes it clear that the call of the Twelve, together with their authoritative designation as *apostoloi*, comes from the earthly Jesus, although at this point in the narrative Luke's readers do not yet know what it means to be an 'apostle'. The important point here is that from the moment of their institution the Twelve are designated 'apostles' by the Lukan Jesus, so that the associated ideas of commissioning and representation are present for his readers from the outset.[17] However, as his narrative unfolds, Luke follows his Markan source in using the designation 'the Twelve' when Jesus first sends his disciples out in mission (Luke 9:1//Mark 6:7).[18] When the Twelve return, Luke also follows Mark in calling the disciples 'apostles'.

Apostles clearly have a missionary function, but not all missionaries are

---

17. For discussion of the background and meaning of the NT idea of apostleship, see for example F. H. Agnew, 'The Origin of the New Testament Apostle-Concept: A Review of Research', *JBL* 105.1 (1986), pp. 75–96; K. H. Rengstorf, ἀποστέλλω, ἀπόστολος, *TDNT* 1, pp. 398–447; C. K. Barrett, *The Signs of an Apostle* (Cato Lecture, 1969; rev. Carlisle: Paternoster, 1996); J. A. Kirk, 'Apostleship Since Rengstorf: Towards a Synthesis', *NTS* 21 (1975), pp. 249–264.

18. Matthew's redaction of Mark, the 'twelve disciples' (Matt. 10:1), avoids the formal title.

called apostles by Luke. Most notably, the Seventy(-Two) sent out in mission in Luke 10 remain for Luke the Seventy(-Two), although this group almost certainly includes the Twelve.[19] In Luke 11:1 the apostles are linked with the prophets, indicating both their role (as the Twelve) in eschatological Israel and, later in Acts, in the suffering of church leaders for the sake of the kingdom (Acts 12:2ff.). In Acts 1:2 there is a reiteration of Luke 6:13, where Luke reminds his readers that the apostles were chosen by Jesus and are the recipients of the dominical teaching, prior to Easter through the person of Jesus, and now 'through the Holy Spirit'. The importance of the Twelve, both as the founding representatives of the church and as keepers of the authoritative dominical tradition, as well as representatives of the new Israel, is emphasized again by Luke in Acts 1:25–26, where he describes the election of Matthias as taking place in order to restore the depleted membership of the apostolic group from eleven to twelve. The election of Matthias is described explicitly by Luke in terms of apostleship, and is central to his understanding of what qualifies a person to be a founding pillar of the church.

As numbers are added to the early Jerusalem community, the focus of their life together is on the apostles' teaching (Acts 2:42; cf. Matt. 28:20) as well as prayer and communal meals. Also, for the first time in Acts, we are told that signs and wonders are a feature associated with the church in Jerusalem, but focused explicitly on the apostles as agents of God's *dynamis* (power) rather than on the wider circle of disciples who have experienced the outpouring of the Spirit and form the body of the community. It is the apostles who are empowered with *dynamis* to perform signs and wonders (Acts 2:43). As I will discuss further below, it is precisely this combination of *pneuma* and *dynamis* that Luke regards as being effective in the performance of signs and wonders, and is limited to the apostolic band together with specifically named heroes of the Spirit who feature as pioneering characters in his narrative of the expansion of the church's mission from Jerusalem to the ends of the earth / Rome (Acts 1:8; 28:11ff.). For Luke, the appointment of the Twelve is divinely inspired and carries an authority that goes back to Jesus himself.

Commentators have pointed out that Luke's use of the noun *apostolos* in contrast to Mark's use of the verb (followed by Matthew), suggests that Luke was introducing his own ideas at this point.[20] Luke has already made it clear

---

19. Luke 10:1, 17. For further discussion, see chapter 15.

20. See for example J. Dupont, 'Le nom d'apôtre a-t-il été donné aux douze par Jésus?', *OrSyr* 1 (1956), pp. 267–290 and 425–444, and especially 435ff.; followed by S. Freyne, *The Twelve: Disciples and Apostles* (London: Sheed & Ward, 1968), p. 93.

that the verb *apostellō* (to send) carries with it the sense of being 'sent with a commission' (Luke 1:19, 26; 4:18, 43).[21] As Green aptly puts it, the naming of the Twelve as apostles here is a 'prolegomenon to instruction in discipleship'.[22] But more than this, having Jesus designate the Twelve as apostles at this point in the narrative serves at least two purposes: it establishes the appointment of the Twelve as apostles firmly in the earthly ministry of Jesus, and this will be of particular significance for Acts (cf. Acts 1:12ff.);[23] it also alerts Luke's readers, even at this early stage, that the Twelve are somehow set apart from the rest of Jesus' disciples, of whom, according to Luke, there were many more than just the Twelve.

## Conclusions

The unique status attributed to the Twelve as 'apostles' by the Lukan Jesus must act as a cautionary note for any exegesis that views the apostles as little more than examples of an intentional model of discipleship that primarily emphasizes the performance of signs and wonders. To do so ignores not only the fuller presentation of Christian discipleship found in Luke-Acts, but also ignores Luke's obvious concern to establish the idea of authority within the church being derived from the earthly Jesus himself and passed on through those whom Jesus appointed to succeed him and act as guarantors of that authority to succeeding Christian generations.

---

21. Johnson, *Gospel of Luke*, p. 103. In the Q tradition, the significance of appointing the Twelve appears to be the inauguration of the new Israel, with the apostles corresponding to the twelve tribes of Israel (Luke 22:30//Matt. 19:28; cf. Jas 1:1). According to G. Vermes, *The Dead Sea Scrolls in English* (Harmondsworth: Pelican, 1962), pp. 17–18, similar ideas are reflected in the way the Qumran community was divided.
22. Green, *Gospel of Luke*, pp. 258–259.
23. Contra G. B. Caird, *The Gospel of Saint Luke* (Harmondsworth: Penguin, 1963), p. 100, who suggests that Luke is guilty here of an anachronism.

# 16. THE MISSION OF THE TWELVE (LUKE 9:1–6)

## Luke's sources

Following Jesus' choosing of the Twelve from amongst the much larger group of disciples (6:13; cf. 6:17–19), Luke continues his narrative by emphasizing Jesus' power to heal as he ministers to the crowds of both disciples and onlookers (6:17). In this summary of Jesus' activities we get a useful insight into Luke's understanding of Jesus' healing ministry (6:18b). Firstly, whilst elsewhere Luke brings out the importance of exorcism for Jesus' healing ministry,[1] he does not appear to differentiate to any marked degree between physical healing and exorcism – both are healed/cured (6:18).[2] Secondly, we are told that as healing takes place, power (*dynamis*) goes out from Jesus (6:19). It appears, then, that for Luke, it is Jesus' *dynamis* through which the miracles are performed.[3]

---

1. Graham Twelftree notes, for example, how in the healing of Peter's mother-in-law the Lukan Jesus *rebukes* the fever, an action that is a characteristic of an exorcism (4:39). G. H. Twelftree, *Jesus the Miracle Worker* (Downers Grove, Ill.: IVP, 1999), p. 176.
2. Noted by Twelftree who makes the further point that 'amongst the gospel writers Luke has the least clear distinction between healing and exorcism . . . he in effect gives all sickness a demonic and cosmic dimension' (ibid.).
3. Ibid. and p. 392 n. 35 notes that of the four places where Luke attributes Jesus'

According to Schweizer, Luke understands the Spirit in typically Jewish terms as the Spirit of prophecy.[4] Consequently, Schweizer argues, Luke never attributes signs and wonders to the Spirit, preferring to associate healing power with either the person of Jesus himself, or faith in the name of Jesus, and later with objects associated with the disciples such as a shadow or handkerchief (cf. Acts 5:15; 19:12).[5] Against Schweizer, Twelftree points to several occasions when Luke uses *dynamis* and *pneuma* together (e.g. Luke 1:17, 35; 4:14; cf. Acts 1:8; 4:7, 8; 10:38),[6] and in Luke 1:17 and Acts 10:38 particularly we have examples of *pneuma* and *dynamis* acting together in close association. Twelftree concludes, rightly, that 'miracles are to be attributed directly to the Spirit or to the power of the Spirit'.[7]

From Luke 6:20 there follows an extended teaching section on characteristics of discipleship that is aimed at the wider group of Jesus' disciples (6:20–49),[8] followed in chapter 9 with a focus on the relationship between Jesus and the Twelve. In sharing his ministry here, Jesus prepares the way for further teaching about discipleship that occurs throughout the rest of the Gospel. In Luke's sources there are two accounts of Jesus commissioning,

---

miraculous power to his *dynamis*, three are redactional (Luke 4:36//Mark 1:26; Luke 5:17//Mark 2:2; Luke 6:19//Mark 3:10; cf. Luke 8:46//Mark 5:30).

4. E. Schweizer, 'The Power of the Spirit: The Uniformity and Diversity of the Concept of the Holy Spirit in the New Testament', *Int* 6 (1952), pp. 264–268; πνεῦμα, *TDNT* 6, pp. 407 and 409; *The Holy Spirit* (ET Philadelphia: Fortress, 1980), pp. 58–60.

5. Schweizer, πνεῦμα, p. 407.

6. Twelftree, *Jesus the Miracle Worker*, p. 171. M. M. B. Turner, *Power from on High: The Spirit in Israel's Restoration and Witness in Luke-Acts* (JPTSup 9; Sheffield: Sheffield Academic Press, 1996), p. 211 n. 78, draws particular attention to Luke 4:14, where the description of Jesus' returning in the power of the Spirit 'reveals the impossibility of Schweizer's claim that Luke makes a clear distinction between πνεῦμα . . . and δύναμις, attributing speech to the former and miracles to the latter'.

7. Twelftree, *Jesus the Miracle Worker*, p. 171.

8. S. Freyne, *The Twelve: Disciples and the Apostles* (London: Sheed & Ward, 1968), pp. 68–69, notes here how, in contrast to Mark, Luke's account of the appointment of the Twelve is presented as an introduction to the Sermon on the Plain, which is addressed to the extended group of Jesus' disciples in contrast to Matthew's Sermon on the Mount, which is a contrasting of old and new demands of the law to the crowd (cf. Matt. 5:1ff.).

empowering and sending the Twelve out in mission – one in Mark (6:7–13), and one in Q. Matthew draws on both sources in his account of the sending out of the Twelve (Luke 9:1–6, 10 // Mark 6:6–13, 30), whereas Luke depends primarily on Mark for his account of the sending out of the Twelve, and material from Q for his unique account of the sending out of the Seventy(-Two) in Luke 10:1–20 (cf. Matt. 9:37–38; 10:7–16; 11:21–23). It seems likely, therefore, that the sending out of the disciples in mission by Jesus goes back to a single dominical tradition,[9] and this clearly has implications for our understanding of the significance of the sending of the Seventy(-Two) for Luke.

## Luke's purpose

How, then, are we to understand Luke's purpose here and how it relates to his understanding of Christian discipleship? Does Luke have a more far-reaching didactic purpose than simply giving a paradigmatic example of Jesus empowering the disciples to perform signs and wonders? Is Luke's purpose perhaps related more to informing his readers at an early stage in his two-volume work about the nature, authority and purpose of the apostolic band and other heroes of the Spirit who are the evangelist's central characters in Acts? It is true that here we have at least superficial evidence for the Third Wave's case, in that the apostles can be described as sharing in Jesus' ministry of proclaiming the kingdom of God and performing signs and wonders. Without further qualification, such an interpretation of the evidence is misleading. In context, Jesus' empowering the disciples here is a necessary corollary of their being commissioned for this particular mission.[10] In other words, at this point in Luke's narrative the commissioning and empowering of the Twelve is better understood in a more discrete sense. So far as Luke's didactic intent is concerned, this can be little more than a foreshadowing for his readers of what is to come later in the post-Easter situation.[11]

---

9. See for example F. Hahn, *Mission in the New Testament* (ET SBT 47; London: SCM, 1965), pp. 41–46; and Marshall, *Gospel of Luke*, p. 350.

10. For the combination of 'preaching and healing', see for example Luke 4:18, 40–44; 6:17–18; 8:1–2.

11. Cf. Marshall, *Gospel of Luke*, p. 350; and for a detailed discussion of the relationship between signs, wonders and preaching in Acts, see L. O'Reilly, *Word and Sign in the Acts of the Apostles: A Study in Lucan Theology* (Rome: Cura Pontificiae Universitatis Gregorianae, 1987).

In Mark's account of the commissioning of the Twelve there is an emphasis on exorcism, with the Twelve being given *exousia* over unclean spirits/demons (Mark 6:7; 6:13), and Mark concludes his narrative in verse 13 by saying that the disciples cast out many demons and healed the sick by anointing them with oil.[12] To Mark's *exousia*, Luke adds *dynamis* in order to describe the power given to the Twelve that enables them to preach and heal (9:1). This combination of 'authority' and 'power' reflects precisely the same combination exercised by Jesus himself (4:14, 36; 5:17; 8:46; 16:19).[13] That for Luke this empowering is also firmly connected with mission was already hinted at in 5:10 when Jesus informed Peter that he would be 'catching men'.[14] According to Bock, Luke is unique in combining the two terms *dynamis* and *exousia*, where Luke's addition of *dynamis* emphasizes the action and appears to underline the fact that the apostles have been commissioned to take a full share in Jesus' ministry on this occasion and (in the name of Jesus) to perform exorcisms and healings.[15]

This raises the question whether the apostles' empowerment was just for this occasion. Marshall thinks not, arguing that Luke's use of the aorist *edōken* (he gave), rather than Mark's *eidou* (he was giving), does not provide sufficient grounds for it to be argued that Luke intended this to be an empowering just for this occasion. Nevertheless, Marshall has to concede that Luke's context does in fact suggest just such a one-off occasion.[16] In Luke 9:1 the apostles are sent out by Jesus to proclaim the kingdom of God, and we have a combination of proclamation accompanied by the miraculous. However, it should also be noted that, in salvation-historical terms, in this first mission the apostles' role is significantly different from their forthcoming role in the post-Easter situation depicted in Acts. In the Gospel they are sent out as participants in the earthly mission of Jesus to Israel, whereas in Acts, with its universal missionary perspective, they receive heavenly *dynamis* to facilitate their empowered witness

---

12. The reference to anointing the sick with oil appears to reflect later Christian practice (cf. Jas 5:14).

13. D. L. Bock, *Luke 1:1–9:50* (Grand Rapids, Mich.: Baker, 1994), p. 814, correctly notes that this power (*dynamis*) to heal will be retained by the Twelve in Acts and extended to others (Acts 3:1–10; 6:8; 8:5–13; 13:9–12; 14:8–15; 15:12; 19:11–16), where their message will have the added dimension of proclaiming Jesus as the risen mediator of their miraculous abilities, which are evidence of the promised kingdom of God.

14. J. B. Green, *The Gospel of Luke* (Grand Rapids, Mich.: Eerdmans, 1997), p. 436.

15. Bock, *1:1–9:50*, p. 813.

16. Marshall, *Gospel of Luke*, pp. 350–351.

beyond Israel to the 'ends of the earth' (Luke 24:47; Acts 1:8; cf. 28:16, 30–31).[17]
It should also be noted that the *exousia* and *dynamis* associated with this commission does not extend to Luke 9:37, where the disciples (apart from Peter,
James and John) are unable to exorcize the boy with a demon and where the
expectation, presumably based on past performance on the part of both the
boy's father and the disciples themselves, was that they would be able to do so.

In Luke 9:2 Johnson insists rightly that the verb 'to send' (*apostellō*) must be
taken in its fullest meaning, since the Twelve have already been designated
'apostles' by Luke's Jesus and they will be called apostles again when they
return.[18] Leaney even suggests that the phrase 'to proclaim the kingdom of
God and to heal' (Luke 9:2) not only summarizes the ministry of Jesus himself,
but for the Twelve should be regarded as a 'formula of apostleship'.[19] Johnson
argues further for the prophetic nature of the apostolic role, where the apostles succeed Jesus as bearers of the Spirit, and that this is clearly foreshadowed
here when the Twelve, as apostles, engage in the same activities as Jesus
himself.[20] Again, this does not necessarily invite the assumption that, at this
point in Luke's narrative, the Twelve play anything more than a unique and for-
mative role foreshadowing their forthcoming role in the life of the early
church. In addition, if we accept Johnson's argument for the prophetic nature
of the apostolic role, including empowerment to perform signs and wonders,
then the evidence in Acts suggests that this often goes hand in hand with missionary activity. If this is the case, it would also explain why, in Acts, Luke
restricts the performance of signs and wonders to the apostles and a few select
individuals who are specifically commissioned by the apostles (e.g. Acts 6:1–6),
or by the risen Lord (e.g. Acts 9:1ff.) or by a local congregation (e.g. Acts
13:1–3) to exercise a similar prophetic/missionary role within the early church.

In other words, there are clear indications elsewhere in Luke's Gospel that
the evangelist views this commission as being of limited duration together
with the accompanying endowments of *exousia* and *dynamis* (Luke 9:40; cf.
24:49 and Acts 1:8).[21] These indications are strengthened further in relation to

---

17. C. K. Barrett, *A Critical and Exegetical Commentary on the Acts of the Apostles.* Vol. 1:
    *Acts I–XIV* (Edinburgh: T. & T. Clark, 1994), p. 81, points out that 'to the ends of
    the earth' is a stock phrase indicating that the mission will be universal.
18. L. T. Johnson, *The Gospel of Luke* (SP 3; Collegeville, Minn.: Liturgical, 1991), p. 145.
    Cf. Luke 9:10a/Mark 6:30, but omitted by Matthew.
19. A. R. C. Leaney, *The Gospel According to St. Luke* (London: A. & C. Black, 1958), p. 160.
20. Johnson, *Gospel of Luke*, p. 145.
21. Cf. R. H. Stein, *Luke* (NAC 24; Nashville, Tenn.: Broadman, 1992), p. 267.

the mission of the Seventy(-Two) when account is taken of Luke 22:35–38, where Jesus deliberately rescinds the prohibition on taking purse, bag or sandals in mission, clearly emphasizing the changed situation faced by Luke's post-Easter readers. Whilst we will discuss this pericope further in the next chapter, the importance of these verses for our understanding of how Luke differentiates between the epochs in salvation-history (then and now) should not be overlooked here. They appear only in Luke and their significance is heightened considerably by the fact that they act as a conclusion to Luke's account of the Last Supper.

Prior to Jesus' earlier rejection by Israel, there was no need for the missionaries to make long-term provision, nor did the eschatological immediacy of the situation that characterized Jesus' earthly ministry warrant such provision. In the post-Easter situation, however, the apostles face an indeterminate period now characterized by a diminishing sense of immediacy, and the church's missionary endeavours must now take a longer-term view with the subsequent need to make provision for an extended period of missionary activity.[22] If, as seems likely, Luke also envisaged the Twelve being part of the Seventy(-Two), the commissioning and empowerment of the Twelve on this occasion is perhaps best understood as being limited for the duration of their mission, with the apostles receiving a further commissioning by Jesus when they were sent out later as part of the larger group.

This is borne out in Luke's account of the disciples' failure to heal the boy possessed by a demon (Luke 9:37–43a pars.), where Luke emphasizes dramatically the disciples' inability to cast out the demon by having the father 'beg' the disciples to act, rather than simply asking them to cast it out as is the case with Luke's Markan source. Luke follows Mark's order, placing this incident immediately after the transfiguration (Mark 9:2–10 pars.). The significance of the incident for Luke may be discerned further by noting Luke's omissions from his Markan source. Luke clearly wants to focus his readers' attention on the person of Jesus. By omitting Jesus' comments about John the Baptist and Elijah (Mark 9:11–13), Luke brings this incident into even closer relationship with his account of the transfiguration.[23] The narrative effect of the disciples' failure acts as a salutary counterbalance to the heavenly glory just revealed on the mount of transfiguration.

As Jesus descends the mount of transfiguration, he is confronted with a sit-

---

22. Evans, *Saint Luke*, p. 805.

23. See for example Marshall, *Luke*, p. 389; and C. F. Evans, *Saint Luke* (London: SCM, 1990), p. 422.

uation where his disciples, although only recently given power and authority by Jesus 'over all demons and to cure diseases' (Luke 9:1, 6), are unable to cast out the unclean spirit. Far from exercising a ministry modelled on that of Jesus, as they had during their recent mission, the disciples now find themselves powerless to act. The reader, in contrast to the portrayal of the post-Easter activities of the apostles in Acts, is left to make a negative comparison between the disciples' recent success, following their being specifically commissioned by Jesus (Luke 9:6) and their present impotence.

Had Luke wanted to promote the model of discipleship claimed by the Third Wave he could easily have done so here, but the changes he has made to his Markan source indicate otherwise. Luke omits any mention of the reason for the disciples' failure being due to the difficulty of this specific case or, more surprisingly for Luke, lack of prayer (cf. Mark 9:29). Rather, Luke's focus is clearly on Jesus himself, whose glory has just been revealed on the mount of transfiguration. In these present circumstances, Jesus acts with authority so that the boy is cured and God's glory is again revealed through Jesus (9:43a).[24]

Luke is not interested here in promoting signs and wonders as a characteristic of the ministry shared between Jesus and his followers. He emphasizes this point clearly in 9:49–50, where exorcism using Jesus' name as a powerful talisman may be practised with effect even by those who are not disciples.[25] And again, in 9:51–56, where the immature attitude to deeds of power evidenced by Jesus' closest confidantes borders on the ridiculous. Having thus put deeds of power into a proper perspective, Jesus' explanation of what is demanded of his followers in 9:57–62 impacts on Luke's readers all the more forcibly and prepares the way for a series of Jesus' instructions to his disciples as he journeys towards Jerusalem (cf. 11:1–13; 12:22ff.; 16:1–13; 17:1–10, 22ff.).

## Conclusions

Whilst it has been argued that, historically, the disciples were probably involved in exorcism prior to Easter,[26] Luke's narrative makes no firm distinction

---

24. Nolland, *Luke 9:21–18:34* (WBC 35B; Dallas: Word, 1993), p. 507, notes that only here does Luke use the Greek 'to astonish' and 'majesty/magnificence' in connection with a healing story.

25. See my discussion of this pericope in chapter 9.

26. See for example G. H. Twelftree, *Jesus the Exorcist: A Contribution to the Study of the Historical Jesus* (Peabody, Mass.: Hendrickson, 1993), p. 124; J. Jeremias, *New*

between healing and exorcism as both are perceived in terms of releasing captives (cf. Luke 4:18). However, Luke does make a firm distinction between the earthly ministry of Jesus and the ministry of the church in the post-Easter situation. The apostles will be empowered in a fuller way by the Holy Spirit in the post-Easter situation. This, in turn, suggests that the two occasions when the disciples are sent out on mission by Jesus in Luke's Gospel are to be regarded as discrete incidents, where the focus is on Jesus' earthly ministry rather than providing evidence that the part played by Jesus' followers indicates a normative state of affairs, where most, if not all, of Jesus' followers are empowered to perform signs and wonders. Even in Acts, Luke makes this clear in the way he restricts the miraculous to a chosen few 'men of the spirit'.[27]

---

*Testament Theology Volume One: The Proclamation of Jesus* (ET London: SCM, 1971), p. 95; M. Hengel, *The Charismatic Leader and His Followers* (ET Edinburgh: T. & T. Clark, 1981), pp. 73–74.

27. For the term 'men of the spirit' and for a discussion of their significance for Luke-Acts, see L. T. Johnson, *The Literary Function of Possessions in Luke-Acts* (SBLDS 39; Missoula: Scholars Press, 1977), pp. 38–60.

## 17. THE SENDING OF THE SEVENTY(-TWO)

### Introduction

As we have seen, Luke's two mission accounts of the Twelve followed by the Seventy(-Two) are of particular importance for the Third Wave's case, and for this reason it is necessary to examine this second mission in detail. Noting the order in which signs and wonders accompany the missionary activity of first Jesus, then the Twelve, then the Seventy(-Two), Williams concludes that Jesus deliberately provides a model for Christian discipleship where the performance of signs and wonders is not restricted to a chosen few but should be regarded as normative for Christian discipleship from the first century to the present day.[1]

We have also seen in the case of the mission of the Twelve that a more critical reading of Luke's narrative leads to the conclusion that Luke regarded the empowering of the Twelve by Jesus to perform healings and exorcisms as a temporary measure firmly aligned to their mission. At best, for Luke's readers this mission foreshadows the widening missionary activities of the church

---

1. D. Williams, 'Following Christ's Example: A Biblical View of Discipleship', in G. S. Greig and K. N. Springer (eds.), *The Kingdom and the Power* (Ventura, Calif.: Regal, 1993), p. 183.

after Pentecost. We must now ask whether a similar conclusion is called for in the case of the mission of the Seventy(-Two)?

Ferdinand Hahn has shown that Luke's two mission accounts are derived from two sources, Mark and Q.[2] Whilst the appointing of the Twelve by Jesus and his sending them out on mission occurs in all three Synoptic Gospels, why has Luke alone, who normally avoids doublets, included two missions in his narrative, one of which is strikingly unique to his Gospel? Does the account of the mission of the Seventy(-Two), chosen by Jesus from his wider circle of followers, support the Third Wave's view that Luke intends to show here that Jesus deliberately widens the authority to heal and perform exorcisms beyond himself and the Twelve to include the wider circle of his followers? In other words, is the mission of the Seventy(-Two) intended by Luke to be paradigmatic for the post-Easter church? Alternatively, does such a reading of the text represent a misunderstanding of Luke's narrative purpose? Does the evidence suggest, contra Williams, that the mission of the Seventy(-Two) had a more discrete purpose in Luke's narrative, as we saw was the case with the mission of the Twelve?

### Seventy or seventy-two?

There is conflicting manuscript evidence about the number of disciples involved. Should we read here, 'seventy' or 'seventy-two'?[3] The evidence is inconclusive either way and arguments in favour of seventy or seventy-two have rested on conclusions drawn about the likely OT background underpinning Luke's narrative at this point. In support of 'seventy' there are two symbolic references in the OT. Firstly, the seventy elders who attend Moses at Sinai (Exod. 24:1) are appointed to share Moses' burden of ministry and are empowered for the role by sharing in the Spirit given by God to Moses (Num. 11:1–2; cf. Exod. 18:21–23; Deut. 1:9–18). It is also argued that the heavenly

---

2. F. Hahn, *Mission in the New Testament* (ET SBT 47; London: SCM, 1965), pp. 41–46. Cf. Also J. Jeremias, *New Testament Theology Volume One: The Proclamation of Jesus* (ET London: SCM, 1971), p. 231.

3. For a full discussion of the textual variants supporting 'seventy' and 'seventy-two', see B. M. Metzger, 'Seventy or Seventy-Two Disciples?', *NTS* 5 (1958–9), pp. 299–306. Metzger concludes that the evidence for both seventy and seventy-two is so evenly balanced that this textual problem cannot be satisfactorily resolved and that both were widely used in the early manuscript tradition.

council of *běnê 'ĕlôhîm* (lit. 'sons of God')[4] are numbered seventy, possibly based on the account of God dividing the nations in Deuteronomy 32:8. The total number of Gentile nations was also thought to be seventy (Gen. 10; *Jub.* 44.34).[5] Interestingly, there are also occasions in contemporary Jewish literature where we read of the appointment of seventy individuals who are sometimes accompanied by a further twelve or seven associates.[6] Alternatively, according to the *Letter of Aristeas*, there were seventy-two translators of the Septuagint made up from six honourable men from each of the twelve tribes of Israel.[7] The LXX itself suggests the number of nations in Genesis 10 – 11 was seventy-two, confirmation of which is found in the number of princes and kings in the world recorded elsewhere in *3 Enoch* 17.8; 18.2–3; 30.2.[8]

Evans maintains that Luke's use of the phrase 'the Lord *appointed*' in 10:1 reflects a technical meaning 'to authorise or appoint to an office' in the church and so is meant by Luke to reflect a later, post-Easter situation.[9] This seems to me unlikely. Apart from the fact that there is no evidence for this in Acts, where, initially at least, any latent idea of 'office bearers' is confined by Luke to the

---

4. Translated as 'angels' in the LXX.

5. As Metzger rightly notes, the number adds up to 72, rather than 70, in the LXX (ibid., p. 303).

6. The following references are noted by C. F. Evans, *Saint Luke* (London: SCM, 1990), p. 445. Josephus, *Life* 52–57 (LCL, p. 23), where Josephus tells us of twelve leading Jews from Caesarea who accompany seventy envoys from Ecbatana back to Caesarea. In *J. W.* 2.569–574 (LCL, p. 543), Josephus tells us of the appointment of seventy mature men who are made magistrates over the whole of Galilee, together with seven individuals in each city who would adjudicate over less petty cases whilst referring more important cases to the seventy. Again in *J. W.* 4.332–338 (LCL, p. 99), Josephus describes the appointment of seventy leading men by the Zealots to act as judges in mock trials and courts of justice.

7. R. J. H. Shutt (trans.), *Letter of Aristeas* 46–50, in J. H. Charlesworth (ed.), *Old Testament Pseudepigrapha*. Vol. 2: *Expansions of the 'Old Testament' Legends, Wisdom and Philosophical Literature, Prayers, Psalms and Odes, Fragments of Lost Judaistic Works* (London: Darton Longman & Todd, 1985), p. 16.

8. All noted by Bock, *Luke 9:51–24:53* (Grand Rapids, Mich.: Baker, 1996), p. 1015, who opts for the originality of seventy-two missionaries in Luke 10. However, Bock downplays the symbolism of the number, arguing that the significance of the pericope lies in the fact that Jesus expands his missionary activity beyond the Twelve (cf. p. 994).

9. Evans, *Saint Luke*, p. 444.

apostolic band, followed by Stephen and his Hellenist colleagues.[10] It should also be noted that Luke's use of the post-Easter title 'Lord' to refer to Jesus is something that occurs throughout Luke's Gospel (e.g. 7:13, 19; 10:1, 39, 41; 11:39; 12:42; 13:15; 17:5, 6; 18:6; 19:8, 31, 34; 22:61; cf. 24:3). Although the evidence for seventy or seventy-two remains inconclusive, whichever the preferred number, most are agreed that the mission of the Seventy(-Two) was intended by Luke to be a symbolic prefiguring of the church's post-Easter mission beyond Israel.

Susan Garrett argues against this prevailing view.[11] In discussing two LXX passages that may inform Luke's second mission (Gen. 10:2–31; Num. 11:16–25), Garrett argues that if Luke had Genesis 10 in mind, then the appointing of the Seventy(-Two) would symbolize the Gentile nations to which the passage refers. Alternatively, she argues, Numbers 11:16–25 contains a number of features that would appeal to Luke, including Moses typology (cf. Acts 3:22; 7:37), the appointment of Seventy(-Two) helpers and empowering for service through sharing Moses' endowment with the Spirit and his resultant charismatic activity (Num. 11:25).

Garrett prefers this second option, where Jesus' appointment of the Seventy(-Two) reflects Moses' sharing of his ministry with appointed helpers.[12] In either case, the number 70 or 72 remains uncertain.[13] Garrett concludes, rightly in my view, that the Lukan context does not suggest a wider mission to non-Jews but a localized mission that precedes Jesus to various towns on his journey to Jerusalem. More widely, Luke may have intended a foreshadowing of the mission of the post-Easter church when many would receive the Spirit, with his resultant charismatic endowments (Acts 2:1ff.).[14] Nevertheless, the fact

---

10.  It is only later in Acts 11:30 that elders are mentioned in connection with the Jerusalem church. From Acts 14:23 we learn that it was Paul's custom to appoint elders in the churches he established as part of his missionary activities. In Acts 15:2, when Paul, Barnabas and other members of the church in Antioch are sent to Jerusalem in order to clarify issues of table fellowship between Jews and Gentiles, 'apostles' and 'elders' are mentioned together by Luke in connection with the leadership of the Jerusalem church. James, the Lord's brother, is not mentioned until Acts 12:7.

11.  S. R. Garrett, *The Demise of the Devil: Magic and the Demonic in Luke's Writings* (Minneapolis: Fortress, 1989), pp. 47–59.

12.  L. T. Johnson, *The Gospel of Luke* (SP 3; Collegeville, Minn.: Liturgical, 1991), p. 167, also argues that Moses typology is reflected here.

13.  Garret, *Demise of the Devil*, p. 48.

14.  Ibid.

remains that for Luke, the church's mission in Acts is entrusted not to the many who have received the Spirit, as evidence of their participation in the post-Easter manifestation of the kingdom of God, but to a chosen few apostles and other heroes of the Spirit.

Was the mission of the Seventy(-Two) intended by Luke to be paradigmatic for the post-Easter church? It seems not, for the following reasons: the Twelve were clearly included by Luke in the larger mission of the Seventy(-Two); this has implications for our understanding of Luke 22:35–36 and the distinction made by the Lukan Jesus during his valedictory discourse at the Last Supper between the situation governing the mission of the Seventy(-Two) and the situation about to face the apostles following Jesus' death; evidence from Luke's narrative of the mission itself.

## The Twelve as part of the mission of the Seventy(-Two)

Are we to understand that the Twelve were included by Luke in the sending out of the Seventy(-Two)? The NT situation is complicated by the fact that in some manuscripts the word 'and' is inserted before 'others',[15] which gives the sense of the Seventy(-Two) being in addition to the Twelve.[16] Conzelmann thinks that the Twelve are excluded from the Seventy(-Two) and suggests that they stayed with Jesus for the duration of the mission.[17] Fitzmyer also argues that the most natural reading is that *heterous* (other) indicates the Seventy(-Two) *excludes* the Twelve.[18] The problem with taking an exclusive view is that it weakens considerably any symbolic significance associated with the numbers 70 or 72. Bock, for example, argues that whilst the word 'others' refers to a group outside the apostolic band, when taken with Luke 22:35–38 it is clear that the Twelve went with, or were part of, the larger group.[19]

It is also clear that Luke has written his accounts of the two missions using

---

15. For example, Aleph, A, C, D, K, W, X. For a full list, see K. Aland, M. Black, C. M. Martini, B. M. Metzger and A. Wickgren (eds.), *The Greek New Testament*, 3rd ed. (Stuttgart: United Bible Societies, 1966), p. 250 n. 1.

16. J. A. Fitzmyer, *Luke (X–XXIV)*, p. 845. I. H. Marshall, *Gospel of Luke*, p. 414, asserts that the insertion of *kai* before *heterous* agrees with Lukan style.

17. H. Conzelmann, *The Theology of St. Luke* (ET London: SCM, 1960), p. 67 n. 1.

18. Fitzmyer, *Luke (X–XXIV)*, p. 845.

19. Bock, *Luke 9:51–24:53* (Grand Rapids, Mich.: Baker, 1996), p. 994. For a similar view, see also Nolland, *9:21–18:34* (WBC 35B; Dallas: Word, 1993), p. 550.

material from Mark and Q, both of which were concerned with the mission of the Twelve. Again, this fact, taken together with Luke 22:35–38, leads to the conclusion that the Twelve formed part of the Seventy(-Two). This being the case, the empowerment of the Twelve in Luke 9:1 is best understood as being specifically for that particular occasion, with the Twelve receiving a second commissioning/empowerment when they were sent out again as part of the larger mission of the Seventy(-Two). Also, we cannot avoid the important fact that Luke 22:35–38 forms part of Jesus' valedictory discourse at the Last Supper, and this would hardly be an occasion for a careless mistake by Luke.[20] When Jesus reverses his previous instructions about not carrying bags, sandals and so on when engaging in mission (cf. Luke 10:4), the meaning is clear: the missionary instructions (and empowerment) given earlier were inspired by the eschatological immediacy of the situation that characterized the earthly ministry of Jesus; times have since changed and the former instructions (together with accompanying empowerment) are no longer appropriate for the longer-term post-Easter situation facing Luke's church. Ongoing empowerment will come after the resurrection, when the Twelve and others are 'clothed with power from on high' (Luke 24:49b),[21] although in Acts empowerment to perform signs and wonders is restricted to a select few.

## Luke 22:35–36

According to Green, Luke's narrative of the sending out of an 'advance party' in 9:51–56 guides our reading towards the commissioning and sending out of the Seventy(-Two), so that the second mission is to be read in light of the first mission, which involved only the apostles.[22] Green concludes that the instructions to the missionaries here and to the Twelve in 9:1–5 provide Luke's readers with a pattern for sending followers of Jesus out in mission.[23] If this is the case, it would, in part at least, support the Third Wave view that here we have a par-

---

20. Contra Nolland, *Luke18:35–24:53* (WBC 35C; Dallas: Word, 1993), p. 1075.

21. Cf. Acts 1:5; 2:1ff. and note there is no evidence that all of the 120 who were present at Pentecost were empowered to perform signs and wonders. Quite the opposite. Luke reserves such empowerment for a selected band of men of the Spirit. This question of Luke's restricting empowerment to perform signs and wonders to a select few in Acts is discussed in detail in chapter 18.

22. J. B. Green, *The Gospel of Luke* (Grand Rapids, Mich.: Eerdmans, 1997), p. 410.

23. Ibid.

adigm for contemporary Christian practice, albeit firmly linked to missionary activity. However, I would argue per contra that the situation envisaged here is intended by Luke to be fluid, rather than paradigmatic. This can be seen from the fact that in 22:35–36 Jesus revokes his former instructions in view of a new situation facing the apostles, and with this revocation the sense of eschatological immediacy that characterized earlier missions. These two verses (22:35–36) form part of a longer discussion (vv. 35–38) that concludes Jesus' valedictory discourse at the end of Luke's version of the Last Supper. How are we to understand the ensuing discussion about buying a sword and, importantly here, the effect this discussion has on the way in which we are to understand the temporal change indicated by the phrase 'but now' (*alla nyn*) (v. 36a)?

I am arguing here that the commissioning, empowerment and instructions given to the Seventy(-Two) were limited in the Lukan narrative to the earthly ministry of Jesus and were not intended by Luke to provide an ongoing contemporary paradigm for mission, accompanied by signs and wonders. This view is strengthened considerably if it can be shown that Luke intends the temporal shift denoted by Jesus' emphatic *alla nyn* (22:36a) to point to a new missionary situation now existing beyond the earthly ministry of Jesus. These verses occur in the context of Luke's description of the Last Supper, and only in Luke's Gospel where the evangelist has shifted the emphasis away from the words of institution to the extended farewell discourse that follows (22:24–38).[24] My primary concern here is how we are to understand these verses in terms of Luke's narrative? More particularly, how are we to understand the temporal shift in verse 36a, and how is it related to mission beyond the earthly ministry of Jesus? Clearly, in order to do this, it will be necessary to take account of the enigmatic two-swords saying and the nature of the new situation to which it alludes. Whatever wider conclusion is reached, Nolland is correct in his view that it seems likely that this material has been transmitted by Luke, at least in part, as teaching on Christian mission in times of crisis.[25]

From as early as 22:31, Luke gives an indication of a shift in the epochs of salvation-history, where Satan, not content with capturing the heart of Judas (22:3) now seeks to subject the apostles to a time of sifting (22:31). In 22:35 Jesus refers back to the sending of the Seventy(-Two) and points out that, although the disciples took little in the way of provisions when they were sent out on mission to Israel, they lacked nothing but could rely on the hospitality of those to whom they were sent. Jesus then makes the emphatic point *alla nyn*,

---

24. P. S. Minear, 'A Note on Luke xxii.36', *NovT* 7 (1964), p. 129.
25. Nolland, *Luke 18:35–24:53*, p. 1075.

indicating that the situation has changed. But how has it changed so far as Luke is concerned, and what is the significance of the dialogue concerning swords (vv. 36b–38), which exegetes find so perplexing? Is it simply that in the changed situation the disciples will also face persecution and suffering because of their close association with Jesus, and for this reason must arm themselves with swords?

According to Conzelmann, Luke uses 22:35–38 to mark the hiatus between the mission of Jesus and that of the church. It was intended by Luke to be figurative in that the swords represent the 'conflict, sacrifice and victory of the disciples' in their forthcoming post-Easter mission.[26] Conzelmann understands the emphatic *alla nyn* as a decisive indication that 'other rules are now in force'.[27] In other words, in view of Luke's understanding of salvation-history, the instructions to the Seventy(-Two) were appropriate to the time in which they were given (the period of Jesus) and, as such, are to be regarded as limited in their application.[28] This reversal of the instructions for mission given to the Seventy(-Two) provides us with an example of commands of Jesus that were intended only for his own contemporary situation and which are to be regarded as temporary and no longer valid in the new, post-Easter situation.[29] Conzelmann argues further that the arming of the disciples symbolizes 'messianic protection' as they face the woes that will accompany the church's mission.[30]

In a short paper discussing Luke 22:36 Paul Minear agrees that Conzelmann rightly recognizes the importance of this final valedictory discourse between Jesus and the apostles, but goes on to argue for a shift in emphasis for *alla nyn* away from Conzelmann's tightly drawn salvation-historical scheme (period of Jesus / period of the church) to the Passion itself and the events preceding it.[31] Minear ignores the change in instructions for

---

26. Conzelmann, *Theology of St. Luke*, p. 84.

27. Ibid., pp. 232–233.

28. Ibid., p. 233.

29. Ibid., p. 13.

30. Ibid., p. 233. Jeremias, *New Testament Theology*, pp. 241 and 294, argues in a similar vein that the change in the situation means that, like their master, the disciples will also face persecution and suffering immediately following Jesus' passion, which marks the 'time of the sword'. For Jeremias, Luke intends the sword as a symbolic illustration of Jesus' prophecy of the forthcoming messianic conflict that was not fulfilled. According to Evans, *Saint Luke*, p. 806, this latter assertion by Jeremias must be rejected on the grounds that it reflects badly on Luke as an editor.

31. Minear, 'A Note on Luke xxii.36', pp. 128–134.

mission whilst concentrating exclusively on the significance of the swords. However, there is no escaping the fact that *alla nyn* refers back specifically to the mission of the Seventy(-Two).

Joseph Fitzmyer regards *alla nyn* as indicating a time shift that begins with the forthcoming Passion and extends into the new period of salvation-history about to be inaugurated. Fitzmyer also makes the important point that the Lukan Jesus is here also addressing the readers of Luke's Gospel. As such, he is looking beyond the Passion to the period of the church indicated by the swords as a period of persecution.[32] By way of caution, R. Maddox makes the important point that the narrative of Acts fails to bear out the notion of the period of the church being a time of danger and distress for the disciples.[33] In a similar vein, S. Brown points out that Conzelmann's identifying of Luke 22:36 as the point of departure between the aeons forces him to include both the Passion and the age of the church in Acts as a time of 'testing' (*peirasmos*) for the apostles.[34] As for regarding the Passion as a time of 'testing', Brown makes the point that this is not so for the apostles, although it is a time of 'sifting' (*siniasai*) that will become a trial only if the apostles fail to pray (Luke 22:46b).[35] Also, it should be noted that *peirasmos* is not used by Luke for the Passion nor does it occur in this sense in Acts.[36] Brown concludes, 'The characteristic of the Age of the Church is rather the presence of the spirit, and the beginning of the Age of the Church is therefore not the passion but Pentecost.'[37]

Whilst most agree that Conzelmann overstates his case, it is important to note that the conversation in Luke's narrative at this point is looking back to an earlier period in Jesus' ministry as well as forward to a period beyond the Passion to the church's mission in Acts, and clearly differentiates between the two. As John Gillmann notes, in Luke 22:35 the disciples' response to Jesus' question about their previous missionary activity, together with Jesus' emphatic interjection of *alla nyn*, prepares Luke's readers for another sending

---

32. Fitzmyer, *Luke (X–XXIV)*, pp. 1431–1432.

33. R. Maddox, *The Purpose of Luke-Acts* (Edinburgh: T. & T. Clark, 1982), p. 154 n. 136. J. Gillmann, 'A Temptation to Violence: The Two Swords', *LS* 9 (1982), p. 143, makes the same point.

34. S. Brown, 'Apostasy and Perseverance', *AnBib* 36 (1969), p. 11.

35. Ibid., p. 10.

36. Ibid., pp. 11–12.

37. Ibid., p. 12. In a similar vein, Gillmann, 'A Temptation to Violence', p. 143, makes the point that the apostles are strengthened by the protection of the Spirit.

out of the apostles, which is confirmed by the issuing of new instructions that are more appropriate for a new time and situation (v. 36).[38]

Gillmann wants to restrict the time frame indicated by *alla nyn* to the Passion and thinks that Luke interpreted the crucifixion in view of Isaiah 53. The lawless (*anomia*) are to be understood in terms of the language and characters who play a part in the Passion.[39] Gillmann argues that Luke's use of 'now' (*nyn*) does not indicate a new mandate extending into the future, but refers to the immediate situation surrounding the Passion and the fulfilment of the prophecy from Isaiah 53 quoted by Jesus in 22:37b. For Gillmann, the quotation by Jesus from Isaiah 53 holds the hermeneutical key to understanding the pericope – the reason for the new instruction is that the scripture must be fulfilled (v. 37). However, the argument fails on two fronts. First, the characters whom Gillmann regards as lawless are not specifically named as such by Luke. According to Acts, in the sermon delivered by Peter at Pentecost, the lawless ones are identified as the Roman authorities responsible for Jesus' execution (Acts 2:23). Second, Gillmann does not pay sufficient attention to the mission context that Luke uses to set up the rest of the discourse. It is in the light of what follows in the post-Easter commissioning of the apostles by the risen Jesus (Luke 24:44–49), taken up at length by Luke in Acts, that we are to understand the clear reference to instructions for mission that are changed by Jesus in their detail rather than the missionary context from which they derive.

In his narrative as a whole, Luke recognizes the changed situation between the ministry of Jesus in the Gospel and the post-Easter situation he portrays in Acts. As Christopher Tuckett has noted, 'the instructions about "ascetic" life style to be adopted by Jesus' own followers on mission during his ministry are cancelled by the Lukan Jesus himself'.[40]

Formerly, the disciples lacked nothing when Jesus sent them out on mission, but now the situation has changed. The apostles must fend for themselves as they move out in mission beyond the boundaries of Israel in obedience to a new commissioning and empowerment from the risen Jesus (Luke 24:44–49; Acts 1:8;).

The implications are clear in that whilst the missionary activities of the

---

38. Gillmann, 'A Temptation to Violence', p. 147.

39. Ibid., p. 148. Cf. Luke 22:52–53; Barabbas, an insurrectionist and a murderer, and Jesus being crucified with criminals.

40. C. M. Tuckett, 'The Christology of Luke-Acts', in J. Verheyden (ed.), *The Unity of Luke-Acts* (Leuven: Leuven University Press, 1999), p. 136.

Twelve and the Seventy(-Two) may in some ways foreshadow what is to follow in Acts, they are clearly not intended to provide the definitive paradigm for mission so far as Luke is concerned. Whatever else the Lukan Jesus signals with the emphatic *alla nyn*, there is a clear indication that, with the rejection of Jesus by Israel, the perspective on mission has changed. With that change comes the need for a new commissioning of the apostles by the risen Jesus, who, following their empowerment by the Holy Spirit, will send them out to all nations (Luke 24:44–49; Acts 1:8). In the final commissioning of his followers (Luke 24:44–49; Acts 1:6–8) Jesus insists that they must now await the necessary empowerment before venturing in mission beyond Jerusalem, a factor hardly necessary if the Twelve and others have already been empowered by Jesus to perform signs and wonders on a permanent basis.

## The mission

Most of the mission charge to the Seventy(-Two) is paralleled in Matthew's version of the mission of the Twelve (Matt. 10:1, 5–16) with Luke's mission charge being drawn partly from Q (vv. 2–3, 8–16) and partly from either Luke's special source or Lukan redaction (vv. 4–7, 17–20).[41] According to Fitzmyer, in the mission charges in chapters 9 and 10 Luke is addressing the Christian community of his own day and, at the same time, providing them with a link between their own missionary activity and that of Jesus and his disciples.[42] This, Fitzmyer argues, should be understood in light of the way in which the importance of the apostles gradually decreases in the first half of Acts. Fitzmyer suggests that the significance of Luke providing his readers with this 'doublet' is to be found in Jesus' widening his commission to an extended number of disciples as missionaries, rather than allowing it to remain limited to the Twelve.[43] If Fitzmyer is correct and Luke's purpose here is to foreshadow the diminishing role of the Twelve in Acts in order to root the situation in his own day more firmly with the earthly Jesus, then it is no more than the evangelist did earlier in his narrative with the designation 'apostle' (cf. Luke 6:13). The designation by Jesus of the Twelve as 'apostles'

---

41. Cf. G. B. Caird, *The Gospel of St. Luke* (Harmondsworth: Penguin, 1963), p. 144. For a full discussion, see Fitzmyer, *Luke (X–XXIV)*, p. 844; and F. Hahn, *Mission in the New Testament* (ET SBT 47; London: SCM, 1965), pp. 41–46.

42. Fitzmyer, *Luke (X–XXIV)*, p. 845.

43. Ibid., p. 844.

was clearly important for Luke. In Acts it is the apostles' known association with Jesus from the beginning of his earthly ministry that was the primary criterion for membership of the apostolic band, thus guaranteeing the authenticity of their teaching (Acts 1:21–22; cf. 2:42).

In many respects, the mission of the Seventy(-Two) resembles the earlier mission of the Twelve (Luke 9:1–6 pars.) to which Luke has added the prophetic denunciation of Chorazin, Bethsaida and Capernaum (10:13–15); a pronouncement from Q on acceptance and rejection (10:16; cf. Matt. 11:21–24); an account of the return of the emissaries, including an account of Jesus' apocalyptic vision of the fall of Satan (10:17–20). Beare suggests that the mission of the Seventy(-Two) is to be located geographically in Samaria, which suggests a foreshadowing of the church's later mission beyond the boundaries of Israel as described in the missionary programme for the narrative of Acts (cf. Acts 1:8).[44] The assumption that the mission took place in Samaria is not borne out by the evidence. We can say that, in narrative terms, the mission of the Seventy(-Two) has something of a 'Samaritan' context in the sense that we have two incidents immediately before and after the mission of the Seventy(-Two) in the Gospel narrative that may be intended to signal what is to come in terms of the church's mission beyond Israel (Acts 8:4ff.). However, it should be noted that the first of these (Luke 9:51–55) is entirely negative towards Samaritans, whilst the second (10:25–37) also plays on the antipathy of Jesus' hearers towards Samaritans in order to drive home the point of the parable (Luke 9:36–37) dramatically.

Details of the mission itself are not given, apart from 10:17, where the disciples report their successful exorcisms in the name of Jesus.[45] The main body of the pericope is concerned with Jesus' instructions to his disciples and the motif of division resulting from the presence of the kingdom of God (cf. Luke 2:34),[46] followed by the return of the Seventy(-Two) and Jesus' vision of the fall of Satan (Luke 10:17–20, 21–24). As Green points out, in proclaiming the kingdom Luke makes it clear that it is not just about human response to the message of restoration or judgment (Luke 10:8–11). It is also about conflict in the heavenly realm between God and Satan and his minions (vv. 13–20).[47]

---

44. F. W. Beare, *The Earliest Records of Jesus* (Oxford: Blackwell, 1962), p. 156.

45. Understood in the sense of their being Jesus' official representatives on this occasion rather than merely using his name as a powerful talisman (cf. Luke 9:49).

46. Noted by Green, *Gospel of Luke*, p. 411.

47. Ibid.

Having said this, Luke makes it very clear in verses 18–20 that victory in the eschatological conflict already belongs to God.

The wider narrative context for the mission of the Seventy(-Two) is that of the journey towards Jerusalem (Luke 9:51ff.).[48] Jesus, who is now on 'the way' to meet his inevitable prophetic fate, sends the Seventy(-Two) out as emissaries as they travel together towards Jerusalem.[49] The journey, which begins in 9:51, has taken on the character of a 'mission'[50] and it is in this context that Jesus commissions the Seventy(-Two), making it clear that they are his representatives, to the point where to reject them is to reject Jesus himself, resulting in inevitable judgment to follow (cf. Luke 10:13–16).

Although Luke was largely dependent on Mark for his account of the mission of the Twelve, he omitted any mention of their being sent out 'two by two' (cf. Mark 6:7). He now applies this instruction to the Seventy(-Two) emissaries who are sent on ahead of Jesus in pairs in order to give their testimony legal status under Jewish law (Deut. 19:15).[51] It seems unlikely that Luke omitted this detail from the mission of the Twelve on the assumption that it was implicit in the text. If this were the case, it would be more logical to include it in his description of the mission of the Twelve and, having established the precedent, to omit it in 10:1.

On the assumption that Luke has carefully crafted his accounts of both missions, why has he inserted in 10:1 and omitted from 9:1–2 a detail that his source attributed to the mission of the Twelve? In both missions the emissaries' testimony, accompanied by signs and wonders, is central (Luke 9:1–2, 6; 10:8–9; cf. 10:1, 16). It is true that it was common practice, as described in Acts, for missionaries to work in pairs (e.g. Acts 13:2; 14:12; 15:27, 39; 17:14; 19:22), but this is not always the case.[52] Therefore, this does not necessarily lead us to

---

48. See especially Luke 9:52, where Luke has already mentioned that Jesus has sent messengers ahead of him in order to prepare the way for his arrival.

49. For a discussion of the 'way' and its antecedents in Qumran usage, see S. V. McCasland, 'The Way', *JBL* 77 (1958), pp. 222–230, and especially p. 230, who argues that 'the way' as a designation for Christianity was derived from 'the way of the LORD' in Isa. 40:3 and was also used in this sense by the Qumran community (see 1QS 8:13–16).

50. Evans, *Saint Luke*, p. 441.

51. See for example A. R. C. Leaney, *The Gospel According to St. Luke* (London: A. & C. Black, 1958), p. 176; and Jeremias, *New Testament Theology*, p. 235.

52. For example, Stephen (Acts 6:8ff.), Philip (Acts 8:4–13, 26–40), Peter (Acts 10:1ff.), Paul (17:16ff.).

the conclusion that Luke's aim here is to mirror the missionary practice of the church of his day.[53] In sending out the Seventy(-Two) in pairs, Jesus ensures that their testimony has formal legal status, which, in turn, would seem to suggest that the mission of the Seventy(-Two) was aimed at (or confined to?) Israel (cf. Matt. 10:5–6), and that Luke intends his readers to understand this mission, as well as the earlier appointing and sending out of the apostles, to be firmly rooted in the life and ministry of Jesus.[54] In towns where the emissaries are welcomed, they are instructed to cure the sick (10:9). Healings and exorcisms are signs of the in-breaking kingdom of God.[55] For those who welcome Jesus' representatives, it is as though they are welcoming Jesus and, in turn, God himself, for whom Jesus claims to act as the emissary (10:16). In such cases the inhabitants will receive healing instead of judgment (cf. vv. 13–15).

The description of the return of the disciples also contains features that are unique to Luke and invite further scrutiny. Just as the sending out in mission of the Seventy(-Two) is unique to Luke, so also is the climax in Luke's narrative. On their return, the emissaries report enthusiastically that even the demons submitted to them as they ministered in the name of Jesus (10:17). Evans comments that this is the only occasion where the disciples make explicit use of the name of Jesus in exorcism during his lifetime. [56] It seems that here we have a further indication that the missionaries' empowerment on this occasion was intrinsically different from the more permanent empowerment promised by the risen Jesus after Easter (24:48–49). Dunn makes the important point that the charismatic power experienced by the Twelve and the Seventy(-Two) was not given for the upbuilding of the community in the sense of post-Easter charismatic gifts of the Spirit, but the disciples were empowered in order to share in Jesus' earthly mission.[57] Dunn concludes, 'It was only

---

53. For example, Acts 2:14ff.; 7:1ff.; 8:4ff.; 9:36ff.; 10:1ff.; 17:16ff.

54. Commenting on Luke 13 – 15, Green, *Gospel of Luke*, p. 416, writes, 'The geographical references indicate that Luke is locating the mission strongly within the temporal ministry of Jesus.'

55. Bock, *Luke 9:51–24:53*, p. 999.

56. Evans, *Saint Luke*, p. 454. The only other occasion in the Gospel is in Luke 9:49//Mark 9:38ff., where the disciples report another exorcist, who was not a disciple, casting out demons in Jesus' name. Presumably, we are to understand that he was successful; otherwise there seems little point in what follows (cf. vv. 50–51).

57. J. D. G. Dunn, *Jesus and the Spirit: A Study of the Religious and Charismatic Experience of Jesus and the First Christians as Reflected in the New Testament* (London: SCM, 1975), p. 80.

as they shared in his ministry that his disciples shared in his authority and char-ismatic power.'[58]

In response to the disciples' claim to have subdued demons in his name, Jesus recalls his visionary experience of seeing Satan fall from heaven in response to the missionaries' activity (10:18–20). This pericope has no Synoptic parallel. Luke places the passage immediately before his descrip-tion of Jesus' rejoicing in the spirit, which Luke takes from Q (Luke 10:21b–22//Matt. 11:25–27). How are we to understand the significance of this apocalyptic scene in terms of Luke's narrative? How does it relate to the mission of the Seventy(-Two) and their empowerment to perform signs and wonders?

First of all, we read in Luke 10:17 that the Seventy(-Two) returned from their mission 'with joy'. The reason for their joy is that they have subdued demons as a result of the commissioning and empowerment they received from Jesus to act in his name. For Luke 'joy' (*charis*) is normally associated with divine revelation (1:14; 2:10; 8:13; 24:42, 51).[59] This element of divine revela-tion is evidenced further in Jesus' response (10:18), which is also unique to Luke's Gospel.

Secondly, in describing his vision of the fall of Satan, the Lukan Jesus alludes to Isaianic imagery, where similar language is used to describe the fall of the king of Babylon (Isa. 14:12ff.)[60] and goes on to link the fate of unre-pentant Capernaum to the fall of Satan himself (10:18; cf. 10:15). In Jesus' vision of the fall of Satan we remain aware that this is not the final end of Satan, but what we might call the beginning of the end. Prior to this, Luke's references to evil personified are to 'the devil' (4:2–12; 8:12), whereas from this point the personification of evil that opposes the work of God's kingdom is named 'Satan' and this name continues throughout the rest of the Gospel (11:18; 13:16; 22: 3, 31). Satan, nevertheless, remains active at the earthly level, entering Judas' heart in 22:3 and opposing the work of the church in Acts (e.g.

---

58. Ibid., p. 81.

59. Whilst the demons submit to the disciples' exorcisms both here and during the mission of the Twelve, as noted previously, this is not always the case (cf. 9:40).

60. Contra Nolland, *Luke 9:21–18:34*, p. 563; and Fitzmyer, *Luke (X–XXIV)*, p. 862. Cf. Marshall, *Gospel of Luke*, pp. 428–429. Whilst the idea of the final defeat of Satan is attested strongly in post-exilic Jewish literature (e.g. 1QM 15.12 – 16.1; 17.5–8; 11QMelch. 13–14; T. Levi 18.12; T. Dan 5.10), in my view the language used here by the Lukan Jesus bears too striking a similarity to Isaiah for this allusion to be dismissed.

204 SIGNS AND WONDERS THEN AND NOW

13:4–12; 26:18). Here Jesus' vision of Satan's fall from the heavenly realm is the direct result of the missionaries' exorcisms.[61] As Green notes, the same eschatological tension that characterizes the 'now' and 'not yet' of the kingdom of God also characterizes the fall of Satan.[62]

Jesus follows this up by confirming that the source of the disciples' success in exorcism and authority over evil is Jesus himself (10:19). This is hardly a promise of 'invulnerability'.[63] The writer of the longer ending to Mark's Gospel (16:9–20; cf. especially v. 15) may have taken this passage from Luke (or an underlying tradition) literally or, alternatively, had Paul's experience in Acts 28:3–6 in mind. It seems to me to be more likely that Luke is using figurative language and his reference to snakes and scorpions would be understood by Luke's readers as symbols for evil (Ps. 91:13; *T. Levi* 18.12; *T. Sim.* 6.6; *T. Zeb.* 9.8).

There is a sense in which the language Jesus uses here ('I have given'; 'nothing shall hurt you') suggests that the authority over Satan that the emissaries enjoyed is not confined just to this particular mission.[64] However, given the apocalyptic nature of the passage, Luke's use of the future tense is more appropriate to an anticipation of Pentecost and beyond rather than indicating that the disciples' empowerment to perform signs and wonders is already established on a permanent basis during Jesus' lifetime. The focus of Luke's narrative at this point is not to be found in an imputed empowerment to perform signs and wonders. Rather, it is Jesus' corrective that provides the lesson in discipleship, taking the focus away from signs and wonders and emphasizing rather the disciples' standing before God. Again it is emphasized by Luke that signs and wonders are not of primary importance for Jesus' disciples. Compared to any authority they may have enjoyed over Satan and his minions in the past or in the future, of overriding importance when it comes to discipleship is the fact that their names are written in heaven (10:20).[65]

---

61. Garrett, *Demise of the Devil*, p. 49, concludes that the use of the imperfect (I was watching) indicates that Satan's fall was seen by Luke's Jesus as occurring simultaneously with (and possibly even caused by) the miraculous activity of the Seventy(-Two).

62. Green, *Gospel of Luke*, p. 419.

63. Evans, *Saint Luke*, p. 455.

64. This is the view of Nolland, *Luke 9:21–18:34*, p. 564; and Garrett, *Demise of the Devil*, p. 50.

65. For references to God's 'book of life', see for example Exod. 32:32–33; Pss. 69:28; 87:4–6; 139:16; Dan. 12:1 and cf. Phil. 4:3; Heb. 12:23; Rev. 3:5; 13:8; 17:8.

## Conclusions

During our examination of the missions of the Twelve and the Seventy(-Two), I have argued that both missions are to be understood as discrete incidents portrayed by Luke during the earthly ministry of Jesus. The mission of the Twelve alerts Luke's readers to the special place held by the apostles in relation to Jesus and the dominical tradition, and subsequently as pioneers leading the initial development of the post-Easter church. The second mission is unique to Luke's Gospel, and the role of the Seventy(-Two) must also be regarded as unique to the situation in which Luke has cast them; namely, that they are sent out by Jesus to prepare for his arrival at various towns as they progress with him to the dramatic climax awaiting them in Jerusalem.

Against the Third Wave, Luke's emphasis here is not intended by the evangelist to provide a paradigm for the normative expectation of 'every disciple'. Beyond Luke's narrative context, we should read no more than a foreshadowing of what is to come in Acts. In other words, the text simply will not bear the weight imposed upon it by the Third Wave's argument that the mission of the Seventy(-Two) provides conclusive evidence from Luke's Gospel that Jesus intended to present the church with a paradigm for contemporary discipleship that includes the normative expectation of empowerment to perform signs and wonders.

In both the missions of the Twelve and the Seventy(-Two), sharing in Jesus' mission during his lifetime was preceded by his commissioning and empowering chosen individuals for a specific purpose, so that receiving the emissaries of Jesus was like receiving the one who had sent them. Similarly, in Acts Luke remains consistent when empowerment to perform signs and wonders is restricted to the apostles and other chosen individuals who are commissioned by the risen Lord or by their Christian community.

In terms of contemporary application, what we can say is that the sending of the Seventy(-Two) illustrates the point that, at least potentially, any of Jesus' followers might be called and commissioned to represent him and share his power.

## 18. RESURRECTION AND COMMISSIONING IN LUKE-ACTS

## Introduction

As with the extended farewell discourse that concludes his account of the Last Supper (22:24–38), Luke has also included a more extended account of the resurrection appearances of the risen Jesus than the other Synoptic Evangelists. The material used is largely peculiar to Luke, although some interesting similarities to John's Gospel may be noted, suggesting perhaps that Luke and the writer of the Fourth Gospel had access to appearance traditions not known to (or at least not used by) Mark and Matthew (cf. 1 Cor. 15:3–8).[1] Why does Luke present us with these extended resurrection narratives? How does the Emmaus story prepare his readers for the final commissioning scene at the end of the Gospel?

A major emphasis throughout Luke's extended resurrection narratives is that events surrounding the life and ministry of Jesus of Nazareth are to be understood in terms of the fulfilment of Scripture (24:25–27, 44–47; Acts 1:16; 2:14; 18:28). This is immediately apparent in the Emmaus story, where

---

1. For a recent discussion, see J. Nolland, *Luke 18:35–24:53* (WBC 35C; Dallas: Word, 1993), pp. 1210–1212 and 1217–1218.

we have a reiteration of this favourite Lukan theme.[2] Also, in the communal life of the church, Jesus' ongoing presence may be experienced within the context of shared meals and the breaking of bread (24:30–31, 35; Acts 2:42), as well as through the Spirit's presence in response to prayer (Acts 13:1–3).

Importantly, Luke also sets out to clarify issues concerning the nature of Jesus' resurrection state that are clearly important for the evangelist and those for whom he was writing. At key points in his narrative, Luke emphasizes that Jesus' resurrection is to be understood in a corporeal rather than a purely metaphysical sense (24:5, 36–43; cf. Acts 1:3). It is clear that the 'materializing tendency'[3] present in Luke's resurrection narratives reflects a similar tendency found elsewhere in Luke-Acts.[4] Dunn suggests that the objectifying of the resurrection appearances by Luke may be due to an 'anti-docetic' motif.[5] Indeed, as I shall argue, Luke's objectifying of Jesus' resurrection state serves to establish for his readers the corporeal, non-angelic nature of Jesus' resurrection body and thus establishes irrefutable continuity between the earthly Jesus and the risen Lord.

Finally, there is the commission to empowered apostolic witness to all nations (Luke 24:47–49; Acts 1:8), which sets out the salvation-historical programme for Luke's narrative in Acts. Luke's form of the Great Commission also contains themes developed later in Acts. For example, the message goes out in the name of Jesus (Acts 2:38; 3:6, 16; 4:7, 10, 12, 17–18, 30; 5:28, 40; 8:12, 16; 9:14–16, 21, 27–28; 10:43, 48; 16:18; 19:5, 13, 17; 21:13; 22:16; 26:9), invites repentance (Acts 2:38; 3:19; 5:31; 8:22; 11:18; 13:24; 17:30; 19:4; 20:21; 26:20) and promises forgiveness of sins and a new relationship with God (Acts 2:38; 5:31; 10:43; 13:38; 26:18).[6]

---

2. N. Perrin, *The Resurrection According to Matthew, Mark and Luke* (Philadelphia: Fortress, 1977), p. 64; and see further below.

3. J. D. G. Dunn, *Jesus and the Spirit: A Study of the Religious and Charismatic Experience of Jesus and the First Christians as Reflected in the New Testament* (London: SCM, 1975), p. 122.

4. Examples include the following: objectifying language used to describe the descent of the Spirit at Jesus' baptism 'in bodily form' (Luke 3:22), and the descent of the Spirit at Pentecost (Acts 2:3); denying or affirming dreams (e.g. Luke 9:32; Acts 9:10; 10:10; 12:9; 16:9); confirming the reality of angelic/epiphanic experiences (e.g. Luke 2:9ff.; 24:4ff.; Acts 1:10–11; 8:26; 12:7, 10, 11; 27:23).

5. Dunn, *Jesus and the Spirit*, p. 122.

6. Noted by D. L. Bock, *Luke 9:51–24:53* (Grand Rapids, Mich.: Baker, 1996), p. 1939; and H. Bietenhard, ὄνομα, *TDNT* 5, p. 278.

## The walk to Emmaus

The first appearance of the risen Jesus described by Luke is to two disciples, who are not part of the apostolic band, and who are journeying from Jerusalem to Emmaus (Luke 24:13–35; cf. Mark 16:12).[7] This resurrection narrative appears only in Luke's Gospel, where the Evangelist has placed it between the empty tomb narrative and his final commissioning scene. Luke's reference to 'two of them' clearly alludes to both the wider circle of Jesus' disciples mentioned in 24:9 as well as serving to establish the forensic validity of the disciples' witness to the resurrection. By naming Cleopas, Luke makes it clear that this appearance is to disciples outside the apostolic band (cf. Acts 13:31; 1 Cor. 15:5–8). This is entirely in line with Luke's tendency to demonstrate that discipleship extends beyond the apostolic circle, and also roots the obligation on all disciples to 'bear witness' firmly in the appearances of the risen Christ.[8]

The journey motif used here by Luke also occurs in Acts 8:26–40, where, as Marshall notes, similar elements occur: journey motif; ignorance of Scripture; sacramental element (baptism/eucharist); sudden disappearance of interpreter of Scripture.[9] The failure of the two disciples to recognize Jesus is attributed by Nolland to 'Satanic binding'.[10] However, this element of incognito on the part of the main protagonist (Jesus) is better understood as a reflection of a common epiphanic element where gods/angels appear at the earthly level.[11] Also, in discussing the Emmaus story, we need to be aware of the apologetic nature of Luke 24:36–43.[12]

---

7. E. Lohse, *Die Auferstehung Jesu Christi im Zeugnis des Lukasevangeliums* (BibS 31; Neukirchen: Kreis Moers, Neukirchener, 1961), p. 25, says of Luke 24:15 that the two disciples followed the Jewish custom of discussing Torah and related issues as they walked along together. Also, cf. Deut. 6:5–7.

8. Bock, *Luke 9:51–24:53*, p. 1907.

9. I. H. Marshall, *Gospel of Luke*, p. 890. For a discussion of sources for Luke's theme of the fulfilment of Scripture, see A. Erhadt, 'The Disciples of Emmaus', *NTS* 10 (1963–4), pp. 187–190.

10. Nolland, *Luke 18:35–24:53*, p. 1201.

11. For examples outside the biblical tradition, see R. Bultmann, *History of the Synoptic Tradition* (ET Oxford: Blackwell, 1963), p. 286 n. 1.

12. Perrin, *Resurrection*, p. 66. Similarly, C. H. Dodd, 'The Appearances of the Risen Christ: An Essay in Form Criticism of the Gospels', in idem, *More New Testament Studies* (Manchester: Manchester University Press, 1968), p. 112, recognizes that

In Matthew's Gospel we have a similar piece of apologetic, but this time aimed at 'Jewish authorities', who claimed that Jesus' resurrection was to be explained by the fact that Jesus' disciples had stolen the body (Matt. 28:11–15). In Luke's Gospel the apology is directed against any notion that Jesus has been transformed into a spiritual or angelic being. David Catchpole argues that Luke is carefully countering a view of the resurrection state of Jesus as being angelic.[13] Whilst I agree with Catchpole that there are some striking similarities between the Emmaus story and Tobias' journey,[14] there are also other OT precedents on which Luke may have called. For example, in the book of Judges the angel who meets Manoah says explicitly that he will not eat the food Manoah offers (Judg. 13:15–16). In Genesis 18:8 the angelic visitors for whom Abraham has a meal prepared, the description of which is quite detailed (cf. Gen. 18:5–7), are actually described as eating the meal prepared for them whilst their host stands by. This passage is edited later by Philo (*Abr.* 115–118), where Philo makes it clear that the angelic visitors, who are incorporeal, have only assumed human form and therefore give only the appearance of eating and drinking.

By the end of the Emmaus story, Luke's readers are aware of a number of factors that the evangelist takes up again in the final commissioning scene. These are as follows:

1. Events surrounding the person and work of Jesus of Nazareth are to be understood in terms of the fulfilment of Scripture (24:26–27; cf. 24:44–46).
2. It is the risen Christ himself who demonstrates from Scripture how these events are fulfilled, thus giving heavenly authority to the theme of fulfilment (24:27; 24:45) for those who are about to bear witness.
3. A shared meal provides the context in which the risen Christ may be

---

Luke's extended recognition scene (24:36–43) serves as an apologetic for faith in the reality of Jesus' resurrection against arguments to the contrary.

13. D. R. Catchpole, *Resurrection People: Studies in the Resurrection Narratives of the Gospels* (London: Darton Longman & Todd, 2000), pp. 91, 93, argues for a pre-Lukan version of the Emmaus story that bears close similarities with Tobias' journey with the (incognito) archangel Raphael in the book of Tobit. For Catchpole's analysis of the Emmaus story, see especially pp. 93–102.

14. For example, travel theme; lack of recognition of Raphael / the risen Jesus; moment of revelation of true identity of travelling companion; the importance of failing to eat / breaking of bread.

recognized truly (24:31, 35), and this theme of using a meal as a vehicle for dispelling doubt and revealing the true nature of Jesus' resurrected state is again taken up in extended form as a precursor to the final commission (24:41b–43).

## Preparing the way for the final commissioning scene

Benjamin Hubbard has established that, although Luke's version of the Great Commission is not as direct as Matthew's, it nevertheless qualifies as a formal commission.[15] In a similar way, James Dunn writes, 'It is characteristic of the resurrection appearances in the gospel that they are commissioning experiences.'[16]

Apart from geographical location,[17] the actual commissions in Luke and Matthew are broadly similar in terms of emphasis in that both commissions are concerned with making disciples and have a universal perspective. The focus of Matthew's commission is on the process of making disciples, whereas Luke's focus is on the witness of Scripture to events surrounding the life and ministry of Jesus:[18] on repentance and forgiveness to be universally proclaimed in Jesus' name (24:47); on the fact that the apostles are to be witnesses; and on the imminent, but still future, expectation of heavenly empowerment. More importantly here, as Perrin has argued, Luke is concerned to provide a bridge between the Gospel and Acts and between the life and ministry of Jesus and the apostles and Luke's own readers.[19] With Luke's bridge-building purpose in mind, my examination of the wording of Luke's final commission(s) will take account of both the commission in Luke 24:44–49 and Acts 1:8.

The text of the final appearance and commissioning in Luke's Gospel clearly falls into two halves: Luke 24:36–43, which provides the link with the Emmaus story, and 24:44–49, where we have Luke's version of the Great

15. B. J. Hubbard, 'Commissioning Stories in Luke-Acts: A Study of their Antecedents, Form and Content', *Semeia* 8 (1977), p. 116.

16. Dunn, *Jesus and the Spirit*, pp. 128–129, who argues that the various versions of the Great Commission (Matt. 28:18–20; Luke 24:44–49; Acts 1:8) are 'expressions of later reflection'.

17. Luke, Jerusalem; Matthew, Galilee (cf. Mark 16:7).

18. Reflected also in the sermons in Acts (e.g. 2:22ff.; 8:30–35; 13:16ff.)

19. Perrin, *Resurrection*, p. 65.

Commission.[20] The words linking the close of the Emmaus story with the final commissioning scene (Luke 24:35–36) give the impression that Jesus' words are to be understood as being addressed to more than just the Eleven (Luke 24:33 and cf. 24:9).[21] At least Cleopas and his companion seem to be present, and this has the effect of widening the circle of disciples/witnesses present for the final commissioning by the risen Jesus. This, in turn, suggests that Luke intends both the final commission and the admonition to wait in Jerusalem until they are clothed with heavenly *dynamis* to apply also to more than just the apostles.[22] If this is Luke's final intention, then the Third Wave's case for all Christians being included in the Great Commission in such a way that they are to consider empowered witness, including signs and wonders, to be a normative expectation is strengthened somewhat. However, the difficulty lies in the fact that Luke corrects himself in Acts, where he names only the apostles as the recipients of the final mission charge (Acts 1:2–7). In his reiteration of the final commission in Acts 1:8 the focus is again specifically on the apostles and the instruction they have received from the risen Jesus over a period of time through the Holy Spirit (Acts 1:2).

As the Acts narrative develops, it becomes clear that it is the apostles who form the transitional unifying group who ensure continuity with the earthly Jesus and his teaching during the initial expansion of the church (e.g. Acts 2:42–43; 6:6; 8:1, 14; 9:27; 15:22–23).[23] Also, as Luke's narrative in Acts progresses, it soon becomes apparent that not all who receive the Spirit at Pentecost, or afterwards, become public proclaimers of the gospel message of repentance and forgiveness. Nor, contra the Third Wave, is it presented by Luke as normative for all who are followers of the Way to engage in empowered witness accompanied by signs and wonders. Luke clearly reserves miraculous

---

20. R. H. Fuller, *The Formation of the Resurrection Narratives*, 2nd ed. (London: SPCK, 1980), p. 117.

21. The link-phrase 'While they were talking about this' in 24:36 is almost certainly Lukan and serves to link the final commission scene with the Emmaus story (cf. vv. 33–35). See for example Nolland, *Luke 18:35–24:53*, p. 1212; and Marshall, *Gospel of Luke*, p. 901.

22. This is clearly the case in Acts, first when the disciples gather to elect a successor to Judas (Acts 1:14, 15, 20) and when Luke describes the descent of the Spirit at Pentecost (Acts 2:1ff.).

23. This important element of continuity between Jesus and the church provided by the apostles is noted by J. D. G. Dunn, *The Acts of the Apostles* (Peterborough: Epworth, 1996), p. 6.

activity for a select few leading characters as he tells his story of the expansion of the church in fulfilment of the Great Commission. According to Acts, during this initial period, miraculous signs and wonders, which by definition must be considered extraordinary, are at first only performed through the apostles, then later through selected individuals rather than by every member of the wider Christian community. In other words, even when Luke's Gospel narrative indicates the possibility of a more general participation by Jesus' followers in ministry accompanied by signs and wonders, Luke's emphasis is to be found in that possibility being realized only by designated individuals who are commissioned and empowered for particular tasks.

An example of this can be seen in the case of the seven 'deacons' in Acts 6, where the prayers and laying on of hands by the apostles/members of the Jerusalem congregation[24] should be seen as a commissioning and conveyance of authority.[25] Also, the impression given by Luke is that these men, whom he describes as being 'full of the Spirit and wisdom', are respected and mature charismatic leaders who are recognized as such by their community (Acts 6:3–5), and thus stand out as exemplars and leaders of their group.[26] Again, the evidence suggests that it is not Luke's intention here to provide a paradigm for the normative expectation of all who have received the Spirit.

Luke's final commissioning scene serves as the finale to his Gospel and points the way forward to Acts. Luke's major soteriological themes are in evidence prior to their being taken up again by Luke in the Acts narrative; namely, proclamation of salvation through repentance and forgiveness of sins (Luke 1:77; 3:3; 24:47; Acts 2:38; 5:31; 10:43; 13:38; 26:18); the universal nature of the gospel (2:31–2; 24:47; Acts 1:8; 2:5; 8:1, 5–8, 14–17, 26–40; 9:15, 31; 10:1–11, 24; 13:1–2, 40–50; 15:1–29; 18:6; 22:13–15; 26:16–18, 23; 27:24; 28:28); salvation is proclaimed in the name of Jesus (Acts 2:38; 3:6, 16; 4:10, 12, 30; 8:12, 16; 10:48; 16:18; 19:5).

More to the point for the purpose of our present investigation, how are we to understand Luke's accounts of Jesus' final commissioning of the apostles in Luke 24:44–49 and Acts 1:8, and where do Luke's emphases lie? How do

---

24. For a further discussion of this point, see chapter 20.

25. B. Witherington III, *The Acts of the Apostles: A Socio-Rhetorical Commentary* (Grand Rapids, Mich.: Eerdmans; Carlisle: Paternoster, 1998), p. 251.

26. Dunn, *Acts of the Apostles*, p. 83, makes the important point that the description 'full of the Spirit and wisdom' is in contrast to Luke's usual verbal phrase that indicates being filled with the Spirit for a particular occasion. Examples of being empowered by the Spirit for a particular occasion may be found in Acts 4:8, 31; 6:5; 7:55; 13:9.

these emphases vary from the Great Commission according to Matthew? Can we say that empowerment to perform miracles features in our understanding of Luke's final commission and, if so, how is this presented by Luke in the ensuing Acts narrative? In what way, if at all, does Luke intend this material to be paradigmatic for his readers, and how does this affect the Third Wave's case?

## The final commissioning scene in Luke's Gospel

As we saw with the resurrection appearance on the road to Emmaus, it is clearly important for Luke to establish the corporeality of Jesus' resurrection body and to establish that the risen Jesus is not a spirit/ghost/angel,[27] so that Luke's resurrection narratives establish continuity between the earthly Jesus and the Risen One. This means that for Luke the words of commission carry at least the same authority, including potential empowerment to heal and cast out demons, as did the earlier commissions of Luke 9 and 10. Uniquely, in the case of Luke-Acts, we have not only Luke's version(s) of the Great Commission (Luke 24:44–49; Acts 1:8), but we also have the author's narrative in Acts that demonstrates for his readers how Luke understands the way in which the fulfilment of Jesus' final commission to his disciples worked out in practice.

As with Matthew 28:16–20, the final appearance of Jesus at the end of Luke's Gospel serves both to establish the fact of Jesus' resurrection to his assembled disciples, and to instruct them in preparation for their future missionary activity of expanding the church. Jesus appears amongst the assembled disciples just as suddenly as he disappeared from the Emmaus narrative. Nolland proposes that Luke's description of the risen Jesus suddenly standing among them may have links with OT stories of angelic appearances found in the LXX (e.g. Gen. 18:2; Dan. 8:15; 12:5; 1 Chron. 21:15–16; cf. Tobit 5:4), and that this suggestion is strengthened by Jesus' greeting 'peace to you' (cf. Dan. 10:19; Judg. 6:23).[28] The assembled disciples are startled and afraid. Their reaction to Jesus' sudden appearance amongst them is reminiscent of reactions classically associated with an epiphany, and they believe they are in the presence of a spirit/ghost.[29]

---

27. John deals with this issue when Jesus confronts Thomas (20:24–29).
28. Nolland, *Luke 18:35–24:53*, p. 1212. See also Bock, *Luke 9:51–24:53*, p. 1932, who agrees that OT traditions may indicate cultural expectations about post-mortem appearances (1 Sam. 28:3–19; Isa. 8:19; 19:3; 29:4).
29. Bock, *Luke 9:51–24:53*, p. 1948, notes that Codex D weakly attests to *phantasma* instead of *pneuma* (cf. Mark 6:49; Matt. 14:26).

As I argued above in my discussion of the Emmaus story, an important aspect of Luke's purpose in having Jesus join the two disciples in the 'breaking of bread' was to dispel their doubts and to reveal the true nature of Jesus' resurrection state. Similarly here, a careful examination of the final appearance scene in Luke and the words of commission themselves reveals a number of interesting factors pointing in the same direction. References to 'flesh and bones' in verse 39, together with the invitation to touch Jesus are all aimed to dispel the doubts expressed in verse 38[30] and to demonstrate that Jesus was not an ethereal spirit. In verse 41a the disciples are literally disbelieving from joy.[31]

Commenting on Luke 24:42, Nolland suggests that here, as well as in the Emmaus story (24:31, 35), Jesus is made known in the 'meal setting', and is rather dismissive of the idea of Jesus' eating being primarily intended by Luke to be proof of the risen Jesus' corporeality and non-angelic status.[32] In other words, for Nolland, here as in the Emmaus story Luke uses the meal setting to explain a eucharistic theology.[33] Fuller takes a similar line when he suggests that Luke has located the final appearance scene within the context of a eucharistic meal.[34] A similar eucharistic view is also taken by Cullmann,[35] but Bock takes a middle line when he writes, 'A meal shows that it is Jesus and not a phantom, and it also indicates table fellowship and oneness.'[36]

However, it should be noted here that there is no indication that this is simply depicted by Luke as a shared or fellowship meal. Rather, it seems clearly to be a way of establishing the corporeal status of Jesus' risen body. Although the language of angelophany is unavoidable, the conclusion to be drawn is similar to that drawn from Luke's following account of Jesus eating a piece of fish before his assembled disciples (24:43); namely that the risen Jesus is not an angel.

---

30. Jesus' words 'Why are you frightened, and why do doubts arise in your hearts?' reflect the doubt theme also present in Matthew's final commission scene (cf. Matt. 28:17).

31. Nolland, *Luke 18:35–24:53*, p. 1214, draws attention to the similar formulation in Luke 22:45 ('he . . . found them sleeping because of grief'), where, in the garden of Gethsemane, the disciples are asleep because of grief.

32. Ibid., p. 1215.

33. Ibid. For further attestation within the tradition of the risen Jesus eating with his disciples, see for example John 21:13; Acts 1:4; 10:41.

34. Fuller, *Resurrection Narratives*, p. 109.

35. O. Cullmann, *Early Christian Worship* (ET London: SCM, 1966), pp. 14–16.

36. Bock, *Luke 9:51–24:53*, p. 1935.

Having firmly established continuity between the earthly Jesus and the Risen One, Luke alerts his readers to the importance of the final commissioning of the disciples by the risen Jesus in two ways. Firstly, in Greek, the opening words of the Lukan Jesus, whom the evangelist regards as a prophet like Moses (Acts 3:22; cf. Deut. 18:18), bear a striking similarity to the introduction to Deuteronomy (Deut. 1:1 LXX).

Secondly, Jesus again opens the Scriptures,[37] reminding his hearers, in similar words to those spoken earlier by the angel to the women (24:6–7) and Jesus' words to the disciples on the road to Emmaus (24:25–27), that all that has happened is in fulfilment of Scripture.[38] In verse 46 Jesus' explicit exposition of Scripture refers to his death and resurrection and leads into the mission charge in verse 47, where we have the kernel of the universal gospel message of repentance and forgiveness of sins in the name of Jesus,[39] which is to be proclaimed to all nations (Isa. 42:6; 49:6; Luke 2:32; Acts 13:47; cf. Acts 10:42–43; 26:22–23).[40]

In verse 49 Luke gives his understanding of the missionary role of the apostles, and here, but apparently not in Acts 1:8,[41] the role of the wider circle of

---

37. Here the entire extent of the Scriptures is specified by Luke ('everything written about me in the law of Moses, the prophets, and the psalms'), and, as J. E. Alsup, *The Post-Resurrection Appearance Stories of the Gospel Tradition* (Calwer Theologische Monographien 5; Stuttgart: Calwer; London: SPCK, 1975), p. 183, notes, this combination occurs only here in the Synoptic tradition.

38. As Bock, *Luke 9:51–24:53*, p. 1936, notes, 'fulfilment' is a key Lukan theme that occurs throughout Luke-Acts (e.g. Luke 1:20; 4:21; 9:31; 21:24; 22:16; Acts 1:16; 3:18; 13:27).

39. Cf. Luke 9:48; 10:17 (cf. 9:49); 21:8, 12, 17; and frequently in Acts – for example, 2:38; 3:6, 16; 4:7, 10, 12, 17–18, 30; 5:28, 40, 41; 8:16; 16:18; 19:2; 22:16.

40. Fitzmyer, *The Gospel According to Luke (X–XXIV)* (AB 28A; New York: Doubleday, 1985), p. 1584, suggests that the gospel message of repentance and forgiveness is the Lukan equivalent of Matthew's 'making disciples'. Alsup, *Post-Resurrection Appearance Stories*, p. 183, notes that the phrase 'all nations' is a combination used throughout the Synoptic Gospels and Acts (e.g. Matt. 24:9, 14; 25:32; 28:19; Mark 11:17; 13:10; Luke 24:47; Acts 2:5; 10:35; 14:16; 17:26; 21:21).

41. In Acts 1:8 Luke appears to have only the apostles in mind (Acts 1:2b), whereas in Luke 24 it is clear from the narrative that more disciples than just the apostles are included in the final commission (cf. 24:33, 36). Fuller, *Resurrection Narratives*, p. 118, maintains that in v. 48 Jesus is addressing the Eleven directly. Whilst this

Jesus' disciples. In the LXX 'witness' (*martys*) is used in a forensic sense in connection with judgment.[42] Luke also uses *martys* here, and in Acts, in the forensic sense of 'witness to the facts'.[43] Disciples are to be witnesses, and the concept of being a witness will be an important theme throughout Acts (1:8, 22; 2:32; 3:15; 5:32; 10:39, 41; 13:31; 22:15, 20; 26:16). More importantly, for Luke these first witnesses have been involved in historical events and are eyewitnesses to the ministry, death and resurrection of Jesus of Nazareth (cf. Acts 1:21–22). The witnesses of later generations – and these include Luke's readers – will not have this direct link to the dominical tradition. Therefore, they will have to rely instead on the apostolic authority of those who accompanied Jesus during his lifetime and who were witnesses of his resurrection – especially those who, according to Luke, were designated 'apostles' by Jesus from the outset (Luke 6:13).

Jesus' reference to the promise of the Father is immediately clarified in verse 49 as 'power from on high'. The disciples are commanded to stay in Jerusalem and to await heavenly empowerment associated with the distribution of the Spirit (cf. Acts 1:8). With the emphatic words 'I am sending upon you what my Father promised' Luke makes it clear that Jesus is now the dispenser of the eschatological Spirit, whereas formerly the Father himself was the dispenser.[44] The idea of being 'clothed with power' reflects OT usage, where we also find the idea of being 'clothed' with power / the Spirit (e.g. Judg. 10:34; 1 Chron. 12:8; 2 Chron. 24:20; Ps. 92:1; Isa. 15:1; cf. Ecclus. 17:3; Wisdom 9:17).[45] Elsewhere in Luke-Acts *dynamis* and *pneuma* appear to be almost synonymous (e.g. Luke 1:17, 35; 4:14; Acts 1:5, 8; 6:8; 10:38), and in this present context *dynamis* may be understood as referring to 'empowered testimony'.[46] Jesus' promise of heavenly *dynamis* in Luke 24:49 becomes a baptism in the Holy Spirit in Acts 1:5 and, in turn, is seen as the source of forthcoming empowerment in Acts 1:8.

---

conjecture may serve to harmonize Luke 24 with Acts 1, it is not borne out by the evidence.

42. H. Strathmann, μάρτυς, *TDNT* 4, p. 463.

43. Ibid., p. 492.

44. Bock, *Luke 9:51–24:53*, p. 1943; L. T. Johnson, *The Gospel of Luke* (SP 3; Collegeville, Minn.: Liturgical, 1991), p. 403. But cf. Acts 5:32, where the source of the Spirit is again God.

45. F. W. Danker, *Jesus and the New Age: A Commentary on St. Luke's Gospel* (Philadelphia: Fortress, 1988), pp. 398–399.

46. Bock, *Luke 9:51–24:53*, p. 1943.

In examining the words of Luke's two versions of the Great Commission there is no mention of signs and wonders, or of disciples performing miracles as part of their remit. It is also worth noting that in Luke 24:49 Jesus instructs the assembled disciples that they are to wait in Jerusalem until they receive the promise of the Father, when they will be clothed with heavenly *dynamis*. Without reading into the text, we cannot assume that, as with Matthew's promise of *exousia*, this will include power over the demonic for all disciples. In any case, our understanding here of being 'clothed with power' must be governed by the clarification in Acts 1:3–8 and, most significantly, by Luke's presentation of signs and wonders in the Acts narrative.

The essence of the Great Commission according to Luke may be summarized as follows:

1. The risen Jesus refers back to his earthly ministry and demonstrates how, in his life, death and resurrection, he has fulfilled Scripture (Luke 24:44–46).
2. The universal gospel message to be preached in Jesus' name is one of repentance and forgiveness (24:47a).
3. Jesus' commission is intended by Luke to be programmatic in that the universal mission begins in Jerusalem before moving out to the rest of the world (24:47b), and this missionary programme provides the narrative framework for Acts.
4. The primary role of those being commissioned is to bear empowered witness to all that has gone before (24:49).

We are now in a position to examine the final commission as it occurs in Acts 1:8 and to note any points of variance between the two versions of Luke's Great Commission.

## The commission according to Acts 1:8

The repeat of the Great Commission in Acts 1:8 forges a narrative link with the Gospel, but more importantly it clarifies and explains for Luke's readers important elements of the gospel commission. This time there is no doubt that it is only the eleven remaining apostles who are being addressed, and the subsequent commissioning by the risen Jesus is for the apostles alone. As might be expected, the missionary outlook remains universal, but the successive stages of Luke's soteriological programme in Acts are now made explicit in chronological detail. This marks the progress that Luke's narrative in Acts will take, beginning in Jerusalem, where the initial outpouring of the Spirit will be experienced by the believers.[47] In Acts 1:8a the *dynamis* imparted through the Holy Spirit not only makes the proclamation of the apostolic witnesses effective; it is also the source through which miracles are performed.[48]

Remaining sensitive to the importance for Luke of the shift in the epochs of salvation-history is of crucial importance if we are to remain sensitive to the outlook of the Acts narrative. Here Luke seeks to embrace both the eschatological reality of the post-Easter situation for the early church, together with the longer-term outlook in which the church in Luke's own day must operate as a result of the delay in the parousia.[49] This historical sensitivity is important for Third Wave and other contemporary commentators to note when seeking NT models that inform contemporary faith and praxis, and cautions against a too direct and uncritical correlation between contemporary experience and praxis and the experience of the early church as Luke portrays it in Acts.

In line with its commission from the risen Jesus, the infant church will expand as it moves out in mission to embrace fellow Jews in wider Judea, Samaritans and Gentiles from Jerusalem to the 'ends of the earth'. Witherington has noted that the phrase 'to the ends of the earth' can simply refer to 'Rome' (cf. *Pss. Sol.* 8.15).[50] This being the case, it bears out the assertion that Acts 1:8 is deliberately setting out the missionary and narrative agenda for the rest of Acts. However, when Acts 1:8 is taken with Luke 24:47, the universal significance becomes clear in that the missionary progress to Rome is to include all peoples.

---

47. J. Fitzmyer, *The Acts of the Apostles* (AB 31; New York: Doubleday, 1998), p. 199. H. Conzelmann, *Acts of the Apostles* (ET Philadelphia: Fortress, 1987), p. 7, comments, 'By means of this outline the delay in the Parousia is transferred into something positive in the course of salvation-history.'

48. F. F. Bruce, *The Acts of the Apostles: Greek Text with Introduction and Commentary*, 3rd ed (Leicester: Apollos, 1990), p. 103; J. Jervell, *Die Apostelgeschichte* (KEK; Göttingen: Vandenhoeck & Ruprecht, 1998), p. 115.

49. S. Brown, 'Apostasy and Perseverance', *AnBib* 36 (1969), p. 12, remarks, 'The characteristic of the Age of the Church is . . . the presence of the spirit, and the beginning of the Age of the Church is therefore not the passion but Pentecost.'

50. Witherington, *Acts*, p. 111.

## Conclusions

In my discussion of Luke's extended resurrection narratives, we have seen that it is important for the evangelist to establish the corporeal, non-angelic nature of Jesus' resurrection state so that his readers may be reassured about the continuity that exists for Luke between the earthly Jesus and the risen Lord, possibly as a defence against docetic tendencies in the church. The first disciples were witnesses to the ministry, death and resurrection of Jesus of Nazareth (cf. Acts 1:21–22) and, as such, the truthfulness of their testimony could be relied upon. The witnesses of later generations, including those for whom Luke is writing, did not have the same direct link with dominical tradition. Therefore, they must depend instead on the reliability of the apostolic testimony that the same Jesus of Nazareth, whose earthly ministry Luke describes in his Gospel, is now also the risen and exalted Lord who has commissioned his church to bear witness to him to the ends of the earth.

Unlike the Great Commission according to Matthew, where the disciples are to share Jesus' authority to teach, forgive sins and cast out demons and heal, the final commission according to Luke-Acts is not so transparent. In Luke's Gospel we are left with the possibility of more than just the Eleven being 'clothed with power from on high', and, without further clarification, this might reasonably be taken to include miraculous power. However, an appropriately critical sensitivity towards the text requires us to note the importance for Luke of the shift in salvation-historical perspective that takes place with the resurrection. This enables us to remain sensitive to the outlook of Acts, where we encounter both Luke's view of the eschatological reality of the post-Easter situation for the early church, together with his own longer-term outlook in view of the delay in the parousia. The need for such sensitivity towards the text has a direct bearing on my engagement with the Third Wave and their tendency towards an homogenous approach to the NT evidence, and cautions us all in the church today against a too direct correlation between contemporary Christian experience and praxis and the experience of the early church as Luke portrays it in Acts.

In this respect we noted that in Acts 1:8 Jesus' commission is addressed only to the remaining apostles, and the enigmatic 'power from on high' is explained by Luke in terms of baptism in the Holy Spirit (Acts 1:5, 8). Whilst the *dynamis* imparted by the Spirit may appear to make empowered witness, including signs and wonders (at least potentially), more widely possible, we are nevertheless faced with the problem that in Acts signs and wonders are restricted to a chosen few. As the Acts narrative progresses, it soon becomes apparent that not all who receive the Spirit become proclaimers of the word and whose activities are accompanied by signs and wonders.

In our next chapter, we will investigate the part played by signs and wonders in Acts, and especially the way in which signs and wonders relate to discipleship and the missionary witness of the infant church.

## 19. SIGNS AND WONDERS IN ACTS

## Introduction

In concluding his detailed discussion of the miracles of Jesus in Luke's Gospel, Graham Twelftree writes, 'Luke was convinced that Jesus' ministry of miracles was to be carried on by his followers.'[1]

This raises the question 'To what extent?' In other words, why, when he has the opportunity to do otherwise, does Luke restrict the performance of miraculous signs and wonders to the apostles and a small number of chosen individuals whom we have designated Luke's heroes of the Spirit? The idea of authoritative commissioning and divine call is a feature in the life of the post-Easter community depicted by Luke in Acts. After Pentecost, it is the apostles together with the Jerusalem congregation they lead who use their authority to commission selected members of their community (Acts 6:2–6), although in the case of Paul his defining commission comes from the risen Lord himself (Acts 9:3ff.; 22:6ff.; 26:12ff. Cf. 1 Cor. 9:1). On other occasions it is the local congregation, acting under the prophetic direction of the Spirit who commission individuals for mission (Acts 13:1–3). In the various post-Easter commissionings described by Luke, the evangelist provides us with a strong echo of

---

1. G. H. Twelftree, *Jesus the Miracle Worker* (Downers Grove, Ill.: IVP, 1999), p. 188.

his earlier presentation of Jesus as a 'man under authority' (cf. Luke 7:8–9), particularly through the prominence given to the name of Jesus in the healing and subsequent discussion in Acts 3 – 4.[2] However, the important point to bear in mind here is that in Acts Luke reserves the performance of signs and wonders to a select few who receive an authoritative commission. Signs and wonders are not, so far as Luke-Acts is concerned, performed by any other members of the Christian community. In terms of contemporary application, I will argue that the evidence from Acts suggests a model where individuals are commissioned by their local congregation, where they are known and in whom the authoritative voice of the Spirit of Jesus rests.[3]

A number of general observations may be made about the miraculous phenomena attributed to individuals in Acts, each of which will be discussed further below.[4] Firstly, individual miracles may not be explicitly designated 'signs and wonders', but it is clear that Luke uses this term as a 'catch-all' for miracles, healings, exorcisms and other miraculous phenomena, all of which contribute to the overall numinous atmosphere of the Acts narrative. Secondly, each of Luke's heroes of the Spirit in Acts to whom he attributes miraculous activity has been commissioned to act with authority. Thirdly, signs and wonders in Acts normally enhance the overall numinous atmosphere of the narrative, serving generally to demonstrate God's validation of the miracle-workers and/or enhance their reputation, normally with a view to creating or supporting the opportunity to preach the gospel and encourage new converts.

There are exceptions, but these are relatively few and when they do occur they also contribute to the overall numinous atmosphere of the narrative. Examples are the building shaken and appearance of fiery tongues during Pentecostal distribution of the Spirit; the building shaken again during prayer

---

2. Discussed further in chapter 20.

3. Acts 13:1–3; and cf. especially vv. 2b–3.

4. For an analysis of signs and wonders in Acts, see the appendix. P. J. Achtemeier, 'The Lukan Perspective on the Miracles of Jesus: A Preliminary Sketch', in C. H. Talbert (ed.), *Perspectives on Luke-Acts* (Danville, Va.: Association of Baptist Professors of Religion; Edinburgh: T. & T. Clark, 1978), p. 165 n. 22, uses a similar grouping. For alternative approaches, see for example J. A. Hardon, 'The Miracle Narratives in the Acts of the Apostles' *CBQ* 16 (1954), pp. 304–305; and F. Neirynck, 'The Miracle Stories in the Acts of the Apostles: An Introduction', in J. Kremer (ed.), *Les Actes des Apôtres: traditions, redaction, théologie* (Gembloux, Leuven: Duculot, 1979), pp. 170–171.

for boldness to preach the gospel (4:30), and it is worth noting here the reference to signs, wonders and healing; angelic aid during Peter's escape from prison
whilst awaiting execution by Herod (12:1–11); and Herod's untimely death
(12:23). Two further incidents are worth mentioning here,[5] Peter's confrontation with Simon Magus (8:18–24), and the exorcism that backfires on the sons
of Sceva (19:13–19), which also results in a general atmosphere of awe (19:17a),
and a number of the residents of Ephesus becoming believers (19:17b).

With the above overview of signs and wonders in Acts in mind, we can now
proceed with our investigation into the way in which Luke understands and
presents signs and wonders in Acts in relation to his heroes of the Spirit.


## Commissioning with power and authority in Acts

We saw in our discussion of authority in Matthew's Gospel that in classical
Greek usage, *exousia* is understood as the right to do something, or authority
over something that is granted by a higher power such as a king or other
authority.[6] However, as Foerster points out, this authority (*exousia*) remains
illusory unless it is accompanied by the power (*dynamis*) necessary in order to
exercise the authority that has been conferred.[7] From here Foerster concludes
that it is 'not always possible to separate between authority and power'.[8] There
are clear implications here for the situation we encounter in Luke-Acts.

First of all, we have seen how both *dynamis* and *exousia* are explicitly present
in the commissionings associated with the two missions in Luke's Gospel
(Luke 9:1; 10:1, 17, 19). Johnson notes how 'power' (*dynamis*) and 'authority'
(*exousia*) are terms used repeatedly of Jesus' ability to deal with demons and
disease (cf. Luke 4:36; 5:17; 6:19; 8:46).[9] Jesus has the *exousia* to expel demons
(Luke 10:19), and this *exousia* presupposes a divine commission.[10] Following
Jesus' Nazareth manifesto in Luke 4:16–30, we find Luke has placed *exousia*
and *dynamis* in juxtaposition in connection with Jesus' exorcisms (4:36), having
previously described Jesus' teaching as being given with 'authority' (4:32).

---

5. Noted by Neirynck, 'Miracle Stories', p. 171.
6. W. Foerster, ἐξουσία, *TDNT* 2, p. 562.
7. Ibid., pp. 562–563.
8. Ibid., p. 563.
9. L. T. Johnson, *The Literary Function of Possessions in Luke-Acts* (SBLDS 39; Missoula:
   Scholars Press, 1977), p. 145.
10. Foerster, ἐξουσία, p. 569. Cf. Luke 3:21–22 and my discussion above.

Secondly, Luke's use of the phrase 'signs and wonders' in Acts, shows that he is conscious of the OT background, and especially the way in which signs and wonders are associated with Moses and the Exodus (Exod. 4:8–9, 17, 28, 30; 7:3, 9; 10:1, 2; 11:9–10; Num. 14:11–12; Deut. 4:34; 6:22; 7:18–19; 11:3; 26:8; 29:3; LXX Pss. 77:43; 104:27; 134:9).[11] In the LXX *dynamis* is used to describe God's mighty liberating acts on behalf of Israel (e.g. Exod. 7:3; Deut. 4:34; 28:46; 29:2; 34:11; 135:9; Isa. 8:18). Wenk rightly emphasizes the point that miracles in Luke-Acts are more than God's validation of the message/messenger: as with the Exodus, they are also evidence of God's 'redemptive intervention'.[12] In this respect, in the OT signs and wonders are of special importance in the portrayal of Moses as a prophet (Acts 7:36; cf. Deut. 34:10–12) who is also a 'type' for Jesus' prophetic ministry that was also validated through powerful deeds, signs and wonders (cf. Acts 2:22; 10:38).[13] This aspect of Jesus' ministry is emphasized by Luke from the beginning of his ministry in Galilee, which the evangelist describes as being 'in the power of the Spirit' (Luke 4:14).

O'Reilly argues that, through his use of Moses typology in Luke-Acts, Luke indicates that signs and wonders associated with both Jesus and his disciples are to be understood as 'inaugurating the time of eschatological salvation'.[14] Just as the signs and wonders of the Exodus demonstrated how YHWH was superior to the gods of those who opposed Israel, so too do the signs and wonders in Acts point to the lordship of the risen and exalted Christ, who is now the dispenser of the Spirit.[15] Similarly, as signs and wonders in the Exodus served to establish Israel as the people of God, so too are signs and wonders in Acts to be understood as being instrumental in the formation of the infant church as the eschatological people of God.[16] This, in turn, suggests that whilst the presence of signs and wonders in Acts serves to enhance the numinous atmosphere of Luke's narrative, they should also be understood as having a more important salvation-historical function. Therefore, it is little

---

11. J. A. Fitzmyer, *The Acts of the Apostles* (AB 31; New York: Doubleday, 1998), p. 255.

12. M. Wenk, *Community-Forming Power: The Socio-Ethical Role of the Spirit in Luke-Acts* (JPTSup 19; Sheffield: Sheffield Academic Press, 2000), pp. 250–251.

13. L. O'Reilly, *Word and Sign in the Acts of the Apostles: A Study in Lucian Theology* (Rome: Cura Pontificial Universitatis Gregorianae, 1987), pp. 174–175; G. W. H. Lampe, 'Miracles in the Acts of the Apostles', in C. F. D. Moule (ed.), *Miracles: Cambridge Studies in their Philosophy and History* (London: Mowbray, 1965), p. 167.

14. Ibid., p. 188.

15. Ibid., pp. 186–187.

16. Ibid., p. 190.

wonder that Luke associated signs and wonders only with those who have a recognized authoritative role to play in the missiological progress of the church.

It has been noted that parallels between the miracles of Jesus and those of the disciples in Acts indicate that, for Luke, Jesus' disciples continue Jesus' charismatic ministry.[17] But again the question is, how widely are we to understand this? O'Reilly understands the relationship between Jesus' working of miracles in the Gospel and the signs and wonders associated with the apostles and other missionaries in Acts in terms of 'prophetic succession'. He articulates this in the following way, 'Jesus is the eschatological prophet-like-Moses whose "signs and wonders" usher in the last days. The apostles and missionaries are prophets-like-Jesus who continue his mission in mighty works as well as in powerful word.'[18]

The Third Wave go much further, arguing that this is intentionally paradigmatic and aimed at all Christians who should, therefore, be encouraged to expect signs and wonders to continue to be a part of everyday Christian experience. However, the evidence in Acts, where signs and wonders are restricted by Luke to the apostles and a select band of heroes of the Spirit, does not appear to support this view.

## Luke's perspective on signs and wonders

Luke does not present the source for the signs and wonders performed in Acts in a systematic way. He attributes them variously to God (Acts 2:22; 15:12), the

---

17. Ibid., p. 182. R. B. Hays, *The Moral Vision of the New Testament: A Contemporary Introduction to New Testament Ethics* (Edinburgh: T. & T. Clark, 1996), p. 122, notes the following examples of miracle stories in Acts that 'mirror' similar miracle stories in Luke's Gospel: Acts 3:1–10 and Luke 5:17–26; Acts 5:15; 19:11–12 and Luke 8:44; Acts 7:59–60 and Luke 23:34; and especially Acts 9:36–43 and Luke 8:40, 49–56. See also C. H. Talbert, *Literary Patterns, Theological Themes, and the Genre of Luke-Acts* (Missoula: Scholars Press, 1974), pp. 23–24. For a discussion of the Lukan parallels between Jesus and Paul and the extensive way in which Luke has modelled Paul's career in Acts on that of Jesus in the Gospel, see W. Radl, *Paulus und Jesus im Lukanischen Doppelwerk: Untersuchungen zu Parallelmotiven im Lukasevangelium und in der Apostelgeschichte* (Bern: H. Lang; Frankfurt: P. Lang, 1975), especially pp. 291–380.

18. O'Reilly, *Word and Sign*, p. 182.

name of Jesus (4:30), and to the Lord (14:3).[19] In Peter's speech to the crowds at Pentecost, the signs and wonders in Acts are the gift of the Spirit in the last days (Acts 2:17), and Luke's redaction of Joel's prophecy makes it clear that signs and wonders are linked with the outpouring of the eschatological Spirit.[20] Miracles occur in Acts in the context of eschatological expectation,[21] and are firmly linked with the missionary activity of the church in its progress from Jerusalem into the Gentile world.[22] As well as having salvation-historical significance, signs and wonders are part of the landscape which contributes to the numinous atmosphere that pervades Luke's narrative of the life and mission of the early church.[23] They also function as God's validation of the proclamation of the gospel by those heroes of the Spirit whom he calls and commissions either though the risen Christ, or through the local Christian community.

### Luke's perspective on the miracles of Jesus

In his study of Luke's portrayal of the miracle-working of Jesus, Achtemeier maintains that the importance of Jesus' miracle-working for Luke can be seen from the fact that it is the miracles he performs that validate him.[24] For example, in Luke 4:36 the evangelist clarifies the adverbial phrase 'with authority' found

---

19.  Cf. J. D. G. Dunn, *Jesus and the Spirit: A Study of the Religious and Charismatic Experience of Jesus and the First Christians as Reflected in the New Testament* (London: SCM, 1975), p. 170. Hardon, 'Miracle Narratives', p. 307, notes how Luke's central characters go to great lengths in order to ensure that those who witness signs and wonders rightly attribute them to their heavenly source.

20.  O'Reilly, *Word and Sign*, p. 187. See my discussion of Acts 2:14ff. below.

21.  Hardon, 'Miracle Narratives', pp. 304–305. Dunn, *Jesus and the Spirit*, p. 163, writes, 'By using the phrase [signs and wonders] so frequently Luke underlines and probably reflects the early community's feeling that they were living in "the new Mosaic age of eschatological redemption", characterized by the same kind of "signs and wonders" that characterized the redemption of Israel from Egypt.'

22.  Lampe, 'Miracles in the Acts of the Apostles', p. 178. A notable exception would be Ananias, who is commissioned by the risen Jesus to minister to Saul/Paul during the conversion process following the latter's encounter with the risen Jesus on the road of Damascus (Acts 9:1ff.).

23.  In Acts 2:43, 5:5, 11, 9:31, 19:17 Luke's use of *phobos* (fear) indicates the numinous atmosphere in which the church operated.

24.  Achtemeier, 'Lukan Perspective', p. 158.

in Mark 1:27 so that it more clearly relates to Jesus' word of command in the exorcism. This has the effect of removing the the alternative possibility in Mark that it relates to Jesus' teaching.[25] Interestingly, Luke also adds *dynamis* in juxtaposition to *exousia*, which is already present in his Markan source (Mark 1:27b).

Again, limiting Jesus' teaching to the introductory verses (4:31–32), Luke ensures that the reaction of the crowd is focused on Jesus' miracle-working, and it is this that leads to the crowd's question about Jesus' teaching in 4:36a. As Achtemeier notes, here the Lukan Jesus' teaching and miracle-working together provide an 'example of Jesus' activity *en exousia*'.[26] A further indication of the validating power of healings and exorcisms in the Lukan Jesus' understanding of his miracle-working may be seen from his response to the Pharisees who warn him that Herod is seeking to kill him (Luke 13:31–33), and where Jesus again points to his exorcisms and healings as expressions of his God-given authority (13:32).[27] This idea of validation can also be seen particularly in the Lukan Jesus' response to John the Baptist's question (Luke 7:18–23//Matt. 11:2–6), where, unlike Matthew's account, the Lukan Jesus' deeds, within the context of his mission, are explicitly powerful miracles, two of which Luke uses to preface the Baptist's question (Luke 7:1–17).[28]

Achtemeier also points to the link between miracles and faith found in the way Luke narrates responses to the miracle-working of Jesus in the Gospel and his heroes of the Spirit in Acts, pointing in both cases to God as the power-source for the miracles.[29] Jesus' miracles in the Gospel have the effect of turning people to God, as indicated in the their response (e.g. Luke 5:25; 7:16; 9:43; 13:13; 17:15; 18:43), and this is also the case in Acts, where Luke

---

25. Ibid., p. 155. C. E. B. Cranfield, *The Gospel According to St. Mark* (Cambridge: Cambridge University Press, 1959), p. 9, gives the meaning in Mark 1:27 as 'What is this? A new teaching with authority! He commands even . . .' (so NRSV).

26. Achtemeier, 'Lukan Perspective', p. 157. Achtemeier argues throughout that Luke's presentation of the miracles and teaching of Jesus is done in such a way as to create a balance between miracle-working and proclamation, and this balance is then carried forward to Acts, where it is continued by Luke in respect of his main characters, his heroes of the Spirit. For detailed evidence of this Lukan trait, see especially O'Reilly, *Word and Sign, passim*.

27. E. Schweizer, *The Good News According to Luke* (ET London: SPCK, 1984), p. 230.

28. Cf. Matt. 11:1, which relates to teaching only.

29. Achtemeier, 'Lukan Perspective', p. 158, for indications of the divine source of signs and wonders in Acts; for example, God (Acts 2:22; 15:12), the name of Jesus (Acts 4:30) and the Lord (Acts 14:3).

retrospectively links Jesus' miracle-working to belief that he was God's chosen agent.[30] This is made clear on the two occasions in Acts when signs and wonders are associated with the ministry of Jesus during evangelistic speeches made by Peter, first to the crowd in Jerusalem following the distribution of the Spirit in the upper room at Pentecost (Acts 2:22), and secondly when Peter addresses the Gentiles of Cornelius' household and circle of friends (10:38).

## The miracles of Jesus in retrospect (Acts 2:22; 10:37–38)

In Acts 2:22 Peter describes Jesus as being approved by God, 'with deeds of power, wonders and signs', thus enabling Luke to make the connection for his readers between the risen and exalted Jesus, who is now the subject of the church's proclamation, and the Jesus presented in his Gospel (Luke 4:14, 36; 5:17; 6:19; 8:46; 9:1; 10:13, 19). Now the embryonic church has received 'power from on high', its missiological activity will also be validated by God through signs and wonders. This becomes clear for Luke's readers during the course of Peter's Pentecost address, where he attributes the distribution of the Pentecostal Spirit to the fulfilment of the eschatological prophecy of Joel (Acts 2:16–21). Although Peter's reference to Joel 3:1–5 follows the LXX closely, Luke has made some significant editorial changes that serve his narrative interest in signs and wonders in Acts. Luke's redactional addition of 'signs on the earth below' to Joel's 'wonders in the heaven' has the effect of making Joel's prophecy foretell the signs and wonders that will accompany the ministry of Luke's heroes of the Spirit in Acts as they operate 'in the last days' (Acts 2:17).[31]

From here Luke makes the link, in terms of the fulfilment of Scripture, between the signs and wonders of Joel's prophecy with the 'deeds of power, wonders and signs' that had demonstrated God's approval of Jesus and his earthly ministry (Acts 2:22).[32] In the Joel text, as it appears in Acts, the normal

---

30. Ibid., pp. 159–60. See also, Hardon, 'Miracle Narratives', pp. 310ff.

31. The introductory phrase 'in the last days' is also a Lukan interpolation (cf. Joel 2:28 LXX), which reads simply, 'And it came to pass . . .'

32. F. S. Spencer, *The Portrait of Philip in Acts* (JSNTSup 67; Sheffield: Sheffield Academic Press, 1992), p. 46, concurs with Dunn, *Jesus and the Spirit*, p. 167, who makes the point that in the extravagant language used here by Luke, and elsewhere in Acts (8:13: 'signs and great miracles' in connection with Philip; 19:11: 'extraordinary miracles' in connection with Paul), Luke betrays a somewhat propagandist attitude to the miraculous in his portrayal of life in the early church.

LXX order of 'signs and wonders' is reversed. This reversal is also continued in Peter's speech, possibly in order to emphasize the theme of fulfilment,[33] or it may be that Luke is emphasizing the order of these validating 'deeds of power', where 'wonders' are assigned to the heavenly realm, which is the source of their origin, and 'signs' are their earthly manifestation.[34]

In Peter's speech the assumption is made that his audience were well aware of the signs and wonders performed by Jesus amongst them. Jervell remarks that, Christologically, Luke appears to understand Jesus' miracles in a subordinationist sense, with his miracles being presented as 'acts of God' performed through Jesus.[35] However, the reader is also made aware that Jesus is accredited by God in more than one way: by acts of power (*dynameis*), signs and wonders, and, supremely, by the resurrection.[36] In Acts 2:22 Luke gives us a succinct summary of his understanding of the significance of the healings and exorcisms performed by Jesus during his earthly ministry and which Luke now carries forward into his presentation of signs and wonders in Acts. Signs and wonders require *dynamis*; God is the source of the signs and wonders performed through a prophetic individual; signs and wonders validate the ministry of God's Spirit-filled agent – all of which is highly relevant for any

---

Dunn, *Jesus and the Spirit*, p. 167, comments, 'the more eye-catching the miracle the greater the propaganda value. All this is in notable contrast to the value placed on signs and wonders elsewhere in the NT.'

33. M. M. B. Turner, *Power from on High: The Spirit in Israel's Restoration and Witness in Luke-Acts* (JPTSup 9; Sheffield: Sheffield Academic Press, 1996), p. 273 n. 14, who points out that this order also occurs in 2:43 in connection with the apostles; otherwise (with the exception of 6:8 and 7:36, where the 'Moses–[Stephen]–Jesus parallel' is again involved) Luke uses the usual LXX order of signs and wonders.

34. See ibid., pp. 273–274.

35. J. Jervell, *The Theology of the Acts of the Apostles* (Cambridge: Cambridge University Press, 1996), p. 20; *Die Apostelgeschichte* (KEK; Göttingen: Vandenhoeck & Ruprecht, 1998), p. 145.

36. I. H. Marshall, *Acts* (TNTC 5; Leicester: IVP, 1992), p. 75; and B. Witherington III, *The Acts of the Apostles: A Socio-Rhetorical Commentary* (Grand Rapids, Mich.: Eerdmans; Carlisle: Paternoster, 1998), p. 144. Both make the point that this supreme mark of divine validation is simply stated by Peter rather than argued for. Also, as noted by E. Haenchen, *The Acts of the Apostles* (ET Oxford: Blackwell, 1971), p. 180 n. 5, the 'completeness' of Jesus' credentials are made plain by reference to God as author of his miraculous ministry, and this, in turn, confirms Jesus as God's 'special agent'.

contemporary understanding of the role of signs and wonders in the church today that seeks support from the narrative of Luke-Acts.

In Acts 10:37–38 Peter refers to Jesus' baptism by John (Luke 3:21–22), which may also be understood as Jesus' heavenly commissioning,[37] in view of the occurrence elsewhere in Acts of Spirit and power in close proximity (e.g. 1:8; 6:5, 8, 10). Barrett is correct to observe that here we have a hendiadys, 'the power of the Spirit' (cf. Luke 4:14). Barrett explains in the following way, 'God bestowed the Spirit upon Jesus and as a result he was filled with power.'[38] Indeed, Jesus' deeds of power were so well known to Peter's audience that the apostle can again speak directly of them as God's validation of Jesus.[39] Furthermore, in Peter's reference to Jesus as the agent of release from Satanic bondage (10:38), Luke's readers are made more acutely aware of Jesus' involvement in the saving work of God.[40] As a consequence, Acts 10:36–38 makes it clear that Peter is not restricting Jesus' commission and anointing with the Spirit just to the message he proclaimed, but to the totality of his ministry, including the signs and wonders he performed (cf. Acts 7:22, 35–38).[41]

## Conclusions

The stress in both Acts 2:22 and 10:38 is clearly on Jesus' validation by God through signs and wonders. The associated notions of power and authority

---

37. For example, C. K. Barrett, *A Critical and Exegetical Commentary on the Acts of the Apostles*. Vol. 1: *Acts I–XIV* (Edinburgh: T. & T. Clark, 1994), p. 524; H. Conzelmann, *Acts of the Apostles* (ET Philadelphia: Fortress, 1987), p. 352; Witherington, *Acts*, p. 358; Turner, *Power from on High*, p. 41. Turner, *Power from on High*, pp. 261–264, argues that it was here that Jesus received his anointing with power and Spirit and that Acts 10:35–38 appears to be modelled on Luke 4:16–30 and to interpret it, and that the reference to Holy Spirit and power in Acts 10:38 'echoes' Luke 4:14 (cf. 4:18a).

38. Barrett, *Acts I–XIV*, p. 524. Turner, *Power from on High*, p. 262, writes, 'Luke understood the Spirit as the power operative through Jesus' proclamation and effective in acts expressive of his kerygma [i.e. signs and wonders].'

39. Conzelmann, *Acts*, p. 353; Dunn, *Jesus and the Spirit*, p. 70.

40. Cf. J. B. Green, '"Salvation to the Ends of the Earth"' (Acts 13:47): God as Saviour in the Acts of the Apostles', in I. H. Marshall and D. Peterson (eds.), *Witness to the Gospel: The Theology of Acts* (Grand Rapids, Mich.: Eerdmans, 1998), p. 94.

41. Cf. Wenk, *Community Forming Power*, p. 129.

that accompany the performance of signs and wonders are terms used repeatedly of Jesus' ability over demons and disease (cf. Luke 4:36; 5:17; 6:19; 8:46).[42]
Similarly, as we shall see in the next chapter, signs and wonders feature in the
Acts narrative to identify and validate Luke's heroes of the Spirit who pioneer
the missionary expansion of the church (cf. 2:43; 4:16, 22, 30; 5:12; 6:8; 8:6, 13;
14:13; 15:12).[43]

---

42. See Johnson, *Possessions*, p. 145.

43. L. T. Johnson, *The Acts of the Apostles* (SP 5; Collegeville, Minn.: Liturgical, 1992),
    p. 45.

## 20. SIGNS AND WONDERS AND LUKE'S HEROES OF THE SPIRIT

### The purpose of signs and wonders in Acts

It is clear from reading Acts that Luke uses the term 'signs and wonders' as a catch-all for healings, exorcisms and other miracles.[1] The summary in Acts 2:42–47 provides us with a vignette of life in the early Jerusalem church, which indicates for Luke's readers the growth and development of the community (cf. 4:4; 5:42).[2] Members of the community devote themselves to the apostles'

---

1. F. Neirynck, 'The Miracles Stories in the Acts of the Apostles: An Introduction', in J. Kremer (ed.), *Les Actes des Apôtres: traditions, redaction, théologie* ( Gembloux, Leuven: Duculot, 1979), pp. 170–171, analyses the references to signs and wonders in Acts as follows. Summary reports: 2:43; 5:12; 5:15; 5:16; 6:8; 8:6–7; 8:13; 14:3; 19:11; 19:12; 28:9. Healing stories: 3:1–10; 9:32–35; 14:8–10; 28:7–8. Exorcisms: 16:16–18; 19:13–19. Raising the dead: 9:36–42; 20:7–12. Liberations from prison: 5:17–21; 12:3–17; 16:25–34. Punishments: 5:1–11; 13:9–12. Nature miracle: 28:3–6. For an alternative approach, see P. J. Achtemeier, 'The Lukan Perspective on the Miracles of Jesus: A Preliminary Sketch', in C. H. Talbert (ed.), *Perspectives on Luke-Acts* (Danville, Va.: Association of Baptist Professors of Religion; Edinburgh: T. & T. Clark, 1978), p. 165 n. 22.
2. M. Dibelius, *Studies in the Acts of the Apostles* (ET London: SCM, 1956), pp. 9–10.

teaching,[3] to fellowship, communal meals[4] and holding all things in common.[5] Luke also states that many wonders and signs were performed through the apostles, resulting in an atmosphere of holy awe/fear descending on the whole community.

In his examination of Luke's presentation of signs and wonders in the early church, Dunn points out that the phrase 'signs and wonders' occurs more frequently in Acts than in any other NT document.[6] The positive attitude to signs and wonders shown by Luke in Acts is contrary to Jesus' negative attitude to 'signs' in the Synoptic tradition.[7] However, in Acts signs and wonders clearly

---

3. For teaching of apostles, see also for example Acts 4:2, 18; 5:21, 25, 28, 42.

4. L. T. Johnson, *The Acts of the Apostles* (SP 5; Collegeville, Minn.: Liturgical, 1992), p. 58, regards the breaking of bread described here by Luke as more than just communal meals, arguing that, for Luke, Jesus' presence has already been indicated in the breaking of bread (Luke 24:35). See also R. Pesch, *Die Apostelgeschichte* (EKKNT 5; Zurich: Neukirchener, 1986), p. 130, who writes, 'Die koinonia ist zunächst charakterisiert durch das (gemeinsame) Brotbrechen.' J. Jeremias, *The Eucharistic Words of Jesus* (ET London: SCM, 1966), pp. 118–119, regards Acts 2:42 as outlining an early form of Christian service of worship rather than a summary of life in the early Jerusalem community. Jeremias argues further (p. 66) that the communal meals of the early church reflected the table fellowship enjoyed by Jesus and his disciples. Against Jeremias, E. Haenchen, *The Acts of the Apostles* (ET Oxford: Blackwell, 1971), p. 191, argues that the summaries in Acts depict all aspects of church life and are not limited just to worship. Whilst F. F. Bruce, *The Acts of the Apostles: Greek Text with Introduction and Commentary*, 3rd ed. (Leicester: Apollos, 1990), p. 132, thinks that Luke's reference to the breaking of bread probably refers to the Lord's Supper and points out that this, together with the prayers, is also an expression of *koinōnia*.

5. Johnson, *Acts*, pp. 58–59, understands *koinōnia* here as referring to the sharing of material possessions (cf. 2:25; 4:32–37). Johnson thinks Luke has in mind the Hellenistic Greek ideal of friendship, where friends hold all things in common. Alternatively, Dunn's proposal that *koinōnia* here reflects Paul's idea of 'the fellowship of the Spirit' (2 Cor. 13:13; Phil. 2:1) may be more likely.

6. Nine times in Acts (Acts 2:19, 22, 43; 4:30; 5:12; 6:8; 7:36; 14:3; 15:12), and no more than once in other NT documents (Mark 13:22//Matt. 24:24; John 4:48; Rom. 15:19; 2 Cor. 12:12; 2 Thess. 2:9; Heb. 2:4). Cf. J. D. G. Dunn, *Jesus and the Spirit: A Study of the Religious and Charismatic Experience of Jesus and the First Christians as Reflected in the New Testament* (London: SCM, 1975), p. 402 n. 47.

7. For example, Mark 8:11–12 pars.

have a missiological significance in that they produce faith in the message of
the witnesses (5:14; 9:42; 13:13; 19:18).[8] Dunn makes the point that Luke's presentation of signs and wonders in Acts is uncritical and may appear to the
modern reader of Acts as somewhat naive (in a non-pejorative sense).[9] Dunn
also observes that Luke supplements his frequent mention of signs and
wonders by describing them as 'miracles/acts of power' (*dynameis*),[10] and
includes miracles that particularly appeal to him.[11] Luke's use of this language
creates an overall atmosphere of religious awe and the numinous where the
focus is on the apostles as the agents of signs and wonders (cf. 5:5–11; 19:17).[12]

The fear that results from witnessing the signs and wonders performed by
the apostles also suggests that the apostolic word is received as a word from
God.[13] Barrett goes even further when he suggests that the fear-language used
here by Luke indicates more than just reverence for God (cf. 9:31): it suggests
fear of the supernatural.[14] Indeed, the text even suggests that this fear of the
supernatural was not just confined to the Christian community, but also
extended to all who witnessed the signs and wonders (5:12; cf. 2:43).[15]

---

8. Cf. H. C. Kee, *Good News to the Ends of the Earth: The Theology of Acts* (Philadelphia:
   Trinity Press International; London: SCM, 1990), p. 10. Dunn, *Jesus and the Spirit*,
   pp. 167–168, notes that this is in contrast to Jesus' healings and exorcisms, where
   faith on the part of the person being healed plays an important role in releasing the
   healing *dynamis* of the Spirit. Even in the Peter/Paul parallel in Acts 3:16 and 14:9
   the faith of the person being healed is primarily in the message.

9. Dunn, *Jesus and the Spirit*, pp. 134ff.

10. For example, 'great miracles' (Acts 8:13) and 'extraordinary miracles' (Acts 19:11
    LXX).

11. Dunn, *Jesus and the Spirit*, p. 167.

12. Cf. J. D. G. Dunn, *The Acts of the Apostles* (Peterborough: Epworth, 1996), p. 35.

13. Cf. R. W. Wall, 'Israel and the Gentile Mission in Acts and Paul: A Canonical
    Approach', in I. H. Marshall and D. Peterson (eds.), *Witness to the Gospel: The Theology
    of Acts* (Grand Rapids, Mich.: Eerdmans, 1998), p. 443.

14. C. K. Barrett, *A Critical and Exegetical Commentary on the Acts of the Apostles*. Vol. 1:
    *Acts I–XIV* (Edinburgh: T. & T. Clark, 1994), p. 166; cf. Haenchen, *Acts*, p. 192.

15. B. Witherington III, *The Acts of the Apostles: A Socio-Rhetorical Commentary* (Grand
    Rapids, Mich.: Eerdmans; Carlisle: Paternoster, 1998), p. 161. H. C. Kee, *To Every
    Nation under Heaven: The Acts of the Apostles* (Harrisburg, Pa.: Trinity Press
    International, 1997), p. 76. H. Conzelmann, *Acts of the Apostles* (ET Philadelphia:
    Fortress, 1987), p. 23, draws attention to the idea of fear being present within the
    holy congregation at Qumran (1QH 4.26).

Importantly, Max Turner notes that, as elsewhere in summary passages in Acts, Luke's focus is on the 'witness and signs of the *apostles*' (Acts 2:42–47; 4:32–37; 5:12–16). He rightly concludes that Luke is 'entirely silent on the matter of congregational witness or evangelism by the rank and file of the church' and that this also applies to the brief summaries in Acts (cf. 6:7; 9:31; 12:24; 16:5 19:20).[16] In a similar vein, Johnson concludes that the clear indication is that signs and wonders were confined to the apostles who were Jesus' successors, receiving both the prophetic *pneuma* and *dynamis* that had previously been at work in Jesus.[17] Just as signs and wonders validated Jesus' words and ministry, so they now validate the words and ministry of the apostles. Thus if the signs and wonders associated with Jesus' ministry are to be understood in terms of what God did through him (cf. Acts 2:22), then the same link is to be made between signs and wonders and Luke's heroes of the Spirit.[18] As we will see, this becomes explicit in the example of the healing sign that follows in Acts 3:1ff., described later in the narrative as a 'notable sign' by the Jewish council (4:16).[19]

By maintaining a sense of the numinous surrounding the activities of the Jerusalem church, Luke shows how, through signs and wonders, the presence of the Lord remained manifest in the community.[20] In 2:41 we read that three thousand persons were added to the new Christian community and in 5:14 further large numbers of men and women joining the church in Jerusalem are described as 'added to the Lord' (cf. 11:24b; my trans.), indicating further that it is the person of the risen Jesus whom Luke regards as still central to the life and activity of the church.[21]

In discussing the earliest communities' sense of charismatic authority, Dunn argues that the principal source of that sense of authority in Acts is clearly the Spirit.[22] However, the evidence in Acts also suggests that

---

16. M. M. B. Turner, *Power from on High: The Spirit in Israel's Restoration and Witness in Luke-Acts* (JPTSup 9; Sheffield: Sheffield Academic Press, 1996), p. 399. Cf. I. H. Marshall, *Acts* (TNTC 5; Leicester: IVP, 1992), p. 104; Pesch, *Apostelgeschichte*, p. 175.

17. Johnson, *Acts*, p. 58; cf. J. A. Fitzmyer, *The Acts of the Apostles* (AB 31; New York: Doubleday, 1998), p. 271; Barrett, *Acts I–XIV*, p. 166.

18. Cf. J. T. Squires, 'The Plan of God', in I. H. Marshall and D. Peterson (eds.), *Witness to the Gospel: The Theology of Acts* (Grand Rapids, Mich.: Eerdmans, 1998), p. 22.

19. See my discussion in the next chapter.

20. Dunn, *Acts*, p. 65.

21. Ibid., p. 66.

22. Dunn, *Jesus and the Spirit*, p. 176.

commissioning is the initiatory vehicle used by Luke in Acts in order to concentrate for his readers the charismatic authority of the Spirit in selected individuals with whom he associates the manifestation of signs and wonders. In
other words, even in light of the outpouring of the Spirit on all Jesus' followers at Pentecost and beyond, the idea of the authoritative commissioning of
selected individuals that we find in Luke's Gospel also extends to his portrayal
of the post-Easter community in Acts. Also in Acts, we see individuals being
commissioned for specific tasks, in some cases of clearly limited duration.[23]
The implications of this for contemporary application are that, contra the
Third Wave model, where signs and wonders are almost commonplace, the
evidence from Acts suggests a model where a limited number of designated
individuals are set apart and commissioned, initially by the risen Jesus but then
more commonly by their local congregation to whom and through whom, as
Luke understands it, the prophetic and authoritative voice of the Spirit of
Jesus speaks.

Just as signs and wonders serve to establish Israel as the people of God,
so too are signs and wonders in Acts to be understood as being instrumental in the formation of the infant church as the eschatological people of
God. This suggests that for Luke, signs and wonders in Acts also have a salvation-historical function that goes beyond creating a numinous atmosphere
for his readers. This, in turn, helps to explain why Luke does not attribute
signs and wonders in a more general way to members of the community as
a whole, but reserves attributing deeds of power to a limited number of
accredited individuals whom he presents as having been commissioned, with
its attendant notion of the conveyance of authority to act on behalf of
another.

There are two further important features closely associated with Luke's
presentation of signs and wonders in Acts that recall for Luke's readers that
the person concerned has legitimate authority to act, and that serve to emphasize further the way in which signs, wonders and the miraculous are restricted
in Acts to a select few individuals; namely, the laying on of hands and the use
of Jesus' name. Finally, it is to these two features that we now turn.

---

23. For example, Paul and Barnabas who are commissioned and sent out as
    missionaries by the church in Antioch but who later part, following the completion
    of Paul's first missionary journey (Acts 13:1–3; 14:26–28; cf. 15:36–41). I would also
    add here Ananias, who is commissioned by the risen Jesus specifically to minister
    to Paul during the latter's conversion experience by laying hands on him in order to
    heal his blindness and impart the Spirit.

## Laying on of hands

In classical Greek the word for 'hand' (*cheir*) is frequently used to mean 'power over others' and this meaning is also present in the OT (e.g. Josh. 2:24; Judg. 3:28; 4:7, 14; 7:9, 15).[24] References to the 'hand of God' in the OT are frequently concerned with God's activity on Israel's behalf where he reveals his might (e.g. Exod. 7:4; 13:3, 14, 16; Deut. 5:15; 7:8; 9:26),[25] and notably with signs and wonders (e.g. Deut. 4:34; 6:21–22; 11:2–7; 26:8). In ancient Israel the laying on of hands conveyed blessing from one person to another (Gen. 48:14) and authority (Num. 8:10; Deut. 34:9), as well as symbolically transferring the sins of the people on to the scapegoat (Lev. 16:21).[26] Similarly, in Leviticus 24:14 the whole congregation are to 'press hands' on a blasphemer's head before carrying out the punishment of stoning.[27] Of particular interest is the fact that in the OT the laying on of hands is also a sign of commissioning that is performed in front of the assembled congregation of Israel (e.g. Num. 27:18–20, 21–23; Deut. 34:9; cf. Acts 6:6; 13:3).

Healings are not normally associated with the laying on of hands in the Old Testament. Lohse points to an exception where the LXX uses *epitithēmi*[28] in the story of the healing of Naaman, translating 2 Kings 5:11 as 'lay his hand upon the place' (LXX 4 Kings 5:11), although here it must be noted that the suggestion that the healer lay hands upon the affected area comes from an affronted 'patient', and the laying on of hands does not actually take place.[29] Of more interest here is an example from Qumran, where, according to 1Qap Gen 20:28–29, the author seeks to protect Sarah's purity whilst she is apart from Abraham in Pharaoh's household, by stating that God afflicted Pharaoh with impotence. Eventually, Abraham lays hands on Pharaoh and heals him, 'So I prayed for him, that blasphemer, and laid my hands upon his head. Thereupon the plague was removed from him, the evil spirit exorcized from him, and he was healed.'[30]

---

24. E. Lohse, χείρ, *TDNT* 9, p. 425.

25. Ibid., p. 427.

26. D. Daube, *The New Testament and Rabbinic Judaism* (London: Athlone, 1956), p. 224.

27. Ibid., p. 227.

28. For NT examples of healing, cf. Matt. 9:18; 19:13, 15; Mark 5:23; 6:5; 7:32; 8:23; Luke 4:40; 13:13. Also used variously in Acts 6:6; 8:17, 19; 9:12, 17; 13:3; 19:6; 28:8 (cf. 1 Tim. 5:22).

29. Lohse, χείρ, p. 428 n. 23.

30. M. O. Wise (trans.) 'Tales of the Patriarchs: 1QapGen', in M. O. Wise,

Fitzmyer argues that the presence of the language of 'rebuke' means that this is to be understood as an exorcism.[31]

The laying on of hands is also an important feature in Acts (5:12; 9:12, 17; 14:3; 28:8; cf. 3:7; 9:41). Dunn suggests that the laying on of hands may have been regarded as an act of 'prophetic symbolism', where the hands of the healer represented the power of the Lord that effected the healing (4:30).[32] It is also true to say that this prophetic symbolism extends in Acts to the formal act of commissioning of individuals by a local congregation (Acts 6:6; 13:3).[33]

Material in Acts that features the laying on of hands may usefully be grouped under three headings, all of which suggest the presence of the element of authority to act on behalf of another. These are laying on of hands as a sign of commissioning (Acts 6:6; 9:10–17; 13:3); laying on of hands and conveying the Holy Spirit (8:17–19; 19:6); laying on of hands and signs and wonders (3:7; 9:12, 17, 41; 14:3; 19:11; 28:8).

## Laying on of hands as a sign of commissioning

In the context of commissioning, the laying on of hands suggests the imparting of authority (*exousia*),[34] as can be seen particularly in the commissionings of the Seven in Jerusalem (Acts 6:6), and of Barnabas and Paul by the church in Antioch (13:3).[35] Prior to the appointment of the Seven, the whole com-

---

M. A. Abegg Jr. and E. M. Cook (eds.), *The Dead Sea Scrolls: A New Translation* (London: Hodder & Stoughton, 1997), p. 75. Also noted by Lohse, χείρ, p. 428 n. 23.

31. J. A. Fitzmyer, 'Some Observations on the Genesis Apocryphon', *CBQ* 22 (1960), p. 284, writes, 'That the laying on of hands was regarded as a sort of exorcism is derived from the verb used in 1QGA 20, 28:29, *titĕ'ar* and *'itga'rat* (or *'itgĕ'ēret*), whose root means "to rebuke" . . .'

32. Dunn, *Jesus and the Spirit*, p. 165.

33. It is also worth noting here the congregational aspect of the election of Matthias as an apostle to replace Judas, where in Acts 1:23 it is the whole community that puts forward the two candidates, Justus and Matthias (cf. Barrett, *Acts I–XIV*, p. 102).

34. Turner, *Power from on High*, p. 372. Turner identifies three paradigms for the laying on of hands in the NT: transference of power in healing; invocatory prayer for healing and/or blessing; identification, representation and transfer of authority.

35. Ibid., pp. 372–373, correctly identifies Paul's appointment of the elders in the churches during his first missionary journey (Acts 14:23) as a form of

munity, consisting of Hebrew and Hellenist Christians, are called together by the apostles in recognition of the need to select leaders from within the Hellenistic Christian community (Acts 6:2).[36] The reason given by the apostles for widening the leadership base is one of administration within the growing community, although the initial complaint on the part of the Hellenists about their widows being neglected (6:1) may indicate more than just the need for the apostles to delegate.[37] This is perhaps further borne out by the fact that the remit of these men of the Spirit (6:3b) extends beyond serving at tables,[38] and their charismatic authority is expressed in mission (6:8; 8:4–8).[39] It is also worth noting here that the choice of the Seven is based on their good standing within the community together with a recognition of their charismatic authority, and the choice of candidates pleases the whole community. The Seven are named and described as being full of the 'Spirit and wisdom' (6:3), with Stephen being singled out in 6:5 as a man 'full of faith and of the Holy Spirit' (6:5).

In the case of Stephen, one of Luke's heroes of the Spirit to whom 'great wonders and miraculous signs' are attributed (Acts 6:8b), the laying on of hands associated with the commissioning of the Seven appears as an expression of solidarity on the part of the apostles and the Jerusalem congregation, as well as conveying authority to act on behalf of the community (cf. Num.

---

commissioning. However, the impression given by Turner that this involved the laying on of hands is not in this case entirely supported by the text. According to Barrett, *Acts I–XIV*, p. 687, the verb 'to appoint' (*cheirotonein*) originally meant 'to stretch out the hand' in the context of voting in the assembly and does not, as it is used here, support the idea of the laying on of hands.

36. It is interesting to note that this is the only occasion in Acts when Luke refers to the apostles as the Twelve and, given the title's close association with Israel (cf. Luke 22:30), may well be understood to emphasize division within the community.

37. The appointment of the Seven may be indicative of growing tensions within the early Jerusalem community between the two groups of Hebrews and Hellenists (cf. 1 Macc. 1:11–15; Acts 8:1b). For a discussion, see for example M. Hengel, *Acts and the History of Earliest Christianity* (ET London: SCM, 1979), pp. 72–80; Dunn, *The Partings of the Ways* (London: SCM, 1991), pp. 60–62; and for a detailed discussion of the encounter between Palestinian Judaism and Hellenism, see M. Hengel, *Judaism and Hellenism: Studies in their Encounter in Palestine during the Early Hellenistic Period* (ET London: SCM, 1974).

38. Cf. Luke 22:27.

39. Dunn, *Jesus and the Spirit*, p. 181.

27:19–23; cf. Deut. 34:9). Although Stephen is further described in 6:8 as being full of grace and power, Luke does not elaborate further. According to Conzelmann, this is because Luke does not know of any 'concrete miracles' performed by Stephen.[40] However, Luke has already established the nature of the signs and wonders performed by his heroes of the Spirit. Stephen's primary role in the narrative is to deliver his extended speech that invokes Israel's history and refers to Moses' rejection despite his prophetic ability to perform signs and wonders in Egypt, at the Red Sea and in the wilderness (7:36),[41] and ends with Stephen condemning the Temple *cultus*, which results in his becoming the first Christian martyr. It is during the narrative of Stephen's execution that, filled with the Holy Spirit (7:55), Stephen confirms for Luke's readers Jesus' exalted status as the Son of Man who stands at the right hand of God. Finally, Stephen echoes the words of his master on the cross, 'Lord Jesus, receive my spirit' (Acts 7:59; cf. Luke 23:46).

There has been some discussion as to whether the laying on of hands in Acts 6:6 is confined to just the apostles or extends to other members of the Jerusalem community. In 6:2 and 6:4 'we' refers to the apostles,[42] but in 6:2 the word 'multitude' (*plēthos*) refers to the whole community.[43] In 6:5 the suggestion made by the apostles pleases the whole community, who then choose the candidates. In 6:6 the candidates are placed before the apostles, and Neil comments that the text is unclear at this point as to whether it is just the apostles or the whole community who lay hands on the Seven.[44] According to Bruce, 'The ceremony in this case indicated the conferring of authority by the apostles on the seven men whom the people had chosen.'[45]

Witherington also thinks that it was just the apostles who laid hands on the Seven,[46] whilst Dunn[47] and Barrett[48] argue that the most natural reading of the

---

40. Conzelmann, *Acts*, p. 47.

41. Noted by Johnson, *Acts*, p. 129.

42. Barrett, *Acts XV–XXVIII*, p. 311.

43. Ibid. Also LXX.

44. W. Neil, *The Acts of the Apostles* (London: Oliphants, 1973), p. 104.

45. Bruce, *Acts*, pp. 184–185.

46. Witherington, *Acts*, p. 251.

47. Dunn, *Acts*, p. 84; *Jesus and the Spirit*, p. 181.

48. Barrett, *Acts I–XIV*, p. 315, asserts that there is no doubt that this is the grammatical meaning of Luke's Greek. However, given the large numbers involved (Acts 1:15; 2:41, 47b; 6:1; and especially 4:4), there are obvious logistic difficulties and this difficulty is recognized by the Western text, where the Seven are placed

Greek suggests that the laying on of hands was carried out by the whole community rather than just the apostles, although logistically this may have been
difficult (cf. Acts 1:15; 2:41; 4:4; 5:14; 6:1a). Nevertheless, it is clear that the
commissioning of the Seven was a communal affair, where the candidates'
charismatic authority was recognized by all, the laying on of hands formalized
their commission and, most importantly here, authority was invested in them
by the whole congregation in Jerusalem.[49]

We find a similar act of commissioning involving the laying on of hands
and the conveyance of authority being used by the church in Antioch when
Barnabas[50] and Paul are commissioned as missionaries (Acts 13:3). Luke elab-
orates the scene in 13:1–2 by mentioning the names of leading prophets and
teachers who are gathered together to worship, fast and to hear the prophetic
word of the Spirit, among whom are Barnabas and Paul themselves. Apart
from the laying on of hands indicating the transference of authority inherent
in their commissioning, it is important to note both the specific nature of the
commission (missionary service, cf.13:4) and the limited duration of their
commission, which is completed on their return to Antioch (13:26).[51] This is
particularly significant in light of what we have seen to be the limited nature
of the commissions of the Twelve and the Seventy(-Two) in Luke's Gospel,
and bears out my conclusion there that Luke envisages situations where individuals are called and commissioned for particular tasks. In these Acts commissionings it is important to note (particularly for contemporary application)
both the criteria used for the selection of individuals, as well as the communal
aspect of the commissioning itself. In both cases it is the whole Christian community that is involved in the appointment and commissioning of the Seven
(6:6) and of Paul and Barnabas (13:3) to act on their behalf. In other words,
precedent is set in the Acts narrative for the ideal conditions for recognizing

---

before the apostles who pray and lay hands on them (Barrett, *Acts I–XIV*, p. 316.
Cf. NRSV).

49. Cf. for example Witherington, *Acts*, p. 251; and Haenchen, *Acts*, p. 264.

50. Dunn, *Acts*, p. 173, suggests that Barnabas is mentioned first here by Luke because
he 'embodies continuity with the Jerusalem church begun in 11:23–26'.

51. Cf. ibid., p. 173; and J. D. G. Dunn, 'Ministry and the Ministry: The Charismatic
Renewal's Challenge to Traditional Ecclesiology', in idem, *The Christ and the Spirit:
Collected Essays of James D. G. Dunn*. Vol. 2: *Pneumatology* (Grand Rapids, Mich.:
Eerdmans, 1998), pp. 305–306, which also notes the limited duration of this
commission and that of Stephen in Acts 6:6. We may also add here the
commissioning of Ananias in Acts 9, which is discussed further below.

and commissioning particular individuals for specific roles within/on behalf of the community.

## Laying on of hands and conveying the Holy Spirit

More briefly, there are three occasions in Acts where we see the laying on of hands involved in the conveyance of the Spirit (Acts 8:4–25; 9:1–19; 19:1–6).[52] For our present purpose, we may simply note here that in each case the act of laying on hands is performed by persons who have received their authority by virtue of their having been commissioned.

The Samaritan Christians receive the Spirit when the apostles Peter and John (8:17) lay hands on them. It is interesting to note that in his confrontation with Peter, we are told that Simon Magus saw that the Spirit was given through the laying on of the apostles' hands (cf. 8:13b), which Simon recognizes in verse 19 as being inexorably linked to the apostles' *exousia*. In the case of Paul's receiving the Spirit when Ananias lays hands upon him, we have an example in Ananias of someone who has received a specific (short-term) commission from the risen Jesus (9:10–12, 15, 17). Finally, in the case of the Ephesian Christians it is Paul, who has been commissioned by the risen Jesus and himself received the Spirit through the laying on of hands by Ananias (Acts 9:17–18), who lays hands upon them (19:6). In all three cases, the laying on of hands is by persons who have been commissioned and whose delegated authority is validated by signs and wonders (e.g. 3:1ff.; 9:12, 17–19; 14:3).

## Laying on of hands and healing

Although in his Gospel Luke faithfully reflects the substance of the miracle stories he finds in Mark, including the laying on of hands by Jesus (e.g. 4:40; 13:13),[53] there are other occasions when he omits this practice by Jesus from

---

52. For a detailed discussion of these passages in relation to conversion-initiation and reception of the Spirit, see J. D. G. Dunn, *Baptism in the Holy Spirit: A Re-examination of the New Testament Teaching on the Gift of the Spirit in Relation to Pentecostalism Today* (London: SCM, 1970), pp. 55–72, 73–78, 83–89; and more recently Turner, *Power from on High*, especially pp. 348–400.

53. G. H. Twelftree, *Jesus the Miracle Worker* (Downers Grove, Ill.: IVP, 1999), p. 181. In

his retelling of his Markan tradition. For example, Luke omits entirely Mark 7:31–37 with its involved description of Jesus healing the deaf man with a speech impediment. For Luke, Jesus' *dynamis* is dispensed with a word or the laying on of hands.[54]

There are just four occasions in Luke's Gospel when Jesus uses his hand(s) in healing (4:40; 5:13; 8:54; 13:3).[55] In Luke 4:40, following the healing of Peter's mother-in-law (4:38–39), the sick are brought to Jesus, who lays hands on each of them as he heals them.[56] In the healing of the leper (Luke 5:13) Luke follows his Markan source in describing Jesus as reaching out his hand and touching the leper as he pronounces the words of healing. Luke omits Mark's direct speech in the healing of Jairus' daughter (Mark 5:23) with its request by Jairus that Jesus should come and lay hands on his daughter so that she may be healed. In describing the healing itself, Luke includes Mark's description of Jesus holding the girl's hand (Luke 8:54), something that also occurs during healings in Acts (cf. 3:7; 9:41).[57] Finally, in the healing of the crippled woman, which appears only in Luke (13:10–17), Jesus is again described as laying hands upon the woman and, as he does so, she is healed immediately.

Luke follows a similar pattern in Acts, except that on two occasions, one ascribed to Peter (Acts 5:14–15) and one ascribed to Paul (Acts 19:11–12), people are healed through contact with items of clothing (Acts 19:12; cf. Mark 5:30b)[58] or even the healer's shadow (Acts 5:15). In general terms, Luke describes signs and wonders being accomplished through the hands of the apostles (5:12), Paul and Barnabas (14:3) and Paul alone (19:11). What evidence there is in Acts for the laying on of hands being associated with specific

---

summaries, Jesus performs his mighty works by the laying on of hands (Mark 6:5; Luke 4:40).

54. On one notable occasion, found in Luke's Markan tradition, Jesus notices that power leaves him when he is touched by a woman seeking healing (Luke 8:45–46//Mark 5:30).

55. For use of the healer's hands in Acts, see for example 5:12; 9:12, 17; 14:3; 19:11; 28:8.

56. The phrase 'and he laid his hands upon each of them' is redactional (cf. Mark 1:32–34). Cf. also Mark 6:5 and its reference to laying on of hands, which is omitted by Luke.

57. In Acts 9:41 Peter simply helps the restored Tabitha to her feet (cf. Barrett, *Acts I–XIV*, p. 486.)

58. Mark 5:30b, 'Who touched my clothes?', is omitted by Luke (cf. Luke 8:46).

healings shows that the healings are performed by those who have been commissioned and are acting with the authority of the risen Jesus.[59] On both occasions where Luke describes the laying on of hands explicitly in connection with a healing (9:17; 28:8), the healer is known to Luke's readers as a person who has been commissioned by the risen Jesus. As I noted earlier in the case of Ananias, his commission appears to have been limited to the specific purpose of ministering to Paul by healing his temporary blindness and helping him to resolve the spiritual turmoil resulting from his being confronted with the risen Jesus on the road to Damascus (9:10–18).

Towards the end of Acts, Luke describes in graphic detail Paul's journey as a prisoner to Rome. Throughout the journey, Paul continues to bear witness to the risen Jesus, and, despite storms at sea and shipwreck, eventually arrives in Rome in fulfilment of his commission (9:15; 22:14–15; and especially 23:11; cf. 1:8). During the journey, Paul and his companions avoid drowning and are shipwrecked on Malta. Upon reaching land, Paul's innocence of any supposed crime (28:4) is demonstrated to all when he shakes off the viper from his wrist (28:3–6; cf. Amos 5:19). This is followed by the healing of Publius by Paul, who prays, lays hands upon him and heals him of his fever and dysentery (28:8–9), followed by Paul healing many who were sick (28:9; cf. Mark 16:18). At key points throughout the narrative Paul's charismatic authority, derived from his having been commissioned by the risen Jesus, is demonstrated.

## Use of Jesus' name

The invocation of the name of Jesus occurs in a wide variety of settings in Acts,[60] and was clearly an expression of the early Christians' sense of authority and power to act on behalf of the exalted Jesus.[61] Of particular relevance is the use of Jesus' name in connection with signs and wonders as validation

---

59. Barrett, *Acts I–XIV*, p. 486. It is worth noting here that when Barnabas and Paul are commissioned by the leaders of the church in Antioch and sent out on mission (Acts 13:2), it is at the instigation of the Holy Spirit whilst the leaders are worshipping the Lord and fasting, and it is also the Lord who is described as the source for the signs and wonders that validate their word of witness (Acts 14:3).

60. For example, preaching/teaching/witness (4:18; 5:28, 40; 8:12; 9:27–28; cf. 19:13, 17); salvation (2:21; 9:15; 10:43); baptism (2:38; 8:16; 10:48; 19:5; 22:16); suffering (5:41; 9:16; 21:13; cf. 9:21); signs and wonders (4:30); healing (3:6, 16; 4:7; 16:18).

61. Dunn, *Jesus and the Spirit*, p. 177.

of the authority invested in Luke's heroes of the Spirit and their word of witness. In Acts, Luke makes it clear that only individuals who have been commissioned may legitimately and successfully (cf. Acts 19:13–16) invoke the name of Jesus, and the authority associated with it.

In the ancient world a person's name was thought to express that person's essence and personality. In the use of the person's name, it is as though the person were actually present, particularly in terms of the authority associated with his or her name.[62] For example, in Acts 4:7 *dynamis* and *onoma* (name) are 'parallel concepts':[63] by invoking the name of Jesus the apostles invoked his power (cf. Acts 2:22, 10:38), and with that power the clear implication that they had the authority to act as they did.[64] Luke makes it clear that Jesus, as the direct representative of God, healed and cast out demons in his own right by virtue of the power and authority he had received directly from God (Acts 2:22; 10:38). In Luke's Gospel we have already seen how the Seventy(-Two) believed that their power and authority to heal and exorcize was operative through the name of Jesus (Luke 10:17, 19). In Acts, Jesus' followers heal by means of the same power that effected Jesus' miracles, but this power is now inextricably linked with the *name* and (authority) of Jesus.[65]

In the narrative surrounding the first healing story in Acts and the subsequent discussion about authority and the use of the name of Jesus, Luke clarifies for his readers his understanding of the relationship between signs and wonders and the invocation of the name of Jesus (Acts 3:1–10, 11–26; 4:1–31). As Fitzmyer has observed, the elements in this healing story are very similar to healing stories in the Synoptic tradition, and may be analysed as follows: situation described (3:2–5); word of command to sick person (3:4, 6); restorative action (3:7); cure effected (3:8); reaction of bystanders (3:9–11).[66]

In Luke's portrayal of Peter healing the crippled beggar, he mentions two key elements that together form a pattern for the apostolic preaching in Acts and provide a further important insight into Luke's understanding of the role of signs and wonders in the early church. Through his main protagonist, Peter,

---

62. H. Bietenhard, ὄνομα, *TDNT* 5, pp. 243–283, and especially 276ff.; Dunn, *Jesus and the Spirit*, p. 164.

63. Bietenhard, ὄνομα, p. 277.

64. Dunn, *Jesus and the Spirit*, p. 177.

65. Ibid., p. 164.

66. Fitzmyer, *Acts*, p. 276. There are clear parallels here with Jesus' healing of the paralytic in Luke 5:17–26 and Paul's healing of the man lame from birth in Acts 14:8–18.

Luke raises the rhetorical question of the source of Peter's healing *dynamis* (3:12), which he identified as coming through faith in the name of Jesus (Acts 3:16). In other words, Peter heals the lame beggar 'in the name of Jesus Christ of Nazareth' (3:6). In his use of the name of Jesus there is a clear implication for the reader of Peter's delegated *exousia*/authority, received by virtue of his having been commissioned by the risen Jesus, and it is by the authority of the name of Jesus that Peter exercises the *dynamis* which effects the miracle (3:12).

Furthermore, the pattern established at Pentecost is again in evidence when the occasion brought about by the presence of signs and wonders is used by Peter to preach to the gathered onlookers.[67] Here Luke also uses the words of Peter in order to make it clear that the healing was not the result of any personal power of Peter's but was a revelation of the power of God through his messiah, Jesus (3:11–16).[68] Importantly, in the preaching that follows, it becomes clear that the miracle is not just an isolated incident but is to be understood in salvation-historical terms as part of the fulfilment of God's promises in Scripture (3:11–16, 18), as can be seen from Acts 4:4, where Luke notes that the number of believers has grown to around five thousand.

As a consequence of the healing and subsequent preaching, Peter and John are arrested and brought before the Council, whose questions ('By what power or what name did you do this?' [4:7]) serve to confirm the understanding of the role of signs and wonders in the church, which Luke has presented in Acts 3. Peter, filled with the Holy Spirit, uses the occasion to repeat the gospel message and to confirm once again the name of Jesus of Nazareth as the source/authority for the healing (4:8–12).[69] In 4:10 in his speech Peter reaffirms that the healing, recognized as a 'notable sign' in 4:16,[70] was effected through the name of Jesus of Nazareth. This makes it difficult for the apostles' opponents to deny their ability to perform miracles and with it the implied

---

67. Ibid., p. 267, notes how Luke ends the healing with a typical reaction from the onlookers who witness the healing so that the miracle has its effect on the observers as well as the person who is healed. In this, the way is suitably prepared for the preaching of the word.

68. Cf. Kee, *To Every Nation*, p. 59.

69. Cf. Luke 12:12, where LkR adds to Mark a reference to the Holy Spirit in the context of being given words to say when appearing before tribunals (cf. Mark 13:11). Matthew's reference to the Spirit of the Father speaking 'through you' (10:20), goes even further.

70. So NRSV. Barrett, *Acts I–XIV*, p. 235, suggests that in context *gnōston sēmeion* is better understood as a 'publicly known' sign.

authority associated with the name of Jesus. Therefore, all they can do is to attempt a damage limitation exercise by forbidding the apostles to teach in the name of Jesus, to which they receive a response from Peter in 4:20 that appears to echo the words of Plato's Socrates spoken during his trial before the Athenian court.[71]

Luke concludes his narrative by summarizing two key aspects of the healing miracle: it was recognized by Peter and John's protagonists as a 'notable sign' (4:16; cf. 4:22),[72] and witnessed by many; the healing of a crippled beggar demonstrates the eschatological restoration of the poor and outcast that was at the heart of Jesus' message of salvation (Luke 4:18–19).[73] In naming the miraculous cure a 'sign', Luke echoes what has been said about Jesus in connection with signs and wonders in 2:22 and clarifies further how signs and wonders, associated with the kerygmatic witness, are to be understood by the readers of Acts.[74]

Following the apostles' release, Luke adds what amounts to a postscript, where the narrative focus is on the community at prayer (4:23–31), and where the prayer and praise of the community again repeats the gospel story (vv. 27–29).[75] Of particular interest is the suggestion in verse 30 of a partnership between the Lord and the witnesses, whereby the Lord will validate their witness with signs and wonders performed through the name of Jesus. This powerful petition is followed in verse 31 with a physical manifestation of God's powerful presence[76] and a further filling of all present by the Spirit,

---

71. 'I owe a greater obedience to God than to you; and so long as I draw breath and have my faculties, I shall never stop practising philosophy and exhorting you and elucidating the truth for everyone that I meet' (Plato, *Apol.* 29D: ET H. Tredennick, *Plato: The Last days of Socrates* [Harmondsworth: Penguin, 1969], p. 61, and noted by Witherington, *Acts*, p. 197). Cf. Peter's response in Acts 4:19b–20.

72. Fitzmyer, *Acts*, p. 304, comments that mention of the fact that the man had been crippled from birth (Acts 3:2) emphasizes the fact that this was a 'notable sign'.

73. Johnson, *Acts*, p. 79. Witherington, *Acts*, p. 176, suggests that in describing the healed man's reaction to his cure as 'leaping and praising God' with the use of the rare verb *exallomai*, Luke may intentionally be reflecting Isa. 35:6 LXX.

74. Fitzmyer, *Acts*, p. 303.

75. Ibid., p. 310, thinks that the petition in v. 29 may echo the prayer of Hezekiah in LXX 4 Kgs 19:19.

76. Cf. Virgil, *Aeneid* 3.89–90 (ET W. F. Jackson-Knight [trans.], *Virgil, The Aeneid* [Penguin Classics; Harmondsworth: Penguin, 1958], p. 77), where Aeneas prays to Apollo for a city that will provide a 'remnant of Troy', and immediately following

which parallels the description Luke gives of the initial distribution of the Spirit at Pentecost followed by bold witness to the gospel[77] – the very thing the Sanhedrin had forbidden (cf. 4:18).

We gain further insight into how Luke understands the ways in which the invocation of the name of Jesus is to be understood in association with signs and wonders through the form of words used in the healing of Aeneas by Peter (Acts 9:32–35). The phrase 'Aeneas, Jesus Christ heals you' (9:34) makes it clear that Peter is the delegated instrument through whom the risen Jesus effects the healing. Again, here, the healing serves the apostolic witness and results in all the residents of Lydda and Sharon turning to the Lord.

In the second half of Acts there are just two occasions that take place during Paul's missionary activities which involve the invocation of the name of Jesus in association with signs and wonders (Acts 16:16–18; 19:13). In Acts 16:18 Luke describes for the first time in Acts a Christian exorcism, when Paul successfully exorcizes the girl with a spirit of divination 'in the name of Jesus Christ'. As Turner rightly points out, previously in Acts 9:34 Luke has reminded his readers of the source of the healing power that lies behind the use of the name of Jesus in connection with signs and wonders, thus showing clearly that Jesus himself is present in the sense that it is 'his authority that is exercised by his representatives in miracles and exorcisms performed in his name'.[78] The efficacy of Paul's use of Jesus' name is underlined in Acts16:18b when we are told that the demon left her at once.[79]

By contrast, in Acts 19:13–19 Luke recounts an incident involving some Jewish exorcists that provides a telling footnote to Luke's understanding of what constitutes the legitimate use of Jesus' name in connection with signs and wonders. The overall context for the story demonstrates how the signs and wonders performed by Jesus' agents exercising the authority associated with

---

his prayer the hill on which Apollo's shrine stood is shaken: 'I had scarcely spoken when of a sudden everything seemed to quake, even the god's entrance door and his bay tree; the whole hill on which we stood appeared to move and the shrine seemed to open and the tripod within to speak with a roar' (*vix ea fatus eram: tremere omnia vis repente liminaque laurusque dei totusque moveri mons cicum et mugire adytis cortina recluses*). Noted by Fitzmyer, *Acts*, p. 35.

77. Barrett, *Acts I–XIV*, pp. 249–250.

78. Turner, *Power from on High*, p. 425. For the use of the name of Jesus in the sense of 'with the authority of', see also for example Barrett, *Acts XV–XXVIII*, p. 787; Bruce, *Acts*, p. 361; Dunn, *Acts*, p. 221; Witherington, *Acts*, p. 495 n. 111.

79. Haenchen, *Acts*, pp. 495–496.

his name are more powerful than the magic associated with the exorcisms practised in a non-Christian context.[80] Luke builds up the dramatic setting by describing the sons of Sceva, who clearly have a reputation as exorcists in the their own right,[81] as having the powerful credentials of being sons of a high priest and numbering seven.

For the Jewish exorcists, the 'name' is deprived of its inherent authority over evil spirits for two reasons: firstly, they are patently not themselves men of the Spirit, nor commissioned agents of Jesus; secondly, they do not invoke the name of Jesus directly, but by proxy through invoking the name of Paul rather than as a direct (authoritative) command (19:13b). The lack of direct authority associated with the legitimate use of the name causes the exorcism to backfire and the result of the incident is that the Christian message and witness prevails. The message for Luke's readers is once again clear: the authority associated with the use of Jesus' name is not available to just anyone but is restricted to those have been commissioned and whose subsequent authority permits them to act legitimately as Jesus' authorized agents.

## Conclusions

As we have seen, the evidence throughout Acts confirms that the laying on of hands is inextricably bound up with the concept of delegated authority linked with commissioning. For contemporary Christians who look to Acts for models in support of their emphasis on signs and wonders it is particularly relevant to note that throughout Acts the laying on of hands for healing is only performed legitimately by those whose authority can be recognized by Luke's readers by virtue of their having been previously commissioned.

Closely linked with the laying on of hands for healing in Acts is the idea of invoking the authority of Jesus through the use of his name so that the healer's authority is expressed in and though the name of Jesus. Indeed, the extensive use of the name of Jesus in healings and exorcisms by Luke's heroes of the

---

80. This can be seen from the fact that the incident is introduced by a reference to the 'extraordinary miracles' performed through the hands of Paul (19:11) and concluded with references to the evangelistic success following on from the incident together with a putting away of previous magical practices (19:18–19), and Luke's final comment that 'the word of the Lord grew mightily and prevailed' (19:20 NRSV).

81. Twelftree, *Jesus the Miracle Worker*, p. 349.

Spirit in Acts (3:6, 16; 4:7, 10, 12, 30; 16:18; cf. 19:13–17), together with the way Luke features the laying on of hands at other significant points in his narrative, may be said to act as a corollary to the idea present throughout Acts of authority exercised by a limited number of individuals being firmly linked to their call/commission, and it is only with these relatively few individuals that Luke associates signs and wonders in Acts.

In the contemporary church the name of Jesus is used too often without due thought being given to the NT implications that lie behind our use of Jesus' name and its subsequent invocation of heavenly authority. According to a wise old saying, too much familiarity breeds contempt. The truth of this can be seen in secular society in the way in which Jesus' name has become a common expletive in a way that does not (yet) apply to Muhammad or Buddha. Christian prayers are rightly made in the name of Jesus, not simply as a way of seeking heavenly endorsement for what we say or ask, but in recognition of the theological truth that it is through Jesus that we gain access to our Father in heaven.

For those in the contemporary church who promote healing, exorcism, signs and wonders as being normative, there are important lessons to be learned from our examination of the use of Jesus' name in connection with signs and wonders in Acts. We saw that at an early stage in his narrative Luke raises a central rhetorical question about the source of Peter's power to heal (3:12). Here, and throughout Acts, Luke makes it clear that the power to heal comes from the legitimate invocation of the name of Jesus by his authorized agents. Their delegated *exousia*, received by virtue of their having been commissioned, qualifies them to exercise the same *dynamis* that effected Jesus' miracles, which is now inextricably bound up with the name and authority of Jesus. Just as in the ancient world a person's name was thought to express that person's essence, the source that lies behind the use of Jesus' name is identified elsewhere in Acts as Jesus himself (9:34).

# 21. CONCLUSIONS TO PART THREE

In Part Three I began by noting that Third Wave commentators rely heavily on Luke's two mission accounts, arguing that Luke's inclusion of the mission of the Seventy(-Two) indicates that the power to heal and exorcize is not to be understood as being restricted just to the apostles but extends to Christians other than the apostles in Acts and, by extension, signs and wonders are to be considered as normative for Christians today. In examining Luke's presentation of commissioning and discipleship during the earthly ministry of Jesus, I concluded that Jesus' baptism is not intended by Luke to be considered as paradigmatic for the church but that Luke portrays Jesus' baptismal experience as being unique to Jesus, having the effect of establishing, from the beginning of Jesus' ministry, the unique place held by the earthly Jesus in the salvation-historical scheme that overarches Luke-Acts, and that Luke has already allotted to Jesus in the birth narrative when he states that Jesus was conceived by the Spirit (Luke 1:39).

In examining Luke's portrayal of the Twelve in his Gospel, we concluded that the unique status attributed to them from the beginning as 'apostles' by the Lukan Jesus (Luke 6:13) is bound up with Luke's concern to establish the idea of authority within the church being derived from the earthly Jesus himself through those whom Jesus appointed to succeed him, acting as guarantors of that authority for succeeding Christian generations. In terms of contemporary application we must note that this acts as a cautionary note for any exegesis that views the apostles as little more than examples of an intentional model of discipleship that primarily emphasizes the performance of signs and wonders.

The two missions of the Twelve and the Seventy(-Two) are portrayed by Luke as discrete incidents, with the mission of the Twelve again alerting us to the special place held by the apostles in relation to Jesus and the dominical tradition. The mission of the Seventy(-Two) illustrates the point that any of Jesus' followers may be called to represent him and to share his power. However, contra the Third Wave, Luke's emphasis here is not to provide a paradigm for the normative expectation of 'every disciple', but foreshadows a model that Luke portrays in Acts, where individuals are commissioned and empowered for particular tasks.

Following our discussion of Luke's extended resurrection narratives, we were led to conclude that it was important for the Evangelist to establish the corporeal, non-angelic nature of Jesus' resurrection state, so that the readers of Luke-Acts might be reassured about the continuity that exists between the earthly Jesus and the risen Lord. A likely reason being that later generations, including those for whom Luke is writing, did not have the same direct link with dominical tradition and, therefore, were dependent on the reliability of those who accompanied Jesus during his lifetime and who were also witnesses to the truth that the same Jesus of Nazareth, whose earthly ministry Luke describes in his Gospel, is now also the risen and exalted Lord who has commissioned his church to bear witness to him to the ends of the earth.

Unlike the Great Commission according to Matthew, where the disciples are to share Jesus' authority to teach, forgive sins, cast out demons and heal, the final commission according to Luke-Acts is not so transparent. Noting the importance for Luke of a shift in salvation-historical perspective enables us to remain sensitive to the outlook of Acts, where we encounter both Luke's view of the eschatological reality of the post-Easter situation for the early church, together with his own longer-term outlook in view of the delay in the parousia. His view, in turn, cautions the contemporary exegete to exercise an appropriate sensitivity towards the text in order to guard against a too direct correlation between contemporary Christian experience and praxis and the experience of the early church as Luke portrays it in Acts.

At the end of Luke's Gospel the evangelist leaves his readers with the possibility of more than just the Eleven being 'clothed with power from on high', but in Acts 1:8 the commission is addressed only to the apostles and the enigmatic 'power from on high' is explained by Luke in terms of baptism in the Holy Spirit (Acts 1:5, 8). Whilst the Pentecostal baptism in the Spirit described by Luke in Acts 2:1–4 may appear to make (at least potentially) empowered witness, including signs and wonders, more widely possible, we are neverthe-less faced with the problem that in Acts signs and wonders are restricted to a chosen few. Here we saw that in Acts commissioning appears as the initiatory vehicle that concentrates for Luke's readers the charismatic authority of the Spirit in selected individuals whom he associates with the manifestation of signs and wonders. In other words, even in light of the outpouring of the Spirit on all Jesus' followers at Pentecost and beyond, the idea of the authoritative commissioning of selected individuals that we found in Luke's Gospel also extends to his portrayal of the post-Easter community in Acts, where we also see individuals being commissioned for specific tasks, in some cases of clearly limited duration.

The implications of this for contemporary application are that, contra the Third Wave model, where signs and wonders are almost commonplace, the evidence from Acts suggests a model where a limited number of designated individuals are set apart and commissioned, initially by the risen Jesus but then more commonly by their local congregation to whom and through whom, as Luke understands it, the prophetic and authoritative voice of the Spirit of Jesus speaks. Just as signs and wonders serve to establish Israel as the people of God, so too are signs and wonders in Acts to be understood as being instru-mental in the formation of the infant church as the eschatological people of God.

In Acts we saw that whilst individual miracles may not be explicitly desig-nated 'signs and wonders' by Luke, it is nevertheless clear that Luke uses this term as a 'catch-all' for miracles, healings, exorcisms and other miraculous phe-nomena, all of which contribute to the overall numinous atmosphere of the Acts narrative. Each of Luke's heroes of the Spirit in Acts to whom he attrib-utes miraculous activity have been commissioned to act with authority. Signs and wonders in Acts both enhance the overall numinous atmosphere of the narrative and serve to demonstrate God's validation of the miracle-workers and/or enhance their reputation, normally with a view to creating or support-ing the opportunity to preach the gospel and encourage new converts.

Finally, we looked at the way in which authority is conveyed in Acts through the laying on of hands and the use of Jesus' name with a view to informing contemporary models within the church today. Our examination of the laying on of hands in Acts showed that this is inextricably bound up for Luke with the concept of delegated authority linked to commissioning. In terms of con-temporary application, this conclusion led us to conclude that for contempor-ary Christians who look to Acts for models in support of their emphasis on signs and wonders it is particularly relevant to note that throughout Acts the laying on of hands for healing is performed legitimately only by those whose authority can be recognized by Luke's readers by virtue of their having been previously commissioned.

Closely linked with the laying on of hands for healing in Acts is the idea of invoking the authority of Jesus through the use of his name. In Acts the healer's authority is expressed in and though the name of Jesus, and throughout Acts Luke makes it clear that the power to heal comes from the legitimate invocation of Jesus' name by his authorized agents. This, together with the way Luke features the laying on of hands at other significant points in his narrative, may be said to act as a corollary to the idea present throughout Acts of the authority exercised by Luke's heroes of the Spirit being firmly linked to their call/commission, and it is only with these relatively few individuals that Luke associates signs and wonders in Acts.

For those in the contemporary church who promote signs and wonders as being normative, there are important lessons to be learned here from our examination of the use of Jesus' name in connection with healings and exorcisms in Acts. We saw that at an early stage in his narrative Luke raises a central rhetorical question about the source of Peter's power to heal (3:12). Here, and throughout Acts, Luke makes it clear that the power to heal comes from the legitimate invocation of the name of Jesus by his authorized agents who have received their delegated *exousia* by virtue of their having been commissioned initially by the risen Lord himself and later by their local Christian community. This, in turn, qualifies them to exercise the same *dynamis* that effected miracles performed by the earthly Jesus and that is now inextricably bound up with the name and authority of Jesus. Just as in the ancient world a person's name was thought to express that person's essence, the source that lies behind the use of Jesus' name is identified elsewhere in Acts as the now risen and exalted Jesus himself (9:34), whose ministry today continues to be one of saving the lost and not simply 'doing the stuff'.

## 22. FINAL REFLECTIONS

In setting the hermeneutical agenda for my engagement with the Third Wave and their influential contemporary theology of signs and wonders, I noted the hermeneutical ambivalence of Third Wave writers. Throughout I have sought to demonstrate a critical approach to the text that is more appropriate to the socio-historical sensitivity required when we seek to hear what the ancient writers are saying on particular issues to the church of their own day and, by extension, what they might be saying to our own Christian generation. From the outset, I also stated my firm belief that the ultimate purpose of Christian biblical scholarship is to serve the community of faith so that any insights gained into the meaning of biblical texts may be applied to contemporary theology and praxis in an informed way. It is my contention that such an approach honours more appropriately the authoritative nature of Scripture, and better facilitates our understanding of what it means to be a follower of Jesus, and a member of the eschatological people of God in the twenty-first century.

Any NT model of discipleship that is put forward as a contemporary paradigm for Christians today must take account of the post-Easter perspective shared by all the NT writers, which naturally colours all that they wrote. The miracles associated with the ministry of the earthly Jesus are understood, by the Synoptic Evangelists, largely in terms of his unique messianic role and, therefore, should be regarded as primarily Christological. In so far as miracles are linked with discipleship, we have seen that they are to be viewed alongside what we have found to be the more fundamental aspects of discipleship taught and modelled by Jesus. Any contemporary model of Christian discipleship that aims to reflect accurately the paradigmatic intentions of the writers of the Synoptic Gospels and the writer of Acts cannot afford to use the blunt instrument of an homogenizing approach to the text that fails to ask each individual Evangelist in turn, 'What does it mean to be a follower of Jesus?'

In a book that seeks to address the community of faith, as well as the academy, it can be tempting to take a more exhortatory approach to these final reflections. However, in seeking to place the emphasis on contemporary application, there is always a danger of overpressing the evidence to the point where the NT writers are no longer permitted simply to speak for themselves, addressing individual readers in their own various situations. Having said this, in terms of informing a model for the contemporary church, a number of common factors have emerged in relation to the NT writers' attitudes to the place of signs and wonders in the church, linked particularly to their presentations of discipleship, commissioning and authority in the Gospels and, by Luke, in Acts. What, then, have we learned from our study about what these NT writers are saying, then and now?

My conclusions throughout this study have shown that all three Synoptic Evangelists leave room for signs and wonders to be associated with the models of discipleship they present. However, then as now, the numinous effect of signs and wonders, healings and exorcisms can all too easily detract from what the Gospel writers consider to be central to their understanding of Christian discipleship, and each of the Evangelists in his own way seeks to restrict the role of signs and wonders in the church.

For *Matthew*, signs and wonders are to come under the authority of the church as a learning community that exemplifies the higher righteousness associated with obeying all that Jesus has commanded. Healings and exorcisms continue to have a part to play in the community's experience of the outworking of the delegated *exousia* entrusted to all disciples, but they must by no means be the predominant characteristic of those who follow Jesus. Indeed, Matthew clearly subordinates healings and exorcisms to doing God's will, even when they are performed in Jesus' name (Matt. 7:21–23). If our reading of the link between the risen Jesus' promise of his abiding presence (Matt. 28:20b) and his authoritative presence in connection with binding and loosing (Matt. 18:20) is correct, then the contemporary model for healings/exorcisms suggested here is one where the invocation of Jesus' name is practised in a setting where the success or otherwise of the claim to authority for healing/exorcism is transparently open to ratification by the church acting in view of their belief in the abiding presence of the risen Jesus / Holy Spirit. Clearly, for Matthew, this could never be at the expense of subordinating what truly characterizes Christian discipleship to simply 'doing the stuff'! In other words, Matthew leaves no room in his church for a charismatic antinomianism that puts signs and wonders before obedience to Jesus.

For *Mark*, signs and wonders have their place particularly in the church's mission, but, as with Matthew, compared to the essentials that characterize discipleship, they are of relatively little importance. In terms of contemporary application from a Markan perspective, the emphasis is clearly on what characterizes authentic Christian discipleship. Mark's paradigm for discipleship is derived from the example of Jesus himself and the correctives we find in Mark's, often negative, portrayal of the disciples. For Mark, Christian discipleship is not particularly characterized by spectacular charismatic activity, but the model for discipleship that Mark's readers are left with – then and now – is one where, despite weakness, misunderstanding and failure, the disciples are called again by the risen Jesus to continue to follow him on the way. This is a model of discipleship that would have brought comfort to Mark's community, and resonates easily with contemporary Christian experience.

Finally, in *Luke-Acts*, the miraculous may potentially be associated with any of Jesus' followers, but, in practice, is restricted to a chosen few whose authority to act is recognized by their Christian community, and again signs and wonders are normally associated with the church's mission. From Luke's perspective, just as the signs and wonders of the Exodus demonstrated how YHWH was superior to the gods of those who opposed Israel, so too do the signs and wonders in Acts point to the lordship of the risen and exalted Christ, who is now the dispenser of the Spirit. Similarly, as signs and wonders in the Exodus served to establish Israel as the people of God, so too signs and wonders in Acts are to be understood as being instrumental in the formation of the infant church as the eschatological people of God. This, in turn, suggests that whilst the presence of signs and wonders in Acts serves to enhance the numinous atmosphere of Luke's narrative, they should also be understood as having a more important salvation-historical function.

This does not mean that from here we should confine signs and wonders to a distant, apostolic past, but it does mean that a theology of signs and wonders that relies on a Lukan model in order to promote their contemporary manifestation as normative should bear in mind what is central to Luke's presentation of signs and wonders in the early church; namely, that Luke associated signs and wonders only with those who had a transparently authoritative role to play in the missiological progress of the church.

In terms of the contemporary application of the overall results gained from our study, it is fair to say that the church in the twenty-first century must remain open to God's sovereign activity, which may on occasion extend to the validation of individuals and their ministries through signs and wonders. However, signs and wonders, by definition, cannot be considered commonplace, and the models of discipleship presented to us in the Synoptic Gospels and Acts do not encourage the expectation that the manifestation of signs and wonders is to be considered normative in the experience of all who seek, through the leading and presence of the Spirit in their lives, to follow Jesus and to model his teaching and example.

# APPENDIX: ANALYSIS OF SIGNS AND WONDERS IN ACTS

| Person involved | Commissioned by | Miraculous phenomena | Effect/Consequence |
| --- | --- | --- | --- |
| Jesus (in retrospect). | God. | Deeds of power, wonders and signs (2:22). | Validation by God. |
| | | Healings/exorcisms (10:38). | Enhances Jesus' reputation. |
| Apostles. | Risen Jesus. | Many signs and wonders performed (2:43). | Numinous awe. |
| | | Many signs, wonders, healings and exorcisms (5:12, 16). | Enhances reputation and believers added (5:13b, 14). |
| Peter (with John). | Risen Jesus. | Healing of crippled beggar (3:2–8). | Opportunity to speak. |
| Peter. | Risen Jesus. | Punishment: Ananias and Sapphira (5:1–6, 7–11). | Numinous fear. |

| Person involved | Commissioned by | Miraculous phenomena | Effect/Consequence |
|---|---|---|---|
| | | Healing via Peter's shadow (5:15) plus miraculous escape from jail (5:19–20). | Attracts populace including sick and possessed, provokes opposition, opportunity to speak (5:16, 17–32). |
| | | Healing (9:32). | Attracts converts (9:42). |
| | | Dead person revived (9:36–41). | Attracts converts (9:42). |
| | | Angelic aid to escape from prison (12:1–11). | Numinous awe (12:15–16). |
| Stephen. | Apostles/church. | Signs and wonders (6:8). | Major character whose reputation enhanced for reader (6:8 – 7:60). |
| Philip. | Apostles/church. | Signs, exorcisms and healings (8:6). | Attracts populace and converts added (8:6). |
| | | Signs and great miracles (8:13). | Numinous awe/Simon's amazement and ref. back to 8:6–7. |
| | | Angel directs Philip to Ethiopian (8:26). | Ethiopian converted (8:38–39). |
| | | Spirit snatches Philip away (8:39). | Opportunities to speak (8:40b; cf. 21:8). |
| Ananias. | Risen Jesus. | Heals Saul (9:17–18; cf. 9:8–9). | Convert added (9:18b). |
| Paul. | Risen Jesus. | Elymas struck blind (13:11). | Convert added (13:12b). |

| Person involved | Commissioned by | Miraculous phenomena | Effect/Consequence |
|---|---|---|---|
| | | Healing (14:9–10). | Reputations enhanced, opportunity to speak (14:11–18). |
| | | Exorcism (16:16–18). | Opportunity to speak, converts added (cf. below 16:32–33). |
| | | Miracles, healings, exorcisms through contact with items of Paul's clothing (19:11–12). | God's validation, reputation enhanced (19:11–12). |
| | | Healing (20:9–11). | Comfort to believers (20:12). |
| | | Paul unharmed by viper (28:5; cf. Mark 16:18a). | Reputation enhanced (28:6). |
| | | Healings (28:8–9). | Reputation enhanced. |
| Paul with Barnabas. | Church in Antioch. | Signs and wonders (14:3). | Opportunities to speak plus validation by the Lord. |
| | | Signs and wonders in retrospect (15:12). | Validation by God. |
| Paul with Silas. | Jerusalem church (15:22, 40).[1] | Earthquake, prison doors open, chains fall off (16:26). | Opportunity to speak, converts added (16:32–33). |

---

1. C. K. Barrett, *A Critical and Exegetical Commentary on the Acts of the Apostles*. Vol. 2: *Acts XV–XXVIII* (London: T. & T. Clark, 1998), p. 757, notes the singular *paradotheis* in 15:40 but argues nevertheless that Silas was almost certainly included in the commendation.

# BIBLIOGRAPHY

ACHTEMEIER, P. J., *Mark* (Proclamation Commentaries; Philadelphia: Fortress, 1975).
— 'Mark as Interpreter of the Jesus Traditions', *Int* 32.4 (1978), pp. 339–352.
— 'The Lukan Perspective on the Miracles of Jesus: A Preliminary Sketch', in C. H. Talbert (ed.), *Perspectives on Luke-Acts* (Danville, Va.: Association of Baptist Professors of Religion; Edinburgh: T. & T. Clark, 1978), pp. 153–167.

AGNEW, F. H., 'The Origin of the NT Apostle Concept: A Review of Research', *JBL* 105.1 (1986), pp. 75–96.

AKER, B., 'New Directions in Lucan Theology: Reflections of Luke 3:21–22 and Some Implications', in P. E. Elbert (ed.), *Faces of Renewal* (Peabody, Mass: Hendrickson, 1988), pp. 108–127.

ALBRIGHT, W. F., and MANN, C. S., *Matthew* (AB 26; New York: Doubleday, 1981).

ALLINSON, D. C., *The New Moses: A Matthean Typology* (Edinburgh: T. & T. Clark, 1993).

ALSUP, J. E., *The Post-Resurrection Appearance Stories of the Gospel Tradition* (Calwer Theologische Monographien 5; Stuttgart: Calwer; London: SPCK, 1975).

ANDERSON, H., *The Gospel of Mark* (London: Oliphants, 1976).

ANDERSON, J. C., *Matthew's Narrative Web: Over, and Over, and Over Again* (Sheffield; JSOT, 1994).

ARCHER, K. J., 'Pentecostal Hermeneutics: Retrospect and Prospect', *JPT* 8 (1996), pp. 63–81.

AUNE, D. E., *Prophecy in Early Christianity and the Ancient Mediterranean World* (Grand Rapids, Mich.: Eerdmans, 1983).

BAILEY, J. L., 'Genre Analysis', in J. B. Green (ed.), *Hearing the New Testament: Strategies for Interpretation* (Grand Rapids, Mich.: Eerdmans; Carlisle: Paternoster, 1995), pp. 197–221.

BANKS, R. J., *Jesus and the Law in the Synoptic Tradition* (Cambridge: Cambridge University Press, 1975).

BARR, J., *Holy Scripture: Canon, Authority, Criticism* (Oxford: Clarendon, 1983).

BARRETT, C. K., *The Signs of an Apostle* (Cato Lecture, 1969; rev. Carlisle: Paternoster, 1996).

— *A Critical and Exegetical Commentary on the Acts of the Apostles.* Vol. 1: *Acts I–XIV* (Edinburgh: T. & T. Clark, 1994).

— *A Critical and Exegetical Commentary on the Acts of the Apostles.* Vol. 2: *Acts XV–XXVIII* (London: T. & T. Clark, 1998).

BARRETT, D. B., 'Global Statistics', in S. M. Burgess, and G. B. McGee (eds.), *Dictionary of Pentecostal and Charismatic Movements* (Grand Rapids, Mich.: Zondervan, 1988), pp. 810–830.

BARTH, G., 'Matthew's Understanding of the Law', in G. Bornkamm, G. Barth and H. J. Held (eds.), *Tradition and Interpretation in Matthew* (ET London: SCM, 1963), pp. 58–164.

BARTON, S. C., 'Historical Criticism and Social-Scientific Perspectives in New Testament Study', in J. B. Green (ed.), *Hearing the New Testament: Strategies for Interpretation* (Grand Rapids, Mich.: Eerdmans; Carlisle: Paternoster, 1995), pp. 61–89.

BARTSCH, H. W., 'Jesu Schwertwort, Lukas xxii, 35–38: Überlieferungsgeschichtliche Studie', *NTS* 20 (1973–4), pp. 190–203.

BAUER, D. R., *The Structure of Matthew's Gospel: A Study in Literary Design* (Sheffield: Almond, 1989).

BEARE, F. W., *The Earliest Records of Jesus* (Oxford: Blackwell, 1962).

— 'The Mission of the Disciples and the Mission Charge: Matthew 10 and Parallels', *JBL* 89 (1970), pp. 1–13.

BEASLEY-MURRAY, G., *Jesus and the Kingdom of God* (Grand Rapids, Mich.: Eerdmans; Exeter: Paternoster, 1986).

BEAVIS, M. A., 'Mark's Teaching on Faith', *BTB* 16 (1986), pp. 139–142.

BEST, E., 'The Role of the Disciples in Mark', *NTS* 23 (1977), pp. 377–401.

— 'Mark's Use of the Twelve', *ZNW* 69 (1978), pp. 11–35.

— *Following Jesus: Discipleship in the Gospel of Mark* (JSNTSup 4; Sheffield: JSOT, 1981).

— *Mark: The Gospel as Story* (Edinburgh: T. & T. Clark, 1983).

— *Disciples and Discipleship: Studies in the Gospel According to Mark* (Edinburgh: T. & T. Clark, 1986).

BICKERMANN, E., 'Das leere Grab', *ZNW* 23 (1924), pp. 218–291.

BIETENHARD, H., ὄνομα, *TDNT* 5, pp. 242–283.

BLACK, C. C., 'The Quest of Mark the Redactor: Why Has it Been Pursued, and what Has it Taught us?', *JSNT* 33 (1988), pp. 19–39.

— *The Disciples According to Mark: Markan Redaction in Current Debate* (JSNTSup 27; Sheffield: JSOT, 1989).

BLOMBERG, C. L., *Jesus and the Gospels* (Leicester: Apollos, 1997).

BLUE, K., *Authority to Heal* (Downers Grove, Ill.: IVP, 1987).

BOCK, D. L., *Luke 1:1–9:50* (Grand Rapids, Mich.: Baker, 1994).

— *Luke 9:51–24:53* (Grand Rapids, Mich.: Baker, 1996).

BOLT, P. G., 'Mark 16:1–8: The Empty Tomb of a Hero?', *TynBul* 47.1 (1996), pp. 27–37.

BONNARD, P., *L'Évangile selon Saint Mathieu* (Neuchâtel: Delachaux & Niestlé, 1963).

BOOMERSHINE, T. E., 'Mark 16:8 and the Apostolic Commission', *JBL* 100.2 (1981), pp. 197–211.

BOOMERSHINE, T. E., and BARTHOLEMEW, G. L., 'The Narrative Technique of Mark 16.8', *JBL* 100.2 (1981), pp. 213–223.

BORING, M. E., *Sayings of the Risen Jesus: Christian Prophecy in the Synoptic Tradition* (SNTSMS 46; Cambridge: Cambridge University Press, 1982).

BORNKAMM, G., 'The Risen Lord and the Earthly Jesus: Matthew 28.16–20'; ET in J. Robinson (ed.), *The Future of our Religious Past* (London: SCM, 1971), pp. 203–229.

— 'The Authority to "Bind and Loose" in the Church'; ET in G. Stanton (ed.), *The Interpretation of Matthew* (London: SPCK, 1983), pp. 85–97.

BORNKAMM, G., BARTH, G., and HELD, H. J., *Tradition and Interpretation in Matthew* (ET London: SCM, 1963).

BOTTOMLY, K., 'Coming out of the Hangar: Confessions of an Evangelical Deist', in G. S. Greig and K. N. Springer (eds.), *The Kingdom and the Power* (Ventura, Calif.: Regal, 1993), pp. 257–274.

BOWDEN, J., 'Narrative Theology', in A. Richardson and J. Bowden (eds.), *A New Dictionary of Christian Theology* (London: SCM, 1983), pp. 391–392.

BRAWLEY, R. L., *Luke-Acts and the Jews* (SBLMS; Atlanta, Ga.: Scholars Press, 1987).

BROADHEAD, E. K., *Teaching with Authority: Miracles and Christology in the Gospel of Mark* (JSNTSup 74; Sheffield: JSOT, 1992).

BROCK, S. P., and PICARD, J.-C., *Testamentum Lobi Apocalypsis Graece* (Leiden: Brill, 1967).

BRODIE, T. L., 'Luke-Acts as an Imitation and Emulation of the Elijah/Elisha Narrative', in E. Richard (ed.), *New Views on Luke and Acts* (Collegeville, Minn.: Liturgical, 1990), pp. 78–85.

BROOKS, O. S., 'Matthew xxviii, 16–20 and the Design of the First Gospel', *JSNT* 10 (1981), pp. 2–18.

BROWN, R. E., DONFRIED, K. P., and REUMANN, J. (eds.), *Peter in the New Testament* (London: Chapman, 1974).

BROWN, S., 'Apostasy and Perseverance', *AnBib* 36 (1969), pp. 5–12.

— 'The Mission to Israel in Matthew's Central Section (Matt. 9.35–11.1)', *ZNW* 69 (1977), pp. 73–90.

— 'The Two-fold Representation of the Mission in Matthew's Gospel', *ST* 31 (1977), pp. 21–32.

BRUCE, F. F., *The Acts of the Apostles: Greek Text with Introduction and Commentary*, 3rd ed. (Leicester: Apollos, 1990).

BUCKWALTER, H. D., 'The Divine Saviour', in I. H. Marshall and D. Peterson (eds.), *Witness to the Gospel: The Theology of Acts* (Grand Rapids, Mich.: Eerdmans, 1998), pp. 107–123.

BULTMANN, R., *Theology of the New Testament*, vol. 1 (ET London: SCM, 1952).

— 'New Testament and Mythology', in H. W. Bartsch (ed.), *Kerygma and Myth: A Theological Debate by Rudolf Bultmann and Five Critics* (ET New York: Harper & Brothers, 1961), pp. 1–44.

— *History of the Synoptic Tradition* (ET Oxford: Blackwell, 1963).

— *History of the Synoptic Tradition* (ET New York: Harper & Row, 1976).

— πιστεύω, πίστις, *TDNT* 6, pp. 174–228.

BUNDY, D. D., 'Keswick Higher Life Movement', in S. M. Burgess and G. B. McGee (eds.), *Dictionary of Pentecostal and Charismatic Movements* (Grand Rapids, Mich.: Zondervan, 1988), pp. 518–519.

BURDON, C., '"Such a Fast God" – True and False Disciples in Mark's Gospel', *Theology* 7.34 (1987), pp. 89–97.

CAIRD, G. B., *The Gospel of Saint Luke* (Harmondsworth: Penguin, 1963).

CARSON, D. A. (ed.), 'A Sketch of the Factors Determining Current Hermeneutical Debate in Cross-Cultural Contexts', in D. A. Carson (ed.), *Biblical Interpretation and the Church: Text and Context* (Exeter: Paternoster, 1984), pp. 11–29.

— *Biblical Interpretation and the Church: Text and Context* (Exeter: Paternoster, 1984).

— 'The Purpose of Signs and Wonders in the New Testament', in M. Scott-Horton (ed.), *Power Religion: The Selling out of the Evangelical Church?* (Chicago: Moody, 1992), pp. 89–118.

CATCHPOLE, D. R., 'The Fearful Silence of the Women at the Tomb: A Study in Markan Theology', *JTSA* 18 (1977), pp. 3–10.

— *The Quest for Q* (Edinburgh: T. & T. Clark, 1993).

— *Resurrection People: Studies in the Resurrection Narratives of the Gospels* (London: Darton Longman & Todd, 2000).

CHAPPELL, P. G., 'Healing Movements', in S. M. Burgess and G. B. McGee (eds.), *Dictionary of Pentecostal and Charismatic Movements* (Grand Rapids, Mich.: Zondervan, 1988), pp. 353–374.

CHARLESWORTH, J. H. (ed.), *The Old Testament Pseudepigrapha*. Vol. 2: *Expansions of the 'Old Testament' Legends, Wisdom and Philosophical Literature, Prayers, Psalms and Odes, Fragments of Lost Judaistic Works* (London: Darton Longman & Todd, 1985).

CHILTON, B. (ed.), *The Kingdom of God in the Teaching of Jesus* (London: SPCK, 1984).

— *Jesus and the Ethics of the Kingdom* (London: SPCK, 1987).

CLARK, A. C., 'The Role of the Apostles', in I. H. Marshall and D. Peterson, *Witness the the Gospel: The Theology of Acts*, pp. 169–190.

COGGINS, J. R., and HIEBERT, P. G. (eds.), *Wonders and the Word: An Examination of Issues Raised by John Wimber and the Vineyard Movement* (Winnipeg: Kindred, 1989).

COLE, A., *Mark* (TNTC; Leicester: IVP, 1961).

COLSON, F. H., and WHITAKER, G. H., *Philo on Abraham* (LCL 261; Cambridge, Mass.: Harvard University Press, 1985).

CONZELMANN, H., *Die Mitte der Zeit* (Tübingen: Mohr, 1953); ET *The Theology of St. Luke* (London: SCM, 1960).

— *The Theology of St. Luke* (ET London: SCM, 1960).

— *Acts of the Apostles* (ET Philadelphia: Fortress, 1987).

COPPENS, J., 'L'Imposition des mains dans les Actes des Apôtres', in J. Kremer (ed.), *Les Actes des Apôtres: traditions, redaction, théologie* (Gembloux, Leuven: Duculot, 1979), pp. 405–438.

CRANFIELD, C. E. B., *The Gospel According to St. Mark* (Cambridge: Cambridge University Press, 1959).

CRAY, G., 'A Theology of the Kingdom', *Transformation* 5.4 (1988), pp. 24–31.

CROSS, F. L., and LIVINGSTONE, E. A. (eds.), *The Oxford Dictionary of the Christian Church* (Oxford: Oxford University Press, 1974).

CULLMANN, O., *Christ and Time* (ET London: SCM, 1951).

— *Peter: Disciple, Apostle, Martyr* (ET London: SCM, 1953).

— *Early Christian Worship* (ET London: SCM, 1966).

DANKER, F. W., *Jesus and the New Age: A Commentary on St. Luke's Gospel* (Philadelphia: Fortress, 1988).

DANOVE, P. L., *The End of Mark's Story: A Methodological Study* (Leiden: Brill, 1993).

DAUBE, D., *The New Testament and Rabbinic Judaism* (London: Athlone, 1956).

DAVIES, M., *Matthew* (Sheffield: JSOT, 1993).

DAVIES, W. D., and ALLISON, D. C., Jr., *A Critical and Exegetical Commentary on The Gospel According to Saint Matthew*. Vol. 1: *Introduction and Commentary on Matthew I–VII* (Edinburgh: T. & T. Clark, 1988).

DEERE, J., *Surprised by the Power of the Spirit* (Eastbourne: Kingsway, 1993).

DELLING, G., ἡμέρα, *TDNT* 2, pp. 943–953.

DELORME, J., 'Luc v.1–2: analyse structurale et histoire de la rédaction', *NTS* 18 (1971–2), pp. 331–350.

DENNEY, J., 'The Word "Hate" in Luke xiv.26', *ExpTim* 21 (1909–10), pp. 41–42.

DIBELIUS, M., *Studies in the Acts of the Apostles* (ET London: SCM, 1956).

— *Die Formsgeschichte des Evangeliums*, 4th ed. (Tübingen: Mohr, 1961).

— *From Tradition to Gospel*, 2nd ed. (ET London: Clarke, 1971).

DODD, C. H., 'The Appearances of the Risen Christ: An Essay in Form Criticism of the Gospels', in idem, *More New Testament Studies* (Manchester: Manchester University

Press, 1968), pp. 102–133.

DONAHUE, J. R., *The Theology and Setting of Discipleship in the Gospel of Mark* (1983 Pere Marquette Theology Lecture; Milwaukee: Marquette University Press, 1983).

DONALDSON, T. L., *Jesus on the Mountain* (JSNTSup 8; JSOT, 1985).

— 'Guiding Readers – Making Disciples: Discipleship in Matthew's Narrative Strategy', in R. N. Longenecker (ed.), *Patterns of Discipleship in the New Testament* (Grand Rapids, Mich.: Eerdmans, 1996), pp. 30–49.

DOWD, S. E., *Prayer, Power, and the Problem of Suffering: Mark 11:22–25 in the Context of Markan Theology* (SBLDS 105; Atlanta, Ga.: Scholars Press, 1988).

DOYLE, R. (ed.), *Signs and Wonders and Evangelicals: A Response to the Teaching of John Wimber* (Randberg, Australia: Fabel Distributors, 1987).

DUNN, J. D. G., *Baptism in the Holy Spirit: A Re-examination of the New Testament Teaching on the Gift of the Spirit in Relation to Pentecostalism Today* (London: SCM, 1970).

— 'Spirit and Kingdom', *ExpTim* 82 (1970–1), pp. 36–40.

— *Jesus and the Spirit: A Study of the Religious and Charismatic Experience of Jesus and the First Christians as Reflected in the New Testament* (London: SCM, 1975).

— 'Has the Canon a Continuing Function?', in idem, *Unity and Diversity in the New Testament: An Enquiry into the Character of Earliest Christianity* (London: SCM, 1977).

— *Unity and Diversity in the New Testament: An Enquiry into the Character of Earliest Christianity* (London: SCM, 1977).

— *Christology in the Making: A New Testament Enquiry into the Origins of the Doctrine of the Incarnation* (London: SCM, 1980).

— 'Levels of Canonical Authority', *HBT* 4.1 (1982), pp. 13–60.

— *The Evidence for Jesus* (London: SCM, 1985).

— *The Living Word* (London: SCM, 1987).

— *The Partings of the Ways* (London: SCM, 1991).

— *Jesus' Call to Discipleship* (Cambridge: Cambridge University Press, 1992).

— 'Baptism in the Spirit: A Response to Pentecostal Scholarship on Luke-Acts', *JPT* 3 (1993), pp. 3–27.

— *The Acts of the Apostles* (Peterborough: Epworth, 1996).

— *The Christ and the Spirit: Essays of James D. G. Dunn.* Vol. 2: *Pneumatology* (Grand Rapids, Mich.: Eerdmans, 1998).

— *The Theology of Paul the Apostle* (Edinburgh: T. & T. Clark, 1998).

— 'What Makes a Good Exposition?', *ExpTim* 114.5 (2003), pp. 147–157.

DUNN, J. D. G. and TWELFTREE, G. H., 'Demon-Possession and Exorcism in the New Testament', *Chm* 3 (1980), pp. 210–225.

DUNN, J. D. G., with MACKEY, J. P., *New Testament Theology in Dialogue* (London: SPCK, 1987).

DUPONT, J., 'Le nom d'apôtre a-t-il été donné aux douze par Jésus?', *OrSyr* 1 (1956), pp. 267–290, 425–444.

DWYER, T., 'The Motif of Wonder in the Gospel of Mark', *JSNT* 57 (1995), pp. 49–59.

ELLIS, E. E., *The Gospel of Luke* (Grand Rapids, Mich.: Eerdmans; London: Marshall, Morgan & Scott, 1981).

ERHADT, A., 'The Disciples of Emmaus', *NTS* 10 (1963–4), pp. 182–201.

ESLER, P. F., *Community and Gospel in Luke-Acts: The Social and Political Motivations of Lucan Theology* (Cambridge: Cambridge University Press, 1987).

EVANS, C. A., *Mark 8:27–16:20* (WBC 34B; Nashville, Tenn.: Nelson, 2001).

EVANS, C. F., *Saint Luke* (London: SCM, 1990).

FARMER, W. R., *The Last Twelve Verses of Mark* (SNTSMS 25; Cambridge: Cambridge University Press, 1974).

FEE, G. D., *God's Empowering Presence: The Holy Spirit in the Letters of Paul* (Peabody, Mass.: Hendrickson, 1994).

FITZMYER, J. A., 'Some Observations on the Genesis Apocryphon', *CBQ* 22 (1960), pp. 277–291.

— *The Gospel According to Luke (I–IX)* (AB 28; New York: Doubleday, 1981).

— *The Gospel According to Luke (X–XXIV)* (AB 28A; New York: Doubleday, 1985).

— *The Acts of the Apostles* (AB 31; New York: Doubleday, 1998).

FLEDDERMANN, H. T., 'The Discipleship Discourse (Mark 9.33–50)', *CBQ* 43 (1981), pp. 60–61.

FLETCHER, D. R., "Condemned to Die: The Logion on Cross-Bearing: What Does it Mean?', *Int* 18 (1964), pp. 156–164.

FOERSTER, W., ἐξουσία, *TDNT* 2, pp. 560–575.

FOWLER, R. M., *Let the Reader Understand: Reader Response Criticism and the Gospel of Mark* (Minneapolis: Fortress, 1991).

FRANCE, R. T., 'The Church and the Kingdom of God', in D. A. Carson (ed.), *Biblical Interpretation and the Church: Text and Context* (Exeter: Paternoster, 1984), pp. 30–44.

— *The Gospel According to Matthew: An Introduction and Commentary* (Leicester: IVP; Grand Rapids, Mich.: Eerdmans, 1985).

— *Matthew: Evangelist and Teacher* (Exeter: Paternoster, 1989).

— *Divine Government: God's Kingship in the Gospel of Mark* (London: SPCK, 1990).

— *The Gospel of Mark: A Commentary on the Greek Text* (NIGTC; Grand Rapids, Mich.: Eerdmans, 2002).

FREYNE, S., *The Twelve: Disciples and Apostles* (London: Sheed & Ward, 1968).

FULLER, R. H., *The Formation of the Resurrection Narratives*, 2nd ed. (London: SPCK, 1980).

GARRETT, S. R., *The Demise of the Devil: Magic and the Demonic in Luke's Writings* (Minneapolis: Fortress, 1989).

GAYLORD, H. E. (trans.) '3 [Greek Apocalypse of] Baruch', in J. H. Charlesworth (ed.), *The Old Testament Pseudepigrapha*. Vol. 1: *Apocalyptic Literature and Testaments* (London: Darton Longman & Todd, 1983), pp. 653–679.

GEISLER, N., *Signs and Wonders* (Wheaton, Ill.: Tyndale House, 1988).

GILLMANN, J., 'A Temptation to Violence: The Two Swords', *LS* 9 (1982), pp. 142–153.

GNILKA, J., *Das Evangelium Nach Markus (Mk 8,27–16,20)* (EKKNT 11.2; Zurich: Benziger; Cologne: Neukirchener, 1979).

GOLDINGAY, J. (ed.), *Signs and Wonders and Healing* (Leicester: IVP, 1989).

— *Models for Scripture* (Grand Rapids, Mich.: Eerdmans; Carlisle: Paternoster, 1994).

— *Models for Interpretation of Scripture* (Grand Rapids, Mich.: Eerdmans; Carlisle: Paternoster, 1995).

GRANT, R. M., 'Literary Criticism and the New Testament Canon', *JSNT* 16 (1982), pp. 24–44; republished in S. E. Porter and C. A. Evans, *New Testament Interpretation and Methods* (Sheffield: Sheffield Academic Press, 1997), pp. 82–101.

GRAYSTON, K., 'The Translation of Matthew 29.17', *JSNT* 21 (1984), pp. 105–109.

GREEN, J. B., *The Gospel of Luke* (Grand Rapids, Mich.: Eerdmans, 1997).

— '"Salvation to the End of the Earth" (Acts 13:47): God as Saviour in the Acts of the Apostles', in I. H. Marshall and D. Peterson (eds.), *Witness to the Gospel: The Theology of Acts* (Grand Rapids, Mich.: Eerdmans, 1998), pp. 83–106.

GREEN, J. B. (ed.), *Hearing the New Testament: Strategies for Interpretation* (Grand Rapids, Mich.: Eerdmans; Carlisle: Paternoster, 1995).

GREIG, G. S., and SPRINGER, K. N. (eds.), *The Kingdom and the Power: Are Healing and the Spiritual Gifts Used by Jesus and the Early Church Meant for the Church Today?* (Ventura, Calif.: Regal, 1993).

GRUDEM, W., 'Should Christians Expect Miracles Today? Objections and Answers from the Bible', in G. S. Greig and K. N. Springer (eds.), *The Kingdom and the Power: Are Healing and the Spiritual Gifts Used by Jesus and the Early Church Meant for the Church Today?* (Ventura, Calif.: Regal, 1993), pp. 55–110.

GRUDEM, W. (ed.), *Are Miraculous Gifts for Today? Four Views* (Leicester: IVP, 1996).

GRUNDMANN, W., δύναμαι, δύναμις, *TDNT* 2, pp. 284–317.

GUELICH, R. A., *The Sermon on the Mount: A Foundation for Understanding* (Waco, Tex.: Word, 1982).

GUNDRY, R. H., *Matthew: A Commentary on His Literary and Theological Art* (Grand Rapids, Mich.: Eerdmans, 1982).

— *Mark: A Commentary on His Apology for the Cross* (Grand Rapids, Mich.: Eerdmans, 1993).

GUNKEL, H., and BEGRICH, J., *Einleitung in die Psalmen*, 2 vols. (Göttingen: Vandenhoeck & Ruprecht, 1928–33).

GUNSTONE, J., *Signs and Wonders: The Wimber Phenomenon* (London: Daybreak, 1989).

HAENCHEN, E., *The Acts of the Apostles* (ET Oxford: Blackwell, 1971).

HAGEDORN, A. C., and NEYREY, J. H., '"It Was out of Envy That they Handed Jesus over" (Mark 15.10): The Anatomy of Envy and the Gospel of Mark', *JSNT* 69 (1998), pp. 15–56.

HAGNER, D. A., *Matthew 1–13* (WBC 33A; Dallas, Tex.: Word, 1993).

— *Matthew 14–28* (WBC 33B; Dallas, Tex.: Word, 1995).

HAHN, F., *Mission in the New Testament* (ET SBT 47; London: SCM, 1965).

HAMILTON, N. Q., 'Resurrection Tradition and the Composition of Mark', *JBL* 84 (1965), pp. 415–421.

HARDON, J. A., 'The Miracle Narratives in the Acts of the Apostles', *CBQ* 16 (1954), pp. 303–318.

HARE, D. R. A., *The Theme of Jewish Persecution of Christians in the Gospel According to St. Mark* (SNTSMS 6; Cambridge: Cambridge University Press, 1967).

— *Mark* (Louisville, Ky.: Westminster John Knox, 1996).

HARE, D. R. A., and HARRINGTON, D. J., 'Make Disciples of All the Gentiles (Matt. 28.19)', *CBQ* 37 (1975), pp. 359–369.

HARLOW, D. C., *The Greek Apocalypse of Baruch (3 Baruch): In Hellenistic Judaism and Early Christianity* (SVTP 12; Leiden: Brill, 1996).

HARPER, M., *Spiritual Warfare* (London: Hodder & Stoughton, 1970).

HARRINGTON, D. J., 'Pseudo Philo', in J. H. Charlesworth (ed.), *The Old Testament Pseudepigrapha*, vol. 2 (London: Darton Longman & Todd, 1985), pp. 297–377.

— *The Gospel of Matthew* (SP 1; Collegeville, Minn.: Liturgical, 1991).

HATCH, E., and REDPATH, H. A., *A Concordance to the Septuagint and Other Greek Versions of the Old Testament*, 2nd ed. (Grand Rapids, Mich.: Baker, 1998).

HAWKIN, D. J.,'The Incomprehension of the Disciples in the Marcan Redaction', *JBL* 91 (1972), pp. 491–500.

HAYA-PRATS, G., *L'Esprit force de l'église: sa nature et son activité d'après les Actes des Apôtres* (FT from Spanish; Paris: Latour-Maubourg, 1975).

HAYS, R. B., *The Moral Vision of the New Testament: A Contemporary Introduction to New Testament Ethics* (Edinburgh: T. & T. Clark, 1996).

HEIL, J. P., *The Death and Resurrection of Jesus: A Narrative-Critical Reading of Matthew 26–28* (Minneapolis: Fortress, 1991).

HENGEL, M., *Judaism and Hellenism: Studies in their Encounter in Palestine during the Early Hellenistic Period* (ET London: SCM, 1974).

— *Property and Riches in the Early Church: Aspects of a Social History of Early Christianity* (ET London: SCM, 1974).

— *Acts and the History of Earliest Christianity* (ET London: SCM, 1979).

— *The Charismatic Leader and His Followers* (ET Edinburgh: T. & T. Clark, 1981).

— *Studies in the Gospel of Mark* (ET SCM, 1985).

— *Crucifixion in the Ancient World and the Folly of the Message of the Cross* (ET republished in *The Cross of the Son of God*; London: SCM, 1986), pp. 92–185.

HIEBERT, P. G., 'Healing and the Kingdom', in J. R. Coggins, *Wonders and the Word* (Winnipeg: Kindred, 1989), pp. 109–152.

HILL, D., 'False Prophets and Charismatics: Structure and Interpretation in Matthew 7,15–25', *Bib* 57 (1976), pp. 327–348.

HOCKEN, P., *Streams of Renewal: The Origins and Early Development of the Charismatic Movement in Great Britain* (Exeter: Paternoster, 1986).

HOCKEN, P. (ed.), *All Together in One Place: Theological Papers from the Brighton Conference on World Evangelization* (Sheffield: Sheffield Academic Press, 1993), pp. 166–180.

HOLLENWEGER, W. J., *The Pentecostals*, 3rd ed. (ET Peabody, Mass.: Hendrickson, 1988).

— 'The Critical Tradition of Pentecostalism', *JPT* 1 (1992), pp. 7–17.

HOOKER, M. D., 'The Prohibition of Foreign Missions (Mt. 10.5–6)', *ExpTim* 82 (1971), pp. 361–365.

— *The Message of Mark* (London: Epworth, 1983).

— *The Gospel According to Saint Mark* (London: A. & C. Black; Peabody, Mass: Hendrickson, 1991).

HORST, P. W. VAN DER, 'Once More: The Translation of οἱ δέ in Matthew 28.17', *JSNT* 27 (1986), pp. 27–30.

HUBBARD, B. J., 'The Matthean Redaction of a Primitive Apostolic Commissioning' (PhD thesis, University of Iowa, 1973).

— 'Commissioning Stories in Luke-Acts: A Study of their Antecedents, Form and Content', *Semeia* 8 (1977), pp. 103–126.

— 'The Role of Commissioning Accounts in Acts', in C. H. Talbert (ed.), *Perspectives on Luke-Acts* (Edinburgh: T. & T. Clark, 1978), pp. 187–198.

HULL, J. M., *Hellenistic Magic and the Synoptic Tradition* (SBT, Second Series, 28; London: SCM, 1974).

HUNTER, H. D., 'Serpent Handling', in S. M. Burgess and G. B. McGee (eds.), *Dictionary of Pentecostal and Charismatic Movements* (Grand Rapids, Mich.: Zondervan, 1988), p. 777.

HURTADO, L. W., *Mark* (NIBCNT; Peabody, Mass: Hendrickson, 1983).

— 'The Gospel of Mark', in S. M. Burgess and G. B. McGee (eds.), *Dictionary of Pentecostal and Charismatic Movements* (Grand Rapids, Mich.: Zondervan, 1988), pp. 573–582.

— *One God, One Lord: Early Christian Devotion and Ancient Jewish Monotheism* (London: SCM, 1988).

— 'Following Jesus in the Gospel of Mark – and Beyond', in R. N. Longenecker (ed.), *Patterns of Discipleship in the New Testament* (Grand Rapids, Mich.: Eerdmans, 1996), pp. 9–29.

IERSEL, B. VAN, *Reading Mark* (ET Edinburgh: T. & T. Clark, 1989).

JACKSON-KNIGHT, W. F. (trans.), *Virgil, The Aeneid* (Penguin Classics; Harmondsworth: Penguin, 1958).

JARVIS, P. G., 'The Tower Builder and the King Going to War, Luke 14.25–33)', *ExpTim* 77 (1965–6), pp. 196–198.

JEREMIAS, J., 'The Freer Logion', in E. Hennecke, *New Testament Apocrypha*, vol. 1 (ET London: SCM, 1963), pp. 188–189.

— κλείς, *TDNT* 3, pp. 744–753.

272 SIGNS AND WONDERS THEN AND NOW

— *The Eucharistic Words of Jesus* (ET London: SCM, 1966).

— *Jesus' Promise to the Nations* (ET London: SCM, 1967).

— *The Prayers of Jesus* (ET London: SCM, 1967).

— *New Testament Theology Volume One: The Proclamation of Jesus* (ET London: SCM, 1971).

— *The Parables of Jesus*, 3rd ed. (ET London: SCM, 1972).

JERVELL, J., *The Theology of the Acts of the Apostles* (Cambridge: Cambridge University Press, 1996).

— *Die Apostelgeschichte* (KEK; Göttingen: Vandenhoeck & Ruprecht, 1998).

JOHNSON, L. T., *The Literary Function of Possessions in Luke-Acts* (SBLDS 39; Missoula: Scholars Press, 1977).

— *The Gospel of Luke* (SP 3; Collegeville, Minn.: Liturgical, 1991).

— *The Acts of the Apostles* (SP 5; Collegeville, Minn.: Liturgical, 1992).

JOHNSON, S. E., *A Commentary on the Gospel According to St. Mark*, 2nd ed. (London: A. & C. Black, 1972).

KÄSEMANN, E., 'Paul and Early Catholicism', in idem, *New Testament Questions of Today* (ET London: SCM, 1969), pp. 236–251.

— 'The Beginnings of Christian Theology', in idem, *New Testament Questions of Today*, pp. 82–107.

— *Commentary on Romans* (ET London: SCM, 1980).

KECK, L. E., 'The Spirit and the Dove', *NTS* 17 (1970–1), pp. 41–67.

KEE, H. C., 'Mark's Gospel in Recent Research', *Int* 32.4 (1978), pp. 353–369.

— *Good News to the Ends of the Earth: The Theology of Acts* (Philadelphia: Trinity Press International; London: SCM, 1990).

— *To Every Nation under Heaven: The Acts of the Apostles* (Harrisburg, Pa.: Trinity Press International, 1997).

KELBER, W. H., *The Kingdom in Mark: A New Place and a New Time* (Philadelphia: Fortress, 1974).

KINGSBURY, J. D., *The Christology of Mark's Gospel* (Philadelphia: Fortress, 1973).

— *Matthew: Structure, Christology, Kingdom* (Philadelphia: Fortress, 1975).

— 'The Verb *akolouthein* ("to follow") as an Index of Matthew's View of his Community', *JBL* 97 (1978), pp. 56–73.

— *Conflict in Mark: Jesus, Authorities, Disciples* (Minneapolis: Fortress, 1989).

KIRK, J. A., 'Apostleship Since Rengstorf: Towards a Synthesis', *NTS* 21 (1975), pp. 249–264.

KNIGHT, H. H., 'God's Faithfulness and God's Freedom: A Comparison of Contemporary Theologies of Healing', *JPT* 2 (1992), pp. 65–89.

KNIGHT, W. F. J. (trans.), *Virgil, The Aeneid* (Penguin Classics; Harmondsworth: Penguin, 1958).

KNOWLES, M., *Jeremiah in Matthew's Gospel: the Rejected Prophet Motif in Matthean Redaction* (JSNTSup 68; Sheffield: Sheffield Academic Press, 1993).

KNOX, W. L., 'The Ending of St. Mark's Gospel', *HTR* (1942), pp. 13–23.

KRAFT, C. H., *Christianity with Power* (Ann Arbor, Mich.: Vine, 1989).

KREMER, J. (ed.), *Les Actes des Apôtres: traditions, redaction, théologie* (Gembloux, Leuven: Duculot, 1979).

KUZMIC, P., 'Kingdom of God', in S. M. Burgess and G. B. McGee (eds.), *Dictionary of Pentecostal and Charismatic Movements* (Grand Rapids, Mich.: Zondervan, 1988), pp. 521–527.

LADD, G. E., *A Theology of the New Testament* (Cambridge: Lutterworth, 1974).

—— *The Presence of the Future: The Eschatology of Biblical Realism* (London: SPCK, 1974).

LAMPE, G. W. H., 'The Holy Spirit in the Writings of St. Luke', in D. E. Nineham (ed.), *Studies in the Gospels* (Oxford: Blackwell, 1955), pp. 159–200.

—— 'Miracles in the Acts of the Apostles', in C. F. D. Moule (ed.), *Miracles: Cambridge Studies in their Philosophy and History* (London: Mowbray, 1965), pp. 165–178.

LANE, T. J., *Luke and the Gentile Mission: Gospel Anticipates Acts* (European University Studies 571; Frankfurt am Main: Lang, Europäischer Verlag der Wissenschaften, 1996).

LANE, W. L., *The Gospel of Mark* (NICNT; Grand Rapids, Mich.: Eerdmans, 1974).

LEANEY, A. R. C., *The Gospel According to St. Luke* (London: A. & C. Black, 1958).

LEWIS, D., *Healing: Fiction, Fantasy or Fact?* (London: Hodder & Stoughton, 1989).

LIGHTFOOT, R. H., *The Gospel Message of Mark* (Oxford: Clarendon, 1950).

LOHFINK, G., *Jesus and Community* (ET Philadelphia: Fortress, 1984).

LOHSE, E., *Die Auferstehung Jesu Christi im Zeugnis des Lukasevangeliums* (BibS 31; Neukirchen: Kreis Moers, Neukirchener, 1961).

—— χείρ, *TDNT* 9, pp. 424–434.

—— *Acts* (Expositors Bible Commentary; Grand Rapids, Mich.: Zondervan, 1995).

—— 'Taking up the Cross Daily: Discipleship in Luke-Acts', in idem (ed.), *Patterns of Discipleship in the New Testament* (Grand Rapids: Eerdmans, 1996), pp. 50–76.

LOUW, J. P., and NIDA, E. A., *Greek-English Lexicon of the New Testament Based on Semantic Domains*, 2nd ed., vols. 1 and 2 (New York: United Bible Societies, 1988 and 1989).

LUNDSTRÖM, G., *The Kingdom of God in the Teaching of Jesus: A History of Interpretation from the Last Decades of the Nineteenth Century to the Present Day* (ET Edinburgh: Oliver & Boyd, 1963).

LUZ, U., 'The Disciples in the Gospel According to Matthew', in G. Stanton (ed.), *The Interpretation of Matthew* (London: SPCK/Fortress, 1983), pp. 98–128.

—— *Das Evangelium nach Matthäus (Mt. 1–7)* (EKKNT 1.1; Zurich: Benziger; Cologne: Neukirchener, 1985).

—— *Matthew 1–7: A Commentary* (ET Edinburgh: T. & T. Clark, 1989).

—— 'Das Primatwort Matthäus 16.17–19 aus Wirkungsgeschichtlicher Sicht', *NTS* 37 (1991), pp. 415–433.

—— *The Theology of the Gospel of Matthew* (ET Cambridge: Cambridge University Press, 1995).

SIGNS AND WONDERS THEN AND NOW

MACK, B. L., *A Myth of Innocence: Mark and Christian* Origins (Philadelphia: Fortress, 1988).

MADDOX, R., *The Purpose of Luke-Acts* (Edinburgh: T. & T. Clark, 1982).

MALBON, E. S., 'Fallible Followers: Women and Men in the Gospel of Mark', *Semeia* 28 (1983), pp. 29–48.

— 'Disciples/Crowds/Whoever: Markan Characters and Readers', *NovT* 18 (1986), pp. 104–130.

— *In the Company of Jesus: Characters in Mark's Gospel* (Louisville, Ky.: John Knox, 2000).

MALINA, B. J., 'The Literary Structure and Form of Matt. XXVIII.16–20', *NTS* 17 (1970), pp. 87–103.

MANN, C. S., *Mark* (AB 27; New York: Doubleday, 1986).

MANSON, T. W., *The Sayings of Jesus* (London: SCM, 1957).

MARCUS, J., 'The Gates of Hades and the Keys of the Kingdom (Matt. 16.18–19)', *CBQ* 50 (1988), pp. 443–455.

MARGUERAT, D., *Le Jugement dans L'Évangile de Matthieu* (Geneva: Labor et Fides,1981).

MARSHALL, C. D., *Faith as a Theme in Mark's Narrative* (SNTSMS 64; Cambridge: Cambridge University Press, 1989).

MARSHALL, I. H., *Luke: Historian and Theologian* (Exeter: Paternoster, 1970).

— *The Gospel of Luke: A Commentary on the Greek Text* (Exeter: Paternoster, 1978).

— *New Testament Interpretation: Essays on Principles and Methods* (Exeter: Paternoster, 1979).

— *Acts* (TNTC 5; Leicester: IVP, 1992).

MARSHALL, I. H. (ed.), *Luke: Historian and Theologian* (Exeter: Paternoster, 1979).

— Marshall, I. H., and Peterson, D. (eds.), *Witness to the Gospel: The Theology of Acts* (Grand Rapids, Mich.: Eerdmans, 1998).

MARTIN, R. F., 'Gift of Healing', in S. M. Burgess and G. B. McGee (eds.), *Dictionary of Pentecostal and Charismatic Movements* (Grand Rapids, Mich.: Zondervan, 1988), pp. 350–353.

MARTIN, R. P., *Mark: Evangelist and Theologian* (Exeter: Paternoster, 1979).

MARXSEN, W., *Mark the Evangelist: Studies on the Redaction History of the Gospel* (ET Nashville, Tenn.: Abingdon, 1969).

MASSEY, R., *Another Springtime: The Life of Donald Gee, Pentecostal Pioneer* (Guildford: Highland, 1992).

MASSON, C., 'La Reconstitution du college des Douze', *RTP* 3 (1955), pp. 193–201.

MATERA, F. J., 'The Prologue as the Interpretative Key to Mark's Gospel', *JSNT* 34 (1988), pp. 3–20.

MAUSER, U., 'Historical Criticism: Liberator or Foe of Biblical Theology?', in J. Reumann (ed.), *The Promise and Practice of Biblical Theology* (Minneapolis: Fortress, 1991), pp. 99–113.

MAY, E., '"... For Power Went Forth From Him ..." (Luke 6,19)', *CBQ* 14 (April 1952), pp. 93–103.

MAY, P., 'Focussing on the Eternal', in J. Goldingay (ed.), *Signs, Wonders and Healing* (Leicester: IVP, 1989), pp. 27–45.

MCARTHUR, H. K., 'Review of B. J. Hubbard "The Matthean Redaction of a Primitive Apostolic Commissioning"', *CBQ* 38 (1976), pp. 107–108.

MCCASLAND, S. V., 'The Way', *JBL* 77 (1958), pp. 222–230.

MCKIM, D. K. (ed.), *A Guide to Contemporary Hermeneutics* (Grand Rapids, Mich.: Eerdmans, 1986).

MEIER, J. P., 'Two Disputed Questions in Matt. 28:16–20', *JBL* 96.3 (1977), pp. 407–424.

— *Matthew* (Collegeville, Minn.: Liturgical, 1990).

MENZIES, R. P., *The Development of Early Christian Pneumatology with Special Reference to Luke-Acts* (JSNTSup 54; Sheffield: JSOT, 1991).

— 'Spirit and Power in Luke-Acts: A Response to Max Turner', *JSNT* 49 (1993), pp. 11–20.

— 'Luke and the Spirit: Reply to James Dunn', *JPT* 4 (1994), pp. 115–138.

MENZIES, W. W., and MENZIES, R. P., 'Luke and the Spirit: A Reply to James Dunn', *JPT* 4 (1994), pp. 115–138.

— *Spirit and Power: Foundations of Pentecostal Experience* (Grand Rapids, Mich.: Zondervan, 2000).

METZGER, B. M., 'Seventy or Seventy-Two Disciples?', *NTS* 5 (1958–9), pp. 299–306.

MEYE, R. P., *Jesus and the Twelve: Discipleship and Revelation in Mark's Gospel* (Grand Rapids, Mich.: Eerdmans, 1968).

MEYER, B. F., *The Aims of Jesus* (London: SCM, 1979).

MICHAELIS, W., μάχαιρα, *TDNT* 4, pp. 524–527.

MICHEL, O., '"Diese Kleinen" – eine Jüngerbezeichnung Jesu', *TSK* 108 (1937–8), pp. 401–415.

— 'Der Abschluss des Matthäusevangeliums', *EvT* 10 (1950–1), pp. 16–26; ET 'The Conclusion of Matthew's Gospel: A Contribution to the History of the Easter Message', in G. N. Stanton (ed.), *The Interpretation of Matthew* (London: SPCK/Fortress, 1983), pp. 30–41.

— μισέω, *TDNT* 4, pp. 683–694.

MINEAR, P. S., 'A Note on Luke xxii.36', *NovT* 7 (1964), pp. 128–134.

MONTEFIORE, C. G., and LOEWE, H. (eds.), *A Rabbinic Anthology* (New York: Schocken, 1974).

MORGAN, R., and BARTON, J., *Biblical Interpretation* (Oxford: Oxford University Press, 1988).

MORRIS, L., *The Gospel According to Luke* (Leicester: IVP, 1974).

MOULE, C. F. D., *An Idiom Book of New Testament Greek*, 2nd ed. (Cambridge: University Press, 1959).

MULLINS, T., 'New Testament Commission Forms, Especially in Luke-Acts', *JBL* 95.4 (1976), pp. 603–614.

MUNCK, J., *The Acts of the Apostles* (AB 31; New York: Doubleday, 1967).

NATHAN, R., and WILSON, K., *Empowered Evangelicals* (Ann Arbor, Mich.: Servant, 1995).

NEIL, W., *The Acts of the Apostles* (London: Oliphants, 1973).

NEIRYNCK, F., 'The Miracle Stories in the Acts of the Apostles: An Introduction', in J. Kremer (ed.), *Les Actes des Apôtres: traditions, redaction, théologie* (Gembloux, Leuven: Duculot, 1979), pp. 169–213.

NICKELSBURG, G. W. E, *Jewish Literature between the Bible and the Mishnah: A Historical and Literary Introduction* (London: SCM, 1981).

NINEHAM, D. E., *Saint Mark* (Pelican Gospel Commentaries; Harmondsworth: Penguin, 1963).

NIXON, R., 'The Authority of the New Testament', in I. H. Marshall (ed.), *New Testament Interpretation: Essays on Principles and Methods* (Exeter: Paternoster, 1979), pp. 334–350.

NOLLAND, J., *Luke 1–9:20* (WBC 35A; Dallas: Word, 1989).

— *Luke 9:21–18:34* (WBC 35B; Dallas: Word, 1993).

— *Luke 18:35–24:53* (WBC 35C; Dallas: Word, 1993).

NUNEZ, E. A., 'The Church in the Liberation Theology of Gustavo Gutiérrez: Description and Hermeneutical Analysis', in D. A. Carson (ed.), *Biblical Interpretation and the Church: Text and Context* (Exeter: Paternoster, 1984), pp. 166–194.

O'CONNOR, E. D., *The Pentecostal Movement in the Catholic Church* (Notre Dame, Ind.: Ave Maria, 1971).

O'REILLY, L., *Word and Sign in the Acts of the Apostles: A Study in Lucian Theology* (Rome: Cura Pontificial Universitatis Gregorianae, 1987).

PARRATT, J. K., 'The Laying on of Hands in the New Testament', *ExpTim* 80 (1969), pp. 210–214.

PENNEY, J. M., *The Missionary Emphasis of Lukan Pneumatology* (JPTSup 12; Sheffield: Sheffield Academic Press, 1997).

PERRIN, N., *The Kingdom of God in the Teaching of Jesus* (London: SPCK, 1963).

— *The Resurrection According to Matthew, Mark and Luke* (Philadelphia: Fortress, 1977).

PESCH, R., *Die Apostelgeschichte* (EKKNT 5; Zurich: Neukirchener, 1986).

PETERSON, N., 'When Is the End Not the End? Literary Reflections of the Ending of Mark's Narrative', *Int* 34 (1980), pp. 151–166.

POWELL, M. A., 'Narrative Criticism', in J. B. Green, *Hearing the New Testament: Strategies for Interpretation* (Grand Rapids, Mich.: Eerdmans; Carlisle: Paternoster, 1995), pp. 239–255.

PRZYBYLSKI, B., *Righteousness in Matthew and in his World of Thought* (SNTSMS 41; Cambridge: Cambridge University Press, 1980).

PYTCHES, D., *Come Holy Spirit* (London: Hodder & Stoughton, 1985).

RADL, W., *Paulus und Jesus im Lukanischen Doppelwerk: Untersuchungen zu Parallelmotiven im Lukasevangelium und in der Apostelgeschichte* (Bern: H. Lang; Frankfurt: P. Lang, 1975).

RENGSTORF, K. H., ἀποστέλλω, ἀπόστολος, *TDNT* 1, pp. 398–447.

RHOADS, D., and MICHIE, D., *Mark as Story: An Introduction to the Narrative of a Gospel* (Philadelphia: Fortress, 1982).

RICHARD, E., 'Pentecost as a Recurrent Theme in Luke-Acts', in E. Richard (ed.), *New Views on Luke and Acts* (Collegeville, Minn.: Liturgical, 1990), pp. 133–149.

ROBECK, C. M., Jr., 'Pentecostal Origins from a Global Perspective', in H. D. Hunter and P. Hocken (eds.), *All Together in One Place: Theological Papers from the Brighton Conference on World Evangelization* (Sheffield: Sheffield Academic Press, 1993), pp. 166–180.

ROBINSON, B. P., 'Peter and his Successors: Tradition and Redaction in Matthew 16.17–19', *JSNT* 21 (1984), pp. 85–104.

ROWLAND, C., *The Open Heaven: A Study of Apocalyptic in Judaism and Early Christianity* (London: SPCK, 1982).

— *Christian Origins: An Account of the Setting and Character of the Most Important Messianic Sect of Judaism* (London: SPCK, 1985).

RUTHVEN, J., *On the Cessation of the Charismata: The Protestant Polemic on Postbiblical Miracles* (JPTSup 3; Sheffield: Sheffield Academic Press, 1993).

SABOURIN, L., *L'Évangile selon Saint Matthieu et ses principaux parallèles* (Rome: Biblical Institute Press, 1978).

— 'Traits apocalyptiques dans L'Évangile de Matthieu', in *ScEs* 33.3 (1981), pp. 357–372.

SALDARINI, A. J., *Matthew's Christian-Jewish Community* (Chicago: University of Chicago Press, 1994).

SANDERS, E. P., *Jesus and Judaism* (London: SCM, 1985).

SARLES, K. L., 'An Appraisal of the Signs and Wonders Movement', *BSac* (January–March 1988), pp. 57–88.

SAUCY, R. L., 'An Open but Cautious View', in W. Grudem (ed.), *Are Miraculous Gifts for Today? Four Views* (Leicester: IVP, 1996), pp. 97–148.

SCHABERG, J., *The Father, The Son and the Holy Spirit: The Triadic Phrase in Matthew 28.19b* (SBLDS 61; Chico, Calif.: Scholars Press, 1982).

SCHNEIDER, J., σταυρός, *TDNT* 7, pp. 568–584.

SCHWARZ, G., 'κυριε, ιδου μαχαιραι ωδε δυο', *BN* 8 (1979), p. 22.

SCHWEIZER, E., 'The Power of the Spirit: The Uniformity and Diversity of the Concept of the Holy Spirit in the New Testament', *Int* 6 (1952), pp. 259–278.

— πνεῦμα, *TDNT* 6, pp. 389–455.

— *Spirit of God* (ET London: A. & C. Black, 1960).

— 'Observance of the Law and Charismatic Activity in Matthew', *NTS* 16 (1969–70), pp. 213–230.

— *Jesus* (ET London: SCM, 1971)

— *The Good News According to Mark* (ET London: SPCK, 1971).

— *The Good News According to Matthew* (ET London: SPCK, 1976).

— 'The Portrayal of The Life of Faith in the Gospel of Mark', *Int* 3.4 (1978), pp. 387–399.

— *The Holy Spirit* (ET Philadelphia: Fortress, 1980).

— *Matthäus und seine Gemeinde* (Stuttgart: Katholisches Bibelwerk, 1974), pp. 138–170; ET 'Matthew's Church', republished in G. Stanton (ed.), *The Interpretation of Matthew* (London: SPCK/Fortress, 1983), pp. 129–155.

— *The Good News According to Luke* (ET London: SPCK, 1984).

— 'Die theologische Leistung des Markus', *EvT* 24 (1964), pp. 337–355; ET 'Mark's Theological Achievement', republished in W. Telford, *The Interpretation of Mark* (Philadelphia: Fortress; London: SPCK, 1985), pp. 42–63.

SCOTLAND, N., *Charismatics and the Next Millennium : Do they Have a Future?* (London: Hodder & Stoughton, 1995).

SEGOVIA, F. F. (ed.), *Discipleship in the New Testament* (Philadelphia: Fortress, 1985).

SHELTON, J. B., 'A Reply to James D. G. Dunn's Baptism in the Spirit: A Response to Pentecostal Scholarship on Luke-Acts', *JPT* 4 (1994), pp. 139–143.

SIM, D. C., *The Gospel of Matthew and Christian Judaism: The History and Social Setting of the Matthean Community* (Edinburgh: T. & T. Clark, 1998).

SMAIL, T., WALKER, A., and WRIGHT, N., *Charismatic Renewal: The Search for a Theology* (London: SPCK, 1993).

SMART, N., *Worldviews: Crosscultural Explorations of Human Beliefs* (New York: Charles Scribner's Sons, 1983).

SMEDES, L. B. (ed.), *Ministry and the Miraculous: A Case Study at Fuller Theological Seminary* (Pasadena, Calif.: Fuller Theological Seminary, 1987).

SMITH, D. L., 'Third Wave Theology: The Vineyard Movement', in idem, *A Handbook of Contemporary Theology* (Wheaton, Ill.: Victor, 1992), pp. 227–241.

SOMMER, A. D., *The Essene Writings from Qumran* (ET Gloucester, Mass.: Smith, 1973).

SOULEN, R. N., *Handbook of Biblical Criticism* (Guildford: Lutterworth, 1977).

SPENCER, F. S., *The Portrait of Philip in Acts* (JSNTSup 67; Sheffield: Sheffield Academic Press, 1992).

SPRINGER, K. N. (ed.), *Riding the Third Wave* (Basingstoke: Marshall Pickering, 1987).

SQUIRES, J. T., 'The Plan of God', in I. H. Marshall and D. Peterson (eds.), *Witness to the Gospel: The Theology of Acts* (Grand Rapids, Mich.: Eerdmans, 1998), pp. 19–39.

STANIFORTH, M., 'Didache', in idem (ed.), *Early Christian Writings: The Apostolic Fathers* (Harmondsworth: Penguin, 1968), pp. 223–237.

STANTON, G. (ed.), *The Interpretation of Matthew* (London: SPCK/Fortress, 1983).

— *The Gospels and Jesus* (Oxford: Oxford University Press, 1989).

— *A Gospel for a New People: Studies in Matthew* (Edinburgh: T. & T. Clark, 1992).

STEIN, R. H., *Luke* (NAC 24; Nashville, Tenn.: Broadman, 1992).

STENDAHL, K., *The School of St. Matthew and its Use of the Old Testament*, 2nd ed. (Philadelphia: Fortress, 1968).

STIBBE, M. W. G., *The Gospel of John as Literature: An Anthology of Twentieth Century Perspectives* (NTTS; Leiden: Brill, 1993).

— 'The Theology of Renewal and the Renewal of Theology', *JPT* 3 (1993), pp. 71–90.

STOCK, A., *Call to Discipleship: A Literary Study of Mark's Gospel* (GNS 1; Delaware: Glazier; Dublin: Veritas, 1982).

STOCK, A., WALKER, A., and WRIGHT, N., *Charismatic Renewal: The Search for a Theology* (London: SPCK, 1993).

STORMS, C. S., 'A Third Wave View', in W. Grudem (ed.), *Are Miraculous Gifts for Today? Four Views* (Leicester: IVP, 1996), pp. 175–233.

STOTT, J. R. W., *Issues Facing Christians Today* (Basingstoke: Marshall, Morgan & Scott, 1984).

STOTT, J. R. W., *Calling Christian Leaders: Biblical Models of Church, Gospel and Ministry* (Leicester: IVP, 2002)

STRACK, H. L. VON, and BILLERBECK, P., *Kommentar zum Neuen Testament aus Talmud und Midrasch*, vols. 1–7 (Munich: Beck, 1922–61).

STRATHMANN, H., μάρτυς, *TDNT* 4, pp. 474–514.

STRECKER, G., *Der Weg der Gerechtigeit: Untersuchung zur Theologie des Matthäus*, 3rd ed. (Göttingen: Vandenhoeck & Ruprecht, 1962).

— 'Das Geschichtsverständnis des Matthäus', *EvT* 26 (1966), pp. 57–74; ET republished as 'The Concept of History in Matthew', in G. Stanton (ed.), *The Interpretation of Matthew* (London: SPCK/Fortress, 1983), pp. 67–84.

— *The Sermon on the Mount* (ET Edinburgh: T. & T. Clark, 1988).

STRONSTAD, R., *The Charismatic Theology of St. Luke* (Peabody, Mass.: Hendrickson, 1984).

SWEETLAND, D. M., 'Following Jesus: Discipleship in Luke-Acts', in E. Richard (ed.), *New Views on Luke-Acts* (Collegeville, Minn.: Liturgical, 1990), pp. 133–149.

TALBERT, C. H., *Literary Patterns, Theological Themes, and the Genre of Luke-Acts* (Missoula: Scholars Press, 1974).

— *Reading Luke: A Literary and Theological Commentary on the Third Gospel* (New York: Crossroad, 1984).

— 'Discipleship in Luke-Acts', in F. F. Segovia (ed.), *Discipleship in the New Testament* (Philadelphia: Fortress, 1985), pp. 62–75.

TALBERT, C. H. (ed.), *Perspectives on Luke-Acts* (Danville, Va.: Association of Baptist Professors of Religion; Edinburgh: T. & T. Clark, 1978).

TANNEHILL, R. C., 'The Disciples in Mark: The Function of Narrative Role', in W. Telford (ed.), *The Interpretation of Mark* (Philadelphia: Fortress; London: SPCK, 1985), pp. 134–157.

— *The Narrative Unity of Luke-Acts: A Literary Interpretation*, vol. 2 (Minneapolis: Fortress, 1990).

TATUM, W. B., 'The Epoch of Israel: Luke I–ii and the Theological Plan of Luke-Acts', *NTS* 13 (1966–7), pp. 184–195.

TAYLOR, V., *The Gospel According to Mark*, 2nd ed. (London: Macmillan, 1966).

THACKERY, H. St. J., *Josephus Antiquities*, books 1–4 (LCL 242; Cambridge, Mass.: Harvard University Press, 1978).

THEISSEN, G., *The Sociology of Early Palestinian Christianity* (ET Philadelphia: Fortress, 1978).

— *Miracle Stories of the Early Christian Tradition* (ET Edinburgh: T. & T. Clark, 1983).

— *The Shadow of the Galilean: The Quest of the Historical Jesus in Narrative Form* (ET London: SCM, 1987).

THEISSEN, G., and MERZ, A., *The Historical Jesus: A Comprehensive Guide* (ET London: SCM, 1998).

THIELICKE, P., 'The Restatement of New Testament Theology', in H. W. Bartsch (ed.), *Kerygma and Myth: A Theological Debate by Rudolf Bultmann and Five Critics* (New York: Harper & Brothers, 1961), pp. 138–174.

THISTLETON, A. C., 'The Use of Philosophical Categories in New Testament Hermeneutics', *Chm* 87 (1973), pp. 87–100.

— *New Horizons in Hermeneutics* (London: HarperCollins, 1992).

TREDENNICK, H. (trans.), *Plato: The Last Days of Socrates* (Harmondsworth: Penguin, 1969).

TRILLING, W., *Das wahre Israel – Studien zur Theologie des Matthäusevangeliums*, 3rd ed. (Munich: Kösel, 1964).

TRITES, A. A., 'The Prayer Motif in Luke-Acts', in C. H. Talbert (ed.), *Perspectives on Luke-Acts* (Edinburgh: T. & T. Clark, 1978), pp. 168–185.

TUCKETT, C. M., *Reading the New Testament: Methods of Interpretation* (London: SPCK, 1987).

— 'The Christology of Luke-Acts', in J. Verheyden (ed.), *The Unity of Luke-Acts* (Leuven: Leuven University Press, 1999), pp. 132–164.

TURNER, C. H., 'Marcan Usage: Notes, Critical and Exegetical, on the Second Gospel', *JTS* 26 (1925), pp. 225–231.

TURNER, M. M. B., 'Jesus and the Spirit in Lucian Perspective', *TynBul* 32 (1981), pp. 3–42.

— 'Spirit Endowment in Luke-Acts: Some Linguistic Considerations', *VE* 12 (1981), pp. 45–63.

— 'The Spirit and the Power of Jesus' Miracles in the Lucian Conception', *NovT* 33.2 (1991), pp. 124–152.

— *Power from on High: The Spirit in Israel's Restoration and Witness in Luke-Acts* (JPTSup 9; Sheffield: Sheffield Academic Press, 1996).

— *The Holy Spirit and Spiritual Gifts: Then and Now*, rev. ed. (Cumbria: Paternoster, 1996).

TWELFTREE, G. H., *Christ Triumphant* (London: Hodder & Stoughton, 1985).

— 'The Place of Exorcism in Contemporary Ministry', *Anvil* 5.2 (1988), pp. 133–150.

— 'Healing, Illness', in G. F. Hawthorne, R. P. Martin and D. G. Reid, *Dictionary of Paul and his Letters* (Leicester: IVP, 1993), p. 380.

— *Jesus the Exorcist: A Contribution to the Study of the Historical Jesus* (Peabody, Mass.: Hendrickson, 1993).

— *Jesus the Miracle Worker* (Downers Grove, Ill.: IVP, 1999).

VERMES, G., *The Dead Sea Scrolls in English*, 2nd ed. (Harmondsworth: Penguin, 1975).

— *Jesus the Jew: A Historian's Reading of the Gospels* (London: SCM, 1983).

WAETJEN, H. C., *A Reordering of Power: A Socio-Political Reading of Mark's Gospel* (Minneapolis: Fortress, 1989).

WAGNER, C. P., *Church Growth and the Whole Gospel* (Bromley, Kent: Marc Europe, 1981).

— *Spiritual Power and Church Growth* (London: Hodder & Stoughton, 1986).

— 'Church Growth', in S. M. Burgess and G. B. McGee (eds.), *Dictionary of Pentecostal and Charismatic Movements* (Grand Rapids, Mich.: Zondervan, 1988), pp. 180–195.

— 'John Wimber', in S. M. Burgess and G. B. McGee (eds.), *Dictionary of Pentecostal and Charismatic Movements* (Grand Rapids, Mich.: Zondervan, 1988), p. 889.

— 'Vineyard Christian Fellowship', in S. M. Burgess and G. B. McGee (eds.), *Dictionary of Pentecostal and Charismatic Movements* (Grand Rapids, Mich.: Zondervan, 1988), pp. 871–872.

— *How to Have a Healing Ministry without Making your Church Sick* (Ventura, Calif.: Regal, 1988).

— *The Third Wave of the Holy Spirit* (Ann Arbor, Mich.: Vine, 1988).

WAGNER, C. P. (ed.), *Signs and Wonders Today* (Altamonte Springs, Fla.: Creation House, 1987).

WAGNER, C. P., and PENNOYER, F. D. (eds.), *Wrestling with Dark Angels* (Eastbourne: Monarch, 1990).

WALL, R. W., 'Reading the New Testament in Canonical Context', in J. B. Green (ed.), *Hearing the New Testament: Strategies for Interpretation* (Grand Rapids, Mich.: Eerdmans; Carlisle: Paternoster, 1995), pp. 370–393.

— 'Israel and the Gentile Mission in Acts and Paul: A Canonical Approach', in I. H. Marshall and D. Peterson (eds.), *Witness to the Gospel: The Theology of Acts* (Grand Rapids, Mich.: Eerdmans, 1998), pp. 437–457.

WANSBOROUGH, H., 'Mark 3:21 – Was Jesus out of his Mind?', *NTS* 18 (1972), pp. 233–235.

WARFIELD, B. B., *Counterfeit Miracles* (Edinburgh: Banner of Truth Trust, 1972).

WATSON, F., *Text and Truth: Redefining Biblical Theology* (Grand Rapids, Mich.: Eerdmans, 1987).

WEEDON, T. J., *Mark – Tradition in Conflict* (Philadelphia: Fortress, 1971).

— 'The Heresy that Necessitated Mark's Gospel', in W. Telford (ed.), *The Interpretation of Mark* (London: Fortress/SPCK, 1985), pp. 64–77.

WENHAM, D., 'The Meaning of Mark 3:21', *NTS* 21 (1975), pp. 295–300.

WENK, M., *Community-Forming Power: The Socio-Ethical Role of the Spirit in Luke-Acts* (JPTSup 19; Sheffield: Sheffield Academic Press, 2000).

WESTERMANN, C., *Basic Forms of Prophetic Speech* (ET London: SCM, 1967).

WHITE, J., *When the Spirit Comes with Power: Signs and Wonders among God's People* (London: Hodder & Stoughton, 1988).

WILCOX, M., 'Peter and the Rock: A Fresh Look at Matthew xvi.17–19', *NTS* 22 (1975–6), pp. 73–78.

WILKINS, M. J., *The Concept of Disciple in Matthew's Gospel: As Reflected in the Use of the Term Μαθητής* (NovTSup 59; Leiden: Brill, 1988).

— 'Discipleship', in J. B. Green, S. McKnight and I. H. Marshall (eds.), *Dictionary of Jesus and the Gospels* (Downers Grove, Ill.: IVP, 1992), pp. 182–189.

WILLIAMS, D., 'Exorcising the Ghost of Newton', in K. Springer (ed.), *Riding the Third Wave* (Basingstoke: Marshall Pickering, 1987), pp. 151–163.

— *Signs, Wonders, and the Kingdom of God* (Ann Arbor, Mich.: Vine, 1989).

— *The God who Reigns* (Basingstoke: Marshall Pickering, 1989).

— 'Following Christ's Example: A Biblical View of Discipleship', in G. S. Greig and K. N. Springer (eds.), *The Kingdom and the Power* (Ventura, Calif.: Regal, 1993), pp. 175–196.

WILLIAMS, G. O., 'The Baptism in Luke's Gospel', *JTS* 45 (1944), pp. 31–38.

WILSON, S. G., *The Gentiles and the Gentile Mission in Luke-Acts* (Cambridge: Cambridge University Press, 1973).

WIMBER, J., 'Theological Foundation: The Kingdom of God', in idem, *Signs, Wonders and Church Growth* (Vineyard Teaching Manual; Placenta, Calif.: Vineyard Ministries International, 1984), pp. 1–16.

— *The Kingdom of God* (Cassette Series; Vineyard Ministries International, 1985).

— 'The Five Key Characteristics of Power Evangelism', *Renewal* 123 (1986), pp. 10–12.

— *Power Healing* (London: Hodder & Stoughton, 1986).

— 'Introduction', in K. Springer (ed.), *Riding the Third Wave* (London: Marshall Pickering, 1987), pp. 17–33.

— *Kingdom Come: Understanding what the Bible Says about the Reign of God* (London: Hodder & Stoughton, 1989).

— *Kingdom Evangelism* (London: Hodder & Stoughton, 1989).

— *Kingdom Suffering* (London: Hodder & Stoughton, 1989).

— 'Power Evangelism: Definitions', in C. P. Wagner and F. D. Pennoyer (eds.), *Wrestling with Dark Angels* (Eastbourne: Monarch, 1990), pp. 21–55.

— *The Dynamics of Spiritual Growth* (London: Hodder & Stoughton, 1990).

— *Power Evangelism: Signs and Wonders Today*, 2nd ed. (London: Hodder & Stoughton, 1992).

WIMBER, J. (ed.), *The Kingdom of God and the Last Days* (Vineyard Teaching Manual; Anaheim, Calif.: Mercy, 1988).

WIMBER, J., with SPRINGER, K., *The Dynamics of Spiritual Growth* (London: Hodder & Stoughton, 1990).

— *Power Evangelism* (rev. ed.; London: Hodder & Stoughton, 1992).

WISE, M. O. (trans.), 'Tales of the Patriarchs: 1QapGen', in M. O. Wise, M. A. Abegg Jr. and E. M. Cook (eds.), *The Dead Sea Scrolls: A New Translation* (London: Hodder & Stoughton, 1997), pp. 74–84.

WITHERINGTON, B., III, 'On the Road with Mary Magdalene, Joanna, Susanna, and Other Disciples – Luke 8.1–3', *ZNW* 70 (1979), pp. 243–248.

— *The Acts of the Apostles: A Socio-Rhetorical Commentary* (Grand Rapids, Mich.: Eerdmans; Carlisle: Paternoster, 1998).

WRIGHT, D. F., 'Why Were the Montanists Condemned?', *Them* 2.1 (1976), pp. 15–22.

WRIGHT, E. E., *Strange Fire? Assessing the Vineyard Movement and the Toronto Blessing* (Darlington: Evangelical, 1996).

WRIGHT, N., 'Weighing up Wimber: Part 1', *Renewal* 152 (January 1989), pp. 22–23.

— 'Asking the Forbidden Questions: Part 2', *Renewal* 153 (February 1989), pp. 11–12.

— 'The Case for Wimber Revisionism: Part 3', *Renewal* 154 (March 1989), pp. 12–15.

WRIGHT, N. T., *The New Testament and the People of God* (London: SPCK, 1993).

— *Jesus and the Victory of God* (London: SPCK, 1996).

# INDEX OF MODERN AUTHORS

# INDEX OF SCRIPTURES AND OTHER ANCIENT WRITINGS